WRITING AND FILMING THE GENOCIDE OF THE TUTSIS IN RWANDA

After the Empire:
The Francophone World and Postcolonial France

Series Editor
Valérie Orlando, University of Maryland

Advisory Board
Robert Bernasconi, Memphis University; Alec Hargreaves, Florida State University; Chima Korieh, Rowan University; Françoise Lionnet, UCLA; Obioma Nnaemeka, Indiana University; Kamal Salhi, University of Leeds; Tracy D. Sharpley-Whiting, Vanderbilt University; Nwachukwu Frank Ukadike, Tulane University

*See www.lexingtonbooks.com/series for the series description and
a complete list of published titles.*

WRITING AND FILMING THE GENOCIDE OF THE TUTSIS IN RWANDA

Dismembering and Remembering Traumatic History

Alexandre Dauge-Roth

LEXINGTON BOOKS
Lanham • Boulder • New York • Toronto • Plymouth, UK

Published by Lexington Books
A wholly owned subsidiary of The Rowman & Littlefield Publishing Group, Inc.
4501 Forbes Boulevard, Suite 200, Lanham, Maryland 20706
http://www.lexingtonbooks.com

Estover Road, Plymouth PL6 7PY, United Kingdom

British Library Cataloguing in Publication Information Available

Library of Congress Cataloging-in-Publication Data

The hardback edition of this book was previously cataloged by the Library of Congress as
follows:

Dauge-Roth, Alexandre, 1967-
  Writing and filming the genocide of the Tutsis in Rwanda : dismembering and
remembering traumatic history / Alexandre Dauge-Roth.
    p. cm.
  Includes bibliographical references and index.
  1. Rwanda—History—Civil War, 1994—Atrocities. 2. Rwanda—History—Civil War,
1994—Personal narratives. 3. Rwanda—History—Civil War, 1994—Literature and
the war. 4. Rwanda—History—Civil War, 1994—Motion pictures and the war.
  5. Tutsi (African people—Crimes against—Rwanda—History—20th century. I. Title.

  DT450.435.D38 2010
  967.57104'31—dc22

                                                                    2010009354

ISBN: 978-0-7391-1229-8 (cloth : alk. paper)
ISBN: 978-0-7391-7282-7 (pbk. : alk. paper)
ISBN: 978-0-7391-4762-7 (electronic)

Printed in the United States of America

To Katherine, Claire & Aymeric
for your unconditional support,
love, patience, and joy

To Jeannette, Berthe, Elise & Gaspard
for sharing your stories, tears, and laughter
Your trust shapes the meaning of this book

To Gasana, Naasson, Esther & Yolande
for all your guidance and wisdom

To Ross & Laure
for your inspiration and ethical generosity

To all the members of Tubeho
& my Rwandan friends

Contents

Acknowledgments

THIS BOOK PROJECT BEGAN WHEN I READ Koulsy Lamko's novel *La Phalène des collines* during the summer of 2002. Haunted by the fates and quests of Lamko's characters, I wanted to know more. I started exploring other voices who bore witness to the genocide of the Tutsis in Rwanda. Along the journey that led to this book, I had the privilege of meeting many survivors and I would like to thank them for their trust. By listening to your attempts to put words to suffering, witnessing your strategies to cope with traumatic loss, and admiring your ability to envision a future despite the destruction of your former life, you shaped my understanding of testimony as a space of encounter. Despite the irreconcilable differences of our past trajectories, together we created a shared space from which a new sense of commonality emerged. I would especially like to thank Esther Mujawayo, Yolande Mukagasana, Berthe Kayitesi, and Gilbert Ndahayo for their inspirational testimonies and their unique ability to help me—the outsider—sense the magnitude of the trauma and the pain of genocide violence. I am indebted to Gasana Ndoba and Naasson Munyandamutsa for their engagement and ethics of listening, which were inspirational as I envisioned the role I ought to play in alleviating survivors' pain. Though no few words of gratitude can mirror the trust and generosity of those who shared their stories, all of whom I unfortunately cannot name here, I wish to thank: Jeannette Kayitesi, Elise Musomandera, Espérance Uwambyeyi, Chantal Kayitesi, Valentina Iribagiza, Gaspard Mukwiye, Julienne Murorunkwere, Carine Gakuba, Thierry Sebaganwa, Martin Muhoza, Géraldine Umutesi, Didier Giscard Sagashya, Abdel Aziz Mwiseneza, Augustin Nkusi, Rose Mukankomeje, Mireille Ikirezi, Christelle Kamaliza, Innocent

Micomyiza, Ildephonse Majyambere, Eugène Mugabo, Jeanine Munyeshuli Barbé, and Ernest Mutwarasibo. Thanks to you all, I have been able to measure the powerful and demanding commitment laid out by Dr. Martin Luther King, Jr.: "All men are caught in an inescapable network of mutuality, tied in a single garment of destiny. Whatever affects one directly affects all indirectly. I can never be what I ought to be until you are what you ought to be. And you can never be what you ought to be until I am what I ought to be. This is the interrelated structure of reality" (*Strength to Love* 1963).

I would like to thank the following friends, colleagues, and mentors whose encouragement, interest, and support played a crucial role in the interrelated process of writing this book: Ross Chambers, whose intellectual generosity and work on testimony have shaped my own and who has been a constant source of inspiration; Laure Coret, through whom I first came to know Rwanda and whose work on genocide constitutes an ethical model; Josias Semujanga, whose analysis of the literary and ideological representations of the genocide of the Tutsis has been inestimable in my understanding of many works; Mária Brewer, whose enthusiasm for this project and insightful approach to the representation of violence have been instrumental; David Scobey, whose passion for oral history helped me to shape what hospitality as a form of civic engagement requires; and Kirk Read, my colleague and friend who embodies academic and human generosity and always finds ways to surprise you with kindness, wit, and humor. Many thanks also to Lynne Tirrell, Catalina Sagarra, Catherine Coquio, Marie-France Collard, Martine Delvaux, Maryse Fauvel, Soko Phay Vakalis, Chantal Kalisa, Rangira Béatrice Gallimore, Erik Ehn, David Collin, Olivier Blanc, Frédéric Jacquet, Bill Blaine-Wallace, Elizabeth Eames, Marie Rice-Defosse, Bill VanderWolk, Susie Dorn, Amy Marczewski and Elizabeth Applegate, whose interest, insight, and comments made the writing of this book an enriching and rewarding experience. My work has also been nourished by numerous discussions with students who took classes with me on the representations of the genocide of the Tutsis and their thought-provoking questions, term papers, and theses. Special thanks to Geordie, Anne, Katie, and Emma and to those who shared three weeks with me and the orphans of Tubeho in Kigali in May 2009. This book would not have been possible without the generous and sustained support of Bates College and its Harward Center for Community Partnership. I am particularly grateful for the College's funding of the conference I hosted in March 2007 on the Bates campus, "Rwanda: From National Disintegration to National Reunification." My warm gratitude and admiration goes to Artie Greenspan, who embarked on the perilous task of translating Koulsy Lamko's *La Phalène des collines* into English, and to Geneviève Creedon, who translated a shorter version of "Screening Memory and (Un)Framing Forgetting." The meticulous readings of Katie Jewett, Kirk Read, and Laura Balladur helped me to craft a hospitable prose for these words of suffering and our duty to respond to them.

I thank my parents, Marion and Michel Dauge, and my second parents, Shirley and George Roth, for their unfailing support these many years. Above all, I wish to express my gratitude to my family who has always believed in me and faced with me the demands of this undertaking. Katherine, Claire, and Aymeric, without your love, understanding, joy, patience, and appetite for life, I would never have succeeded in giving hospitality to all the voices who shape the "inescapable network of mutuality" that now defines my life, our life.

Early versions of chapters 5 and 6 appeared as "Passing On Voices, Going on Haunted: Witnessing and Hospitality in the Play *Rwanda 94*" in *L'esprit créateur* XLV.3 (Fall 2005): 85–102. I thank Mária Brewer and Dan Brewer for soliciting this article and their helpful comments. A shorter version of chapter 18 appeared as "Testimonial Encounter: Esther Mujawayo's Dialogic Art of Witnessing," in *French Cultural Studies* XX.2 (May–June 2009): 165–180. Many thanks to Piotr A. Cieplak and Emma Wilson for including me in this special issue on "Material Manifestations of Memory: Genocide and Commemoration in Rwanda."

INTRODUCTION

I continue to be troubled by the unsettling spectacle offered by an excess of memory here, and an excess of forgetting elsewhere, to say nothing of an influence of commemorations and abuses of memory—and of forgetting.

Paul Ricoeur (*Memory, History, Forgetting* xv)

I can tell you, in one sentence, why, as survivors, we remained silent after the genocide: we could feel that we were disturbing presences.

Esther Mujawayo (*SurVivantes* 20)

This new period was marked by an excess of memory, which made me face the difficulties of bearing witness, of speaking the pain of genocide. During this period, I often spoke about the genocide, the horrific death of my people, without realizing that it was a sacred knowledge, that can only be voiced in certain places—a disturbing knowledge. Very few people are capable of listening to what a genocide is. Just listening. Some people asked me questions, and then were unable to lend an ear.

Berthe Kayitesi (*Demain ma vie* 264)

1

Excess of Memory?

R EADING THE LITERATURE AND WATCHING THE FILMS that bear witness to genocide is an unpleasant and troubling encounter. It forces on us a proximity
with death and cruelty, confronts us with the most radical consequences of
hatred and racism, and asks us, ultimately, to face, here and now, what we
would like to believe is something that happened "over there" and that is over.
"Never again," "*Plus jamais cela*," "*Ntidigasubire*" we are inclined to repeat,
again and again, as we articulate the relationship we establish with such a
traumatic past and define its remembrance. Yet, in the midst of our moral
indignation, sympathy for the victims, and frenzy for memorials, interjec-
tions such as "It's history!" and "Let's turn the page!" betray a symptomatic
desire to confine, if not dismiss, genocide's disturbing legacy and interpellation: namely, that no society is immune to genocide. By framing genocide as
what happened "over there" and "being over," while constantly celebrating
this past as being precisely "the past," we wish to avert any links it may have
with the present. We wish to bypass the responsibilities that the recognition
of the political and ideological nature of genocide entails within our own
societies today—not to mention the systematic planning of the killings and
the complicity or indifference they required among ordinary citizens. In this
sense, the reassuring belief that by remembering the past we will exorcise its
atrocities and not repeat its failures betrays a collective fantasy, not to say an
hypocrisy, if this "excess of memory" does not translate into concrete forms
of action within the present. What should not be forgotten is that the present
social order in the name of which certain facets of the past are remembered
within a society, is a process that engages as much "the" past of this society

than its present order. Any memorialization of "the" past functions always to a certain degree as a powerful legitimizing gesture directed toward the present. Finally, to proclaim that we need "to turn the page," represents a call for a collective memory that tends to silence and disfranchise the needs of survivors who, still today, must negotiate the long lasting scars and traumatic aftermath that genocidal violence inscribed within them.

How shall we then understand this archival fervor and reverence for past genocides, especially the Holocaust, while we elude within our present the call for action and avoid the disturbing legacy survivors of genocide attempt to pass on to us? Facing this paradoxical relationship toward past genocides, we must ask ourselves if our current "Holocaust consciousness"[1] and the duty of remembering its uniqueness have not become our moral and political excuse for remaining blind to the ongoing genocide in Darfur and deaf to the long-lasting needs of survivors of more recent genocides perpetrated in Cambodia, the former Yugoslavia, and Rwanda. Furthermore, as Henry Rousso points out in his analysis of the correlation between the fetishization of memory and an obsessive fear of the past, an excessive attention to certain facets of the past signals both a difficulty to assume this past and a desire to elude the challenges of the present: "The overflow of the past, which is equally a result and a cause of the ideology of memory, constitutes a phenomenon as worrisome as the denial of the past. Both are in fact the inverted symptoms of a same difficulty to assume this past, which is to say to face the present and to imagine the future."[2] For Rousso, there is a symptomatic link between an ideology advocating an overflow of memory and the denial of certain facets of the past to mute their implications within the present—especially when this past concerns the involvement of the State and collective forms of responsibilities as it is the case with genocide. Thus, any society facing its former implication and role regarding past genocides must define rituals and forms of transmission of this disturbing past so that its heirs "can live *with* the memory of the tragedy rather then trying to live *without* it, . . . or *against* it" (*Hantise* 47).

In "*A Problem from Hell*": *America and the Age of Genocide*, Samantha Power gives a striking and symptomatic example of this unwillingness to translate the remembrance of genocide into political action within the present while professing a duty to remember:

> At a State Department press conference on April 8 [1994, one day after the beginning of the mass killings in Rwanda], Bushnell made an appearance and spoke gravely about the mounting violence in Rwanda. . . . After she left the podium, Michael McCurry, the department spokesman, took her place and criticized foreign governments for preventing the screening of the Steven Spielberg film *Schindler's List*. "This film . . . ," McCurry said "shows that even in the midst of genocide, one individual can make a difference. . . . The most effective

way to avoid the recurrence of genocidal tragedy," he declared, "is to ensure that past acts of genocide are never forgotten." (352–353)

Needless to say, while everybody agreed on the necessity to remember the Holocaust, nobody saw in these two successive declarations any correlation, or tried to remind the U.S. administration, when it became clear a couple of days later that a genocide of the Tutsis was underway in Rwanda, that if "one individual can make a difference," what about a country like the United States and its lobbying power within the United Nations.[3] As Susan Sontag has shown in *Regarding the Pain of Others*, it is therefore insufficient to document the horror humans can inflict on other humans if one addresses neither the ethical dimension of remembering nor the implications the awareness of the past generates within the present of our actions:

> To designate a hell is not, of course, to tell us anything about how to extract people from that hell, how to moderate hell's flame. Still, it seems a good in itself to acknowledge, to have enlarged, one's sense of how much suffering caused by human wickedness there is in the world we share with others. . . . No one after a certain age has the right to this kind of innocence, of superficiality, to this degree of ignorance, or amnesia. There now exist a vast repository of images that make it harder to maintain this kind of moral defectiveness. Let the atrocious images haunt us. Even if they are only tokens, and cannot possibly encompass most of the reality to which they refer, they still perform a vital function. The images say: This is what human beings are capable of doing—may volunteer to do, enthusiastically, self-righteously. Don't forget.
>
> This is not quite the same as asking people to remember a particularly monstrous bout of evil ("Never forget"). Perhaps too much value is assigned to memory, not enough to thinking. Remembering *is* an ethical act, has ethical value in and on itself. (114–115)

As one of the haunting voices of the dead staged in the five-hour-long play *Rwanda 94* asserts, if the encounter with the voices and mediations bearing witness to genocide is so disturbing, it is mainly because this encounter can not be confined to the past nor to the question of remembering. The subtitle of *Rwanda 94—An Attempt at Symbolic Reparation to the Dead, for Use by the Living*—asserts clearly the connection between the symbolic act of remembering and the social and political implications of this act of memorialization within our present.[4] For Jacques Delcuvellerie and Groupov, any attempt to remember the genocide of the Tutsis in 2000 must be understood as an uneasy and disturbing quest for justice so that the dead are not erased within the memory of the living. In staging the voices of the dead, Delcuvellerie dramatizes the fact that the dead have not yet lost everything since they can die a second time due to our indifference to fight impunity and our unwillingness to see ourselves as the heirs of those who are no longer alive to tell their stories:

> Through us, humanity looks sadly at you.
> We, who died unjustly, hacked, mutilated, dismembered,
> today already: forgotten, denied, insulted.
> We are this million of cries that hang over the hills of Rwanda.
> We are forever this accusatory cloud.
> We will forever make our claims, speaking in the name of those who are no
> more and in the name of those who are still there;
> we who are stronger today than when we were alive, for alive we had but a
> short life to bear witness.
> Dead, it is through eternity that we will claim our due. (211)

As Rousso has shown in his work on the competing interpretations of Vichy's legacy in France after World War II, each representation of the past must also, if not primarily, be examined as an attempt to legitimize a certain social order within the present.[5] Hence, any collective and political mediation of the past constitutes a carefully crafted version of what should be remembered and forgotten, of what is significant and insignificant. Thus, regardless of its intended symbolic gesture, each act of personal or collective remembrance, while it inscribes and actualizes a certain visibility of the past within the present, performs at the same time a silencing gesture institutionalizing forgetting. Moreover, when a representation of the past attempts to position itself as "the true remembrance," it exercises a form of "symbolic violence" since it occults the socially negotiated and culturally determined process that defines what is worthy of memory. According to Pierre Bourdieu, dominant discourses commit "symbolic violence" by grounding their legitimacy in the ignorance of their conditions of production and thus operate a contextual erasure that prevents any positional awareness.[6] As a result, the power of their eloquence to cast what must be passed on as a given—rather than the explicit result of social negotiation—goes hand in hand with the silencing of any dissenting voices that might initiate a dialogue or question "the order of things," be they past or present.

The representation of the genocide of the Tutsis in Rwanda is no exception. The "symbolic violence" of its memorials—where they exist—combined with the political control of survivors' memory and testimonies, too often censor the survivors' voices. Furthermore, by imposing official versions and injunctions "to turn the page," the government generates a representation of the past in which survivors too often do not recognize themselves and may feel alienated. The tense relations between Paul Kagame's government and the Rwandan survivors association "Ibuka" (Remember) during the first decade after the genocide offers a symptomatic example of the control exercised by the government on the voices of survivors. One of the key points of contention has been survivors' claim for compensation within a political context where national reconciliation and unity is paramount for Rwanda's future as a nation. As Catherine Coquio shows, Tutsi survivors were never fully in a position to decide, according to their specific needs, how to remember their dead. "Ibuka" had to negotiate constantly how the genocide and the remains of its victims should be displayed, the government being more concerned with the symbolic and political capital they could gain from sites and memorials that maintained a vivid visibility of the past, than interested in the individual needs of survivors facing the traumatic aftermath of genocide.[7] If current President Paul Kagame rightly underlines the fact that the genocide of 1994 affected everyone and that it requires, therefore, all Rwandans to define their present actions in relationship to this common but highly divisive past, his reading of history, because it is motivated by the necessity of reunification, tends to play down the fact that the collective aftermath of the genocide is lived very differently if one is a survivor, a perpetrator, a bystander, or an exile who came back to Rwanda after 1994: "How do we now go about rebuilding a Rwandan society that was so decimated—physically, emotionally, psychologically and spiritually—by the genocide? How can we ensure that such destruction is not wrought again in Rwanda or anywhere else in the future? The events of 1994 reverberate through the daily lives of all Rwandans and all inhabitants of the Great Lake region, just as they should reverberate through the memories and consciences of all humanity. The genocide touched the lives of all Rwandans; no individual or community was spared. Every Rwandan is either a genocide survivor or a perpetrator, or the friend or relative of a survivor or perpetrator" (xxi).

In *Accounting for Horror: Post-Genocide Debates in Rwanda*, Nigel Eltringham underlines therefore the importance to keep in mind the ideological use—and sometimes abuse—of an official history since the writing of history played such a crucial role throughout Rwanda's past. Without denying the appeal to history, Eltringham urges us to be highly critical and careful as history has been one of the most powerful tools for maintaining divisions and justifying various politics of discrimination among Rwandans:

> The appeal to history was a central component in constructing and maintaining division in Rwanda and was intrinsic to genocidal propaganda. There is a danger that actors continue to appeal to history in this absolutist fashion. The instrumental power inherent in a belief that a single, absolute history is attainable (and preferable) has not only proved to be deadly, but overestimates the capacity and misunderstands the nature of historiography. While there may be non-negotiable *chronicle of events*, the narratives that actors recognize (and value) as history are

the product of an interpretative exercise that inevitably generates different narratives. . . . Given the role played by history in Rwanda's past, a recognition of the limits of historiography should be encouraged. (181–182)

Today the Rwandan government, in its will to move beyond the social tensions and ideology that lead to the genocide of 1994, is promoting a program of national reconciliation and unity, which requires new compromises and sacrifices for survivors. If everyone agrees that it was imperative to eliminate the "ethnic" mention on all identity cards and ban their use for political purposes after the genocide, recent legislation has placed some additional burdens on survivors. The government's refusal to create a specific compensation fund for the victims of the genocide has been seen as unfair by most survivors when many perpetrators benefit from reduced sentences if they confess their crimes under the *gacaca* laws. Furthermore, the accelerated release of more than forty thousand genocide suspects and criminals within their communities represents a heavy emotional challenge for survivors who are not psychologically ready to coexist with those who killed their relatives— a scenario that too often contributes to their silencing.[8] In a political climate where all Rwandans are seen as equal and judged on their merits and competence regardless of their past trajectories and sufferings, survivors often find themselves struggling to establish their place and to have a voice within a rapidly growing economy. Oriented toward the future, the Rwandan political vision is increasingly reluctant to make special arrangements for those who struggle to "turn the page"—an injunction that equates to repress traumatic memories instead of giving survivors the means to negotiate their past and ongoing suffering as they face the demands of the present. If these political choices and priorities make sense—since any lasting perception that the current government is a pro-Tutsi regime could only lead to future chaos and nourish hatred and divisions among Rwandans—it places many survivors in a precarious position. It tends to radically redefine the historical recognition of their suffering and the social resonance of their ongoing struggle with the traumatic aftermath of genocide. Furthermore, survivors embody a disturbing memory, which revives a chapter of Rwanda's history that most people would like to see closed, while its aftermath still constitutes an open wound for those who survived. Survivors find themselves in an anachronistic relationship with their contemporaries, since for them the past is more than ever what defines their present. Thus, as Innocent Rwililiza underlines through his testimony recorded by the French journalist Jean Hatzfeld who interviewed both victims and perpetrators in the region of Nyamata over several years (1999–2007), survivors like him are seen as a parasitic presence today, a disturbance that prevents others from fully embracing the present by obliterating the traumatic legacy of the genocide: "I see today that there is still uneasiness in talking about the survivors, even among Rwandans, even among Tutsis. I think that everyone would like the survivors to relinquish the genocide, in a way. As if people wanted them to leave the task of dealing with it to others, who have never been in direct danger of being sliced up by machete. As if we were from now on somewhat superfluous. . . . We survivors, we are growing more like strangers in our own land—which we have never left—than all the foreigners and expatriates who consider us so anxiously" (Rwililiza quoted in *Life Laid Bare* 111 and 114–115).

The tension between competing personal, collective, and official processes of memorialization is at the center of this book, which examines how literature, testimony, and film offer different configurations, accounts, and venues to bear witness to the genocide of the Tutsis either as an outsider or as a survivor. Relying on Omer Bartov's work on the Holocaust and David Apter's analysis of political violence, Eltringham underlines the complexity of the process of remembering the unsettling magnitude of genocidal violence and advocates that any narrative attempt to account for an event such as a genocide needs to address the double set of issues implied by the imperative to "account" and to "account for":

> "Account" both in the sense of "to account for" (to provide adequate explanation) and "account" as in "provide a processual narrative." To an extent, "devastation of such proportions destroys our ability to imagine it" (Bartov 798). We are required to reduce it "to a more manageable size and more conventional nature, so that the mind can take it rather than totally blot it out" (Bartov 799). The question remains however, whether in making things "manageable" and achieving some sense of order we inadvertently (re)deploy the same ways of "worldimagining" upon which perpetrators of genocide rely. Our attempts to "account" must be tempered by a recognition that genocide itself "disorders explicitly for a . . . *reordering* purpose" (Apter 5). (Eltringham xi)

Thus, acknowledging the positionality of literary, testimonial, and cinematic mediations, which are always in dialogue with competing and former representations of the genocide of the Tutsis, my reading of these works examines the various narrative strategies used by authors, survivors, and filmmakers. Moreover, I focus on how some of these narratives deploy a haunting esthetic capable to inscribe a long-lasting, disturbing, and demanding legacy within the cultural scene of their readers or viewers knowing that they will ultimately turn the page and go on with their lives despite their initial interest. Subsequently, by analyzing how these works seek to position us as heirs of this genocide, I explore what this status entails for those who, like me, have become secondary witnesses and what it might imply to go on, haunted by knowing that we will never fully know the experience that is passed on to us as Rwililiza reminds us:

> I also see a gulf is opening between those who lived through the genocide and everyone else. Someone from outside, even a Rwandan, even a Tutsi, whose whole family was lost in the slaughter, this person cannot completely understand the genocide. Even someone who has seen all those bodies rotting in the bush, after the liberation, and the heaped-up corpses in the churches—this person cannot look at life with our eyes. . . . A Rwandan outside from the genocide . . . believes whatever the survivor tells him and then, a moment later, he begins to forget. He accepts the principle of the genocide, but has doubt about the details. Anyone who has not experienced the genocide wants life to go on as before, wants to press on toward the future without too many delays. . . . The Tutsi from away, who lived in Bujumbura during the genocide, or in Kampala, or Brussels, does not understand these commemorations, these ceremonies of mourning, these memorials. He tires of these constant observances, he does not want his conscience to traumatize him relentlessly. . . . To a survivor, he recommends, "My friend, stop brooding, try to forget, think of yourself now." (Rwililiza quoted in *Life Laid Bare* 114–115)

What does it mean then to listen to survivors, to read literary accounts and view cinematic representations of the genocide of the Tutsis in Rwanda? What resonance and place are we willing to give to this experience we will never fully comprehend but whose remembrance constitutes nevertheless a traumatic dissonance within our present? What does it entail personally and collectively to listen and give assurance to survivors that their testimonies carry a meaningful knowledge while recognizing that those who have not experienced the genocide can neither identify with survivors nor speak for them? As Dominick LaCapra suggests in *Writing History, Writing Trauma*, can and should one "develop what might be called an ethics of response for secondary witnesses" while it is "important to recognize that an historian or other academic, however attentive and emphatic a listener he or she may be, may not assume the voice of the victim" (98)? What social will, collective responsiveness, and personal ethics do literary, testimonial, and cinematic representations of the genocide of the Tutsis advocate and require of us who have not experienced the abyss, so that the words and mediations bearing witness to this genocide not only generate social resonance but, more crucially, impact the way we position ourselves within the present?

Notes

1. Peter Novick, *The Holocaust in American Life* (1999), 1. On this topic, see also Tim Cole, *Selling the Holocaust: From Auschwitz to Schindler: How History is Bought, Packaged, and Sold* (1999).

2. Henry Rousso, *La hantise du passé. Entretien avec Philippe Petit* (1998), 30. Henceforth, all quotes from this work are my translations.

3. Samantha Power, "*A Problem from Hell": America and the Age of Genocide* (2003). Regarding the role the US played in Rwanda, see Power's chapter 10 "Rwanda: 'Mostly in a Listening Mode'" (328–389) and Jared Cohen, *One-hundred Days of Silence: America and the Rwanda Genocide* (2007).

4. Groupov (Collectif théâtral. Jacques Delcuvellerie director). *Rwanda 94. Une tentative de réparation symbolique envers les morts, à l'usage des vivants* (2002). If not indicated otherwise, the quotes of this play refer to the bilingual edition *Rwanda 94. Une tentative de réparation symbolique envers les morts, à l'usage des vivants—Rwanda 94: An Attempt at Symbolic Reparation to the Dead, For Use by the Living* (2000), which reproduces most of the dialogues in French and in English with 2 CDs featuring the music score of the play. Nevertheless, the opening testimony of Yolande Mukagasana is not reproduced in this 2000 bilingual version published by Carbon 7 Records and Groupov. Thus, when the translation is mine for this play, the page number refers to the French text *Rwanda 94* published in 2002 by les éditions théâtrales.

5. Henry Rousso, *The Vichy Syndrome: History and Memory in France since 1944* (1991).

6. On Pierre Bourdieu's concept of "symbolic violence," see the chapter "The Economy of Symbolic Good" in *Practical Reason: On the Theory of Action* (1998).

7. For more details, see Catherine Coquio, "Aux lendemains, là-bas et ici: l'écriture, la mémoire et le deuil" (2003): especially 8–12. Henceforth, all quotes from Coquio's works are my translations.

8. On this topic see chapter 18, "Testimony, Memory, and Reconciliation in the Era of *gacaca*." See also Phil Clark and Zachary D. Kaufmann eds., *After Genocide: Transitional Justice, Post-Conflict Reconstruction and Reconciliation in Rwanda and Beyond* (2009).

2

Historical Preamble to Set the Scene

BETWEEN APRIL 7 AND MID-JULY 1994, more than one million people were killed in Rwanda, the vast majority for the unique reason of being Tutsi; the others, for being Hutus who refused to embrace the extremist Hutu power ideology and regime responsible of the last genocide of the twentieth century. Thousands of people were slaughtered each day by the Hutu-led Rwandan Armed Forces (RAF), by Hutu extremist militias known as *Interahamwe*,[1] by their neighbors, teachers, friends, and even, in some instances, by their own relatives. On April 6, 1994, only a few hours after the plane of Rwandan president Juvénal Habyarimana was shot down, lists of prominent Hutu and Tutsi politicians opposed to the Parmehutu ideology and Habyarimana's regime were distributed to ensure their systematical assassination. In the evening of the next day, massacres were perpetrated throughout the country. Habyarimana's death gave Hutu extremists the pretext they needed to seize power and disregard any political promises made during the 1993 peace negotiation in Arusha. More fundamentally, it allowed them to radicalize the conflict by declaring that all Tutsis were traitors allied to the Rwandan Patriotic Front (RPF)—Paul Kagame's Tutsi-led army and party "responsible" for the ongoing war in Rwanda since 1990. The possibility for a progressive implementation of multiparty democracy as a means to move beyond the era of the single-party dictatorship was suddenly history, as was the chance to put a peaceful end to the war between the RPF and the Habyarimana regime, which had been in power since 1973.

Casting Habyarimana's assassination as the decisive factor to explain how an allegedly "ethnic" civil war transformed "itself" into genocide is a tempting rationale to which many narratives have subscribed in their desire to explain what happened. But no social reality transforms "itself" into anything, especially not into a genocide! Genocides are the result of long and precise political planning that gradually implements the social conditions making mass killing not only historically possible but endorsed by the majority[2]—cultural and international indifference constituting here essential forms of endorsement that were as decisive as the fact that a war had been raging since 1990. As Hatzfeld highlights in *Machete Season: The Killers in Rwanda Speak*:

> All genocides in modern history have occurred in the midst of war—not because they were its cause or consequence but because war suspends the rule of law: it systematizes death, normalizes savagery, fosters fear and delusions, reawakens old demons, and unsettles morality and human values. It undermines the last psychological defenses of the future perpetrators of the genocide. . . . In Germany as in Rwanda, genocide was undertaken by a totalitarian regime that had been in power for some time. The elimination of the Jew, the Gypsy, or the Tutsi had been openly part of the regime's political agenda from the moment it took power, and it had been repeatedly stressed in official speeches. The genocide was planned in successive stages. It thrived in the disbelief of foreign nations. It was tested for short periods on segments of the population. It was tested in the Bugesera, for example. (54–58)

The task of explaining why so many ordinary Rwandans—more than half a million—took part in the genocide of the Tutsis is a very complex endeavor. According to Peter Uvin, author of *Aiding Violence: The Development Enterprise in Rwanda*, the desire of a Hutu elite to stay in power by all means is not a sufficient explanation, since this thesis attributes too much weight to state power, propaganda, and ideology while undermining the will and response of the civil society's members. For Uvin, Rwandans are not more obedient or permeable to ideology than any others and would not, therefore, more easily renounce their moral and social values. Other factors were at play within the civil society to explain such a massive participation in the killings. Among these factors, Uvin mentions in addition to the long history of discriminations defined along ethnic lines: decades of socio-psychological racism that instilled the prevalence of an imaginary where Hutus and Tutsis are morally, intellectually, and physically so different that they can not live together peacefully; an economic recession and rising poverty that instilled a climate of crisis and resentment; a polarized political context that excluded compromise; an inherited culture of impunity regarding violence against Tutsis; an absence of external constraints; opportunistic attitudes when violence becomes socially acceptable; and a culture of the State inherited from the colonial period where governing is a means to accumulate wealth and privileges for the minority in power. All these factors played a role in why so many Rwandans took part in the killings of people they often knew as neighbors, childhood friends, and even family members:

> To understand the genocide, then, three elements are necessary: the anomie and frustration caused by the long-standing condition of structural violence; the strategies of manipulation by elites under threat from economic and political processes; and the existence of a socio-psychological, widespread attachment to racist values in society. It is the specific interaction of these three processes that allowed the genocide to occur in Rwanda.
>
> Four other factors are of secondary importance; they contributed to the genocide but did not cause it directly. Foremost among them is the occurrence of past violence, both in Rwanda and in Burundi. The others are opportunism, the absence of external constraints, and the colonial legacy. Virtually all these factors far predate the 1990s. Many of them involve the international community. (Uvin 223)[3]

The "us" or "them" (di)vision has deep roots in Rwanda's history since it goes back to the Hamitic myth[4] introduced by colonizers to justify a hierarchy between three groups: first were the Twas (hunters and potters who were native to the region), then came the Hutus (cultivators identified as Bantu from Western Africa) and finally arrived the Tutsis (settlers who came from Egypt or Abyssinia). The Hamitic myth developed by the British explorer John Hanning Speke (1827–1864) was supposed to explain the arrival of "civilization" in this part of Central Africa and legitimize the political superiority of the Tutsis since a powerful and centralizing court based on the Tutsi Nyiginya lineage was ruling the kingdom in the nineteenth century. According to this myth, Tutsis were descendants of the biblical figure Ham, had lighter skin and held more European intellectual and social qualities than the Hutu who were Bantu and the Twa who were identified as pygmies. During the colonial period, this narrative, which had originally three distinct moments, was transformed within the political sphere and became the narration of a duel that totally eclipsed the Twas who represented only 1 to 3 percent of the population. For Coquio, "This erasure should deserve close attention in the process of a rewriting of the country's history since it proved to be the necessary condition to impose within Rwanda's society an implacable binary logic—Hutu/Tutsi—which seems to have conditioned in this country all public discourses and, certainly, the majority of private discussions as well" (*Rwanda. Le réel et les récits* 26).

This polarization between two distinct identities not only eclipsed the native Twas but replaced them by the Hutus as the natives in most colonial and postcolonial discourses. At the same time, this Hamitic myth and its rewritings imposed a social imaginary where Twas, Hutus, and Tutsis had irreconcilable values and qualities, which allowed a framing of social relations in a recurrent history of natives and settlers, superiority and inferiority, dominance and servitude, economic control and discrimination. During the colonial period, Belgians relied on this binary narrative to justify the privileges they attributed to a Tutsi elite and went so far as to institute the ethnic declaration on Rwandan identity cards in 1933. During the decolonization era, pro-Hutu discourses depicted themselves as not only the real natives constituting the majority of Rwandans, but also as historical victims with all the rhetorical weight and legitimacy that this enunciative position carries, not to mention its mobilizing power. The political use and abuse of the Hamitic myth rewritings progressively essentialized and naturalized two antagonistic ethnicities that no longer referred to social categories or economic occupations as they did originally.[5] Hutu and Tutsi came even to designate different races, as in the "Bahutu Manifesto" of 1957.

After Rwanda's independence in 1962, the Hutu/Tutsi and native/invader narrative continued to prevail as the paradigm to define national identity and positioning between Rwandans. The Hamitic myth and its dualistic revisions, by legitimizing an interpretation of Rwanda's history as a constant fight between the "indigenous" and "native" Hutus against the "foreign" and "invading" Tutsis, proved to have terrible long-lasting consequences. It allowed those in power to mute existing or emerging political positions, dismiss cultural practices transcending this exclusionary divide, downplay the weight of regional solidarities, and obliterate inter-ethnic marriages within Rwanda's civil society before and after independence.[6] This ethnicist rhetoric not only attempted to reify national identity but was meant to abrogate all forms of past and present coexistence between Hutus and Tutsis. Indeed, breaking all family ties between Hutus and Tutsis was advocated by the three first commandments of the Bahutu Manifesto of March 1957, which was reedited in December 1990 by the extremist pro-Hutu journal *Kangura*.[7]

Unlike in 1959, 1963, 1973, and 1992, when previous massacres of Tutsis already occurred in total impunity, in 1994 churches proved to be deadly traps rather than safe sanctuaries respected by political, military, religious, and civilian authorities. The violation and profanation of churches in a country where 90 percent of the population was Christian was a telling symptom of how far extremists were ready to go and how low moral values and social ties had fallen within the civil society.[8] This time, weakened and threatened by the Arusha agreements which imposed a multiparty system giving unprecedented political rights to Tutsis and moderate Hutus, the Hutu extremists who seized power after the president's death opted to radicalize the situation by carrying out the ultimate consequences of their ideology grounded in pro-Hutu ethnicism and nativism. Controlling official and extremist media like the journal *Kangura* and *Radio-Télévision Libre des Mille Collines* (*RTLM*) during the years leading to the genocide, they revived the specter of Tutsi's power monopoly in force before the Hutu revolution of 1959 as these polarizing excerpts of the journal *Kangura* attest in their attempt to rally all Hutus to their cause:

> Tutsis invaded us in Rwanda, they oppressed us, and we endured it. But now that we have freed ourselves from servitude and that they want to reinstate the morning whip, I think that no Hutu will tolerate this. The war that Gahutu leads is right, it is a fight for the republic. All Hutu need to know that when the feudal lords will arrive in Rwanda, they won't make any distinction between Hutu from the north and those from the south, they need to know that it will be the end for all of them.[9]
>
> Rediscover your ethnicity because the Tutsis have taught you to disregard who you are. You are an important ethnicity of the Bantu group . . . Be aware that an arrogant and bloodthirsty minority operates between you to dilute you, to devise you, to dominate you and to massacre you . . . The nation is artificial, but the ethnicity is natural.[10]

Capitalizing on years of such ethnist nationalism that instilled the fear that a victory of the Tutsi-led RPF would necessarily translate into the subjection of all Hutus, an extremist pro-Hutu minority viewed Habyarimana's death as the pretext to rally all Hutus to their cause. They did so by implicating as many as possible in the killings of all Tutsis—labeled as RPF sympathizers and spies—and Hutus opposed to Habyarimana's regime—labeled as traitors selling out the country to the enemy. Killing the "Other," as a patriotic gesture of self-defense justified by an ethnist and nativist interpretation of all social relations, was the perverse way to shed blood on the hands and consciousness of the vast majority of Rwandans and force them to back the extremist views and legitimacy of the pro-Hutu elite in power who called itself the "government of the saviors" (Chrétien, *Rwanda, les médias du génocide* 297).

In retrospect, one could argue that the genocide was foreseeable and could have been prevented. Foreseeable not only because of the impunity of *Kangura*'s promotion of genocidal ideology, but more importantly because several generations of Rwandan leaders had been unwilling to "re-imagine" the perverse colonial legacy they inherited when the Belgians left in 1962. Rather than dispelling the ethnic visions and divisions used by the German and Belgian administrations, visions that favored a small elite of the Tutsi minority in their indirect ruling of the colony, the Hutu revolution of 1959 put in power a small Hutu elite with the consent of the Belgian colonizers and the help of the Church. This reversal of allegiance in favor of the Hutu, who represented the majority of the population, was an opportunistic attempt by the colonial authorities to keep their grip on Rwanda when the Tutsi elite—which had been favored since the beginning of the colonization—sought independence for Rwanda during the 1950s.[11] The Hutu elite who came in power through the Party of the Movement of Emancipation of the Bahutu (Parmehutu) simply inverted the existing ethnic hierarchy in their favor and professed a pro-Hutu ideology and discrimination.

Needless to say, the Tutsis—and not the Belgian colonizer who had just propelled this new Hutu elite into power—were designated as the cause of all Rwanda's trouble and problems, a rhetoric that quickly lead to Tutsi bashing and slaughter with total impunity. Consequently, postcolonial Rwanda never freed itself from the politics of ethnicity inherited from the colonial era. Instead, a Hutu elite used ethnicity politically and economically to its advantage (see Braeckman, Chrétien, Des Forges, Franche, Prunier, and Semujanga). After the RPF attack in October 1990, the Hutu extremists were quick to revive the Hamitic myth, a vision of Rwanda's history that casts the Tutsis as invaders and oppressors and Hutus as the natives: "The Tutsis found us in Rwanda; they oppressed us; and we put up with this. But now that we have left serfdom and they want to reinstall the morning *chicotte* [whip], I think that no Hutu will be able to support this. The war Gahutu leads is just. It is a battle for the republic" (*Kangura* May 1991).[12] In order to unify all Hutu behind the Habyarimana regime, Hutu extremist ideologues translated a historical fact into an immutable trait of character and ideological permanency that rhetorically superimposed the past on the present in order to obliterate historical and social change and eliminate the possibility of a negotiated solution since "a Tutsi is always the same" and will never have any intent other than to exploit Hutus.

Obviously the Western powers also have their share of responsibility, since they have been equally unwilling to "re-imagine" their relationship with Africa in a postcolonial world. Short-term alliances and profits, geo-political influence, economic interest, and disregard of human rights have remained the pillars of Western engagement in Africa. Thus, it is not surprising that the world and its media—who had all the necessary information to foresee the genocide (see Brauman, Des Forges, and Thompson)—looked the other way while one million Tutsis were killed, more inclined to celebrate the end of Apartheid in South Africa than to question the acquisition of six hundred thousand machetes by the Rwandan Government between January 1993 and March 1994 thanks to a loan from the World Bank (Chrétien, *L'Afrique des Grands Lacs* 369). While the military victory of the RPF in July 1994 stopped the genocide, the four years of civil war that preceded the genocide also played an ambiguous role in the conditions that led to the genocide. The fact that the RPF was a mostly Tutsi army composed of Rwandan refugees exiled in Uganda and financed by neighboring countries only added to the complexity of the situation preceding the genocide. Some historians claim therefore that this "war of liberation" was one of the factors that precipitated the genocide, since it allowed Habyarimana's regime and pro-Hutu extremists to radicalize the politics of ethnicity by equating any Tutsi in Rwanda to foreign invaders. Such a reading is highly problematic, since it inverts—like the rhetoric adopted by many deniers' discourses—the primary responsibility of the genocide by placing it on the victims and minimizing the fact that the anti-Tutsi ideology and the planning of their extermination was solely the doing of an Hutu elite and minority determined to remain in power by all means.

Sixteen years have now passed since the pro-Hutu regime that planned and carried out the genocide was overthrown. The new government headed by Paul Kagame since 2000—who led the RPF to victory in 1994—has officially banned the use of ethnic categories such as Hutu, Tutsi, and Twa for the sake of national reconciliation and has undertaken sweeping judicial and economic reforms under the plan "Rwanda Vision 2020." While this ban represents a decisive and welcomed rupture with the past, it must also be read as a political move. Through the implementation of economic reforms combined with the promotion of a renewed conception of identity favoring national belonging,[13] the current government aims at transcending long term "ethnic" divisions and promoting social reconciliation in a country where the majority of the population remains self-identified as Hutu.

Moreover, to accelerate the process of national reconciliation also required the government to address the fate of more than one hundred thousand inmates accused of killings during the genocide. Aware that it could take close to a century to judge all of the suspects, the new regime decided to remedy this politically explosive situation by reviving and revising in 1996 the *gacaca*, a traditional judicial forum based on public confession during local hearings led by elders called *Inyangamugayo*—which means in Kinyarwanda "uncorrupted" or literally "those who hate evil." The *gacaca* jurisdictions as defined by the 1996, 2001 and 2004 organic laws differ from the traditional *gacaca* since they have been given the competence to judge murders and crimes of genocide—which was not at all the case in the past socio-historical function of the *gacaca*. The highly decentralized and local *gacaca* courts convene weekly, are mandatory and open to the public. Furthermore, beyond their judicial function they serve as a public reminder of the new government's authority while reaffirming the end of impunity and the rule of law. Under the *gacaca* law, the perpetrators who admit their crimes can hope to see the duration of their sentences reduced by half in exchange for their public confession. This restorative justice furthermore promotes at a local level the social reinsertion of the killers through community service and aims to accelerate the political process of national reunification. The *gacaca* courts are open to the majority of the presumed perpetrators of the genocide as long as they are not accused of having played any influential role in the planning of the genocide and did not commit sexual violence against their victims (Digneffe & Fierens).

While such salutary measures and pragmatic dispositions have been put in place for the thousands of perpetrators, where do they leave the victims and the survivors who seek justice, social recognition of their trauma, and forms of material compensation? What possible reparation might there be for survivors who have all too often endured seeing all of their relatives killed, who now find themselves living with AIDS as a result of organized rape, and who frequently claim they are "dead" despite their physical survival? As Anne Aghion's documentaries have shown (2002, 2004 and 2009), by asking the people of Rwanda to turn the dark page of their past in the name of national reconciliation, Kagame's primary concern was not the fate of the direct victims and survivors of the genocide. Numerous survivors, therefore, see the *gacaca* as a politically driven form of justice, which generates new forms of censorship for many survivors who still feel psychologically very vulnerable if not threatened by perpetrators' relatives or influent circles seeking to silence them. In the eyes of many survivors, the value of the *gacaca* resides more in the possibility it represents to find out how their relatives were killed and where their remains are located so that they can bury them with dignity.[14] According to a 2008 study by African Rights and REDRESS, "Assessments of gacaca vary, but for the most part gacaca has not met survivors' expectations. Their fears, particularly about the leniency of the sentences for crimes of the utmost gravity, have been borne out by the process. . . . Some survivors . . . feel they have been vindicated in their refusal to engage with gacaca. At the other extreme, Alphonse, the gacaca judge . . . , though aware of its many shortcomings, is 'convinced that for survivors, gacaca remains the only system of justice in which we can have confidence.'"[15]

Once more, at the very moment a society claims to face the disturbing realities and implications of genocide, it finds ways to keep this legacy present, but at a distance, by confining it to a very strict realm within society. The current "order of things" and the present priorities and interests prevail over the needs and desires of those for whom there cannot be any clear borderline between the past and the present, or definite forms of closure in which they can believe as they seek to define their place and their voice within Rwanda's post-genocidal society. If the mediation of genocidal violence and trauma is such a sensitive topic for survivors and governments, it is not necessarily for the same reasons: for the former, it is the social recognition of the genocide and the personal negotiation of its present aftermath that matters, while for the latter, it is how certain mediations of the past can help to legitimize the present order of things or contest it.

This brings us to the official politics of remembrance in Rwanda and how the memorialization of the genocide has been progressively crafted and politically orchestrated to ensure political stability and social reconciliation. Though the numerous memorials scattered throughout the hills of Rwanda have conferred for more than a decade a haunting visibility to the genocide—forbidding its obliteration and breaking away from a culture of impunity—ultimately, the vivid memory of the victims they symbolize and invite to mourn has been "reinterpreted for political gain" (Pottier 11). While these memorials undoubtedly offer a public space to mourn the dead, as is the case in Gisozi and Nyamata, they have also too often deferred for years the possibility of more personal rituals of mourning, since many exposed corpses that composed numerous memorials could not be buried for several years, even when they had been identified. Moreover, by privileging a visibility of the massive killings through anonymous piles of skulls and bones for more than a decade—and still today in Murambi—these memorials functioned as potent symbols of the legitimacy of the new government controlled by the RPF. Finally, on the international scene, these memorials legitimized Kagame's aggressive military activity within the Great Lakes region during the late 1990s, since the genocide could be mobilized as a shield against any criticism of his politics. By reminding the United Nations or countries like France, Belgium, and the United States how they criminally looked the other way in 1994 and did everything they could to pull out their troops from the United Nations Mission to Assist Rwanda forces (MINUAR), the official memorialization of the genocide offered a powerful rebuttal to any interference from foreign powers (Vidal 1998 and 2001).

By briefly mapping out some contextual and representational trends that led to the genocide of the Tutsi minority in Rwanda in 1994, I wanted to offer a minimal historical framework and highlight how the mediations of certain historical "facts" depend on their conditions of production and circulation as "the facts." In other words, we need to keep in mind how mediations of the past are themselves "facts" capable of exercising, after the facts, a "symbolic violence." The clarity of these prevalent and accepted accounts has been forged at the expense of the complex nexus of facts, discourses, historical legacies, collective beliefs, conflicting interests, and power struggles that ultimately made this genocide possible and still weigh on the analysis of its aftermath—not to mention the discourses that deny the occurrence of a genocide in Rwanda.

As we will see, by equating truth with clarity and coherence, literary and cinematic representations of the genocide institute a narrative conformity, which might, ultimately, contribute to silence survivors' views and their ability to tell their story in their own terms. As survivors see themselves obliged to follow narrative models and cultural expectations that do not necessarily correspond to their perception, many remain silent rather than risk a public disavowal or invalidation of their views regarding their past and present survival. In the aftermath of the genocide, survivors thus face not only the trauma generated by the suffering they have experienced, but also the rhetorical pressure and narrative conformity imposed by competing discourses positioning themselves as the true mediations of the genocide of the Tutsis in Rwanda. Furthermore, as Esther Mujawayo stresses in her first testimony *SurVivantes* (2004), the belated intervention of the international community had also long-lasting consequences regarding the identification of the perpetrators of the genocide. By covering events in the region only once the genocide of the Tutsis had been stopped by the RPF in mid July, the Western media generated a perverse inversion between victims and perpetrators. Their focus on the humanitarian crisis in eastern Congo created by the massive exodus from Rwanda of Hutus perpetrators and civilians led the world to see the Hutu refugees as victims, their plight overshadowing the fate of Tutsi survivors:

> . . . right after the genocide, you, as a survivor you were expecting compassion, and, in fact, you had again to defend yourself. Very rapidly, the situation reversed itself, the victims became the perpetrators, and the perpetrators, victims. And this reversal happened extremely fast: just as they were done exterminating, a whole wave of killers left . . . and, while you remain silent, the entire world sympathizes for them because their pain was more visible: their families were in exile, were decaying because of the cholera in the camps, or they were arrested and jailed, meanwhile, on the side of the real victims, you can't see anything: the badly wounded are not hanging around on the roads, survivors are mute, nor are regrouped into camps . . . The survivors' wounds are interior and often invisible ones. How many years did it take for the women who had been raped to be able to speak? . . . As for being listened. . . (54)[16]

This belated arrival of the media, the silencing of the survivors, and the political tensions at play in post-genocide Rwanda explain why so few narratives, testimonies, and films depart from expected references and consensual tropes; they explain why these representations reproduce chronological and causal storylines so that everything happens for a reason, follows a clear chain of events, can be explained, and, thus, ultimately leads to a foreseeable epilogue, moral, or political lesson.

Among these accepted narrative constraints lies the quest for "the" origin of the genocide, as if one single historical factor, cultural practice, or decisive moment could contain—literally and figuratively—the key that sparked off a massive and systematic killing of one million people. The ability to reduce the genesis and implementation of the genocide to a single and key factor would offer a reassuring rhetorical *trompe l'œil* while confronting the complex and troubling interactions that bring into play social factors such as the will to power, material greed, colonial legacy, the hatred of the Other, institutionalized discrimination, decades of Tutsi-bashing, not to mention a culture of impunity increased tenfold by the collapse of the rule of law during the war.

My questioning of the appeal of chronological configuration and these commonly anticipated and accepted tropes such as the quest for "the" origin or "the" beginning of the genocide applies equally to survivors' testimonies and literary and cinematic accounts. In their desire to be believable and in compliance with the cultural scene and expectations of their audience, many witnesses, authors, and filmmakers are more inclined to reproduce such illusion of mastery in their mediation of the genocide rather than to admit that its complex political genesis and aftermath cannot be encapsulated in ninety minutes or two hundred pages. Thus, one central question is how fictional and personalized representations of the genocide take into account in their esthetics and care for realism, the incommensurable gap highlighted by Rwililiza, namely that viewers and readers like me will always remain outsiders to survivors' experiences since they cannot "look at life with [the] eyes" of those who went through the abyss. Raising this issue is by no mean to suggest that the genocide of the Tutsis in Rwanda, because of its existential alterity and traumatic nature, is ineffable. Nor is this what I am advocating. Endorsing silence, behind its ethical desire to assert that no one can speak for the survivor without trivializing the radical evil of genocide through commonly accepted modes of representation, ultimately runs a greater risk, namely to legitimize a social silence that not only leaves unexamined the conditions of possibility of genocidal massacres, but also inhibits survivors' ability to forge the recognition of their survival and reclaim their due within our cultural "scene."[17] Thus, one of the major issues that this book explores is how various mediations negotiate the impossibility of speaking like and seeing as survivors while acknowledging the social necessity for survivors to bear witness to the genocide and, for their interlocutors, to socially advocate for an ethics of listening and secondary witnessing. Subsequently, my analysis focuses on how testimonial, literary, and cinematic works position their respective audience and what kind of response these works seek from our cultural scene by exposing us to an unsettling knowledge that defies the values and beliefs defining our shared humanity and sociability.

Notes

1. This name was given to the armed militia created as early as 1992 by the National Republican Movement for Democracy (MRND), President Habyarimana's party. In

Kinyarwanda, the word means "those who fight together." These militiamen played a primary role in massacres of Tutsis during the genocide.

2. For an analysis of the context that led to the genocide and the Arusha talks, see Alison Des Forges, *Leave no One to Tell the Story: Genocide in Rwanda* (1999); Colette Braeckman, *Rwanda. Histoire d'un genocide* (1994); and Mahmood Mamdani's chapter "The Civil War and The Genocide" in *When Victims Become Killers: Colonialism, Nativism, and the Genocide in Rwanda* (2001), esp. 210–218. For the long-term ideological genealogy that progressively shaped the social conditions leading to the possibility of the genocide of the Tutsis, see Gérard Prunier, *The Rwandan Crisis: History of a Genocide* (1995); Josias Semujanga, *Origins of Rwandan Genocide* (2003) and "Les mots du rejets et les récits du génocide" (2003); Scott Straus *The Order of Genocide: Race, Power, and War in Rwanda* (2006); and Yves Ternon, "Rwanda 1994. Analyse d'un processus génocidaire" (2009).

3. For a detailed analysis about the various factors and their relevance to explain the genocide of the Tutsis in Rwanda, see especially Uvin's conclusions exposed in the chapter "Why Did People Participate in Genocide? A Theoretically Informed Synthesis" (205–223) in *Aiding Violence: The Development Enterprise in Rwanda* (1998).

4. For an analysis of this myth see Gerard Prunier's first chapter, "Rwandese Society and the Colonial Impact: The Making of a Cultural Mythology (1894–1959)" (1–40) in *The Rwanda Crisis: History of a Genocide* (1995); Mahmood Mamdani's third chapter, "The Racialization of the Hutu/Tutsi Difference under Colonization" (76–102) in *When Victims Become Killers* (2001); Josias Semujanga's fourth chapter "Propagandist Discourse, or the Art of Manipulating Myths" (135–169) in *Origins of the Rwandan Genocide* (2003); Catherine Coquio, "1894–1994 La Fable du Hamite. Exotisme racial et idéologie génocidaire" (9–67) in *Rwanda. Le réel et les récits* (2004); and Nigel Eltringham's first chapter "'Ethnicity': The Permanent Debate" (1–33) in *Accounting for Horror* (2004).

5. That is to say that this biblical and racial explanation missed the complexity of pre-colonial Rwanda where the terms "Tutsi," "Hutu," and "Twa" designated economic occupations such as cattle owners and farmers. Most Tutsis were as poor as Hutus depending on their lineage or clan, and in some regions, some Hutu chiefs had power over Tutsis depending on their clan and which economic activity was prevalent in the region. Moreover, "Hutu" could become "Tutsi," and "Hutu" farmers became wealthy and could acquire cattle. Rwanda was a society where fights for political authority and economical power existed, but there were no fixed, immovable, and racialized hierarchies. The Nyiginya Tutsi dominance over the royal court was counterbalanced by social rules that gave authority to certain Hutu chiefs, and imposed certain obligations on Tutsi leaders. For more information on pre-colonial Rwanda see Servilien Sebasoni, *Les Origines du Rwanda* (2000).

6. See Mahmood Mamdani, *When Victims Become Killers: Colonialism, Nativism, and the Genocide in Rwanda* (2001), especially chapters 1–3: "Defining the Crisis of Postcolonial Citizenship: Settler and Native as Political Identities," "The Origins of Hutu and Tutsi," and "Racializing the Hutu/Tutsi Difference."

7. For an analysis of the ideological attempt to equate the struggle for power in 1994 to the situation before the Hutu Revolution of 1959 in order to naturalize a bi-

nary and divisive vision of Rwandans in the 1990s, see Marcel Kabanda, "*Kangura*: the Triumph of Propaganda Refined" (2007) and Assumpta Mugiraneza, "La dynamique discursive dans l'idéologie génocidaire" (2004).

8. Regarding the role played by various religious authorities and ecclesiastics as well as the complicity of the Catholic Church due to its close ties with the Habyarimana's regime, see Carol Rittner, John K. Roth, and Wendy Whitworth eds., *Genocide in Rwanda: Complicity of the Churches?* (2004) and Paul Rutayisere "Le remodelage de l'espace culturel rwandais par l'église et la colonisation" (2009).

9. "Le Rwanda souverain a besoin de l'unité et de la solidarité des Hutu" (*Kangura* 16 [May 1991]: 6) quoted in Jean-Pierre Chrétien ed., *Rwanda. Les médias du génocide* (2002), 143. Translation mine.

10. "Le Front commun des Bahutu: une nécessité absolue" (*Kangura* 7 [March/ April 1992]: 11–12) quoted in Jean-Pierre Chrétien et al. eds., *Rwanda. Les médias du génocide* (2002), 112. Translation mine. For an insightful analysis of *Kangura*'s self-defense rhetoric see Marcel Kabanda "*Kangura*: The Triumph of Propaganda Refined" (2007).

11. After the Belgian administrators transformed the three social groups—Hutu, Tutsi, and Twa—into official ethnic categories and decided in the early 1930s to mention explicitly these ethnicized affiliations on the Rwandan identity card, more than 80% of the population was identified as Hutu.

12. Quoted in Jean-Pierre Chrétien, *The Great Lakes of Africa: Two Thousand Years of History* (2003), 324.

13. Rwanda adopted a new flag and a new national anthem in 2002 and, more important, a new constitution in June 2003 whose article 2 stipulates that "All the power derives from the people. No group of people or individual can vest in themselves the exercise of power. National sovereignty belongs to the people who shall exercise it directly by way of referendum or through their representatives." The preamble of the 2003 constitution is also instructive as it underlines several points that can be read as a history lesson indicative on how the past will be interpreted officially and which references will be legitimate: "We, the People of Rwanda 1. In the wake of the genocide that was organized and supervised by unworthy leaders and other perpetrators and that decimated more than a million sons and daughters of Rwanda; 2. Resolved to fight the ideology of genocide and all its manifestations and to eradicate ethnic, regional and any other form of divisions; 3. Determined to fight dictatorship by putting in place democratic institutions and leaders freely elected by ourselves; 4. Emphasizing the necessity to strengthen and promote national unity and reconciliation, which were seriously shaken by the genocide and its consequences; 5. Conscious that peace and unity of Rwandans constitute the essential basis for national economic development and social progress; 6. Resolved to build a State governed by the rule of law, based on respect for fundamental human rights, pluralistic democracy, equitable power sharing, tolerance and resolution of issues through dialogue; 7. Considering that we enjoy the privilege of having one country, a common language, a common culture and a long shared history which ought to lead to a common vision of our destiny; 8. Considering that it is necessary to draw from our centuries-old history the positive

values which characterized our ancestors that must be the basis for the existence and flourishing of our Nation. . . ."

14. See on this topic Gilbert Ndahayo's remarkable documentary *Rwanda: Beyond The Deadly Pit* (2008) and the testimonies written by Annick Kayitesi *Nous existons encore* (2004) and Esther Mujawayo and Souâd Belhaddad *La Fleur de Stéphanie. Rwanda entre réconciliation et déni* (2006).

15. African Rights and REDRESS, *Survivors and Post-Genocide Justice in Rwanda: Their Experiences, Perspectives and Hopes* (2008), 28.

16. Henceforth, all quotes of Esther Mujawayo and Souâd Belhaddad's testimonies are my translations.

17. On this topic, see the polemic surrounding the publication of Georges Didi-Huberman's essay *Images in Spite of All: Four Photographs from Auschwitz* (2008) where he discusses the status of photographs taken by members of a *Sonderkommando* in Auschwitz.

3

Testimony, Literature, and
Film as Vectors of Memory

THE LAST DECADE HAS SEEN THE EMERGENCE of a multi-faceted literature bearing witness to the genocide of the Tutsis in Rwanda and the publication of numerous testimonies written by survivors. Mostly published in French, they seek to assert, within the Francophone world, that a genocide against the Tutsis occurred in Rwanda in 1994. They attempt to forge social recognition for the personal and collective trauma that continues to haunt the victims of this genocide, so that their loss and suffering can no longer be ignored. This testimonial literature written by survivors and authors who have not directly witnessed the genocide is thus engaged in the social negotiation of the cultural place and political response the West gives to the genocide's aftermath. As Kalí Tal asserts in *Worlds of Hurt*, what is crucial in this analysis of testimony in the context of extreme violence is that the meanings of personal trauma cannot be separated from the collective memory shaped by literary authors and filmmakers through and within which survivors seek forms of social recognition:

> Bearing witness is an aggressive act. It is born out of a refusal to bow to outside pressure to revise or to repress experience, a decision to embrace conflict rather than conformity, to endure a lifetime of anger and pain rather than to submit to the seductive pull of revision and repression. . . . If survivors retain control over the interpretation of their trauma, they can sometimes force a shift in the social and political structure. If the dominant culture manages to appropriate the trauma and can codify it in its own terms, the status quo will remain unchanged. (7)

The narratives witnessing the genocide of the Tutsis in Rwanda can be grouped into three main categories: First, testimonies written by survivors such as Vénuste Kayimahe, Annick Kayitesi, Berthe Kayitesi, Esther Mujawayo, Yolande Mukagasana, Scholastique Mukasonga, or Révérien Rurangwa; second, edited compilations of collected testimonies that sometimes bring together both survivors' and killers' accounts—the most well-known being Jean Hatzfeld's trilogy; and finally, works of fiction that have been mainly created as part of "Rwanda: Writing As a Duty of Memory" ("Rwanda: Écrire par devoir de mémoire") a literary project initiated in 1998 by "Fest' Africa" festival's directors Nocky Djedanoum and Maïmouna Coulibaly. Among the Francophone writers who collaborated in this undertaking, which gave unprecedented cultural visibility to the genocide of the Tutsis within Francophone literature were Boubacar Boris Diop (Senegal), Maïmouna Coulibaly (Ivory Coast), Nocky Djedanoum (Chad), Koulsy Lamko (Chad), Tierno Monénembo (Guinea), Jean-Luc Raharimanana (Madagascar), Véronique Tadjo (Ivory Coast), and Abdourahman Ali Waberi (Djibouti).[1]

As to the cinematic representations of this genocide, numerous feature films and documentaries have been produced both in English and in French. Though Terry George's *Hotel Rwanda* (2004) managed, ten years after the genocide of the Tutsis, to put this slaughter in the West's imaginary and consciousness, it was not the first film nor the only one created after 2000. Six other major films were produced and, moreover, shot in Rwanda by filmmakers of different nationalities: Nick Hughes (2001), Raoul Peck (2004), Michael Caton-Jones (2005), Robert Favreau (2006), Roger Spottiswoode (2007), and Alain Tasma (2007). Several documentaries shown on various national television channels played also a significant role in conferring a visibility to the genocide of the Tutsis in various countries as they were often followed by debates and roundtables. To name a few: Robert Genoud's *Rwanda: How History can lead to Genocide* (1995), Danièle Lacourse and Yvan Patry's *Chronicle of a Genocide Foretold* (1996), Fergal Keane's *Valentina's Nightmare: A Journey into the Rwandan Genocide* (1997), Anne Lainé's *Rwanda, un cri d'un silence inouï. Témoignages de rescapés du génocide* (2003), Anne Aghion's *In Rwanda We Say . . . The Family That Does Not Speak Dies* (2004), Greg Barker's *Ghosts of Rwanda* (2004), Raphaël Glucksmann, David Hazan and Pierre Mezerette's *"Tuez-les tous!" Rwanda: Histoire d'un génocide "sans importance"* (2004), Peter Raymont's *Shake Hands with the Devil: The Journey of Roméo Dallaire* (2004), Eric Kabera's *Keepers of Memory* (2005), Jean-Christophe Klotz's *Kigali. Des images contre un massacre* (2005), Laura Waters Hinson's *As We Forgive* (2008), Gilbert Ndahayo's *Rwanda: Beyond the Deadly Pit* (2008), and Anne Aghion's latest documentary on post-genocide Rwanda *My Neighbor My Killer* (2009).

Given these numerous and diverse representations of the genocide of the Tutsis, what does it mean, then, for authors, filmmakers, or survivors to bear witness? For survivors, what testimonial resonance and social recognition are then possible in the face of so many competing and seductive accounts, not to mention numerous forms of denial? Are fiction writers and filmmakers equally entitled to decipher the experience of genocide, the sequence of events leading to its implementation, or assert its readability for a readership that is foreign to the genocide and often immune to the politization of memory, preferring sympathy and sorrow to ideological scrutiny and historical guilt? Furthermore, what does it mean for readers and viewers to face these various accounts? What does this knowledge passed on to us require from us to prevent it from being confined to the past and to a distant society? If "transforming is what art does" according to Sontag, then how should literature and film define an esthetic of indirect witnessing (76)? More than ever we are inscribed in the "Age of Testimony" and need to respond to its obligations as defined by Shoshana Felman in her analysis of Albert Camus' novel *The Plague*:

> *Age of Testimony*: an age whose writing task (and reading task) is to confront the horror of its own destructiveness, to attest to the unthinkable disaster of culture's breakdown, and to attempt to assimilate the massive trauma, and the cataclysmic shift in being that resulted, within some reworked frame of culture or within some revolutionized order of consciousness. . . . The literature of testimony, therefore, is not simply a statement (any statement can but lag behind events), but rather a performative *engagement* between consciousness and history, a struggling act of readjustment between the integrative scope of words and the unintegrated impact of events. (*Testimony* 114)

* * *

The first part of this book, "The Testimonial Encounter," analyzes texts written by Tutsi survivors such as Esther Mujawayo and Yolande Mukagasana who bear witness to their past sufferings and present challenges. I show how survivors appropriate various rhetorical and narrative strategies to negotiate their *state of out-of-jointness* (Chambers) generated by the status of being estranged to oneself and to society. Despite this double estrangement, the testimonial impulse to have it acknowledged signals, on the survivors' part, a desire of connectedness that requires survivors to forge the social recognition of their *ob-scene* (Chambers) disconnection. In this sense, I explore how the witness to an experience that has no cultural precedent and is, furthermore, perceived as a disruption of the social body must poetically, tactically, and rhetorically create the conditions of testimonial readability. Thus, I especially focus on the narrative strategies deployed by survivors to engage and implicate their readers, so that the latter become haunted by and thus *co-witnesses* (Felman) to the genocidal experience and the demands for justice that are passed on to us. In this first part focused on testimonial representations, I introduce the key questions and concepts that prompted the writing of this book through an analysis of the unique and remarkable play *Rwanda 94. An Attempt at Symbolic Reparation to the Dead, for Use by the Living*. Created by the Belgian collective Groupov in collaboration with survivors of the genocide of the Tutsis, this play, more than five hours long, premiered in Belgium in 2000 and toured Rwanda for the tenth commemoration of the genocide. The five parts of the play feature a dialogic configuration staging conflicting voices both in French and Kinyarwanda and rely on a multimedia setting that embarks its spectators on a polymorphous journey confronting them with the genealogy of the genocide, the horror of the killings, the role of the media, the indecent apathy of Western countries, and, above all, the voices of those who died and those who survived. My choice for this play as a gateway to this book is also grounded in the fact that it combines the various genres and media bearing witness to the genocide examined in the following chapters, namely, literary representations and cinematic attempts to confer a visibility to the genocide of the Tutsis—an event that remained culturally off-screen in the Western world until 2004 when Terry George's movie *Hotel Rwanda* forbade to reproduce any longer this denial. My reading of Groupov's five-hour play highlights the difficulties and the conditions of possibility in passing on survivors' *ob-scene knowledge* given of the social and *cultural scene* of their audience. In order to address the various strategies of resistance and denial of the Western audience targeted by this play, I demonstrate how works and testimonies bearing witness to genocidal violence and its aftermath require a renewed understanding of *hospitality* (Derrida) as an experience of interruption and *co-witnessing*.

The second section, "Dismembering Remembering," examines the possibilities and the limits of the literary attempt "Rwanda: Writing as a Duty to Remember" to forge, within the Francophone world, a social recognition for the personal and collective trauma that continues to haunt the victims of this genocide. This collective artistic project, initiated in 1998 by Djedanoum and Coulibaly, led two years later to an unprecedented visibility of the genocide of the Tutsis and therefore functions, within the Francophone world, both as one of the major symbolic memorials to the million who died anonymously and a site of commemoration fraught with political and judicial implications. Faced with readers who would prefer to silence the genocide's legacy and responsibilities, I discuss how some authors use various narrative strategies to seek political recognition of the genocide's victims and their suffering. I show how these works written by authors who have not directly experienced the genocide, while giving voice to the dead and the survivors, question the problematic status of their own voice and its relationship to this traumatic past. What does it mean for these narratives to acknowledge their inadequacy even as they testify to this traumatic past? I argue that the questioning of their authorial voice and the inability of their text to represent the genocide is, paradoxically, what allows these writers to testify by engaging in a virulent criticism of acts of commemoration that are, inevitably, also invitations to forget. In this light, I examine the conjunction between an esthetics of *dis-membering* and an ethics of *re-membering* advocated by this collective literary project in its attempt to testify to a traumatic experience both personal and collective. In my critique of configurations favoring realism, chronological progression, and causality to account for the genocide of the Tutsis, I show the ideological implications and benefits of an esthetic of fragmentation and interruption that does not put readers in a position of mastery. By forcing us to question their attempt to account for genocidal violence in Rwanda, these works engage us in *a self-reflexive work of remembering* while fulfilling the intended *duty to remember.*

In the third part, "Screening Memory and (Un)Framing Forgetting," I examine the cinematic representations that have been produced on the genocide of the Tutsis between 2001 and 2007. Facing a mounting number of discourses denying a genocide has occurred in Rwanda and political forms of denial aiming at obscuring Western responsibilities in the genocide of the Tutsis in Rwanda, I examine how each film confers a visibility and readability to a genocide that has been maintained culturally and ideologically off-screen. In particular, I explore how each filmmaker positions himself through various *history lessons* given either at the beginning and at the end of the films or through *erudite dialogues* on Rwanda's history between characters clearly identified as legitimate truth tellers. My analysis aims at highlighting that too often the history lessons staged by these films, despite their intention to pay tribute to survivors' traumatic experience, are highly problematic as they simplify or distort the complexity of the genocide's genesis and perpetration, too anxious to allow their viewers to articulate a coherent and intelligible diegetic world from the facts and characters presented. As in my reading of "Rwanda: Writing as a Duty to Remember," I focus on how the viewer's position is constructed through various dynamics of identification and differentiation and what understanding of *hospitality* is imagined through the multiple Western characters that are fictionally added to bridge the gap between Rwanda and the Western audience targeted by these films. By examining the diegesis and the characters' distribution, I analyze whether these various cinematic representations call for a *self-reflexive work on remembering* in their framing of the past—a gesture that would invite their audience to question their historical and cultural role, be it during the genocide or today regarding its aftermath. As Michel-Rolph Trouillot reminds us in *Silencing the Past*, what we should never lose site of in the writing of history is positionality: "The past does not exist independently from the present. Indeed, the past is only past because there is a present, just as I can point to something *over there* only because I am *here*. But nothing is inherently over there or here. In that sense, the past has no content. The past—or more accurately, pastness—is a position" (15).

Ultimately, this book questions how communities and individuals define *hospitality* in the face of a traumatic experience, how we address our silencing power toward those who speak a foreign language, embody a disturbing experience, and seek from us an acknowledgment of their shared humanity and the radical difference of their gaze. In this sense, how we position ourselves as heirs through the relationships we establish with the haunting voices of an *ob-scene* experience and the disturbing aftermath that survivors' testimonies inscribe within our present *scene*, is the question that weaves together the pages of this book.

Note

1. The works and authors mentioned here are only representative of these three categories and do not amount to an exhaustive list. Furthermore, one could add a fourth category since several comics focusing on the genocide have been published. See especially the works of Rupert Bazambanza, *Smile Through The Tears: The Story of the Rwandan Genocide* (2005); Willy Inongo and Senga Kibwanga, *Couple modèle— couple maudit* (2001); Pat Masioni, Cécile Grenier, and Ralph, *Rwanda 1994. Tome 1. Descente en enfer* (2005); Pat Masioni, Cécile Grenier, and Alain Austini, *Rwanda 1994. Tome 2. Le camp de la vie* (2008); and Jean-Philippe Stassen, *Déogratias. A Tale of Rwanda* (2000) and *PAWA Chroniques des monts de la lune* (2002).

I

THE TESTIMONIAL ENCOUNTER

You start to tell your story, you go on, and they refuse to listen, and this is terrible. They say: "It is too horrible." They say: "It is too much, too much . . ." It is too much for whom? It is too much for me or for you who listens? . . . As a survivor of the genocide, you don't have the luxury to put it aside: you are in it, in it.

Meanwhile the other, the one who listens, he just receives the horror through words and he, he has the luxury, or the choice to be outside it, to declare that he is unable to bear this and say: "Here stops the horror." Myself, I do not have this choice not to bear it because I had to bear it and still have to bear it.

Esther Mujawayo (*SurVivantes* 20–21)

4

The Hospitality of
Listening as Interruption

RWANDA 94. *An Attempt at Symbolic Reparation to the Dead, for Use by the Living* is a performance created by the Belgian collective Groupov[1] and written by Marie-France Collard, Jacques Delcuvellerie, Tharcisse Kalisa Rugano, Yolande Mukagasana, Jean-Marie Piemme, Dorcy Rugamba, and Mathias Simons. Directed by Delcuvellerie, it premiered at the Théâtre de La Place in Liège (Belgium) in March 2000 and at the Théâtre National in Brussels in April of the same year. A preliminary version was presented at the Avignon Festival (France) in July 1999 as a work-in-progress.[2] Since then, it has played in France, Belgium, Germany, Switzerland, Canada and, for the tenth anniversary of the genocide, Rwanda in numerous locations in 2004.[3] A first version of the text was published in a bilingual edition with two CDs of the music composed by the American musician Garrett List and the Rwandan singer Jean-Marie Muyango. The musical pieces, like the play, were the result of a four-year collaboration between Western and Rwandan artists. The second version, which includes the opening testimony of the survivor Yolande Mukagasana, was published in 2002 in France. In 2007, a DVD of the play with French and English subtitles was produced by Marie-France Collard and Patrick Czaplinski.

Rwanda 94 is a five-and-half-hour performance targeting a Western audience. It follows no linear plot besides the quest of the journalist Bee Bee Bee as she seeks to understand how this genocide was possible in Rwanda and the role played by the media in our understanding of the killing of one million people in 1994. Opting for a kaleidoscopic and polyphonic composition, the authors stage multiple voices and characters throughout five parts using various media.

Moreover, they do not shy away from pointing out the responsibility of Western nations and leaders, and offer no reassuring epilogue. As Delcuvellerie's
introduction to the 2000 edition underlines, *Rwanda 94* is a highly interdis-
ciplinary and polyvocal production, has a very explicit agenda regarding the
responsibilities of the West, and positions itself clearly within the history of
genocide representation by crafting an esthetic that recognizes its own limits
and the impossibility of remaining neutral:

> The *Rwanda 94* project was born out of an extremely violent revolt in the face
> of the events themselves and the indifference and general apathy toward the
> genocide. The dead were anonymous, faceless, unimportant. At the same time,
> it was a revolt against the process which created the news out of these events
> on television, on the radio, and in the press. This "dramaturgy" of information
> is one subject of the production. With a few rare exceptions, the "Rwandan
> tragedy" was presented as a "tribal war," an interethnic massacre between the
> Hutus and the Tutsis, a "typical African" problem. . . . Groupov then embarked
> on a long enquiry amongst ethnologists, historians, journalists, survivors of
> the massacres, and witnesses, and made three field trips to obtain information.
> . . . Why? Why did it happen? Why this hatred, these dead, why this indifference
> to the genocide, why this complicity with the murderers? It is pointless to keep
> repeating: Never again! describing the horror, but identifying the causes as being
> beyond human comprehension. . . . *Rwanda 94* tries, of course imperfectly, but
> resolutely, not only to do justice to the victims but also to examine the motives
> for their killing. (11–13)

My analysis of this play will also include a reading of the testimonies published by Yolande Mukagasana and Esther Mujawayo as I seek to expose the
rhetorical, social, and cultural issues at stake when bearing witness to the
genocide of the Tutsis. In this first part, "The Testimonial Encounter," I lay
out a general framework for this book focusing on testimonial, literary, and
cinematographic representations of the genocide. Furthermore, the fact that
Rwanda 94 combines testimonies, fictional accounts, instrumental compositions, historical archives, and visual representations offers a unique opportunity to examine what it means to mediate the radical violence and traumatic
aftermath of genocide for authors who are themselves survivors and those
who do not share this traumatic fate. As Delcuvellerie underscores in his
essay on theatrical representation, the stage—like the page and the screen—
functions as a figuration of the world, which is not the world, even though it
establishes a specific mode of communication with an audience who is part of
the world. Thus, what is enacted never equates to a "presentation" of reality
but has to be approached as a "re-presentation," which does not attempt to
substitute itself for the experience it "re-presents," since it confers a visibility

to historical events and social interactions that are culturally marginalized if not ideologically censored ("La représentation en question" 127 and 136).

Furthermore, agreeing with Cathy Caruth that "history, like trauma, is never simply one's own, that history is precisely the way we are implicated in each other's traumas," (24) this opening section explores how the play *Rwanda 94* and Mukagasana's and Mujawayo's testimonies stage a demanding relation between the dead, the survivors, and the living who seek to understand what happened, to identify who is responsible, to explore what form of justice can be implemented, and to grasp the challenges of genocide's aftermath. But if we agree that we are "implicated in each other's trauma," then ultimately, reading, listening, and watching testimonial accounts bearing witness to the genocide demand from us—the Western audience targeted by these works—that we see ourselves no longer in a position of exteriority but one that requires us to redefine our responsiveness and agency. As Patricia Yaeger highlights in her essay "Consuming Trauma," the task to confer a social visibility and a historical resonance to the dead is not an easy endeavor and requires from those, who like me, position themselves as the survivors' interlocutors to examine critically the "ventriloquism" we are socially performing through our readings as we seek to be faithful *porte-paroles* for those who can no longer speak and act on their behalf:

> . . . how do we narrate or speak for the dead? What allows this speech to grant them proper weight, substance, dignity? If this weight is too heavy, can we go on writing? Do we want to? If the weight is too light, can we do justice to the injustices endured by the specter? . . . The ventriloquism we lend to the dead, the tropes we clothe them in, can have the power to re-dress their bodies, to speak volumes. . . . At the same time . . . we inhabit an academic world that is busy consuming trauma . . . through its stories about the dead. We are obsessed with stories that must be passed on, that must not be passed over. But aren't we also drawn to these stories from within an elite culture driven by its own economies: by the pains and pleasures of needing to publish. . . . Given the danger of commodification and the pleasures of academic melancholy—of those exquisite acts of mourning that create a conceptual profit—what are our responsibilities when we write about the dead? (28–29)

The play *Rwanda 94* opens with the testimony of a Tutsi survivor—Yolande Mukagasana—who, sitting alone on a small iron chair, tells her own story entitled "Death does not want me."[4] During the account of her nightmarish survival, she narrates how her husband, who despite being a Hutu, was killed by neighbors with a machete. Separated from her children as they were hiding in a different place, Mukagasana learned their fate from her niece Spérancie who told her how two of her kids were killed and thrown in a pit. The third,

afraid of the machete, jumped in it alive and died asphyxiated under the bodies
of Tutsi neighbors. Her monologue lasts forty minutes, but her words witnessing the death of all those who were massacred around her are more than words;
they are a performance through which she asserts the refusal of her social death
and her new identity as a survivor: "Even though I didn't hope I would survive,
I was telling myself: *I will bear witness*. . . . It is true that it is very difficult to
constantly repeat my testimony but I know that nothing could prevent me
from doing so. It is the only thing I can do for my people and for humanity.
. . . I would rather faint in front of you than fall silent" (22. Translation mine).
At the same time, the memory of a traumatic past represents a double-edged
sword for the survivor, since the memory of those who died in the genocide
embodies a past that should not be forgotten socially—its forgetting would signal the success of the genocidal obliteration—and cannot be forgotten personally because of its painful traumatic nature. As Régine Waintrater underlines in
her analysis of testimonies as a venue for genocide survivors to negotiate their
return among the living and being alive, the survivor must undertake a memorial fight on several fronts: "against forgetting and against memory . . . and foremost against himself or herself. . . . For a victim of a powerful trauma, memory
has an ambiguous status: at the same time a source of consolation and suffering, it contains the memories of the period that preceded the trauma and the
one that encapsulates the scenes of extreme trauma" (*Sortir du génocide* 100).[5]

Even if genocide survivors are socially perceived as the legitimate speakers,
to testify does not put their suffering at a more tolerable distance, nor does
it amount to a personal resolution. As Ross Chambers suggests in *Untimely
Interventions*, testimony is driven by a desire to voice the fact that survivors,
rather then "having survived a trauma," are "still surviving experiences that
were already themselves an experience of being, somehow, still alive although
already dead." What is here at stake is the social acknowledgment of an aftermath defined as a "state of out-of-jointness . . . of perpetually surviving a
trauma that is never over" (43). Mukagasana frequently stresses this feeling of
being in a "state of out-of-jointness" in her second testimony entitled *Don't
Be Afraid to Know* (1999).[6] She describes this fracture instilled within her by
the genocide through the dissociation she perceives between her body and
herself, a divorce that maintains her in a state of being a stranger to herself,
both incapable of reuniting with and afraid of facing herself as she seeks to be
one with herself:

> Something is wrong in my head. Again, I have this feeling of shame, this inexpli-
> cable shame. I work like hell . . . to forget myself. It is as if I began being afraid
> of those moments when I can reconnect with myself. I try to escape from myself.
> But what is going on then inside me? (164)

Survivor who lost more than two hundred members of her family in 1994 and co-author with Souâd Belhaddad of two testimonies, Esther Mujawayo echoes this fracture that lies at the heart of bearing witness to genocide. Like Mukagasana, Mujawayo envisions testimony as a social practice of reconnecting with oneself and with one's community while remaining aware that the process of bearing witness to her trauma and loss does not amount to a definitive catharsis: "The power of a genocide resides precisely in this: a horror during, but also a horror after. It is not the end of a genocide that puts an end to genocide, because within survivors there is no end to genocide. There is just a cessation of the killings, the massacres, the hunts—crucial, of course—but there is no end to the destruction" (*SurVivantes* 197). As Mujawayo testifies to a disruptive legacy whose stranglehold cannot be easily undone, she acknowledges the feelings of mourning, guilt, inner and social estrangement she must negotiate throughout the testimonial process:

> For the last ten years, to keep alive their memory and that of one million Tutsis who were eliminated, my life is a frantic race that will never know an end. Bearing witness, bearing witness, always bearing witness. For them, Innocent, my husband, my father, my mother, my sister Stéphanie, my sister Rachel, my nieces, my relatives, all my absent relatives that I have accounted for, do you remember. The more I testify, the more I hammer their memory. But the more I testify, the more their memory hammers me. Maybe, one day, I will be able to be done mourning my relatives, but never will I be able to make peace with what they have endured. (*Stéphanie* 13–14)

The wounds remain open, the scars visible, as does the feeling of being a stranger to oneself and to society while simultaneously seeking to reassert the necessity and negotiate the possibility of one's belonging to a community. As Delcuvellerie reminds us, "The machete inscribes a discourse in the body."[7] And yet, despite this double estrangement, the testimonial impulse to have it acknowledged signals a desire of connectedness that requires survivors to forge the social recognition of their disconnection. This desire of connectedness through testimony must be envisioned in the first place as a performance of survival, an act through which the survivor attests publicly her social survival and reaffirms her ongoing and current presence despite the obliteration to which she had been subjected: "The essence of testimony cannot necessarily be reduced to narration, that is, to descriptive, informative relations, to knowledge or to narrative; it is first a present act" (Derrida, *Demeure* 38). This insistence of being there, of being alive, is highlighted by the title Mujawayo chose for her first testimony: *SurVivantes*. Through this title, she asserts that those who escaped death are not only survivors, but also persons who need to find ways of being first and foremost Alive with a capital "A"—*Vivantes*.

The act of bearing witness to her survival played then for Mujawayo during many years a crucial role as it helped her to be sometimes "just alive"—even though she acknowledges that she faces moments of staggering doubt since the tenth commemoration: "Until then, this determination to bear witness to what I have lived during the extermination of the Tutsis, but also to testify to our difficulty or impossibility to bear witness to it, this determination was a sufficient counterpoint to the painful effort required by the remembrance of the conditions in which one's relatives were killed, but especially to the feeling emanating from the cruel absurdity of their annihilation. That is to say, as long as I was explaining how I succeeded in resisting annihilation, I didn't feel annihilated. I narrated what happened after: how, as a survivor, I rebuilt myself and decided to believe again in the Other, despite everything . . . and, suddenly, there, I tell myself that I am deluding myself. I tell myself that everything is moving forward, that we are going to get out of it, but fundamentally our reality is inexpressible because what we went through has been just that" (*SurVivantes* 244–45).

In the specific context of genocide, to bear witness as a survivor represents the social claim that the genocidal project—here the extermination of Rwanda's Tutsis—has failed even if this failure in the eyes of those who have survived represents more a chance for future generations than for themselves as Mujawayo highlights when she acknowledges the difficulty for the victims to overcome the imprint of genocidal ideology and violence:

> The accomplishment, I mean "the success" of a genocide, precisely resides, among others, in this principle: to make you feel guilty of being and then, as a survivor, to make you feel guilty of having survived. If being a Tutsi condemned me to death, why did I escape death . . . ? Why them and not me? To free oneself from this dilemma takes you years. . . . Today, remarried with Helmut, I live in Germany where I work as a therapist in a center for refugees. My three daughters are doing wonderfully well. Of course, almost each day, I weigh the ineffable luck that I didn't loose any of them. But this thought does not chase away the feeling of pain, nor the dull madness that torments my life since the genocide. A feeling of failure too: to be named Esther did not help me at all. I only saved three persons out of the two hundred and eighty-two who were exterminated. Queen without a King nor power, Esther failed in her mission. (*Stéphanie* 40–41)

The overwhelming feeling of guilt to which Mujawayo bears witness has been stated by numerous genocide survivors. All have to face the fact that their survival just happened by chance, thanks to a succession of events and coincidences that are beyond their grasp. To acknowledge that one's survival has nothing to do with one's beliefs or actions proves to be a highly destabilizing and undermining revelation as Mukagasana eloquently dramatizes the shame of being a survivor:

> *Why did I not die instead of this child?*
> *Why did I not die instead of my children?*
> *Why did I not die instead of those who died while saving the Tutsis?*
> *Why did I not die instead of all those who died for who they were?*
> *Why did I not die instead of all those who were wrongly identified as being me?*
> (*N'aie pas peur* 173)

Thus, in the aftermath of genocide, survivors have to confront a double dynamic, which insidiously suggests that their lives are "unjustified." First, they have to overcome the legacy that they were designated as unworthy of living because of who they are—Tutsis—that is to say that they were destined not to be: "This feeling of 'being illegitimate,' I have always experienced it" (*Stéphanie* 27). Second, for those who survived, they must come to term with the feeling that they are alive, but that nothing justifies their survival while so many relatives died: "An inner voice accompanies me everywhere and always whispers the same sentence. 'Yolande, you have no right to be alive.' . . . I am ashamed that I am not even wounded because of the genocide, that I was not raped, that I didn't have at least one arm cut off" (*N'aie pas peur* 205). This feeling of shame runs very deep for many survivors and affects their ability to interact with others and fully engage within their respective communities, as Nancy Miller underlines: "Shame reshapes identity, becomes a way of life, becomes almost invisible, as though it had entered the body itself. The secret knowledge of shame that excludes you in your own eyes from decency operates *regardless* of whether others know about it" (198). Third, many survivors experience a feeling of being alive but somehow dead, since their former self had been obliterated and the relatives who shaped their community and sense of belonging killed: "You tell yourself that you are alive, but that in fact, since they wanted to exterminate everything of yours, your family, your ethnic group, you shouldn't be there. You shouldn't be there, and yet you are there. But are you really there? . . . since you don't have any support, no interlocutor, no mirror to reflect love for yourself . . . In fact, you are just a zombie, the living dead. Yes, that's it: after the genocide, I was a zombie" (*SurVivantes* 223). In this situation, often the opportunity to take care of other relatives or orphans reintroduces the ability to project oneself in the future by proxy as it is the case for Mujawayo whose three daughters survived: "In fact, it is more they who saved me. I was able to hold on thanks to them: to save a child is such an obsession that it restores a meaning to a situation that no longer had any" (*Stéphanie* 25). To dedicate one's life to future generations has proven to be a vital counterpoint for those survivors who always run the risk to find themselves again, trapped in a past without means to re-envision themselves outside of its haunting and alienating potency. As Waintrater underlines, one of the major challenges for genocide survivors is the ability to negotiate a new form of psychological continuity after the radical gap that the genocide generated within themselves, cutting them from who they were by obliterating the community of those with whom they were: "Genocide cuts life in two. There is always a before and an after. And yet, the human being needs a continuity within identity. . . . Testimony carries therefore this double function to be a mandate and an attempt of reuniting the parts of one's life that have been deeply split into heterogeneous pieces by the radical event that genocide represents" ("Dix ans après" 59).

In the context of genocidal survival and its aftermath, to bear witness represents then the possibility of and the call for a dialogic space where survivors seek to redefine the present meaning derived from the experience of genocide and the weight of its haunting resonance within themselves and their community. In their attempt to re-envision themselves through testimony, survivors move from a position of being subjected to political violence to a position that entails the promise of agency and the possibility of crafting the meaning of who they are: "April 2004, ten years later. Ten years later, and finally the beginning. Yes, but the beginning of what? The beginning of living again? Finally? Moving from the condemnation of being alive . . . to the *choice* of living, this is the path that I have traveled during these last ten years" (*SurVivantes* 29). To bear witness is then to generate a social space within which survivors can negotiate and, eventually, reclaim on their own terms the meanings of their survival and assert the demands of the traumatic aftermath they face in order to lighten its disruptive burden: "I will write in their memory. . . . My books will be my fight. To write about the genocide in Rwanda is a way to make humanity face its own cowardice. And I know already that voices will rise up to smother mine and to ridicule it. . . . But one day, truth will conquer" (*N'aie pas peur* 106–107).

Testimony must therefore be understood not only as a personal and social endeavor through which survivors assert their survival and the memory they embody, but also as the assertion of one's own uniqueness—that is to say that no one else can bear witness for the witness—and the reassurance that survivors are not carriers of a knowledge deprived of any social resonance and legacy. The paradox survivors have to negotiate is then, in part, related to the fact that they voice a unique and disturbing knowledge, which must be universalized under certain conditions even though those who have not experienced genocide will never be able to know absolutely or identify with survivors' experience and ongoing trauma. Jaques Derrida captures this tension at the heart of the uniqueness of an enunciative position that needs to overcome the risk of solipsism by creating the narrative means to fulfill the promise of its communicability, as follows:

> When I testify, I am unique and irreplaceable. . . . In saying: I swear to tell the truth, where I have been the only one to see or hear and where I am the only one who can attest to it, this is true to the extent that anyone who *in my place*, at that instant, would have seen or heard or touched the same thing and could repeat exemplarily, universally, the truth of my testimony. The exemplarity of the "instant," that which makes it an "instance," if you like, is that it is singular, like any exemplarity, singular *and* universal, singular *and* universalizable: this is the testimonial condition. Simultaneously, at the same instant, in the "I swear, you must believe me," I am claiming, I am demanding, I am postulating the possible and necessary universalization of this singularity: anyone who is in my place, etc., would confirm my testimony, which is thus both infinitely secret and infinitely public. . . . (*Demeure* 40–41)

For those who survived, the task of testifying and performing "this singular *and* universal exemplarity" is a daunting one that should not be confined to the sole witness, since it involves us, the listeners who have to reflect on the crucial role we play within the testimonial process and how we weigh on its conditions of possibility. As Belhaddad—Mujawayo's interlocutor and co-author— underlines, for survivors "to remain silent is forbidden, but telling is impossible," which leaves only a third option: being listened to: "if telling does not provide relief to the survivors, listening to them, on the other hand, might contribute to do so" ("Dire est impossible" 178). But are we willing and capable to listen? What does it entail and require to listen to a survivor of genocide? How does one envision, define, and become a listening community for survivors? To which extent can we, listeners, be implicated *in* and *through* the act of listening to survivors?

Bearing witness to the genocide of the Tutsis and one's own ability to face its aftermath, then, implies a daily negotiation both personal and collective, where the gesture of passing on one's pain becomes one of the possible affirmations of one's survival. But in order to perform this negotiation, survivors must invent, within and through testimony, the conditions of their social recognition. Faced with a society and politicians who too often speak for them and not to them or with them, survivors must craft textual configurations able to anticipate the potential reluctance and denial their testimonies will encounter, so that they may pass on their disturbing stories on their own terms. Since their experience is perceived as atypical, foreign, disturbing, and unbearable, their voice always faces the risk to be socially muted, euphemized, ventriloquized or interrupted as one of Mujawayo's chapters entitled "Testifying, Testifying,

Testifying, Testi . . ." symptomatically suggests: "I am convinced that my whole life long I will continue to testify—if only because everyone else wants solely to forget . . . Forget that 'this' happened again, that the survivors are still alive, with cut jaws, blocked Fallopian tubes, broken backs. We, on the other hand, we will have no means to forget" (*SurVivantes* 265).

As Derrida has shown in his analysis of Maurice Blanchot's short testimony *The Instant of My Death* (2000), the witness to an experience that has no cultural precedent, and is, furthermore, perceived as a disruption of the social body, must poetically, tactically, and rhetorically create the conditions of his testimony's readability: "For the witness must both conform to given criteria and at the same time invent, in quasi-poetic fashion, the norms of his [or her] attestation" (*Demeure* 40). Since trauma defies our preestablished mediations and eludes our social lenses, the necessity to work on the readability of one's witnessing is even more crucial in the context of testimony bearing witness to a traumatic event such as genocide: "Trauma is enacted in a liminal state, outside the bound of 'normal' human experience, and the subject is radically ungrounded. Accurate representation of trauma can never be achieved without recreating the event, since, by its very definition, trauma lies beyond the bounds of 'normal' conception" (Tal 15). As he attempts to answer the question "What is the place of the other?" in his reading of Montaigne's essay "Of Cannibals,"[8] Michel de Certeau underlines the necessity for testimonial literature bearing witness to the other to craft its own cultural and textual attestation as it disrupts the established (di)visions of the readers' cultural scene:

> On the one hand, the text accomplishes a spatializing operation which results in the determination or displacement of the boundaries delimiting cultural fields (the familiar vs. the strange). In addition, it reworks the spatial divisions which underlie and organize a culture. For these socio- or ethno-cultural boundaries to be changed, reinforced, or disrupted, a space of interplay is needed, one that establishes the text's difference, makes possible operations and gives it "credibility" in the eyes of its readers, by distinguishing it both from the conditions within which it arose (the context) and from its object (the content). . . . These two aspects are only formally distinguishable, because it is in fact the text's reworking of space that simultaneously produces the space of the text. . . . It combines a *representation of the other* . . . and the fabrication and accreditation of the *text as witness of the other*. (*Heterologies. Discourse on the Other* 67–68)

Only the testimonies that acknowledge the symbolic violence and strategies of denial they face might therefore be able to alleviate the enunciative trauma survivors endure when being spoken rather than being recognized as legitimate speakers of their pain. It is this enunciative trauma of being silenced by discourses claiming to speak in the name of survivors, testimonial literature and theatrical performances such as *Rwanda 94* can undo. At stake here is the ethical aim to no longer reinforce the social and political confinement of the genocide's aftermath and its disruptive implications to a personal matter. Mukagasana bluntly asserts this refusal to confine her pain to the private sphere and to mourn her dead in silence as follows: "When one mourns, one should shut up and simmer down one's sorrow without being a pain in the ass for others. But I, I am not like that. I am Yolande Mukagasana. When I am mourning, I rebel. I am too indebted to my dead children to subject myself to the expected good behavior required by funerals. I yell. And I will yell to the end of my days. . . . I do not have any other weapons, besides my pain" (*N'aie pas peur* 124).

Only through uncovering the silence we impose on survivors can we grasp our role in continuing their suffering, a suffering I refer to as "enunciative trauma" and that Sarah Kofman identifies as *Smothered Words.*[9] Dori Laub, one of the founding member of the *Fortunoff Video Archives for Holocaust Testimonies*, frames as follows the need for survivors to speak and even more so to be listened: "Lies are toxic and silence is suffocating. Each survivor has an imperative need to tell his or her story so that he or she can piece together its fragments; a need to free oneself from the ghosts of the past, need to know the buried truth in order to reimmerse oneself in the flow of life. It is a mistake to believe that silence favors peace." Furthermore, Laub underscores the fact that "a testimony to which nobody listens represents a trauma equally serious as the initial ordeal."[10] Thus, reading the literature bearing witness to the genocide of the Tutsis makes us face the forgetting we have sanctioned, the "symbolic violence" (Bourdieu) in which we are complacent, and the voices we have muted despite our claim to remember.

In *SurVivantes*, Mujawayo narrates the story of Alice whose survival and attempt to tell her story are emblematic of the "enunciative trauma" that most survivors experience in addition to the trauma related to their own survival:

> There are sometime stories that nobody wants to hear or can hear the whole way through, like Alice's story, for instance. I have a friend, Alice . . . who had been thrown in a mass grave with other corpses and she was in the pit . . . Oh, they are always the same stories! . . . Each time that the truck came back to dump more corpses, Alice tried to hold on. "Esther, she told me, the survival instinct is something crazy, because at this moment I realized that I was alive, that I didn't want to let myself be buried." She started to climb on top of the cadavers and each time that a new load was dumped on her, she had to reach the surface again, and always positioned herself above the other corpses; finally, during the night, she was able to get out of the pit. That very night, she was able to get out of there. But even now, she still lives in it. She tells me: "The children who I left inside . . ." because there were many dead mothers with their babies still alive wrapped around their backs who were crying, and she knew that if she succeeded

to save herself, she would only be able to save herself alone and would not be able to save the babies. And this, this has tormented her for a long time, a very long time. . . .

When Alice told her story, she was always asked to stop when she reached the moment about the babies who were crying and when she couldn't take any with her out of the pit where she had been thrown alive among the cadavers. That moment, it was too horrible for people and they interrupted her in the middle because it was too unbearable. "It's too horrible, stop!" But it was even more horrible for her not to be able to finish. Alice, her story, she had never been able to tell it to the end. One day, when I found her in Kigali in August 1994, after the genocide, that was the first time she was able to tell it to the end. She was relieved that she could tell it to the end. (21–23)

Mujawayo's testimony demonstrates here the importance of listening to the whole story and for those who have become the heirs of these stories, to tell them in their entirety instead of euphemizing or censoring them to manage the sensitivity of their audience. As the title of the chapter devoted to Alice indicates—"For Once, telling Alice's story to the end . . ."—what matters here for Mujawayo, is the importance of telling Alice's whole story and refusing to stop where Alice's interlocutors interrupt her—as Mujawayo did a couple chapters before mimicking the censuring and muting Alice faces (37). By doing so, Mujawayo's testimony performatively undoes the cultural silencing Alice faced each time she tried to testify. By narrating Alice's story, Mujawayo confers a social resonance to her suffering and, by bearing witness to it in its entirety, she refuses to reproduce the censuring gesture through which Alice's interlocutors attempted to protect themselves. If the fate of the babies is indeed sickening and horrible, the attempt to silence Alice is, as Mujawayo's account underlines, equally violent. Her listeners reject her because of the guilt she embodies and voices. Alice's testimony functions then as a double-edged mirror because it reflects not only Alice's guilt, but also the guilt of her interlocutors who, in their overwhelming majority, in the end are no better than she is because they too—we—did nothing to save those babies. Envisioned in this light, the genocidal violence to which survivors bear witness is just as "horrible" and disturbing as the violence we exert on them, since they embody and mirror our own haunting and disturbing failure to act while the babies were still crying.

The title of Mukagasana's second testimony puts this cultural silencing center stage: *Don't Be Afraid to Know. Rwanda: One Million Deaths. A Tutsi Survivor Testifies.* Mukagasana suggests up front that her ability to pass on her legacy cannot be separated from our willingness to see reading as a form of social witnessing. How shall we then read the fear her title anticipates—*Don't Be Afraid to Know*—if not as our belief in the duty to remember but yet, at a safe distance—more inclined to confront the genocidal aftermath through the petrified monologues of official memorials than through the cultural dialogues and social spaces of encounter testimonies seek to provoke. In Groupov's play, Mukagasana, therefore, reasserts as follows the importance of the audience's duty to listen and to act upon the knowledge passed on to its members: "I, Yolande Mukagasana, declare before humanity that whosoever refuses to acknowledge the torture of the Rwandan people is an accomplice to the crime. . . . I do not wish to either terrify or to seek pity. I wish to testify" (21). Her demand for a social space and cultural scene where survivors' experiences could be audible both to themselves and their interlocutors is not foreign to the literary endeavor if literature is understood as a social practice that allows members of a society to reflect through innovative written works on their shared humanity and negotiate a renewed common belonging.

In *Rwanda 94*, bearing witness to the dead and to one's own survival goes, therefore, hand in hand. It represents a social gesture that inscribes survivors like Mujawayo and Mukagasana—and the victims for whom they have become the spokespersons—within the process of remembering. By refusing to remain silent, Mukagasana claims a voice in the midst of the political struggles defining the memory of the victims and the fate of survivors of the genocide of the Tutsis in Rwanda. Moreover, her testimony, envisioned as a social gesture directed toward the living—here symbolized by the audience of the play and her readers—inscribes us within the polemical and ideological process of shaping the memory of this genocide. Mukagasana's testimonial interpellation ultimately demands that we overcome the fear leading us too often to silence survivors. She knows that her interlocutors are prone to confine her disturbing knowledge to the past, to what happens only to others. Thus, from the outset, she anticipates our attempt to reassure ourselves of our innocence by invoking our ignorance and by reproducing it socially through our refusal to "hear" her. Mukagasana's testimony is therefore not only directed toward the past but also equally toward the present since she demands that we confront our unwillingness to face radical challenges to our beliefs and values so that her testimony does not remain *lettre morte*. As such, we must then define throughout the testimonial encounter the resonance we want to give to the victims and survivors of this genocide within our respective communities and what our desire to listen entails.

As in her written testimonies like *Death Does Not Want Me* (1997) and her numerous public appearances,[11] Mukagasana's "performance" in the play *Rwanda 94* stresses from the outset the disturbing potential of her testimony and how demanding testimonial encounters with survivors of genocide can be. Aware that she embodies a traumatic experience whose deepest scars and meaning ultimately escape her as much as they baffle her audience, she anticipates the

dismissal of her testimony by asking her interlocutors to question why her suffering is so disconcerting. In her effort to sound out the depth of our desire and
our ability to listen to her story, she also addresses the pain our rejection would
inflict on survivors of genocide who, like her, seek social and personal recognition in order to restore their sense of humanity and belonging. After having
been dehumanized as treacherous cockroaches to justify their massacre, survivors exploit the capacity to provoke, negotiate, and revive through testimony a
space of encounter and social recognition that is crucial for their survival.

While Mukagasana stresses the importance for survivors to provoke social
dialogues that bear witness to the dead and engage in an intersubjective relationship that reasserts her humanity among the living, she also declares that
her testimony always runs the risk of becoming, to quote Charlotte Delbo,
"useless knowledge" if it fails to be read and translated into action. In all her
efforts and rhetorical ingenuity, Mukagasana is very aware that the willingness
of her interlocutors to engage in the dialogue she seeks to provoke is volatile,
since the suffering and aftermath to which she bears witness radically question
the assumptions and legitimacy of our will to know. By explicitly addressing
the resistance her testimony encounters within a society that claims to fulfill
a duty to remember, Mukagasana highlights not only the limits of our will to
know but, furthermore, also reveals its ideological function when it comes to
face the genocide of the Tutsis: "*Let anyone who does not have the will to listen
to this, denounce himself as accomplice of the genocide in Rwanda*" (*Rwanda 94*,
21). Therein, Mukagasana assigns her audience and readers a place defined
by an imperative. This obligation imposed upon the readers is a response, as
Alain Parrau underscores it, to the oppressive and silencing strategies readers
and interlocutors adopt within the testimonial process. These interlocutors,
Parrau attests, are more inclined to protect themselves from the extreme
violence to which survivors bear witness than to respond to their power of
interruption: "The event that became visible through the process of mediating it (that is to say configured, represented, depicted) imposes on the reader
. . . the visibility of what he could not see, of what he didn't want to see. It is
through this visual imposition . . . that the 'mirror' of the mediation defines
its power of mobilizing the real" (71–72).[12]

This cultural resistance that Mukagasana denounces as a form of genocidal
complicity is mainly linked to the fact that encountering her voice amounts
to an encounter with the "ob-scene," with what is culturally excluded, a disruption that is—and should remain—beyond the realm of what is commonly
accepted as legitimate. I borrow this concept of the "ob-scene" from Chambers who associates it etymologically to what is culturally "obscured" and,
therefore, somehow known but not readily acknowledged:

The cultural obscene is "obscured" or "covered" with respect to a scene of culture, but without being discontinuous with it. And it is tinged with a sense of the sacred (Latin *obscenus* meant of ill augur), but also of stigma and abjection, both of which refer to a mixture of fascination and repulsion exerted by objects [and experiences] that are expelled from within the social or physical body. (*Untimely* 23)

It is this liminal experience that we fear in testimonies bearing witness to genocide, since it questions the assumptions of our "signifying scene," challenges its social conformity, not to mention the fantasy of our neutrality or innocence. Therefore it is crucial, as Waintrater asserts, to depart from the common perception that reduces testimony to a form of catharsis. This understanding of testimony bearing witness to genocide, by confining the meaning of testimony and its implication within the survivor, signals rather our discomfort and a social attempt to contain survivors' words beyond our cultural scene: "Under the cover of a wrongly understood cathartic ideology, one trivializes testimony by taking off its irreducible scandalous dimension" (*Sortir du génocide* 16). Suddenly positioned by the testimonial encounter as heirs to a traumatic experience no longer culturally disconnected from our own, we find ourselves challenged in our belief that we should never have inherited this experience of genocide because it was supposed to be and remain an "ob-scene" reality. But, as Chambers underlines, the very act of witnessing redefines our thresholds when it proves capable of foiling the filters and gatekeepers of our cultural scene: "Because witnessing 'turns' what would otherwise be an infraction or an error, through the power of troping, into a meaningful if disturbing utterance that can participate in the exchanges and interactions that constitute culture, it is an act of *détournement* in all those senses. The culture is hijacked, its conventions appropriated for new purposes; audiences are turned from the circle of their everyday concerns toward what they may least wish to hear about." (21). To listen to testimonies and read the literature witnessing the genocide of the Tutsis questions then both our willingness to confront disconcerting human behaviors and our sense of cultural "hospitality," when "hospitality" is understood as "interrupting oneself."

As Derrida suggests: "This interruption of the self by the self, if such thing is possible, can or must be taken up by thought: this is ethical discourse—and it is also, as the limit of thematization, hospitality. Is not hospitality an interruption of the self? . . . One will understand nothing about hospitality if one does not understand what 'interrupting oneself' might mean, the interruption of the self by the self as other" (*Adieu* 51–52). At the end of her first testimony,

Mujawayo identifies as follows the challenges inherent in testifying to her "ob-scene" experience and to the hospitality she seeks through the testimonial encounters she culturally and ethically provokes:

> Indeed, the content of my public testimonies can make people feel uncomfortable, like the narratives that illustrate it. But I generate discomfort at a bearable level. The story of Rachel asphyxiated in the shit, before this book, I never told it to anyone. By respect also: it is my people who have been soiled in this genocide, so why would I tell this offense easily? Furthermore, I terribly fear pity, this is the last thing I want. During conferences, I rarely use numbers, especially rounded ones. When one says that one million people have been exterminated, it's enormous, it's horrible, scandalous, and then you close your eyes, you turn off the television and you go back to your normal life the next morning, without having memorized the number that was quoted. And yet, I would like to disturb. . . . I don't want you to sleep peacefully; you have some power, use it. (*SurVivantes* 260)

The encounter with the "ob-scene" experience of genocide can thus provoke in us one of two responses. It may, on the one hand, impose on us a duty to rethink how we position ourselves within the present and among the living in relationship to this "ob-scene" past in order to recognize both its long-lasting aftermath and the possibility of its repetition. Or, on the other hand, this encounter will affirm us in our unquestioned belief that our "order of things" is the only viable one, that it is immune to the possibility of genocide and, consequently, that survivors' testimonies are nothing but "ob-scene"—which does not preclude feelings like pity or call for a duty to remember, on the contrary. The first response represents an intersubjective dialogue where the survivors and their interlocutors engage in a mutually transformative relation, while the second symptomizes a social and cultural monologue where survivors' voices are cast as interferences or noise with respect to an exclusive harmony that defines the existing social order and what is culturally audible and appropriate. As Stevan Weine underlines in his analysis of testimony bearing witness to trauma generated by political violence, through "testimony, survivors and receivers engage with some of the most critical political, existential, and moral questions that a society can ask concerning identity, otherness, existence, values, and enemies. . . . These questions are at the core of how society and its people redefine themselves and the codes by which they live" (135).

Like the other representations of genocide I will explore throughout this book, my reading of the testimonial literature bearing witness to the genocide of the Tutsis is grounded in the concept of "hospitality" as defined by Derrida, namely as an encounter where the host must position himself or herself as the guest. As we find ourselves positioned as guests within the testimonial encounter, we must then, through the eyes of the foreigner, reenvision the assumptions of our laws and the evidence of the language regulating our space and belonging. This inversion of positions means becoming foreign to one's home and oneself rather than imposing one's views on foreigners with whom we cannot identify as we become "co-owners" of the legacy they pass on to us: "As though the foreigner were first of all *the one who* puts the first question or *the one to whom* you address the first question. As though the foreigner were being-in-question, the very question of being-in-question, the question-being or being-in-question of the question. But also the one who, putting the first question, puts me in question" (*Of Hospitality* 3). Derrida's conception of "hospitality" must then be understood as a space of encounter that requires of readers of testimony bearing witness to genocidal violence—as they face "someone who speaks an odd sort of language"—an interruption of oneself as an other (5). As *Rwanda 94* performatively demonstrates, the duration of the play combined with the multiplicity of survivors' voices represents a double form of interruption within our cultural scene and our ways of thinking. Rather than an interruption of the voices culturally identified as "ob-scene," which is to say foreign to the cultural and moral "scene" of the readers and viewers we represent, *Rwanda 94*, like Mujawayo and Mukagasana's testimonies, expose us to mediations bearing witness to experiences and suffering, which instill a sense of unhomeliness within ourselves at the very moment we are called to offer a home to those who have been estranged from themselves and their community. Naasson Munyandamutsa, a psychiatrist who works with survivors of the genocide of the Tutsis in Rwanda, phrases as follows the demanding hospitality required by the testimonial encounter: "Building peace with survivors of extreme violence, and therefore with the world, requires the determination to help them reinstitute their love for themselves, rebuild the trust in themselves, and by doing so, recuperate their self-esteem for those who have lost it—this is the supreme objective for those who have not yet been wounded" (166).[13] For those who have been spared, this objective can only be embraced by departing from the evidence of who we are as we accept to negotiate with survivors the estrangement provoked by the testimonial encounter with an "ob-scene" reality. This shift within the practice of listening is precisely what calls for a renewed conception of hospitality that can no longer rely on a principle of identification, since the interruption of oneself as another becomes here the new paradigm within the testimonial encounter.

Notes

1. Groupov was founded in 1980 in Liège and is made up of artists from various disciplines and nationalities who collaborate in experimental creations and dramatic

productions. Focusing on "the question of truth," Groupov has explored innovative modes of scenic representation that question the social and political function of theater within society. Groupov has performed and staged *Trash (a lonely prayer)* by Marie-France Collard, Berthold Brecht's *The Mother* and after *Rwanda 94*, Aimé Césaire's *Discourse on Colonialism*, and *Bloody Niggers!* written by the Rwandan actor and playwright Dorcy Rugamba. Groupov redefined itself as an "Experimental Center for Active Culture" since its activities were no longer limited to theater productions as Marie-France Collard's film *Ouvrières du Monde* (2000) exemplifies.

2. For additional information on the genesis of the play and its performance, see: Jacques Delcuvellerie, "La représentation en question" (2005); Sylvie Chalaye, "Entretien avec Jacques Delcuvellerie" (1999) and "*Rwanda 94*, du Groupov (Belgique) et *Méfiez-vous de la pierre à barbe* de la Madani Compagnie. Que peut le théâtre face à l'horreur génocidaire?" (2000); Marie-France Collard, "Le génocide continue" (2005); Jean-Christophe Planche, "Une réparation symbolique" (2000); and Dorcy Rugamba, "Nécessité de dire" (2005).

3. For Groupov's tour in Rwanda in 2004, read Laure Coret, "*Rwanda 94*, au Rwanda, dix ans après" (2005) and see Marie-France Collard's remarkable film *Rwanda. Through us, humanity . . .* (2006), which follows the performances of the play *Rwanda 94* throughout Rwanda in 2004 and addresses the fate of survivors ten years after the genocide.

4. Which is the title of her first testimony *La mort ne veut pas de moi* (1997).

5. Henceforth, all quotes from Régine Waintrater's works are my translations. On this issue see also Marie-Odile Godard *Rêves et traumatismes* (2003).

6. Henceforth, all quotes from Yolande Mukagasana's works are my translations.

7. "Rwanda 1994. Une réparation symbolique" (2000). Henceforth, all quotes from this work are my translations.

8. Thanks to my colleague Kirk Read for having brought this essay of de Certeau to my attention.

9. In *Smothered Words*, Sarah Kofman, through a discussion of Robert Antelme, Maurice Blanchot, and Emmanuel Levinas, exposes the trauma of having outlived her father and survived the Holocaust. She committed suicide on October 15, 1994, the date of Nietzsche's 150th birthday.

10. Quoted in Cojean. "Les voix de l'indicible." Translation mine.

11. Mukagasana's public engagement in the aftermath of the genocide is unique: she has published three testimonies *La mort ne veut pas de moi* (1997), *N'aie pas peur de savoir* (1999), and *Les blessures du silence. Témoignages du génocide au Rwanda* (2001); she has performed in *Rwanda 94*; she has given numerous lectures around the world; and she has created in Rwanda "La Fondation Nyamirambo-Point d'appui" and an orphanage where she has adopted seventeen children. For her outstanding engagement, the UNESCO gave her, in September 2003, the prize for education and peace (Coquio, "Aux lendemains" 17–20).

12. Translation mine. Henceforth, all quotes from Parrau's works are my translations

13. Henceforth, all quotes from Naasson Munyandamutsa's work are my translations.

5

Staging the Ob-Scene

I F MUKAGASANA'S TESTIMONY FORCES US to acknowledge that we cannot identify with her experience and survival while it forces us to witness her suffering and loss, the rest of *Rwanda 94* even more explicitly carries on this disconcerting conception of hospitality. The play employs numerous electronic ghosts who constantly interrupt the communication among the living and harass the media to denounce their preconceived frame and vision of what is newsworthy. As such, *Rwanda 94* implements a powerful and haunting esthetic of interruption. The recurrent and sudden appearance of electronic faces and voices not only disrupts the usual flow of communications all around the world, but also progressively succeeds in "making the news." They defy inscription into the media's preformatted gaze and rhetoric. The fact that the media and the Western audience of the play are, initially, unable to understand these ghosts who speak an incomprehensible language is key to the play's ability to make one question the pertinence of commonly accepted representations of this genocide and signals an impossibility to reproduce them unchanged. Facing a language that escapes our understanding, we are forced to estrange ourselves from our ordinary frames of reference in order to be able to listen to an "ob-scene" experience or we will never be able to decode what we hear. As the psychiatrist Munyandamutsa underlines in his comments to a quote from Léo Rosten, it is imperative to believe survivors' words and to question the evidence of our rationality if we want to hear the suffering they cryptically attempt to express while protecting both themselves and their listeners from the traumatic detonation they attempt to communicate: "'It is imperative not to think that they talk nonsense all day long. Most of the time, what they

say is very coherent. This trick to understand them, is that we need to listen
to them patiently. They have their own vocabulary. It is English, French (or
Kinyarwanda), and yet it is as if they were speaking a foreign language: it is the
language of suffering. . . .' [Rosten] The challenge is then to practice listening
to them and to succeed in decoding their foreign language. This is strange,
but even more so estranging—estranging because the wound is invisible and
cannot be seen" (161–162). By underscoring the selective lenses of the media
and the dead angles they legitimate, the electronic ghosts of *Rwanda 94* place
center stage the media's limited ability to frame, decode, and comprehend the
"ob-scene" experience to which these ghosts bear witness. This initial failure
of the media to inform compels us—the audience—to revise our perception
and understanding of the genocide of the Tutsis since this experience is voiced
in a language foreign to us.

The discursive and narrative tension between the ghosts and the TV host
symptomizes then the existence of a "cultural trauma," which Weine defines
as follows: "The idea of cultural trauma is linked to larger ethical questions
concerning people's obligations to their history and culture, questions such
as: Who are we? Who are our friends and who are our enemies? What is the
purpose or our existence as a society? What are the values that unite us? . . .
One thing for certain is that after cultural trauma, a culture can no longer go
back to what it once was. Therefore responding to cultural trauma requires
finding ways to creatively combine some of the old with some things new in
ways that may better facilitate peace and reconciliation" (129–130).

Rwanda 94 stages this cultural trauma by undermining our reliance on the
media's ability to inform us and invites us therefore to question the means
through which we try to confer a meaning to these electronic ghosts whose
language exceeds our cultural and linguistic scene. Here is how these interruptions are described in the stage directions provided by Delcuvellerie:

> The huge red wall of red Rwandan earth, the only essential element of the stage
> décor, opens up to reveal a screen. Images from all over the globe flash on the
> screen to the accompaniment of commentaries in different languages: sports,
> the Pope's message against abortion, the Peking Opera, a speech by President
> François Mitterrand, the pilgrimage to Mecca. . . . Each sequence is suddenly
> interrupted and disturbed by the face of an African man, woman, or child.
> These "electronic ghosts" speak to us in an incomprehensible tongue. We are
> in a special TV broadcast "Mwaramutze 1995" in the company of the TV star
> Bee Bee Bee and her assistant, Paolo Dos Santos. For several weeks (April 95)
> communications across the globe, including television, are being saturated with
> such "interferences." (31)

It is not coincidental that these ghostly interferences occur as the world is
about to commemorate the first anniversary of the genocide, since the re-

membrance of this event and its ongoing aftermath seem to be completely absent from the media. It is as if their coverage, rather than fulfilling a duty to inform and remember, orchestrates a historical cover-up leading to a Western amnesia regarding Rwanda. It is in this context of (dis)information that the dead must make the news from beyond the grave to interrupt our belief in the established media. *Rwanda 94* reminds us from the beginning on that the various lenses, screens, and stages through which we perceive the genocide of the Tutsis hide the reality of what happened as much as they reveal it—which is not to say, hide the reality of what happened at the very moment they affirm to reveal it.

The fact that these ghosts speak to the audience in an "incomprehensible" language not only dramatizes their power of interruption, but also allows them to elude any quick appropriation by the media, since they remain obscure to our reasoning. When the language of the ghosts is revealed to be Kinyarwanda, nothing is resolved for the Western audience who is then forced to reflect on the issue of translation. A linguist is invited on stage to offer a literal translation of what the ghosts are saying. But quickly, it becomes clear that the representation of genocide cannot be confined to such an exercise, since the messages of the "electronic ghosts" do not make sense if they are uprooted from the personal and socio-historical context of their enunciation. Throughout the play, these ghostly interferences function then as a recurrent reminder of the gap between the discourses defining our cultural "scene" and the "ob-scene" experience they try to comprehend and render. To be able to establish a dialogue with these voices from beyond the grave will require, from those of us who are foreign to the traumatic experience of the genocide, a long journey; if we engage, this labor of translation will not leave us unchanged if we truly seek to expose ourselves to the genealogy and aftermath of an experience that is, *a priori,* foreign to us.

As Derrida puts it in his reading of *The Apology of Socrates,* the question of the foreigner is intimately linked to the ability of the foreigner to master the "appropriate" language in order to be understood by the audience from which he or she seeks a form of social recognition despite his or her disturbing otherness. In this sense, the survivor who embodies an experience and trauma foreign to us questions the evidence of our commonly accepted language and our thresholds:

> He [Socrates] has to ask for hospitality in a language, which by definition is not his own, the one imposed on him by the master of the house, the host, the king, the lord, the authorities, the nation, the State, the father, etc. This personage imposes on him translation into their own language, and that's the first act of violence. That is where the question of hospitality begins: must we ask the foreigner to understand us, to speak our language, in all senses of this term, in all its

possible extensions, before being able and so as to be able to welcome him into our country? If he was already speaking our language, with all that that implies, if we already shared everything that is shared with language, would the foreigner still be a foreigner and could we speak of . . . hospitality in regard to him? (*Of Hospitality* 15–17)

What is at stake in our encounter with works bearing witness to the genocide—an experience whose language we do not speak—is their ability to pass on the haunting power of the trauma they voice, stage, or depict visually, and our willingness to expose ourselves to the foreign voices they convey. To do so requires us to question the silencing violence generated by our cultural scene, since we are more inclined to reproduce than to question its boundaries.

Reading this body of testimonies and literature devoted to the genocide of 1994 and viewing critically its cinematic representations must then be understood as a practice that cannot be confined to the exposition of the "true" meaning of these texts or films—an approach that allows us all too easily to just pass by or to remain at a safe hermeneutical distance. Experiencing works that confer an unprecedented visibility to the genocide of the Tutsis and inscribe this "ob-scene" experience within our social scene requires us to measure what it means to expose ourselves and our cultural scene to the aftermath generated by experiences of pain and suffering. What kinds of hospitality are we ready to offer to those who embody an experience we wish could not exist and remain culturally "ob-scene"? Estranged through our encounter with works bearing witness to genocidal violence, can we still "be at home while in another's home"?[1] And if so, what kind of hospitality can we offer when reading and listening to works bearing witness to an "ob-scene" reality that interrupts our sense of self and questions the evidence of our belonging?

What is remarkable in *Rwanda 94* is the link that the play stages between the social performance of bearing witness, the cultural function of mourning, and a self-reflexive awareness regarding the challenges survivors face while testifying and mourning. In other words, the *duty to remember* to which Groupov subscribes necessarily implies *a self-reflexive work of remembering* without which there can be no awareness of what is socially and ideologically silenced. During the entire play, numerous voices and discourses compete and complete each other to impose a representation of this traumatic and conflicting past that cannot be separated from the position from which this past is mediated. To stress the importance of positionality and spur the audience to think critically with and against Groupov's representation, the play uses different strategies to orchestrate heterogeneous points of view facing the "same" traumatic past and its legacy.

First, it refuses a stable and reassuring form of narration in order to engage the audience in the production of meaning. It abruptly juxtaposes moments of meditation, prayer, chorus, and dance with witty dialogues about the mediation of the genocide, scenes of smothered voices speaking up, and interpellations from beyond the grave that accuse Mitterrand or Dallaire for their role in the genocide. Second, it stages a genuine Western journalist who—like the audience—wants to understand how this genocide happened and who constantly assesses out loud the ability of her coverage to make sense of the genocide but not at the expense of the experience's reality. Constantly anticipating the sanctions of her Western audience, she engages us to think about our willingness to know and highlights the role we play in the process of shaping the form and social resonance of the genocide and what it means to be informed by it. Third, the surreal and anachronistic dialogues between survivors, dead victims, killers, journalists, experts, not to mention one Holocaust survivor, blur the reassuring borderline separating the present from the past as well, and the "here" from "there." Groupov's staging fully subscribes to Tal's assertion that "bearing witness is an aggressive act." As a result, the play exposes us to spatial and temporal encounters that challenge our conventional sense of liminality and, thus, performs an inscription of the genocide's "ob-scene" within our cultural "scene."

Groupov's testimonies have to be approached as "estranged conceptual prisms through which we attempt to apprehend—and to make tangible to the imagination—the ways in which our cultural frames of reference . . . which delimit and determine our perception of reality have failed, essentially, both to contain, and to account for, the scale of what has happened in contemporary history" (Felman xv). Groupov's play *Rwanda 94*, through its "dismembering" of the genocide's history into a polyphonic orchestration of voices and genres, stages a remembrance that calls for a *self-reflexive work of remembering*—travail de mémoire—which I oppose to a *duty to remember*—un devoir de mémoire. Moreover, in its attempt to bypass the silencing effect of official and media representations, *Rwanda 94* explores dialogic configurations as a way to stage a dialogue with survivors' points of view and, in many cases, with the dead whose chorus refuses to let the living speak on their behalf, well aware that we are prone to minimize their traumatic experience and mute their posthumous request for justice. Often suspicious of the now commonly evoked *duty to remember*—a duty that official accounts, memorials, and some testimonies claim to fulfill without questioning their conditions of production and ideological purpose—Groupov's mediation performs a provocative *work of remembering* that questions the potential inadequacy and "symbolic violence" of its own configuration, not to mention the discomfort and guilt of speaking in the name of those who died.

Rwanda 94's opening underscores the existential and cultural loneliness of the survivor by confining Mukagasana to the deserted scene of an empty stage. She faces the "social scene" of an audience whose members have yet to acknowledge that the "ob-scene" aftermath of the genocide she embodies is an integral part of their "cultural scene"—which requires the public to redefine the limits of its "scene" and refuse to reproduce the gap or disconnection that separates the audience from the witness on stage. Mukagasana's initial loneliness reminds us that ultimately, to quote Paul Celan, "No one bears witness for the witness" who must therefore negotiate the loneliness of a responsibility and the responsibility of this loneliness (Felman 3). In this opening scene of *Rwanda 94*, then, Mukagasana not only bears witness to her traumatic experience but asks the audience to envision her testimony as the social performance through which she voices a double refusal: to remain silent and confined to the "ob-scene" and to have others speak for her, which would equate to her social death. Mukagasana's testimony represents therefore not only a theatrical performance, but also a form of social action through which she performs her survival and her belonging to the community from which she seeks recognition:

> The testimony is, therefore, the process by which the narrator (the survivor) reclaims his position as a witness: reconstitutes the internal "thou," and thus the possibility of a witness or a listener inside himself. In my experience, repossessing one's life story through giving testimony is itself a form of action, of change. . . . (Felman 85–86)

What ultimately matters in Mukagasana's performance "of *living through* testimony" is the possibility for her, as a survivor, to engage in a dialogue both with herself and the community from which she seeks social recognition by bearing witness to her suffering. By giving testimony, she seeks a form of hospitality that no longer presupposes an interruption of her voice, but an interruption within the community of her listeners—interruption that would signal our willingness to "hear" her suffering rather than declare it socially and existentially ineffable.

To remember then must be understood both as *a duty to remember* and *a work of remembering*, since it constitutes a social practice that allows members of a social scene to remember who they were, but equally important, who they are in relation to whom they want others to believe they were. Remembering functions then among the living as a social reminder of how we ought to position ourselves in relation to what is commonly accepted as worthy of remembrance. In *The Writing of History*, de Certeau analyses the historiographic operation of bearing witness to the dead through writing not only as a testimony to the importance a society wants to give them, but also as a testimony to all that the living claim in the name of the dead:

One the one hand, writing plays the role of a burial rite, in the ethnological and quasi-religious meaning of the term; it exorcises death by inserting it into discourse. On the other hand, it possesses a symbolizing function; it allows a society to situate itself by giving itself a past through language, and it thus opens to the present a space of its own. "To mark" a past is to make a place for the dead, but also to redistribute the space of possibility, to determine negatively what *must be done*, and consequently to use the narrative that buries the dead as a way of establishing a place for the living. (100)

This explains why survivors of traumatic events see their testimonies contested and face various injunctions to remain silent. For survivors, to bear witness is not only a question of being able to remember, but also a question of conformity to how, today, within our cultural scene, we are *supposed* to recall the past as it weighs on the relation among the living. Moreover, fulfilling a duty to remember also raises the question of who is authorized and able to tell "the facts." Among the living, the literary and cinematic mediations of this disturbing past both honor and bury the past as they point to a desired place within the present that the remembrance of certain facets of the past values and legitimates. The retelling of the genocide of the Tutsis through literature or cinema must consequently be seen as a disputed process. This process both contests and legitimizes various positions claimed by the heirs of this traumatic legacy. For de Certeau, to narrate the dead—be it testimonial, literary or cinematic—"furnishes death with a representation that, in placing the lack within language, outside of existence, has the value of an exorcism against anguish. But, through its performativity, historiography fills the lacuna that it represents; it uses this locus to impose upon the receiver a will, a wisdom, and a lesson" (101). What are then the will, the wisdom, and the lesson that survivors' testimonies and fictional accounts seek to pass on to us?

The end of the first section of *Rwanda 94* offers a first hint by staging a series of short testimonies performed by those who compose the Choir of the dead. Each of its members, while surrounding Mukagasana, posthumously narrates how he or she was killed during the genocide. Each testimony given by the Choir of the dead was written by Rwandan members of the show and is based on a story that happened to known relatives. This juxtaposition of voices highlights the uniqueness of each destiny, asserts the personal and intimate character of pain, and underlines the thin and unpredictable line separating those who survived from those who died. Here is the testimony of the fifth dead:

I can never stop enumerating the tragedies I went through during this same period. They are infinite. I don't even know where to start. I can only say that wild animals are not only the ones who live in the jungle!

Here is why: five Interahamwe (among them was my servant whom I had always treated like my own son), arrived in my house. Before my eyes, they successively raped my loving wife as I was unable to do anything to help her. And the poor woman did not survive this collective rape. And then they told me: *You are so damn selfish! Why didn't you have us taste this delicious dish?*

They killed my baby and cut his arms. They offered them to me parodying Jesus-Christ: *Take them,* they told me, *eat them, this is my flesh offered to you, the Batutsi, in remission of your numerous sins, you will do this in memory of us.* Proud of their exploit, they left after they told me: *Die of sorrow, we will be back tomorrow to send you there where your wife and baby already are.*

After the gunfire, an Interahamwe militiaman came to search the corpses around me. He found the identity card of a Hutu man, and he turned toward me and asked: *Is this ID yours, so that I spare your life?* And I who played the dead during all this time, answered him: *I have no more legs, my head has been broken by a hammer. If you want to save me, then kill me. I am not Muhutu, I am a Mututsi.* The Interahamwe left. He probably wanted me to die suffering for a long time. (31–32)

For Groupov, each testimony matters, since no survivor can speak for all and no lesson of the genocide can be achieved if the living are not willing to depart from the silencing injunctions that surround the genocide of the Tutsis. Rhetorically, these ghosts play a crucial role in the ability of the play to engage us in a haunting dialogue with voices from beyond the grave, voices to which we should not have been exposed, since they were, without appeal, reduced to silence. But in *Rwanda 94*, the dead will constantly assert and exercise a right to appeal, forcing us to face our complacency in the symbolic violence of our accepted mediations and the smothered voices we culturally contain by proclaiming them "ob-scene" if they do not conform to ours.

Like the Rwandan actors in the Choir of the dead who narrate the fate of their killed relatives, the witness to the dead must be envisioned with respect to the living's own sense of belonging to a community. We cannot be alive if we do not acknowledge those who preceded us, those with whom we shared past moments, those who help us to position ourselves within the present as we celebrate their legacy. For Dorcy Rugamba who plays the role of the dead number 1—none other than his own brother who died on April 7, 1994, at the age of sixteen—to bear witness to the dead is a social gesture that cannot be confined to simply reviving their memories within the present. For him, narrating the fate of his relatives aims also to give voice to their unanswered questions regarding why they died and how is it possible for survivors to go on with their life when the community at the foundation of their sense of self has been destroyed:

When a single person dies, we can hear it, perceive it. But how can one approach this obligation to define oneself, without others, without parents, without friends, without neighbors? Suddenly one perceives oneself as having no reality. . . . If the world of the people with whom I lived before the genocide has revolved, so have I. I am then completely outdated, I belong to the past. And I cannot come back to life. I can no longer invent myself, since I always used to define myself in relation to those who no longer are.

At this point comes the absolute necessity to write, to speak, to tell. It is like a desire to resuscitate those people because they cannot be erased. One must absolutely bring back their words, bring them back to life, and continue to hold on to something so that oneself can exist: because if they are not, neither am I. Through my collaboration in this play, through writing . . . I reconnected with myself through the questions asked by the victims who died during this genocide. Because they could have a voice again, the victims were able to exist somewhere, even though it was only on the stage. They were able to engage with the world. They were no longer disembodied. (142–143)[2]

Mirroring Rugamba's relation to his deceased brother, the relation that the Choir of the dead's testimonies establish with its audience or readers seeks to provoke a form of cultural survivorhood through listening and reading. Chambers defines this "readerly survivorhood" in his analysis of AIDS diaries when he underlines how authors position readers as heirs of their social survival—a positioning that consciously instills a feeling of inadequacy and guilt aimed at anticipating our "readerly indifference":

. . . every reader must also face an awareness of the responsibilities of readerly survivorhood, which are those of ensuring the survival of a text whose author is dead, and of prolonging its witness, responsibilities that, because of the inevitable difference (named by death) between readerly survivorhood and the authorial project of which the text is the only surviving evidence, are necessarily tinged with a sense of inadequacy and, almost as inevitably, with a sense of guilt. Every reading confirms . . . the death of the author, which is why every reader, as survivor, stands accused in advanced of indifference to the author's fate. (*Facing It* 22)

By giving voice to the dead, *Rwanda 94* grants the victims who did not have the time to engage in—and thus engage us in—any form of testimonial survival a posthumous chance to remedy this silence thanks to the haunting voices composing the Choir of the dead.

The second section of the play entitled "Mwaramutse"—a morning greeting that literally means in Kinyarwanda "Did you pass the night?"—opens with Bee Bee Bee, the Francophone journalist working for the European Union of Broadcasting whose programs on the genocide of the Tutsis are watched throughout Francophone Africa via the channel TV5. Through this scenario, *Rwanda 94* directly addresses the abilities of Francophone media and literature to bear witness to the genocide by questioning where and how its representations are produced and distributed. Meanwhile, since this play was created in Belgium, the character of Bee Bee Bee must also be seen as a self-critical device in the play. She represents a *mise en abîme* that inserts, within the play's *duty to remember*, a salutary call for a *self-reflexive work of remembering*. The progressive invalidation of the journalist's initial expectations and modes of seeing will lead the audience in the exploration of a co-witnessing esthetic that no longer silences those in whose name one claims to speak. Through the evolution of Bee Bee Bee's gaze and her growing awareness that, despite her best intentions, she ultimately silences the victims and trivializes their testimonies, the play highlights how she—like us, the audience—condemns the survivors to remain "ob-scene" as long as she exposes the genocide without exposing herself to her own silencing role at the very moment her journalistic gaze aims to address and voice the genocide of 1994 and its aftermath.

In her broadcasts, Bee Bee Bee is constantly interrupted by parasitic messages sent electronically by ghosts of the genocide. These aired fragments of testimonies in Kinyarwanda interfere in the pre-established format and rhetoric of her journalistic discourse as the dead call for a work of remembering that questions commonly accepted mediations of the genocide.[3] The use of the word "tragedy" by the journalist generates, for example, a vehement critique from the ghosts who see in this word not only a euphemism of the systematic and planned massacres, but also an unwillingness to define any responsibilities. Echoing the international reluctance to use the word "genocide" to qualify the mass killings that were taking place in Rwanda, one of Bee Bee Bee's guests reminds her that each of her words matters here greatly because of the implicit presuppositions each word carries and naturalizes: "I think that just before the interruption, Bee Bee Bee innocently used the rather usual, clichéd phrase by referring to the 'Rwandan tragedy.' . . . I think that the dead, among other things, can't stand such nebulous language anymore, which refers neither to victims nor perpetrators. Do you see? 'Tragedy' implies fate or destiny. The ghost insisted strongly on the definition of the crime: 'genocide'"(45).

All this happens while Bee Bee Bee is broadcasting live, suggesting symbolically that the voices of the dead are still alive. Furthermore by casting these testimonies as parasites, the play dramatizes both their power of interruption and their dependency on the hospitality of their audience, since parasites live off their host's generosity without doing anything in return, a dynamic that defines precisely the unconditional laws of hospitality according to Derrida

(*Of Hospitality* 83). At first, the messages of these ghosts are incomprehensible, since they do not speak the language of the host: if it had not been the case, the question of the foreigner and the issue of hospitality would never have become a question. Bee Bee Bee's symptomatic failure to translate them casts the suffering to which these voices bear witness as present, yet opaque, and thus highly troubling for the transparent mastery that the journalist's commentary is ideologically supposed to produce. Fundamentally at stake here is "the haunting power of the residual" of that which is socially denied and existentially repressed, but nevertheless does not disappear because of its traumatic nature. As Chambers shows in *Untimely Interventions*, "The potential power of the residual to become haunting is realized through writing that rewrites its own representational inadequacy as an index of the survival that is denied, and thus as the haunting power to become a marker of liminality" (xxvii). In their groundbreaking work on testimony, Felman and Laub present the question of the "residual" in their analysis of Holocaust testimonies as follows: "The collection of the fragments does not yield . . . any possible totality or any possible totalization: the gathering of testimonial incommensurates does not amount either to a generalizable theoretical statement or to a narrative monologic sum" (223).

Rwanda 94 stages this inadequacy and impossible totality through the outright refusal of any possible coherent whole, but even more so because the staged dialogues between the living and the dead rely on and perform a haunting use of hypotyposis—this trope that confers a sense of immediate presence to a mediate reality (Chambers, *Untimely* 203). Commonly used to erase the consciousness of reading or watching a distant reality by immersing the audience in the midst of the action as if we were part of it, hypotyposis is used in *Rwanda 94* in a parasitic dynamic that complexifies its intended effect. On the one hand, it confers an immediate presence to the absent victims by collapsing the ontological frontier between the present of the audience and the distant past to which the dead bear witness. On the other hand, the abrupt interruptions of the dead within the present, each time they feel their legacy betrayed or distorted, draws a recurrent attention to the bias of the mediations used by the living to speak about the traumatic experience of the dead and confine them at a safe distance. By imploring a reflexive consciousness about language to address the legacy of the genocide, Delcuvellerie highlights the fact that the visibility we confer to the past through our mediations matters, a metanarrative debate that the ordinary use of hypotyposis seeks precisely to muzzle. The absence of mastery achieved through a fragmented configuration combined with a sense of hyperreadability achieved through hypotyposis confers a haunting power to the play's dialogic mosaic as it renders presence to absence. The skillful polyphony, the refusal of a linear exposure favoring a reassuring sense of causality, and the constant desire to inform without putting the listener and viewer in a position of mastery regarding the genocide of the Tutsis enact the "empathic unsettlement" that defines the writing of trauma according to LaCapra:

> Trauma is a disruptive experience that disarticulates the self and creates holes in existence; it has belated effects that are controlled only with difficulty and perhaps never mastered. . . . Being responsive to the traumatic experience of others, notably of victims, implies not the reappropriation of their experience but what I would call emphatic unsettlement, which should have stylistic effects or, more broadly, effects in writing which cannot be reduced to formulas or rules of method. . . . At the very least, emphatic unsettlement poses a barrier to closure in discourse and places in jeopardy harmonizing or spiritually uplifting accounts of extreme events from which we attempt to derive reassurance and benefit. . . . Trauma brings about a dissociation of affect and representation: one disorientingly feels what one cannot represent; one numbingly represents what one cannot feel. Working through trauma involves the effort to articulate or rearticulate affect and representation in a manner that may never transcend, but may to some viable extent counteract, a reenactment, or acting out, of that disabling dissociation. (41–42)

To remember in *Rwanda 94* is then to orchestrate a collision of collected voices rather than to forge a consensual chorus that would silence any dissenting points of view or claims. Drowned out by these parasitic voices, Bee Bee Bee suddenly finds herself unable to perform the social and ideological function of her enunciative position. Here she is, on television, live but speechless, unable to report the news, that is to say, failing to translate into the signifying "scene" of her viewers the "ob-scenity" of the genocide and, therefore, failing to render and neutralize it culturally. The ongoing encounters between Bee Bee Bee and various interlocutors throughout the play will progressively inflect her preestablished discourse and approach and empower her to envision new modes of seeing and passing on the genocide of the Tutsis in Rwanda. As she learns to understand not only the language but also the trauma that motivates the recurrent interventions of the electronic ghosts and the Choir of the dead, we, the living, are invited to join her and debate within our respective communities how we can alleviate some of the pain survivors face daily as they negotiate the scars—too often invisible—that the machetes have inscribed within them.

Notes

1. I translate here one of Derrida's subheadings of his article "Responsabilité et hospitalité" (2001), which eloquently captures the paradoxical issue we are facing here: "*Être chez soi chez l'autre*" (142).

2. Henceforth, all quotes from Dorcy Rugamba are my translations.

3. At one point in her first testimony, Mukagasana recounts her refusal to sub-scribe to the preestablished role of the "generic survivor" interviewed for a couple of minutes to generate pity and sympathy among viewers and fulfill a perverse voyeur-ism and esthetic, which is more concerned about ratings than listening to survivors and giving them the possibility to negotiate the representation of their experience: "A television crew just arrived in a mini-van. A woman, I am told, is already interviewing the survivors, a cameraman frames the emaciated faces, a soundman immortalizes the trembling voice of those who are dead in their hearts. 'It's CNN, I believe!' shouts a fifteen-year old boy. . . . The TV? The TV of the White people? Never! The TV of those who have helped the genocide to occur? Never! No way! Exhibiting my little face to distract the world? They don't know me! . . . I feel that I am as much in danger if photographed in my current condition as I felt my life was in danger one week ago. To accept being photographed in my current condition, this would be accepting death and dishonor. No, I will not come forward. If one day I bear witness to the genocide, it will not be for satisfying the curiosity of the lazybones. It will be to point at the as-sassins" (137–138).

6

Becoming Heirs and Going on Haunted

T HE THIRD SECTION OF THE PLAY in which Bee Bee Bee doesn't appear is entitled "The Litany of Questions." It stages a series of interrupted communications from beyond the grave, which harass the living as the Choir of the dead questions what will be remembered and what will be concealed. Moreover, the chorus invites us not to trust blindly the various sources of information on which we, the living, depend as we seek to understand this genocide and address the issue of justice. Rhetorically, the recurrence of the same question over and over—"Will they say . . . ? Will they speak of . . . ?"—for more than half an hour achieves a double purpose. First, it makes the audience aware that the representation of the genocide of the Tutsis is polemical and that each mediation is selective; each purposely omits certain facts as it tailors a representation that is not only about the past but also about positioning oneself within the present. In this sense, the litany of questions underscores the fact that certain facets of this painful past are obliterated or distorted to neutralize their long-lasting consequences and reverberations within the present. Remembering this genocide is not a neutral endeavor. It requires to take a stand within a specific context of enunciation and define the intent of one's discourse. Second, by systematically mentioning within the questions facts and information that are likely to be concealed or denied, Groupov's play offers a history lesson that positions the Choir of the dead—and thus the play itself—as a disturbing truth teller. *Rwanda 94* functions therefore as a transgressive counterpoint or countervoice to dominant representations of the genocide.

As such the Choir of the dead and the performance *Rwanda 94* by Groupov (whose first name when created was "Group-off") performatively represents a "new public site of discourse" able to instill within the cultural and social scene of its audience transgressive ways of seeing, since the play departs with the common representations of the genocide. Thus, *Rwanda 94* functions as a vector of social change, as Peter Stallybrass and Allon White understand it in their analysis of transgression:

> Discursive space is never completely independent of social place and the formation of new kinds of speech can be traced through the emergence of new public sites of discourse and the transformation of old ones. Each "site of assembly" constitutes a nucleus of material and cultural conditions which regulate what may and may not be said, who may speak, how people may communicate and what importance must be given to what is said. An utterance is legitimated or disregarded according to its place of production and so, in large part, the history of political struggle has been the history of the attempts made to control significant sites of assembly and spaces of discourse. (80)

Thanks to its rhetorical use of paralepsis or preterition,[1] the genocide victims are no longer silenced in *Rwanda 94* as they denounce the omissions and ellipses of other discourses that aim to speak on their behalf. The litany of questions represents therefore a rhetorical device or posture, which functions more as a litany of historical facts absent from the dominant representations of the genocide of the Tutsis. Because of length, this litany erodes the reliability of other legitimate sources of information that shape our memory and understanding of this genocide. If it matters to the dead that we, the living, gain a complex understanding of what happened and how what happened could happen, it is because our knowledge of this past will influence how we, today and tomorrow, will define personal and collective justice, historical liability, and moral responsibility. As one of the dead reminds us: "The path of reconciliation does not lead to forgetting" (89):

> *Dead 1.* Will they speak of Léon Mugesera's speech on November 22, 1992?
>
> *Dead 5.* Will they say that he asked the Bahutu to send back the Batutsi to their homeland Ethiopia by the shortest route, the Nyabarongo river, because, as they said, "They must all be liquidated"? (54)
>
> *Dead 3.* Will they speak of Colonel Bagosora sent on December 22, 1992, to Arusha to destroy the peace agreements and who declared: "I am returning to Kigali to prepare the apocalypse"?
>
> *Dead 3.* Will they say that the cover of the sixth issue of *Kangura* carried a photo of Mitterrand, saying: "It is when times are bad that you discover your true friends"?(55)
>
> *Dead 3.* Will they say that the Americans opened a bureau in Nairobi to cater for the dogs and the cats of the white expatriates?

Dead 5. Will they speak about the French aircraft, which on April 9, 1994, without the knowledge of the media, evacuated high dignitaries of the genocidal regime, among them Agathe Habyarımana and her brothers! (63)

Dead 1. Will they say that if our history, like that of any nation, is not without wars of conquest or palace intrigues. Never in living memory, before the colonization of Rwanda, was there any ethnic conflict between Bahutu and Batutsi? (79)

The litany of questions has seven verses, each one introducing a central aspect that needs to be taken into account if one seeks to understand the genocide's genesis and the challenges of its aftermath: "RTLM," "The U.N.," "1959," "The Colonizers," "Precolonial Rwanda," "Church," "Mourning." Each series is introduced by the same chorus inviting the audience to question what they hear and see: "Listen to them, but be on guard. Look at them, but beware of them. These machines, which spread information, they infect our hearts and pollute our minds"(89). The recurrence of this warning invites the audience to examine the origin and intent of each discourse on Rwanda's history, society, and culture. By examining the role played by the pro-Hutu extremist radio station RTLM, the hypocrisy of the United Nations, the racial views of German and Belgian colonizers, the opportunism of the "Françafrique,"[2] the influential role of the Catholic Church, the social relations defining the precolonial era, and the current politization of mourning, *Rwanda 94* forces the audience to fully envision the enunciative complexity of the genocide's representations. Finally, the decision to compose this litany of questions in seven verses carries also a symbolic metanarrative meaning that links this litany to the Rwandan rituals of mourning, as Marie-France Collard—one of the co-authors of the play—indicates: "To write the litany of questions, we opted for a structure that corresponds symbolically to the ceremony of mourning in Rwanda, a ceremony that lasts eight days: the eighth day, the mourning period is over, the dead are honored, life regains its rights. Inspired by this ritual, the litany of questions is composed of seven choruses and seven verses: the eighth being the play as a whole. Operating to some extent as a metonymy of the play, this third section questions and accuses: mourning cannot be fully achieved without justice, without the truth being unveiled. This must be done without any concession, the dead have nothing to lose, they are therefore the ones who speak" ("Le génocide continue" 145. Translation mine).

In the absence of any omniscient perspective or master narrative, we are compelled, based on the information that the dead pass on to us, to filter critically the dominant readings of the genocide and to postpone any hasty and reassuring judgment. Furthermore, this litany, because it is performed by ghosts and by the Choir of the dead, infuses in the audience a sense of guilt as it continues to blur the discontinuity between our "scene" and the "ob-scene" suffering witnessed on stage. By questioning what might remain behind the scene of our commonly accepted representations of the genocide, the litany of the dead opens our political "scene" to disturbing revelations regarding the complicity of the media, the United Nations, the Church, and the West in general. This litany, denying its Western audience the possibility of knowing at a safe distance, not only connects us to the questions and demands raised by these voices from beyond the grave, it also predisposes us, as we come to envision ourselves as their hosts, to be haunted by them through remorse as we listen to the Choir of the dead: "May our bones be picked from the marshes, from the hillsides, and from the common graves. May our names be written on a cross. We are these million cries suspended above the hills of Rwanda. We are this accusatory cloud. We expect reparations from you. For us, the dead, and for all who survived. For all Rwandans and for all men on earth. . . . Through us, humanity looks sadly at you. What are you waiting for? We are not at peace" (89–91).

The fourth section of the play is entitled "Ubwoko,"[3] which means "clan" in Kinyarwanda—a term that the colonizers translated by "ethnic group." This colonial misunderstanding not only introduced ethnic divisions within the Rwandan society, but also led to institutionalize "ethnicity" in the 1930s by assigning an ethnic status to all Rwandans and inscribing it on all identity cards until 1994. This section sees the return of Bee Bee Bee who continues her challenging journey to understand how it is possible to kill one million human beings so easily (95). In her quest, she finds herself more and more frequently interrupted by the Choir of the dead who remains on stage for the rest of the play—a way of asserting that their voices are no longer "ob-scene," but are actively involved in the making of any representation aiming to pass on this traumatic past that does not pass away. But in order to be passed on, testimonies as well as literary, cinematic or journalistic accounts must, in most instances, forge within their audience a desire to know, a willingness to expose one's cultural scene and question its premises through the encounter with works bearing witness to genocide. Too often, despite a declared desire to know, the living confine the pain and trauma of their interlocutors as foreign to their "world" and, ultimately, declare them "ob-scene" thanks to various strategies of denial involving pity and compassion, if not declaring survivors' experiences simply unbearable.

Thus, the fundamental conversion Bee Bee Bee must achieve in her desire to fulfill a duty to remember is to become simultaneously a listener who opens her "scene" to the "opacity" of an experience that exceeds hers, a host who is willing to be interrupted and disrupted by those who speak a foreign language, and a witness to the survivors bearing witness to the traumatic aftermath of genocide. I understand the "opacity" to which survivors' testimonies are bearing witness as defined as follows by Edouard Glissant in his essay *The Poetics of Relation*: "The thought of opacity distracts me from absolute truths whose guardian I might believe myself to be. . . . I thus am able to conceive of the opacity of the other for me, without reproach for my opacity for him. To feel in solidarity with him . . . it is not necessary to try to become the other (to become other) nor to 'make' him in my image" (192–193). Following the litany of questions, which leaves no doubt about the gruesome planning of genocide, its horrific implementation, and the inexcusable indifference of the world, Bee Bee Bee continues her quest by requiring her audience to subscribe to the following will to knowledge—a prerequisite, in her eyes, to the very possibility of truth:

> There is no truth possible where one does not listen with every fiber of their being. Thus, you are here with me because truth needs the desire for truth. The person who does not want to know will never know. One can show him or her a thousand times the evidence, and the evidence of the evidence, and a thousand times the one who does not want to know will say: *Things certainly happened the way you told them, yet I can't make myself believe them. Didn't you exaggerate? Is it not in your own interest to present the facts in this light? I do not shut the door to the truth but you have to understand that I want to be careful, measured, balanced, slow if necessary.* (80–81)

Admitting her ignorance and her inability to grasp the traumatic experience she is supposed to pass on to her audience, Bee Bee Bee asks Jacob, a survivor of the Holocaust, to accompany her in her quest. She also invites a historian played by Delcuvellerie—who as the director takes here full responsibility for the historical knowledge the play conveys—to deconstruct at great length the political use of "ethnic" differences during the colonial era and the decades leading to the genocide. In this fourth section, sitting on the edge of the stage, Bee Bee Bee becomes more and more an active listener, is no longer a "TV host" but a host who accepts interruption and haunting by the voices she seeks to pass on. Moreover, she comes to question her own position of enunciation and concludes that any *work of remembering* within the *duty to remember* presupposes questioning the constraints of the medium she is working with as well as its ideological role. As Jacob tells her at the beginning of this fourth section, the enunciative challenge she faces is to find a mediation capable of reconciling her desire to pass on the complexity of the genocide and the demands of survivors while obeying the rules that define television's production: "How can one express . . . the infinite complexity of cause and effect in a media space where speech is measured, where formula is more valuable than reason and emotion pays better than conviction? How?"

How can noise become sound analysis? How can the temple of show-business content itself with the austerity of truth?" (97)

At this point in the play, Bee Bee Bee has to acknowledge fully that the testimonial encounter with voices bearing witness to the "ob-scene" reality of genocide generates fear and insecurity, and represents a disconcerting interruption. Ultimately, it requires from her, the host, a departure from any former and preestablished script as she aims to answer to and for the litany of questions performed by the Choir of the dead. Is Bee Bee Bee—and thus the audience—willing to take such a risk? A risk that is not only at the core of hospitality understood as an interruption of oneself as an other, but also a source of uneasiness and "malaise" leading to the possibility of being mutually changed by the testimonial encounter as Mireille Rosello suggests it in her analysis of *Postcolonial Hospitality*:

> . . . if the guest and the host are not willing to take that risk and do not welcome the possibility of being challenged, shaken, changed by the encounter, then there is no hospitality. . . . The very precondition of hospitality may require that, in some ways, both the host and the guest accept, in different ways, the uncomfortable and sometimes painful possibility of being changed by the other. Some degree of mutual metamorphosis, brought about by the presence of the other, of his or her different values or points of view, will undoubtedly constitute the by-product and the visible evidence of hospitality gesture. Perhaps then, it is this paradoxical nature of conditional and unconditional hospitality alike to be a practice that . . . constantly tests the host's and the guest's thresholds of fear, and their willingness to live with that fear, and with their malaise. (175–176)

Reflecting on her self-critical work of remembering as a host, Bee Bee Bee confronts her producer with a transgressive report—eight minutes of images documenting the genocide without any commentary, nor music, just silent images of the killings, except for one extract of a radio broadcast in Kinyarwanda from the pro-Hutu Radio Télévision Libre des Mille Collines (RTLM) urging and celebrating the killing of all the cockroaches.[4] The producer's immediate response is symptomatic of the rules that guide and define news production—laws to which Bee Bee Bee now refuses to conform in her attempt to pass on what she has learned by exploring an esthetic that favors an ethic of interruption. In her eyes, to report as usual would only distort the complexity of the genocide, be disrespectful to the dead, euphemize genocidal violence and ideology, and trivialize survivors' daily challenges. In short, to report as usual would amount to misinformation. Ultimately, the media's unwillingness to provoke within its audience any "malaise" by infringing on the scripted format represents a form of censorship where the respect of the format prevails on the content of what is making the news and is worthy of remembrance:

> *The producer.* That's heavy. You are not scared of knocking out the spectator? . . . It is impossible to put it out like that, it needs an introduction.
>
> *Bee Bee Bee.* That is the introduction. There is killing, which produces corpses, then bones, then nothing: the grass is already growing. It is up to us to ensure that the memory does not disappear with the bones.
>
> *The producer.* All the same. Let's look at things clearly. It's 8:40 p.m. The ads are over. People are getting ready to eat. What do they find on their plates? That! Eight minutes of that! Excuse me, it's a bit difficult to digest. It's a bit too much. . . . The world has its laws. Television too has its laws. The viewer should not be brutalized, or demoralized! Nor made to feel guilty. What happens in Africa is hardly his fault. . . . If one puts in a rapid, sustained rhythm, I am sure it will have a different impact altogether. We would have said the same thing, the essential, without harassing the viewer. Don't you think so? And this silence in the images! What's that meant to be? I don't suppose this is the final version?
>
> *Bee Bee Bee.* Yes. (203–207)

By refusing to euphemize her account of the genocide and the discomfort generated by her iconoclastic report, Bee Bee Bee, of course, never gets a chance to officially broadcast what the audience of the play just saw. This censoring in *Rwanda 94* stigmatizes the practice of *a duty to remember* that refuses to expose itself to the cultural transgression testimonies perform when they maintain an exposure to the liminality they expose rather then concealing it. By abrogating her enunciative authority to the victims, Bee Bee Bee not only casts them as the legitimate speakers of their suffering, but also testifies to the fact that she—as a host and producer of our cultural "scene"—has understood the interruption and "malaise" that the practice of hospitality demands, namely "an interruption of oneself by oneself as an other."

If this multi-media play that confronts us with the genocide of the Tutsis in Rwanda is disturbing, it is not only because of the horror and suffering it stages, but also because of its emphasis on the *work of remembering* the dead and the survivors' request from their audience. Delcuvellerie presents this *work of remembering* as follows when he defends his choice to show these eight minutes of raw footage of the killings:

> What is appropriate to show or not on screen, and how? In other words, the spectator receives the shock of the slaughter through the chilling platitude of a trace while he is simultaneously invited to think about the way his main source of information defines the images' pertinence or inadmissibility, that is, the "conditions" that structure this discourse through which one pretends to communicate with him. ("Entretien avec Jean-Christophe Planche")

If the silence surrounding these images is eloquently disturbing, it is because the absence of commentary and music paradoxically succeeds at underlining the silencing that is at play in the practices of remembering and the role we are called to play not as passive consumers of images but as active communities of viewers. As Sontag underlines, "One can feel obliged to look at photographs that record great cruelties and crimes. One should feel obliged to think about what it means to look at them, about the capacity actually to assimilate what they show" (95). By refusing to screen out the institutionalization of forgetting and the work of remembering at play in *Rwanda 94*, Delcuvellerie refuses to duplicate the radical enterprise of silencing that the genocide is all about. On the contrary, his *mise-en-scène* puts this enterprise of silencing center stage to voice its cultural and ideological functions. The subtitle of the play— *Attempt at Symbolic Reparation to the Dead, for Use by the Living*—explicitly formulates this process of ongoing negotiation with a past that we, the living, inherit, and to which we have to respond according to our present willingness to expose ourselves to its disturbing scars:

> Once we had let the dead *disturb* us, once we had tried to listen to what they could tell us and demand from us, this scenic work took shape and evolved, constantly reformulating itself, never satisfied with any of its approaches nor with their complementarities. It is this disturbance that we wish to make contagious through our *Attempt at Symbolic Reparation to the Dead, for Use by the Living*. ("La représentation en question" 140)

For those who do not write and speak as survivors—Bee Bee Bee in the play, and me, here—what is then decisive is our willingness to be disturbed and interrupted by voices that are existentially and culturally "ob-scene." In our encounter with the testimonial literature bearing witness to the genocide of the Tutsis in Rwanda, we must therefore face not only the horror and pain of genocide, but also our complicity in a political and symbolic violence that silences the survivors. When mainstream documentaries and news reports privilege, for instance, outsiders' analyses of what happened in Rwanda—like those offered by Canadian General Dallaire who led the failing and fleeing U.N. peace keeping force in Kigali—over testimonies of Tutsi survivors who saw most of their relatives killed, we must ask ourselves what kind of encounter we are meant to avoid, and, to a certain degree, we want to avoid. One of the most symptomatic examples of the silencing of Tutsi survivors at the very moment a representation claims to give visibility to the genocide of the Tutsis can be found in Greg Barkers' documentary *Ghosts of Rwanda* (2004). In the trailer that presents the documentary produced for the tenth anniversary of the genocide, a Western narrator promises the viewers that they will be presented with all the voices implicated in the genocide and its aftermath:

"Tonight on *Frontline*, the full story of perhaps the darkest and most brutal tragedy of our time. It's a story told by the victims and by the killers, by those who turned away and by those who stayed to save as many lives as they could" (*Ghosts of Rwanda*). The promise of a polyvocal account of the genocide, which gives precedence to the victims' voice, is quickly deceived. In the documentary, the main witness through which the viewer is invited to discover the genocide and to identify with is General Dallaire and his guilt of having failed in his mission to prevent the genocide. Viewers have to wait fifteen minutes before they can hear the first Tutsi survivor bearing witness to the genocide and this for less than a minute! In Barker's *Ghosts of Rwanda*, the survivors' voices are filtered, contained, framed by experts allegedly more knowledgeable. This silencing hierarchy casts the survivors' voices bearing witness to the genocide and its aftermath as residual interlocutors, attesting presences of a discourse that ventriloquizes them and maintains them performatively "obscene" since they are portrayed as being passive, unable to produce a coherent account of their own trajectories and suffering, thus distant ghosts who can only be heard through the mediation of a Western narrator and the mastery instilled by the (ab)use of voice-over.[5]

What becomes then imperative to question is our willingness to create ways to pass on survivors' voices as hosts in order to generate an interruption within our respective communities. At stake in the testimonial encounter provoked by works such as *Rwanda 94* is a cultural willingness to position ourselves as heirs to an experience that remains opaque to us. Thus, bearing witness to the survivors' direct witnessing—or its indirect mediations through fictional works—requires us to see the writing of the genocide as the writing of a past that does not pass *away* but can only be passed *on* through *a work of remembering*. In such a venue the living "determine negatively what *must be done*, and consequently use the narrative that buries the dead as a way of establishing a place for the living" (Certeau, *The Writing of History* 100).

This is precisely what the last section of *Rwanda 94* aims to accomplish with the powerful "Bisesero Cantata," which draws its inspiration from an investigation carried out by African Rights on the killings that were perpetrated on the hills of Bisesero near Kibuye.[6] There, during the three months of the genocide, a handful of Tutsis survived thanks to their organized and heroic resistance on the hill of Muyira—of the fifty thousand who sought refuge at Bisesero, approximately one thousand people survived. The cantata weaves together for one hour voices of numerous witnesses, alternating solos, duets, recitatives, and a chorus to narrate the fate of the Abasesero people and the refugees who joined them in their resistance. That fate is poignantly captured in the refrain: "On the hill of Muyira covered with the bushes and forests lived many strong men before the genocide. . . . Between bushes and forests on the hill of Muyira remain a mere handful of men. A handful of men who now die of grief" (217).

The play ends by stressing, on the one hand, the fate of the main perpetrators, some having been arrested and sentenced, numerous others still at large, and, on the other hand, the loneliness and precariousness of the survivors of Bisesero where a memorial to the resistance fills the void and aims to preserve the memory of those who are no longer: "On the hill of Muyira stands the memorial to the resistance. There, where men once lived, there are only stones, skulls, bones" (261). After a moment of silence, to emphasize the individual cost and human suffering inflicted by genocide, the Choir of the dead begins to read the names of the victims of the genocide at Bisesero while the stage imperceptibly fades into total darkness and silence.

Derrida's conception of the "heir," as he exposes it in "Choosing One's Heritage,"[7] can help us to envision the act of inheriting as a multi-relational and dynamic process as we listen to the names of the dead and risk finding ourselves petrified by the weight that is passed on to us. According to Derrida, the process of passing on a legacy demands that both survivor and audience respect and transform the heritage one transmits or receives in order to ensure that the heritage remains still relevant within the present. To inherit, then, necessarily implies an engagement with memory: both to remember the genocide's traumatic past and to pass on "the haunting power of the residual" (Chambers) requires a transformative process where the heir, according to Derrida, must be "faithful *and* unfaithful, unfaithful *out of* faithfulness" ("Marx & Sons" 219). Hence, the heir cannot "remember" the past he or she inherits without "dis-membering" and "re-membering" it, that is to say without rewriting it in order to keep this past that is passed on to him or her alive in the eyes of the living. Fundamentally at stake here is the heir's ability to negotiate within the present the conditions of possibility that allow one to sign both in the name of the past and in one's own name:

> Even before saying that one is responsible for a particular inheritance, it is necessary to know that responsibility in general ("answering for," "answering to," "answering in one's name") is first assigned to us, and that it is assigned to us through and through, as an inheritance. One is responsible before what comes before one but also before what is to come, and therefore *before oneself.* A double *before,* one that is also a debt, as when we say *devant ce qu'il doit: before* what *he ought to do* and *owing* what he *owes,* once and for all, the heir is doubly indebted. It is always a question of a sort of anachronism: to come before [*devancer*] in the name of what came before us, and to come before the name itself! To invent one's name, to sign otherwise, uniquely in each case but in the name of the name passed down, if that's possible! ("Choosing" 5–6)

The reading of the names that concludes Groupov's *Attempt at Symbolic Reparation to the Dead, For Use by the Living* functions therefore as a double injunction addressed to us, the living who inherit the violence and suffering that these names embody. First, we can no longer go on as if nothing had been passed on to us and, therefore, we must invent a response to these voices, which have inscribed within our "scene" a haunting legacy. Second, while there is a duty to answer for and to this past, we can only do so by "dismembering" and "re-membering" this traumatic past in order to render its pertinence within our present as we position ourselves both in the name of the past and in our difference with this past. It is this contradictory injunction and dynamic that is at the core of the writing of history, which ultimately enables us, the living, to invent and sign in our own name without having to write off our debt toward the dead.

The great value of *Rwanda 94*—like certain testimonies and novels written as part of the project "Rwanda: Writing As a Duty to Remember"—lies in its willingness to stage its own representational inadequacy so that the audience faces the limits and symbolic violence of their commonly accepted mediations of the genocide perpetrated in Rwanda.[8] Through the dismembering work of remembering, through the rhetorical use of hypotyposis to instill the voices of the dead within our present, and through the call for a self-reflexive work of remembering on the part of hosts who pass on this genocide's legacy, *Rwanda 94* not only testifies to the violence of genocide and the scars of its long-lasting aftermath, but also stresses the residual dimension of traumatic suffering that denounces our complicity in various forms of denial and exclusion survivors must face. Moreover, through the ongoing and transformative dialogue that the play stages between the Choir of the dead who bears witness to the genocide and the host Bee Bee Bee without whom there would be no testimonial encounter, *Rwanda 94* acknowledges the powerful link between testimonial inadequacy and the haunting power of the residual as a symptom of the specters that haunt our imaginary and consciousness:

> After all, the most unequivocally genuine of Holocaust testimonies themselves frequently bear witness to their own utter inadequacy as testimonial. That is, they cannot report the full enormity of the Holocaust in such a way that this enormity might be, once for all, recognized. Their testimony is haunting enough but it is itself also haunted; it testifies that there is no end to the business of laying our ghosts. Specters, as Derrida has said, are always plural; one reason for that is that they have specters of their own. . . . My thesis, then, is that there are . . . orphaned memories, who haunt the collective consciousness but *need* . . . a "host" if they are to achieve some sort of vividness, some degree of discursive status within culture, and force our acknowledgment that they do indeed haunt us . . . . (Chambers, "Orphaned Memories" 98)

In *Rwanda 94*, Mukagasana's testimony, Bee Bee Bee's self-critical endeavor, and the audience's dialogues with the Choir of the dead seek to create
the conditions through which the residual dimension indexed by survivors'
testimonies and the malaise they embody can be passed on within society. The
hope is that the residual's haunting power can engage our sense of hospitality and redraw the threshold of what is culturally "ob-scene" and obscured.
As Lawrence Kritzman stresses in his introduction to *Realms of Memory:
Rethinking the French Past*, the promise of the testimonial encounter resides
in the possible actualization of a social space of distanciation and hospitality where the "rewriting of the history of memory can forge new paradigms
of cultural identity" (xiv).[9] Envisioned as a space of social dialogue bearing
witness to a trauma that does not pass away and can only be passed on, testimony offers then the possibility to negotiate the emergence of new paradigms
leading to a common belonging that does not erase cultural differences and
equate identity to sameness. On the contrary, in the aftermath of genocide it is
imperative to depart from an ideology of sameness and advocate a conception
of identity that acknowledges differences and defines belonging through an
ethics of mutual interdependence and a sense of hospitality where the suffering of others always already positions and owns me. For Weine, in his analysis
of testimony after catastrophe, "listening to testimonies means joining the
survivor and crossing a boundary into the world of trauma" so that "survivors
feel less alone" and "the receiver of testimony may learn something new from
survivors, which would change his or her views about war and peace, conflict
and reconciliation" (134).

Through its cultural transgressions and haunting positioning of the audience, *Rwanda 94* ultimately calls for a practice of "co-ownership" throughout
the testimonial encounter, which Laub defines as follows in his work with
Felman on testimony:

> By extension, the listener to trauma comes to be a participant and co-owner of
> the traumatic event: through his very listening, he comes to partially experience
> trauma in himself. . . . While overlapping, to a degree, with the experience of
> the victim, he nonetheless does not become the victim—he preserves his own
> separate place, position and perspective. . . . The listener, therefore, has to be at
> the same time a witness to the trauma witness and a witness to himself. (57–58)

Through Bee Bee Bee's resolute desire to understand and bear witness to the
genocide's "ob-scene" experience and her willingness to forge a new esthetic
of interruption to pass on the voices and demands of the dead, *Rwanda 94*
invites us to challenge not only the limits of history, testimony, and literature,
but also their mutual claims and disclaimers regarding their ability to represent this traumatic past. The questioning of the host's authorial voice when

it comes to witnessing the genocide—critical discourse performed through
Bee Bee Bee   allows Rwanda 94 to engage in a virulent criticism of the media's intent and dominant representations. Moreover, by reminding us that
the media are fundamentally preoccupied with conforming the reality of the
events to their preestablished format and their audience ratings, Bee Bee Bee's
trajectory denounces the cultural and ideological function of the media and
their invitation to forget.

Ultimately, exploring the representations of the genocide of the Tutsis in
Rwanda questions the means and the desire of a community to face its present
through the relationship this community seeks to establish with the haunting
voices from its past. The testimony of Innocent Rwililiza, a thirty-eight-year-
old teacher in Nyamata, a town whose church has now become one of many
official memorials of the genocide in Rwanda, offers a haunting allegory for
my reading of *Rwanda 94*, by way of conclusion:

> I feel, I repeat, that they cut and mutilated to take humanity away from the
> Tutsis and kill them more easily that way. And they made a dreadful mistake.
> I learned for example of a killer who had buried his Tutsi neighbor completely
> alive in a hole behind the man's house. Eight months later, he felt himself called
> by his victim in a dream. He went back to that garden, he dug up the dirt,
> unearthed the corpse, and got himself arrested. Since then, in the prison, he
> wanders day and night with that man's skull in a plastic bag he holds tight in his
> hand. He cannot let go of the bag even to eat. He is haunted to the last extremity.
> (quoted in Hatzfeld, *Life Laid Bare* 113–114)

The skull of this Tutsi teacher that his killer is doomed to carry not only
symbolizes the haunting power of the residual, it also evokes the disturbing
exchange that the literature witnessing the genocide of the Tutsis seeks to
enable among the living, thanks to its esthetic and ethic of interruption and
haunting tenacity. If the genocide's ghosts point toward the cultural existence
of a haunted identity, it is not because the dead have died in horrific ways, but
rather because their capacity to haunt the living signals a social consciousness
of injustice and guilt. Chambers underlines this dynamic in his analysis of the
cultural "success" that Wilkomirski's testimony *Fragments* enjoyed during a
couple of years before it was denounced as a hoax, since its author—Bruno
Dössekker[10]—appropriated the identity of a Holocaust victim he wasn't in
order to express his own orphaned identity and gain social recognition:

> Ghosts are not easily laid, however. The reason for this is that their presence
> signifies the sense the living have of an injustice that has gone unrepaired (and
> may indeed be irreparable). It always seems easier to lay the ghost than to repair
> injustice—but "seems" is the operative word because ghosts ultimately refuse
> to lie down and be still, for the very reason that the consciousness of injustice,

otherwise known as a sense of guilt, inhabits the living, not the dead. . . . we may think that the dead should feel less alive and act more dead, they remain restless because the living remain anxious, being prevented by guilt from completing the normal process of mourning that would lay them to rest. ("Orphaned Memories" 95–96)

Testimony thus conceived becomes furthermore one of the social means for survivors to re-engage in what the philosopher Martin Buber defines as the "I-Thou" relationship. Considered in Buber's perspective, the dialogue between the survivor and her audience is not only about the remembrance of the past, since dialogue enacts the true interpersonal dimension of human nature and rouses the survivor from the loneliness of the monologue, which Buber designates by the "I-It" relationship. Felman and Laub underscore this necessity to reinscribe oneself within an intersubjective dialogue where the promise of a genuine interlocutor is crucial for survivors of genocide, as follows: "When one cannot turn to a 'you' one cannot say 'thou' even to oneself. The Holocaust created in this way a world in which one *could not bear witness to oneself*. . . . This loss of the capacity to be a witness to oneself and thus to witness from the inside is perhaps the true meaning of annihilation, for when one's history is abolished, one's identity ceases to exist as well" (82). Mukagasana in her second testimony, *Don't be Afraid to Know*, poetically signifies this need to restore an "I-Thou" relationship within herself—while she seeks the strength to respond to the legacy that defines her new identity of survivor—by bearing witness to the genocide and becoming a *porte-paroles* who gives a voice to the dead and maintains their memory alive and a defining issue of our time:

> *I need to live.*
> *I need to reunite with my inner self.*
> *I need silence.*
> *I need loneliness.*
> *I need to listen to myself, to hear myself, to understand myself.*
> *I need my harshest memories, my most bitter ones. And the others as well.*
> *I need to touch myself to reassure myself of my own presence.*
> *I need a mirror to be certain of my smile.* (*N'aie pas peur* 128)

The ability to write a testimony constitutes then precisely for Mukagasana the mirror she needs for herself in order to reconquer within herself a distance that opens the possibility of inner and social dialogue. More precisely, the experience of hearing her co-author read her own story and especially the passages bearing witness to the death of her children proves to be a pivotal experience: "My co-author reads, I listen. . . . It is the first time I succeed to shed tears over my children. I have the feeling that this manuscript is the first stone of a new house that I will build, a house for all the children of the world, the dead and the living. My words became a book and the book speaks in my name. The book finally is published with the title *Death Doesn't Want Me.* . . . Publishing a testimony on what I have endured is the beginning of the end of my inner roving" (*N'aie pas peur* 273).

Regarding the ability of the survivor to restore an "I-Thou" relationship, one of the distinctive marks of Mujawayo witnessing resides in the fact that her testimonies do not erase the dialogue through which they have been generated. As it has been the case with *SurVivantes, La Fleur de Stéphanie* presents itself as a co-authored work by Esther Mujawayo and Souâd Belhaddad where the co-author's role does not limit itself to "translate" into a captivating narrative the story of the survivor—a form of collaboration that is very common in the case of survivors who are not professional writers. Here the co-authorship takes another dimension, since the interlocutor's presence is not erased within Mujawayo's testimony. On the contrary, Belhaddad's presence is constantly acknowledged by Mujawayo whose enunciation repeatedly acknowledges the presence of her interlocutor, valorizes her ongoing presence, and highlights her willingness to listen. The recurrence of the "you," which Belhaddad performatively embodies, represents therefore in the survivor's eyes the promise of being heard and not judged. If Mujawayo explicitly renders within her narrative the dialogic nature of testimony, it is not only to underline the central role listeners are called upon to play, but also to anticipate our reluctance to engage truly in the testimonial encounter she seeks to provoke. As she underlines in her first testimony—see the epitaph to this chapter—she is only too aware that many of those who profess an interest in her testimony are neither willing to implicate themselves *in* the testimonial encounter nor are they willing to be implicated *through* it, since it challenges the foundations of their beliefs and generates a cultural malaise calling for social change in order to make the violence she has been subjected audible. One of the key challenges for survivors is to negotiate the state of loneliness and interior violence in which they find themselves trapped. For Mujawayo,

> This loneliness is triggered by an impossibility to share, to tell the horror that inhabits each of us, impossibility due to the fact that it is too horrible and that those who listen have the remote control in their hands and can stop the tape when it becomes unbearable. Alas, the survivors have lost the remote control. The movie plays without interruption, over and over, and even when their interlocutors stop listening, for the survivors, the tape is still playing. The film plays endlessly. And the images like the sounds or the odors are incredibly violent. Real violence that cannot be voiced, screamed; the hatred of the perpetrator, of the rapist that cannot be expressed and that, ultimately, turns itself against the survivor. The silence, the rules of politeness, the fear to annoy, the fear to be

noticed, of always being the one who is different, the spoilsport . . . therefore you end burying in yourself all this violence, all this unspoken—impossible to tell because deprived of appropriate spaces to share it! And thus, from everywhere, our bellies explode, these constant back pains, these headaches that we cannot explain. ("Postface" 177–178)

Aware that she embodies a traumatic experience whose deepest scars and meaning ultimately escape her as much as they baffle her interlocutors, Mujawayo anticipates the dismissal of her testimony by asking us to question why her suffering is so disconcerting. In her effort to sound out the depth of our desire and our ability to listen to her story, she also addresses the pain our rejection would inflict on survivors of genocide who, like her, seek social and personal recognition to restore their sense of humanity and belonging. After having been dehumanized as treacherous cockroaches to justify their massacre, survivors exploit the capacity to provoke, negotiate, and revive through testimony a space of encounter and social recognition that is vital. In this sense, Belhaddad's presence as an explicit listener within the process of bearing witness is decisive, since, by the only virtue of being there, she asserts in the survivor's eyes the belief that someone is listening to her, that her experience is worthy of memory, her survival worthy of being acknowledged, and her hope that it carries a value for others reinforced. Without a listener "being there," there would be no encounter, no shared social space, no promise of belonging—all these factors that precisely both allow and motivate Mujawayo's testimony.

Mujawayo's art of bearing witness is, in this sense, fundamentally dialogic as she does not cast herself as being the only one in possession of the truth but casts herself as being engaged in a dialogue through which she succeeds to confer a resonance to her past thanks to the relational dynamic of speaking *to* a listener and, even more decisively, *with* a listener. My analysis of Mujawayo's art of witnessing borrows here from Weine and his alternative understanding of Bakhtin's "dialogic work" when applied to the analysis of testimony to trauma of political violence:

> The perspective of dialogic work does not depend on the claim that traumatic memory is the source and memory disorder is the form of survivors' suffering. Rather, Bakhtin's dialogic work suggests approaching suffering following catastrophe as a metalinguistic condition. In testimony, the survivor works with a receiver to create a story that, as a polyphonic and dialogic narrative, offers the survivor potential for growth in consciousness and ethics in regard to his or her experience of political violence. (95)

The demand for a social space and cultural scene where survivors' experiences could be audible both to themselves and their interlocutors is then not foreign to testimonial literature if it is understood as a social space and practice that

allows members of a society to reflect through innovative written works on
their shared humanity, and negotiate a common belonging. As Coquio eloquently underlines in her analysis of the role "writing" plays as a "third party"
within the memorial and mourning process of bearing witness, the distinction
between literary and testimonial enunciation is often blurred in the genocidal
aftermath. Survivors who have experienced a traumatic violence that is both
physical and symbolic speak and write from a position that requires them to
craft their testimony both within and against the vacuum generated by the
loss of their relatives, the collapse of their former sense of self and of belonging, and the cultural disconnectedness of their experiences and their narrative
translation. In this particular context of enunciation, writing functions then
as *a call for* as well as *a performance of* remembrance and mourning, as Esther
Mujawayo's second testimony attests.

In *The Flower of Stéphanie*, she concludes the narration of her failed attempt to find the body of her sister Stéphanie and her three children by
declaring performatively that her book constitutes her sister's symbolic sepul-
ture in order to uproot her from the anonymity and indecency of the yet still
unidentified mass grave or pit in which her body lies as well as those of the
other women and children killed with her: "I offer you this book as a sepul-
ture, Stéphanie, I have invited many people, all the readers will be present to
your burial, to your children's one, to Antoinette's and her young children's
one, and to Immaculée's one" (228).[11] Nevertheless, one of the major ob-
stacles to envision writing and testimony under such a symbolic and literary
light resides in the disbelief and negation survivors too often meet when they
tell their disturbing stories. According to Coquio, this potential disbelief tends
to confine testimonies to a *proof* rather than a place of *creation*, which would
allow to craft new ways of mourning and remembering:

> Beyond *proving what happened*, often an impossible task when confronted with
> infinite negation, the witness attempts to reinscribe her life within a meaning
> based on annihilating nonsense. Thus, testimony always exceeds its juridical
> framing and its historiographic exploitation, which with particular violence
> reduces it to the status of *proof* and *document*. This excess often leads to a form
> of writing, sometimes literary, which functions as a substitute for mourning. . . .
> The surviving witness is forced to make of her survival, if not an active despair, a
> continual effort of transmission. The prohibition of mourning intrinsic to geno-
> cidal logic, whether or not the witness evokes it, is at the core of the testimonial
> act: the search for words and meaning takes the place of impossible funeral ritu-
> als, destined to counter the disappearance of the living and the dead. (*Rwanda.
> Le réel et les récits* 105)

As Felman and Laub have demonstrated in their crucial work on testimony,
the truth of such a traumatic event cannot be possessed by one single survivor

or witness. It takes more than one person to bear witness, since the very act of bearing witness constitutes a social performance that has to be understood more as an access to the truth than a statement of the truth in the context of genocide and its traumatic legacy (15–16).

Given the dialogic nature of truth and its indirect and mediated access through testimony, how does Mujawayo's dialogic account weigh in the reconciliation process and allow her to position herself within and through her desire to bear witness? The dialogic staging of Mujawayo's words is crucial not only for herself but also for a wider audience, since she finds in Belhaddad a listener who tells her that her history and suffering are worthy of memory and deserve social recognition even though her interlocutors cannot identify with her experience. Thus, as Wendy Hui Kyong Chun highlights in her attempt to define "a politic of listening," our task as interlocutors must be envisioned as follows: "The important task in listening, then, is to feel the victim's victories, defeats, and silences, know them from within, while at the same time acknowledging that one is not the victim, so that the victim can testify, so that the truth can be reached together. In this model, distance must be maintained between listener and speaker" (162). This dialogic format also indirectly inscribes the reader in a more intimate position of listening, since Mujawayo's is talking to us through Belhaddad. Weine highlights as follows the interactive relational context at play and at stake in the testimonial encounter: "In testimony . . . there are two parties directly present who are occupying the role of the 'I for another.' There is the actual giver of testimony who is a listener to himself or herself. And there is also an actual "another" present in the room, the listener and recorder of testimony" (110–111).

Because the genesis of her testimony is dialogic, the staging of Mujawayo's enunciation functions then as a constant reminder that her testimony has an addressee who assures her that she is alive, heard, and acknowledged in her humanity despite the trauma she faces and the inhuman behavior and violence she has endured. The possibility of engaging in an intersubjective relation and the human recognition it entails is the first crucial dimension of a dialogic approach to testimony. Reading testimonies bearing witness to the "ob-scene" experience of the genocide must then be envisioned as entering a social space of encounter where the affirmation of a mutual and shared humanity is at stake and where the host and the witness are willing to be mutually interrupted and transformed by each other.

Notes

1. A figure by which, in pretending to pass over a fact, a mention of it is made while the speaker or narrator denies doing it. Common examples of this artful way of assert-

ing while pretending to omit are: "It is unnecessary to remind you . . . / I will not say . . . / I will not mention. . . ."

2. For an analysis of the concept of "Françafrique" see François-Xavier Verschave, *Françafrique: Le plus long scandale de la République* (2003).

3. Thus, one of the cultural translations of the Western term "genocide" in Kinyarwanda is "Itsembabwoko," which was the title of the opening scene staging Mukagasana's testimony and those bearing witness to the death of the various members composing the Choir of the dead. For a detailed discussion about the issue of naming the genocide of the Tutsis in Kinyarwanda, see Assumpta Mugiraneza's discussion of the terms *Itsemba-tsemba, Itsembabwoko, Isembabatutsi,* and *Jenoside y'Abatutsi* in "Les écueils dans l'appréhension de l'histoire du génocide des Tutsi" (2009).

4. The RTLM excerpt: "The truth is all Tutsis will perish. They will disappear from this country. They believe that they will revive but they will progressively disappear thanks to the arms which shoot them down but also because they are killed like rats. . . . Come and sing: Come dear friends, let us congratulate ourselves! They have been exterminated! Come, dear friends, let us congratulate ourselves! God is just!" (201)

5. Among the documentaries on the genocide of the Tutsis, Lacourse and Patry's documentary *Chronicle of a Genocide Foretold* (1996) offers a salutary counterexample to Barker's approach.

6. African Rights' report "Bisesero: Résistance au Génocide. Avril-Juin 1994" (1998). At the end of the report, one can find a preliminary list of Bisesero's victims. This impressive list is established cell by cell and totals close to 5,000 names (84–112).

7. See also on the question of the "heir" as someone who not only receives but also elects certain meanings in relation to his present situation, Derrida's *Specters of Marx* (1994).

8. If we follow Giorgio Agamben's reading of Primo Levi according to which "The authority of the witness consists in his capacity to speak solely in the name of an incapacity to speak—that is, in his or her being a subject," (158) then we only start to discern the difficulties we are facing to make textual crossroads encounters.

9. A great example of the residual's haunting power and social malaise generated by orphaned memories can be found in Vénuste Kayimahe's analysis of the political fear of ghostly information buried yet still "alive" in classified documents. In his article, Kayimahe exposes the efforts of the French government to cease—more than ten years after the genocide—the circulation of a secret document highlighting the knowledge and actions of the French army prior to April 1994—even though this document was in the open more than a year: "The fear of ghosts can turn into persecution. Like the truth, ghosts can suddenly appear anywhere and anytime: in the sunlight or in the middle of a dark night; in a rosy dream or in the midst of a horrible nightmare; in the street under the form of a protest or in a newspaper kiosk thanks to a headline; and recently on the internet under the appearance of virtual documents sealed by the magical and relevant 'confidential secret defense' be they classified or not" ("La peur des fantômes" 68. Translation mine).

10. Bruno Dössekker was born Bruno Grosjean in 1941 but because he was the illegitimate child of Yvonne Grosjean, he was abandoned and grew up in an orphanage in Switzerland.

11. After *La Fleur de Stéphanie* was published, Mujawayo was finally able to locate the place where Stéphanie and her family members had been thrown: "As the repentant killer Pierre always said, they had been thrown into Pascal's latrines. It was true, there they were. We were able to identify them thanks to the famous ID card that was so important that we had protected it with a plastic cover. Indeed, we found along with the remains of bodies we unearthed, a small handbag in imitation leather that belonged to Stéphanie, there was the rest of a bible, a hymnal, the famous ID card still readable with her name and those of her parents!" ("Postface" 178).

II

DISMEMBERING REMEMBERING: "RWANDA: WRITING AS A DUTY TO REMEMBER"

Cornelius was slightly ashamed of having entertained the idea of a play. But he wasn't giving up his enthusiasm for words, dictated by despair, helplessness before the sheer immensity of evil, and no doubt a nagging conscience. He did not intend to resign himself to the definitive victory of the murderers through silence. . . . He would tirelessly recount the horror. With machete words, club words, words studded with nails, naked words . . . because he saw in the genocide of Rwandan Tutsis a great lesson in simplicity. Every chronicler could at least learn—something essential to his art—to call a monster by its name.

Boubacar Boris Diop (*Murambi* 179)

7

We Came, We Saw . . . We Listened

O N APRIL 14, 1994, one week into the systematic killings of the Rwandan Tutsis and Hutus opposed to the ideology of hatred, three thousand Tutsis were slaughtered in the Catholic Church of Nyamata, a small town in the Bugesera region, south of Kigali. Four years later, in July 1998, a group of Francophone African writers visited the church of Nyamata, since then transformed into a memorial by the new Rwandan government. What kind of encounter were these writers expecting and what kind actually took place? What representation did this memorial intend to provide and allow them to experience? As they faced the remains of those killed, how did these writers respond to the staged and memorialized legacy that was being passed on to them? How did they position themselves in their attempt to answer the call that drove their collective enterprise, "Rwanda: Writing As a Duty to Remember"? Furthermore, when they later wrote about Nyamata's memorial and its dead, what kind of encounter did they want us as readers to experience? Within their narratives, how did they anticipate our resistance to admit that the genocide of the Tutsis in Rwanda was part of a shared history defined by human and political failure? Would this genocide that killed more than one million people be forgotten, and its perpetrators remain unpunished because, in the words of French President François Mitterrand, "In those countries, what's another genocide?"[1] And now, as I write these lines, how will I pass on the consciousness and agency my narrative and personal encounter with the dead and survivors of Nyamata require within our present? Furthermore, if no one can speak for survivors nor fully comprehend their traumatic experience, how can fictional characters ethically bear witness to their suffering? To what extent can the literary imagination bridge such "ob-scene" trauma by disinterring the victims, and, for the duration of our reading at least, disallow our futile belief that we might find some sense of immunity from the horror they embody?[2]

Before I analyze some of these authors' literary works and how they might fulfill the duty to remember that prompted them to go to Rwanda, see various memorials, and listen to many survivors, let us examine how their writing was shaped by their journey throughout Rwanda and the project they joined. As James Young underlines in *Writing and Rewriting the Holocaust: Narrative and the Consequences of Interpretation*, the context in which genocide's representations are forged must be an integral part of the work on remembering, which I was advocating in the first part of this book:

> The aim of an inquiry into "literary testimony" is rather to determine *how* writers' experiences have been shaped both in and out of narrative. Once we recognize that the "facts" of history are not distinct from their reflexive interpretation in narrative, and that the "facts" of the Holocaust and their interpretation may even have been fatally interdependent, we are able to look beyond both the facts and the poetics of literary testimony to their consequences. (39)

The project "Rwanda: Writing as A Duty to Remember" was conceived in 1998 by two African artists living in France, Nocky Djedanoum from Chad and Maïmouna Coulibaly from the Ivory Coast, joined in their initiative by Rwandan journalist Théogène Karabayinga of Radio France International. This literary project, which aimed to bear witness to the genocide of the Tutsis, was initiated in conjunction with "Fest'Africa," an annual African arts and literature festival that Djedanoum and Coulibaly began in the French city of Lille in 1992.[3] "Rwanda: Writing as A Duty to Remember" filled a literary and cultural void; for four years after the genocide, no major work had yet been written by an African author on the genocide of the Tutsis in Rwanda. Djedanoum's motivation was both personal and ideological:

> If the genocide of Tutsis and the massacre of the moderate Hutus in 1994 has prompted many thoughts in Europe among journalists, writers, politicians, researchers etc., it is deplorable to notice the silence of African intellectuals on the issue. . . . Artists, especially writers, wanted to fill a gap in their hearts; we wanted to take a position. . . . The mourning for Rwanda, Africa, and the world had to take an immortal dimension. And therefore we came to Rwanda, listened to the Rwandese, and thus produced works, thereby opening an important page in the history of Rwanda. It was a case of Africa being committed to Africa.[4]

In addition to the organizers Djedanoum and Coulibaly, the non-Rwandan authors were Boubacar Boris Diop (Senegal), Monique Ilboudo (Burkina

Faso), Koulsy Lamko (Chad), Tierno Monénembo (Guinea), Jean-Luc Raharimanana (Madagascar), Véronique Tadjo (Ivory Coast), and Abdourahman Ali Waberi (Djibouti). Some of these authors were already established Francophone writers in 1998 who had published poems, novels, or plays with renowned French and Francophone publishing houses such as Le Seuil (Monénembo),[5] Stock (Diop),[6] Hatier (Tadjo),[7] Actes Sud (Lamko),[8] L'Harmattan (Diop, Tadjo),[9] Présence africaine (Tadjo),[10] and Le Serpent à Plumes (Waberi).[11] Only two authors were Rwandan: Jean-Marie Vianney Rurangwa, who embarked on this project with the others, and Vénuste Kayimahe, who joined it once underway.

Kayimahe was himself a genocide survivor. He was working at the French Cultural Center when the genocide started and, despite being a targeted Tutsi, was not evacuated like his French colleagues when the Center closed two days after Habyarimana's death. In 2002, he wrote *France-Rwanda: Behind the Scenes of a Genocide. Testimony of a Survivor*,[12] a compelling account of France's diplomatic involvement in Rwanda before and during the genocide and on how he managed to survive despite having been left behind to die. For Kayimahe, the desire to embrace the duty to remember of this collective effort initiated by "Fest'Africa" was also a response to the guilt he felt for having survived and remained silent for so many years:

> Due to my unjustifiable silence, my spirit has been constantly tormented by a deep and tenacious remorse for years: the remorse of having abandoned to anonymity and oblivion my brothers and sisters, victims of the hatred of their fellow citizens; the remorse of finding myself satisfied by this abdication; the remorse of seeking refuge in the unreal comfort of cowardice and voluntary amnesia at the detriment of remembrance and memory. Moved by the specters of my daughter, my mother, and many other close friends savagely killed during the genocide of 1994 in Rwanda, I finally felt a pressing duty to publish this testimony. (7)

Rurangwa's trajectory was very different, since he left Rwanda in the 1960s and has lived since then in Burundi, Italy, and Belgium. His contribution to "Fest'Africa" was a short essay entitled *The Genocide of the Tutsis Explained to a Foreigner* (2000), targeting readers unfamiliar with Rwanda's colonial and postcolonial history.[13] In his foreword, Rurangwa highlights the conflicts and tensions surrounding survivors' testimonies to make readers aware of the polemical context of enunciation in which he offers his explanation of the genocide:

> Testifying is not always easy. Testifying is synonymous with exposing oneself and exposing one's people. It means exposing oneself to the calumnies of those who do not have a clear consciousness or of those who have still not understood that "justice is not a vendetta," to borrow Simon Wiesenthal's words. . . . For

those who are afraid of the truth, the genocide survivor is a disturbing presence. This is why some prefer his silence. But it is this very silence that kills the survivor. To bear witness to his people, to speak for them and in their name, gives the only meaning to his survival. And some want him to remain silent! But to remain silent is for him synonymous with death. (12–13)

Beyond their desire to pass on the voices of victims and survivors and to counter the political obliteration of the genocide outside Rwanda, the authors who took part in "Fest'Africa"'s initiative had to negotiate two other major issues. First, their writing had to denounce the racist framework of ethnic killings commonly reproduced and accepted in the Western world to justify its politics of nonintervention in 1994. Second, they had to refute the thesis of a double genocide promoted by various deniers of the genocide of the Tutsis in Rwanda—deniers who try to blur the distinction between a state-planned genocide against the Tutsis and the war opposing the RPF and the Habyarimana regime. These authors' desire to publicly assert and insist that a genocide against the Tutsis had been perpetrated in Rwanda in 1994 must therefore be read as a response to the deniers' discourses emanating from pro-Hutu ideologues and exiled perpetrators throughout the Francophone world and especially in France—which has been a safe heaven for them. "Rwanda: Writing as A Duty to Remember" was therefore not only a moral and ethical tribute to the dead, but also a vital political rebuttal. For Djedanoum and Coulibaly, it was imperative that African writers assert in their own words that the genocide of the Tutsis in Rwanda had occurred, that it had happened for political and historical reasons, and that its moral obligations and political responsibilities could be consigned neither to the past nor to Rwanda. Targeting a French-speaking audience in Belgium, France, and Canada—countries that are home to the largest Rwandan diasporas outside of Africa—"Rwanda: Writing as A Duty to Remember" sought to show survivors that they had not been forgotten and to raise awareness about the challenges they face in a post-genocidal society trying to implement national reconciliation and unity. By its very premise, behind the call to fulfill a duty to remember, the project intimately intertwined the literary and the political in order to promote the social recognition of the genocide of the Tutsis throughout the Francophone world.

For Diop, Lamko, Tadjo, and the other authors who traveled to Rwanda in 1998, it was imperative to encourage a reflection on the conditions that made the genocide possible, to highlight the manipulation of history it required, and to refute its various denials. As African writers, all wanted to denounce the political abuse of ethnic categories and the rhetoric of hatred that led to the genocide, stressing their lethal consequences in today's postcolonial era. Djedanoum and Coulibaly saw in literature, with its symbolic capital in the

Western world and the activist role it had played in shaping the memory of the Holocaust, an effective vehicle for spreading knowledge of what had happened in postcolonial Rwanda. Inherent in the duty to remember this past was also the need to provoke a long overdue debate concerning the role France and Belgium had played in the genocide's genesis and implementation, as well as their current responsibilities in its aftermath and their potential collaboration toward bringing the main perpetrators, all living in exile, to justice.[14]

Having won approval for their project from the Rwandan government, the authors came to Rwanda in 1998, where they resided in Nyamirambo, a popular neighborhood of Kigali, during the months of July and August, living in a small hotel made available to them by the Rwandan government. They met numerous survivors, listened to their testimonies, and visited memorials and places where mass killings occurred. They discovered the different regions of Rwanda, saw the gap between urban and rural areas, familiarized themselves with aspects of Rwandan history and culture, and observed the state of social relations in this post-genocide era and the challenges facing the implementation of justice and reconciliation. However, these authors could not travel freely throughout the whole country because of fierce battles that were still raging, mostly in the northwest region bordering the Democratic Republic of Congo.

Following their two-month residency in Rwanda, these authors went on to create a unique body of literature that explores the complexities of the genocide of the Tutsis and its aftermath through various lenses and genres. In addition to Kayimahe's testimony and Rurangwa's essay (see above), Djedanoum composed *Nyamirambo!* (2000), a long poem inspired by the diverse and lively neighborhood of Kigali where the group stayed. Véronique Tadjo published a literary chronicle of her journey, *The Shadow of Imana: Travel in the Heart of Rwanda* (2000), while Jean-Luc Raharimanana and Abdourahman Ali Waberi opted for a series of short texts gathered under the titles *Under the Shroud* (1998) and *Harvest of Skulls* (2000).[15] Finally, Boubacar Boris Diop, Monique Ilboudo, Koulsy Lamko, and Tierno Monénembo choose the novel for its ability to create a polyvocal and intimate representation of victims and perpetrators' feelings and thoughts.[16] Presented during the eighth annual "Fest'Africa" in 2000, these works generated unprecedented visibility for the genocide of the Tutsis within the French media and cultural scene.[17] To highlight the shared European-African commitment required by this duty to remember, the initiators of "Fest'Africa" chose, for the first time, to organize the event on both continents: first in Kigali and Butare from May 27 to June 5, and later in Lille from November 8 to 11 of the same year.

For the Rwandan edition of "Fest'Africa," numerous authors, artists, and intellectuals whose work was directly related to the genocide of the Tutsis and its legacy joined eight of the ten authors who had gone to Rwanda in 1998—Monénembo and Waberi being unable to travel to Rwanda in 2000. These additional voices, visions, and media gave a broader status and resonance to the event, especially the inclusion of African Anglophone writers such as Antjie Krog and Goretti Kyomuhendo and Rwandans like Yolande Mukagasana and John Garuka Rusimbi. The South-African journalist Krog was invited for her work on the Truth and Reconciliation Commission published in *Country of My Skull: Guilt, Sorrow, and the Limits of Forgiveness in the New South Africa* (2000). Kyomuhendo from Uganda presented *Secrets No More* (1999), a fictional narrative about the genocide of the Tutsis. Mukagasana, survivor of the genocide, shared her testimonies, *Death Doesn't Want Me* (1997) and *Don't Be Afraid to Know* (1999) (see part 1). John Garuka Rusimbi brought to the event his focus on the refugee crisis he had detailed in *By the Time She Returned* (1999). Other important Francophone voices were: Benjamin Sehene, a Rwandan who had lived in exile since the 1960s, author of *Le piège ethnique* (1999), an essay on the political exploitation of hatred between Tutsis and Hutus in Rwanda's history that lead to a deadly *Ethnic Trap*; two historians from the École des Hautes Études en Sciences Sociales (EHESS) from Paris, the Congolese Elikia M'Bokolo, author of *Au cœur de l'ethnie* (*In the Heart of Ethnicity*) (1985), and the Rwandan José Kagabo who worked on Muslim communities in Rwanda. In addition to public readings, roundtables, and art exhibits, one of the festival's highlights was the play created and directed by Lamko, *Body and Voice, Rhizome Words.*

The play represented a patchwork of characters and scenes selected from the texts created for "Rwanda: Writing as A Duty to Remember." To stage these many voices, he adopted as his narrator Ilboudo's main character, Murekatete, a Tutsi woman raped by a soldier who, in exchange, saved her life.[18] As she remembers her traumatic past, Murekatete functions as the prism through which the various voices that bear witness to the genocide enter the stage and weave together in a polyvocal homage to the dead.[19] Lamko staged the two-and-a-half-hour-long play in French, English, and Kinyarwanda. *Body and Voice, Rhizome Words* was performed again a year later in both Kigali, at the summit on Unity and Reconciliation, and in France.[20] Intimately marked by his stay in Rwanda, Lamko worked for several years as the director of the University Arts Center in Butare while teaching creative writing and drama at the National University of Rwanda. Emblematic of the authors who embarked in the project "Rwanda: Writing As a Duty to Remember," Lamko's work aimed to enable Rwandans to find their voice and to create cultural spaces of dialogue within Rwanda's post-genocide society.

This overview of the Rwandan edition of "Fest'Africa" would not be complete without mentioning a documentary film and a memorial project that marked the event. *Nous ne sommes plus morts* (*We Are No Longer Dead*), produced by Francois Woukoache, was shown during the festival. On June 5, the last day of the festival, "The Garden of Memory," created by South-African artist Bruce Clarke, was inaugurated in Nyanza Kicukiro in the presence of numerous Rwandan personalities involved in the defense of survivors' memory, voices, and rights.[21] This memorial was meant to contain one million stones, each bearing the name or distinctive sign of a victim, on a site of one square kilometer. For Clarke, the specificity of his artistic project resided in the symbolic gesture that The Garden of Memory makes possible in the act of deposing a stone with the name of a dead relative: "To lay down a stone represents . . . both a duty to remember and a very concrete act. It was an occasion to make a statement and affirm: 'this stone represents one member of my family,' psychologically this is huge! . . . Thanks to this memorial, my artistic work allowed a work of mourning. . . . People have been for the last six years in a stage of non-mourning, therefore it is vital they find spaces to mourn" (19. Translation mine). Today, a decade after the dedication of the inaugural stone engraved with the name of the site in French, English, and Kinyarwanda, only a few personalized stones have been deposited due to a lack of funding once the attention generated by "Fest'Africa" dissipated. Another factor that explains why Clarke's Garden of Memory never became "the" national memorial to the victims as intended is linked to the evolution of official memorials that progressively became sites combining the display of remains and spaces of mourning, as Clarke's project envisioned them.[22]

In addition to being a space of remembering and mourning, several memorials also offer a chronological and illustrated version of Rwanda's history in an effort to explain the roots of the genocide and promote national reconciliation. These official history lessons highlight the political manipulation of ethnicity inaugurated by the colonial period, and favor a peaceful cohabitation of all Rwandans during the pre-colonial era regardless of clan affiliation or social identities such as Tutsi, Hutu, and Twa. These official versions of history can be found in The Gisozi Memorial Center in Kigali since 2004 and in the Murambi memorial since 2009. This evolution of the museographic narratives in Rwanda highlights the fact that the pertinence of any memorial project is defined by the relevance of what must be remembered—and forgotten—and of the priorities a community, a society, or a nation elects and aspires to be identified with as it seeks to implement them. Moreover, the fate of Clarke's Garden of Memory—and this is also true for works published in association with "Fest'Africa"—underlines the importance of the dialogic and evolving context of production and usage of mediations that bear witness to the genocide of the Tutsis. The simultaneously complementary and competing dialogue surrounding the remembrance of the genocide stresses the need for the authors of "Rwanda: Writing as A Duty to Remember" to position themselves within their narratives in regard to survivors' testimonies, official Rwandan accounts and politics of memory, perpetrators' confessions, judicial verdicts, scholarly works, journalistic reports, and international inquiries from groups like Human Rights Watch, not to mention deniers.

One might ask if literature represents the most effective and appropriate medium for fulfilling a duty to remember in the case of the genocide of the Tutsis. In targeting a mainly Western audience in the Francophone world, it may risk leaving survivors behind. How can such a project touch the survivors themselves, given that many of them are illiterate and only an educated minority can read French?[23] Moreover, Rwandan survivors had another major issue with literature as a medium for generating social and international visibility for the genocide and the challenges of their survival—that of being misrepresented. Those who told their stories to "Fest'Africa"'s authors often addressed the dangers they perceived in the rewriting of their testimonies through literary lenses. Diop responds to this social perception and cultural fear that equate literary works of fiction with inauthenticity, betrayal, and misrepresentation, as follows:

> The Rwandans themselves told us: "Above all, don't write novels of our sufferings." We responded that it was, on the contrary, the best way to speak about them because a genocide is a phenomenon of such extreme violence that it situates itself necessarily within the realm of emotions. And as long as the task is to communicate intimate sufferings, to present them as a reality and not as disembodied numbers, novelists are in well-known territory. I wanted to give a face and a soul to the victims so that each reader must ask himself: "What would I have done in their place?" ("Le Rwanda m'a appris à appeler les monstres pas leur nom" 16. Translation mine)

Diop justifies the use of fiction for its ability to personalize the genocide's mediation and to invite readers to engage with his characters' choices and actions, which echo those survivors had to face. Because he firmly grounds his writing in Rwanda's complex history and colonial legacy, his novel never falls in the trap of identification. Moreover, by setting his narrative in the aftermath of the genocide—the main character Cornelius comes back for the first time to Rwanda four years after the end of the genocide, after having spent twenty-five years in exile—Diop's novel maintains a chronological gap that functions as an invitation to maintain a critical distance between our position of indirect witnessing through reading and the position of survivors and their points of view. Another advantage of not being contemporaneous to the event one describes is that it allows Diop—like Cornelius—to address not only the genesis and perpetration of the genocide in 1994, but also the multiple challenges of its legacy. Among these are: the difficulty Rwandans have to speak publicly about their very recent past, whose scars are only too visible and sensitive; the current politics of memory; the daunting task of defining who is responsible and how to judge them; and the politics of reunification and reconciliation. Lamko's narrative follows a similar retrospective timeline since most of the novel takes place five years after the genocide, so that it might assess how the genocide can be remembered and what its implications are within the present in the eyes of the survivors. Like Diop and Lamko, by opting to write the diary of her two journeys to Rwanda, Tadjo also maintains a distance within her work, which separates her from the genocide and her words from the reality they try to mediate.

Reflecting on the role and potentialities of writing from a distance, Tadjo asserts that the belatedness of their position can help to understand the genesis of the genocide, the mechanisms of hatred, and the various discourses that instill divisions within a society. It not only constitutes a prerequisite for fulfilling the duty to remember, but also enables these authors to shape the resonance and consciousness of this past that threatens our collective present and puts "our humanity" at risk (*Shadow* 118). Well aware that a decontextualized work of fiction could be all too easily dismissed or used to distort the truth, Tadjo, Lamko, and Diop show without any ambiguity that the genocide of the Tutsis necessitated careful political planning, resulted from an ideological manipulation of both Rwanda's pre-colonial and colonial history, and must be envisioned as the most horrific means to satisfy a will to power. Thus, for Diop, it is imperative that the genocide be analyzed as the result of various political factors and struggles for power in order to fight racist Euro-centric views that would dismiss the genocide of the Tutsis as ethnic massacres only Africans could commit against each other:

> As with the Holocaust, which was not the Europeans' fault, the genocide of 1994 and all the civil wars on the African continent cannot be attributed to being African. In both cases, very precise political mechanisms were at work. An artist cannot pretend he doesn't see them. . . . African political leaders are at the origin of these horrors and we know very well who puts them in command of our different countries. A large section of the Western public prefers to forget this political reality, we have to remind them of it. ("A la découverte" 34. Translation mine)[24]

To fulfill the duty to remember in the case of the genocide of the Tutsis reveals itself to be a gesture far less consensual than writing about other past events that have already gained a legitimate status. When it comes to remembering Rwanda's past, competing interests and divergent wills for knowledge are present. Thus, the authors of the "Fest'Africa" project must envision their writing as a social practice directed not merely toward the past, but also toward their

readers' present and future willingness to remember a disturbing past, the actions this legacy demands within their societies, the dialogue they are ready to
envision with genocide survivors in Rwanda, and the role the West and the
Francophone world play in Rwanda's politics of memory and reconciliation.

Once again, "the literary imagination" as defined by Lawrence Langer in
his early work on the Holocaust (1975) was called upon in 1998 to forge,
within the Francophone world, socially unprecedented mediations capable of
bearing witness to the most horrific acts and sufferings humans could inflict
on other humans. Once more in our face-to-face with extreme violence and
genocide today, the literary is convened to offer a symbolic and social space
that not only acknowledges what happened, but also helps us to reflect on
this legacy within our present so that we can respond to it as informed heirs.
Defining our engagement and relationship to others in the name of the past
is what is at stake as we embark in the reading of literary accounts of the
genocide of the Tutsis:

> The mind resists what it feels to be imaginatively valid but wants to disbelieve;
> and the task of the artist is to find a style and a form to present the atmo-
> sphere or landscape of atrocity, to make it compelling, to coax the reader into
> credulity—and ultimately, complicity. The fundamental task of the critic is not
> to ask whether it should or can be done, since it already has been, but to evalu-
> ate *how* it has been done, judge its effectiveness, and analyze its implications for
> literature and for society. (Langer 22)

In the following chapters of this second part, I will focus on three works written and published within the realm of the collective project "Rwanda: Writing
as a Duty to Remember": Tadjo's *The Shadow of Imana: Travels in the Heart
of Rwanda*, Lamko's *A Butterfly in the Hills*, and Diop's *Murambi: The Book
of Bones*.

Notes

1. "Dans ces pays-là, un génocide, ce n'est pas trop important." *Le Figaro* January 12, 1998.
2. For a definition of the "ob-scene" see part 1, end of chapter 4, "The Hospital-ity of Listening as Interruption." Henceforth, I will use ob-scene without quotation marks.
3. For more information on the genesis of this project see the interview of Dje-danoum and Coulibaly, "'Nous avions l'obligation morale d'aller jusqu'au bout' Entretien" (2000); Nocky Djedanoum, "Le partage du deuil: entretien avec Sylvain Marcelli" (2000), Samba Félix N'Diaye's documentary *Rwanda, pour mémoire* (2003); and Boris Diop, "Génocide et devoir d'imaginaire" (2009).

4. "Interview of Nocky Djedanoum by Chaacha Mwita" (2000).

5. *Les Crapauds-brousse* (1979); *Les Écailles du ciel* (1986) which received the "Grand Prix de l'Afrique noire"; *Un rêve utile* (1991); *Un attiéké pour Elgass* (1993); *Pelourinho* (1995); and *Cinéma* (1997).

6. *Le cavalier et son ombre* (1998).

7. *Latérite* (poems) (1984).

8. *Le Mot dans la rosée* (1997).

9. Diop's works published by L'Harmattan: *Le Temps de Tamango* (1981); *Thiaroye terre rouge* (theater) (1981); *Les Tambours de la mémoire* (1990), which received the "Grand prix de la République du Sénégal pour les Lettres"; and *Les Traces de la meute* (1993). Tadjo's works published by L'Harmattan: *Le Royaume aveugle* (1991) and *A vol d'oiseau* (1992).

10. *Champs de bataille et d'amour* (1999).

11. *Balbala* (1996).

12. My translation for *France-Rwanda, les coulisses du génocide. Témoignage d'un rescapé* (2002). Henceforth, all quotes from Kayimahe's works are my translations. See also Robert Genoud's documentary on Kayimahe: *Rwanda—Récit d'un Survivant* (2001).

13. My translation for *Le génocide des Tutsi expliqué à un étranger* (2000). Henceforth, all quotes from Rurangwa's works are my translations. Rurangwa's title is a direct reference to the book published in 1999 by the renowned French Holocaust scholar Annette Wieviorka, *Auschwitz expliqué à ma fille* [*Auschwitz Explained to My Daughter*].

14. For the French involvement in Rwanda see especially the findings of La Commission d'Enquête Citoyenne <www.enquete-citoyenne-rwanda.org> published by Laure Coret and François-Xavier Verschave under the title *L'horreur qui nous prend au visage. L'État français et le génocide au Rwanda* (2005). See also Medhi Bâ, *Rwanda, un génocide français* (1997); Jean-Paul Gouteux, *Un génocide sans importance. La Françafrique au Rwanda* (2001); Géraud de La Pradelle, *Imprescriptible. L'implication française dans le génocide tutsi portée devant les tribunaux* (2005); and Patrick de Saint-Exupéry, *L'inavouable: La France au Rwanda* (2004) and *Complices de l'Inavouable. La France au Rwanda* (2009). Regarding U.S. responsibility, see Samantha Power, *"A Problem from Hell": America and the Age of Genocide* (2003) and Jared Cohen, *One-hundred Days of Silence: America and the Rwanda Genocide* (2007).

15. My translation for Raharimanana's title *Rêves sous le linceul* and also for Waberi's *Moisson de crânes. Textes pour le Rwanda.* For an analysis of Waberi's novel see Josias Semujanga's third chapter of *Le génocide, sujet de fiction?* (2008) entitled "'L'autre génocide'. Échos intertextuels dans *Moissons de crânes*" (99–123).

16. Diop published *Murambi, The Book of Bones* (2000), Ilboudo *Murekatete* (2000), Lamko *La Phallène des collines [A Butterfly in the Hills]* (2000), and Monénembo *The Oldest Orphan* (2000). For an analysis of Monénembo's novel see Semujanga, "Les méandres du récit du génocide dans *L'aîné des orphelins*" (2003) and the second chapter of *Le génocide, sujet de fiction?* (2008) entitled "L'aîné des orphelins. Au-delà du bien et du mal ou la quête d'une parole sur le génocide" (71–97). For an analysis of Ilboudo, see Semujanga's sixth chapter entitled "*Murekatete* ou le mythe d'Abel et Caïn comme métaphore de la fraternité brisée" (185–217).

17. For additional information see also Audrey Small's essay, "The Duty of Memory: A Solidarity of Voices after the Rwandan Genocide" (2007).

18. For a reading of *Murekatete* as a testimonial attempt through a fictional character, see Monique Gasengayire's pertinent analysis, "*Murekatete*, un témoignage (im) possible" (2005).

19. For a comparative analysis of Lamko and Ilboudo's work, see Odile Cazenave's essay, "Writing the Rwandan Genocide: African Literature and the Duty of Memory" (2004).

20. See Chantal Kalisa's article on Lamko's dramatic work related to the process of reconciliation in Rwanda: "Theater and the Rwandan Genocide" (2006) and her interview of Lamko, "Le Gos au Rwanda. Entretien avec Koulsy Lamko" (2005).

21. Officially present along with Djedanoum, Clarke, and the writers of "Rwanda: Writing as A Duty to Remember" were: The First Lady, wife of the President, Jeannette Kagame; The Speaker of the National Assembly, Vincent Biruta; The Minister of Youth, Sport and Culture, François Ngarambe; The Prefect of Kigali, Marc Kabandana; The Chairperson of the Rwandan Human Rights Commission, François Ndoba Gasana; The Executive Secretary of the Unity and Reconciliation Commission, Aloisea Inyumba; The Vice-Chairman of Pro-Femmes, Suzanne Ruboneko; The Vice-Chairman of Ibuka, Antoine Mugesera; and The Chairman of the Memorial Commission, Louis Kanamugire.

22. For more information, see the official site of the project: <http://www.rwanda-garden-memory.org>. The memorial site of Nyanza Kicukiro hosts since 2009 the headquarters of the Association IBUKA and has been completely reorganized for the 2009 official commemoration of the genocide of the Tutsis. In this revamping, Clarke's Garden of Memory has been preserved and is now located next to the main entrance of the memorial. Even though the Garden of Memory remains yet unfinished, the new spatial planning of the memorial projects the future completion of Clarke's Garden of Memory.

23. French is one of the three national languages of Rwanda, along with Kinyarwanda and English. English was added as the third national language after the genocide to reflect the demographic change that occurred in 1994 due to a massive return of Anglophone Tutsis who, like President Paul Kagame, either fled the country in the 1960s or the 1970s at a very young age to find refuge in Uganda and Tanzania or were born in exile during the thirty years of discrimination and persecution of Tutsi citizens in Rwanda.

24. See also on the this issue "Stephen Smith, passeur du racisme ordinaire" (2005), Diop's response to Stephen Smith's *Négrologie: Pourquoi l'Afrique meurt* (Paris: Calmann-Lévy, 2003). In this essay, Diop virulently criticizes Smith, a *Le Monde* journalist who has become the epigone of the official French position of no wrong doing in Africa and who uses his influential position as "the" French expert on Africa's politics and history to legitimize deniers' discourses regarding the genocide of the Tutsis in Rwanda and to promote one of the most racist visions of Africa out there through his articles, television appearances, and essays such as *Négrologie*.

8

Belated Witnessing and Preemptive Positioning

IN THE SUMMER OF 1998, the authors of "Fest'Africa" discovered a country where the duty to remember was a preoccupation directly linked to the political handling of the genocide's aftermath. The government was trying to stabilize the military situation in the Great Lakes region and had launched radical reforms in Rwanda in the midst of political, social, and economic turmoil. Pasteur Bizimungu, a Hutu from the North who had represented the FPR during the Arusha negotiation, had been president of Rwanda since 1994 while Paul Kagame, who had led the RPF during the war between 1990 and 1994 after the death of its leader, Fred Rwigema, was vice-president and secretary of defense.[1] In 1998, Rwanda's security still suffered from repercussions of the Great Lakes refugee crisis caused by the exodus of two million Hutus from Rwanda to former Zaire in 1994 and Mobutu's fall in 1997. Despite the return in 1996 of most displaced persons and the destruction of refugee camps in the Kivu used by pro-Hutu extremists, the new Rwandan government was still conducting military operations—sometimes in violation of human rights—to assert its authority over the entire national territory. Moreover, it continued to defend its borders from incursions launched by exiled Hutu militias in the Congo who were backed by the newly installed Laurent-Désiré Kabila after he toppled the dictator Mobutu in May 1997 with Rwanda's help.[2]

The year 1998 was also marked by an era of suspicion and fear between the different communities within Rwanda where the prospect of peace and reconciliation was very uncertain. Thousands of Rwandan civilians found themselves caught in-between the government army and pro-Hutu rebels

Chapter 8

like the Army for the Liberation of Rwanda (ALIR) and members of the former *Interahamwe* militia or Rwandan Armed Forces (ex-FAR). Thousand of
Rwandans, both Hutu and Tutsi, died as a result of these ongoing struggles
which also generated instability and economical distress. In 1998, more than
120,000 Rwandans, most of them accused of genocide crimes, awaited trial
in overcrowded prisons, engulfing a judicial system incapable of process-
ing so many cases only four years after the genocide that had left it in ruins.
Meanwhile, also in 1998, The International Criminal Tribunal for Rwanda
(ICTR) based in Arusha, Tanzania pronounced its first guilty verdicts for
the crime of genocide against Prime Minister Jean Kambanda and Jean Paul
Akayesu, who were both sentenced to life imprisonment. 1998 was also the
year during which a French investigating committee on Rwanda examined
France's military operations in Rwanda and those led by other countries and
the United Nations between 1990 and 1994. The report of the commission led
by Paul Quilès not only cleared the French army and its government of any
wrongdoing in the genesis and perpetration of the genocide, but also went so
far as to assert that the French-led "Opération Turquoise" at the end of the
genocide saved many lives.[3] While the authors of "Rwanda: Writing as a Duty
to Remember" visited several sites and memorials of the genocide, the French
magazine *Marianne* of August 28 called the genocide of the Tutsis one of "the
misleading ideas of our time," and several notorious editorialists of French
newspapers backed the theory that the Tutsi-led RPF was responsible for the
"genocide," which therefore was no longer one since the killings were the result of an ethnic and/or a civil war (Verschave, "Dix ans de désinformation"
146).[4] In France, a concerted effort to put the blame on Kagame's RPF and the
current government was evident as part of a political strategy to clear France
of any wrong doing.

   1998 was also the year when two political figures who played a key role in
the genocide of the Tutsis came to honor the victims and to reflect on their
past (in)actions. First, on March 25, Bill Clinton stopped briefly for two hours
at Kigali-Kanombe Airport to express his remorse for not having intervened:
"All over the world there were people like me sitting in offices who did not
fully appreciate the depth and the speed with which you were being engulfed
by this unimaginable terror. . . . Genocide can occur anywhere. It is not an
African phenomenon. We must have global vigilance. And never again must
we be shy in the face of the evidence" (quoted in Power 386). Then, on May
7 and 8, the Secretary-General of the United Nations, Kofi Annan, visited
Rwanda and was greeted with hostility after he did not express personal remorse for his actions in front of the Rwandan National Assembly, who then
boycotted the reception to follow in his honor. The next day, while visiting
the Mulire memorial, he found himself heckled by a survivor, Charles Butera,

who told him, "We waited for Kofi Annan's UN, but it never came. You have piled evil upon evil."[5] Another unpleasant moment of his journey was Annan's visit to the cemetery of Nyanza close to the École Technique Officielle (ETO) of Kicukiro where more than two thousand Tutsis were killed after UN forces abandoned them on April 11.[6] Rwandan reactions to these belated performances of remorse by Annan and Clinton demonstrated that the government did not fear conflict at this time when the remembrance of the genocide was being shaped. When these international powers later tried to interfere in Rwandan politics and military decisions, the government knew how to use the past failures of the international community diplomatically. As one can imagine, this complex and tense political context surfaces in numerous literary works, since the writing of the past cannot be separated from its ability to legitimate present actions and confer political capital within the present. Remembering the genocide of the Tutsis is therefore not only a moral and ethical duty, but also a social and political practice of positioning within one's present, since the responses to the legacy of this genocide are highly disputed, be it four years after the killings or today.

By 1998, the genocide of the Tutsis had already been mediated through a complex chain of narratives and images that impacted the literary responses of the Francophone authors who visited memorials like Nyamata and Murambi. Their mediated and belated encounter with the genocide therefore imposed on them a double duty of positioning. In addition to envisioning how their writing could echo survivors' suffering and respond to their demands as they passed them on, they also had to determine what kind of resonance their literary works could shape for such a traumatic past within their readers' present, keenly aware that the echoes and cries of the past always run the risk of being muted or too nicely orchestrated when officially scripted for political gain. Thus, the authors of "Rwanda: Writing as a Duty to Remember" not only struggled with the question of the literary representation of the genocide, but also found themselves forced to take a position in regard to the dominant and ever-evolving mediations bearing witness to the genocide of the Tutsis. As Andreas Huyssen highlights in his analysis of the Holocaust's monuments envisioned as sites that institutionalize and promote social memory, the gesture of memorialization is never achieved once for all, since the meaning of its museographic narrative is inscribed in the history of its genesis and the successive presents of its reception and evolving interpretations:

A society's memory is negotiated in the social body's beliefs and values, rituals and institutions, and in the case of modern societies in particular, it is shaped by such public sites of memory as the museum, the memorial, and the monument. Yet the promise of permanence a monument in stone will suggest is always built on quicksand. . . . Given this selective and permanently shifting dialogue between present and past, we have to come to recognize that our present will inevitably have an impact on what and how we remember. The point is to understand that process, not to regret it in the mistaken belief in some ultimately pure, complete, and transcendent memory. It follows that the strongly remembered past will always be inscribed into our present, from feeding our subconscious desires to guiding our most conscious actions. At the same time, this strongly remembered past may turn into mythic memory. It is not immune to ossification and may become a stumbling block to the needs of the present rather than an opening in the continuum of history. (9)

One of the challenges for the authors of "Rwanda: Writing as A Duty to Remember" resides therefore in the need to position themselves within the process of memorialization contemporaneous to their own writing. Since the memory of the genocide of the Tutsis in Rwanda did not benefit in 1998 from the same social recognition and hermeneutic stability as did the Holocaust, it was crucial for these authors to address the social and political roles "writing," defined as an injunction to remember, might be able to play. This self-reflexive assessment and positioning appears even more crucial today because of the numerous forms of denial that seek to undermine, if not completely negate, that a genocide against the Tutsis was perpetrated in Rwanda in 1994.[7]

For these authors, then, the call for *a duty to remember* goes hand in hand with a call for *a self-reflexive work of remembering* and a need to position oneself within the competing mediations of the genocide. Furthermore, their works must not only take into account the power relations that govern the present from which this past is declared worthy of memory, but must also equally seek to invent narratives that invite their readers to reflect on the never-ending process that reasserts or undermines the accuracy of the commonly accepted mediations that shape the understanding of the genocide. In order to fulfill this *self-reflexive work of remembering*, many authors like Lamko and Diop will stage one main character who functions as the writer's fictional double: Pelouse plays this role in *A Butterfly in the Hills*, as does Cornelius in *Murambi*. Mirroring their authors' dilemma, these characters find themselves struggling in their attempt to apprehend, represent, and render the ob-scene violence and traumatic aftermath of this genocide that they—like their authors—have not themselves experienced.

This ongoing process of re-envisioning the past through the lens of the present intensifies the intertextual legacy already at play within any process of remembering. It led authors like Diop and Lamko to take into account the representations that preceded theirs as well as those contemporaneous to their own work with which they engaged in a "dialogic relation."[8] Consequently, these authors had to dialogically negotiate the stories, testimonies, historical accounts, political speeches, and museographic narratives that preexisted their works. In other words, they were not only heirs to the stories they collected, but also heirs to a narrative history that shaped their representations, challenged their authorial legitimacy, and weighed on their ability to voice the fate of those who died. Furthermore, they had to demonstrate the pertinence of the mediation they had elected, since it is seen by many as an impertinent choice. That is to say, they had to answer the following undermining question: what social pertinence has fiction as a genre when it comes to passing on the words and experiences of those who witnessed the genocide of the Tutsis and its aftermath? And if it does, how are we to define this social pertinence in the face of the impertinence of an enunciation that can speak neither from the position of the dead nor from that of the survivor?

Reflecting on this issue, writer Abdourahman Ali Waberi—a contributor to "Rwanda: Writing as a Duty to Remember"—underlines the fact that no writing or memorialization, no matter what its genre or intimacy to the event, can be seen as a neutral practice, as the role played by the media in the genocide of the Tutsi demonstrated:

> One asks oneself, what can fiction remedy in such a context . . . Immediately, one recalls that the machete was not the unique tool at the executioner's disposition: the pen and the symbolic power of numerous Hutu intellectuals like the historian Ferdinand Nahimana[9] or the scholar Léon Mugesera[10] . . . had been mobilized to legitimate the final solution. . . . One tells oneself that what was dismantled by the deadly power of the pen can be healed today by the pen—or at least that it is not forbidden to give it a try. (16–17. Translation mine)

Throughout the history of Rwanda, relations between Tutsis, Hutus, and Twas have been rewritten numerous times with different agendas. Too often, this rewriting of the past carried extreme consequences. In the wake of the genocide, one of the challenges awaiting the authors engaged in its literary remembrance was to create mediations capable of "re-mediating" this prewritten past in order to denounce its political manipulation and counter its symbolic and ideological violence. The various novels, poems, journals, and essays published within the project "Rwanda: Writing as a Duty to Remember" had, therefore, to stage and question their own acts of memorialization as they grew out of the critical dialogues they had with other representations of the same event. It is this double awareness that this second part, "Dismembering, Remembering," aims to explore: namely, that any process of memorialization also institutionalizes forgetting and that any *duty to remember* requires *a self-reflexive work of remembering*. My analysis examines the *dismembering* esthetics that Tadjo's, Lamko's, and Diop's works propose in their ethical *remembering* of the genocide of the Tutsis.

The fact that these three Francophone authors are neither survivors nor direct witnesses of the genocide perpetrated against the Tutsis in Rwanda means that they had to rely on their encounters with survivors, visits of memorial sites such as Ntarama, Nyamata, or Murambi, recorded testimonies in French and English, or documents like *Leave No One to Tell the Story*, the monumental report published by Human Rights Watch in France in 1999. In *The Shadow of Imana*, Tadjo quotes the following passage of this report as she tries to define the purpose of her literary engagement: "By mobilizing fear and hatred against the Tutsis, the organizers hoped to forge a kind of solidarity among the Hutus. But beyond that, they intended to build a collective responsibility for the genocide. People were encouraged to involve themselves in group killing . . . so that no individual can be held separately accountable or solely responsible for the execution. 'No person killed another person single-handed,' declared one of those who participated" (892). In response to this political attempt to make the genocide a collective enterprise where the notion of responsibility gets dissolved, Tadjo defines the personal duty she sees for herself and all of us—since genocide constitutes a menace to our sense of humanity—as follows: "Yes, to remember. To bear witness. That is what remains for us in our attempt to combat the past and restore our humanity" (*Shadow* 84–85). It is thus the turn of these Francophone writers to build a collective awareness and responsibility through "Fest'Africa"'s project. It is their turn to counter any ideology where hatred of the Other leads to a culture of impunity, where the killing of those who have been portrayed as others is acceptable, where killing is expected to prove, if not reward, one's legitimacy. For Tadjo, the fact that "no person killed another person single-handed" reveals a collective and symptomatic failure that threatens our humanity and that, therefore, cannot be confined to Rwanda, since the potential of its recurrence menaces us all.

While visiting the memorial that the church at Ntarama became after the genocide, Tadjo and the other authors of "Fest'Africa" met a survivor who escaped death and now serves as a gatekeeper of the memorial. As he guided the visitors through the graphic aftermath embodying the wake of genocidal violence, Tadjo became aware of the limits of her ability to imagine what happened. She realized her inability to fully encounter the reality and experience to which this survivor bore witness. As he testified to the death of his relatives, friends, and neighbors and talked of his present suffering with the hope of having it acknowledged, she wondered how long his words would be able to delay our forgetting, which would equate his social death. In her account of this moment, while showing immediate sympathy and understanding, Tadjo underlines the insurmountable gap between her and the survivor: "He talks, knowing that our imagination will never be able to get anywhere close to the reality. Deep down, he does not understand why we are coming to stir up Evil. . . . He cannot understand what we have come here to seek, what is concealed in our hearts. What hidden motive drives us to gaze wide-eyed at death distorted by hatred?" (*Shadow* 15) What would it take to interrupt our juxtaposed monologues in order to recast them into a dialogue that could be mutually transformative and lead to mutual understanding of one's reciprocal positionality regarding a shared past—not to be confused with a same common past?

To narrate her visit of Ntarama's church, Tadjo stages a double dialogue. One, out loud, in which the guide responds to the visitors' questions, and a second one, unspoken, between her consciousness of being foreign—to both the history of Rwanda and the experience of the genocide—and the skeptical thoughts she attributes to the survivor who wonders what these authors are looking for and are able to see, grasp, and comprehend. Through these concurrent dialogues that each create interference for the other, Tadjo questions the limits and meaning of the exchange that is taking place at the memorial site and invites the reader to do the same in relationship to her journal entries. Philip Gourevitch, author of *We Wish to Inform You That Tomorrow We Will be Killed With Our Families: Stories from Rwanda* (1998), prolongs Tadjo's questioning by doubting the possibility of a dialogue that would not be shaped by belatedness: "Quite often, I felt that these stories were offered to me the way that shipwrecked people, neither drowned nor saved, send messages in bottles: in the hope that, even if the legends they carry can do the teller no good, they may at some other time be of use to somebody, somewhere else" (183).

The inner voice Tadjo attributes to the guide creates an interference during the visit of the memorial, which shifts the reader's attention to the act of witnessing itself by stressing the gap between the survivor's perspective and the author's own, as one who has not experienced the genocide and can therefore only encounter its violence and trauma indirectly through testimonies and memorials. As she seeks to know what happened, she is quick to point out the belatedness and limits of her understanding of the survivor's experience and the limits of the knowledge his testimony is able to pass on to her. Thus, one of the first lessons regarding her desire to remember the genocide of the Tutsis is to accept that the experience of surviving genocidal violence requires an encounter that cannot be grounded in a relationship of identification—which is not to suggest that this experience is ineffable, nor that we should renounce attempting to understand its genesis and implementation. By highlighting the distance that separates her from the man guiding her through Ntarama's memorial, Tadjo dramatizes the difficulty of defining the nature of the dialogue she seeks to establish between survivors who have suffered horrific acts of violence and cannot put this traumatic experience at a distance once and for all and those who like Tadjo and myself, have been spared such traumatic violence and can only try to imagine its aftermath from a distance. From the beginning on, Tadjo admits that her quest to fully account for the experience of genocide is, in one sense, doomed to fail. Consequently, she does not hesitate to question the legitimacy of her authorial ability to fulfill a duty to remember since she exposes the flawed status of her belated and foreign position of enunciation.

In her narrative, which reads like a travel journal of her two trips to Rwanda, Tadjo encourages us to wonder if she is truly in a position to bear witness to what happened in 1994 and if she is well suited to lead her fight against inhumanity and hatred. Though she obtains answers to all her questions, she does not cast her encounter with Ntarama's survivor as a rhetorical move to present herself as a legitimate author. On the contrary, through this encounter, she denies herself the presumption of being in the know and capable of deciphering the survivor's experience, thoughts, feelings, and hopes. By staging her dialogue with this survivor as a "missed" encounter, Tadjo questions the reasons of her presence, the relevance of their dialogue, and the meaning of this visit that bars the possibility of fully understanding what survivors went through and are still enduring when they talk to her. The issue Tadjo underlines in these very first pages of her account is that the failure to know the experience of the genocide from within signals a fundamental schism between her position of enunciation and that of the survivor. This leads to a paradox that her narrative must address in order to reconcile her desire to bear witness to the genocide with her awareness that the survivor's experience exceeds her "willingness to know." In short, how can Tadjo's narrative work toward the remembrance of an experience whose knowledge seems to escape her? As she refuses to leave unquestioned the relationship between her visit and the act of remembrance she wants to perform, we, her readers, are invited to question the relationship we aim to establish between our reading of *The Shadow of Imana* and our duty to remember and to fight genocidal ideology within our present. In their attempt "to restore our humanity," all the authors who visited Rwanda with her in 1998 will have to do the same: negotiate the implications of this incommensurable distance and belatedness while postulating a common sense of humanity shared by all—survivors, killers, and foreigners alike.

Diop, Lamko, and Tadjo write from a specific position of exteriority as they respond to the duty to bear witness to the genocide of the Tutsis, a position that should not be confused with that of the survivor despite their respective claim "to remember" and "to bear witness." This indirect and mediated relationship to the genocide is an intrinsic dimension of their writings' genesis, which they all address in different ways since it impacts their narrative authority and ability *to tell the story*. By exploring the imperatives of their commitment as they are reshaped through their encounters with survivors, these authors find ways to inscribe within their narratives the awareness that their positions of enunciation are defined by a double process of witnessing.[11] While they are witnesses to survivors testifying to the existence of the genocide and its aftermath, they are also witnesses to themselves as they become heirs of survivors' stories and find themselves engaged in elaborating a response to this legacy. Diop powerfully stages this Cornelian issue in the epilogue of his novel, which ends with Cornelius deciding that he must expose himself to the testimony of a young widow haunting the petrified remains of the massacre planned by his own father. His encounter ultimately leads him to become the *porte-parole*, or spokesperson, of the dead of Murambi. The response Cornelius seeks to elaborate by listening to this survivor's testimony is driven by the hope that both could, to a certain extent, offer each other a space of mutual recognition where a certain belief in humanity could be restored and a sense of belonging to the living revived through listening:

> She herself, was she dead or alive? Cornelius would have liked to be able to ask that question to those who, under the pretext of drawing up the exact figures of the genocide, threw numbers around furiously. . . . He wanted to ask them where the young woman in black should go in their graphs. But it was easy to understand: after such an ordeal, there was a little bit of death in everyone. Maybe there was less life left in the veins of that unknown woman than among the remains of Murambi. . . . Cornelius decided to wait for her.
>
> He had to see her face, listen to her voice. She had no reason to hide, and it was his duty to get as close as he could to all suffering. He wanted to say to the woman in black . . . that the dead of Murambi, too, had dreams, and that their most ardent desire was the resurrection of the living. (*Murambi* 181)

The authors' willingness to expose themselves—and us, their readers—to the challenges raised by the duty to remember the genocide of the Tutsis is not foreign to the ethical responsibility they associate with the distance that separates them from survivors. Paradoxically, it is precisely because Tadjo, Diop, and Lamko enjoy an existential distance from the traumatic aftermath of the genocide, and that they are aware of it, that they can reflect on the distance and difference between their ability to bear witness indirectly to the genocide and survivors' knowledge and ability to testify. This dual act of witnessing signals our good fortune in being able to listen from a distance in their encounter with genocidal violence and its traumatic effects. Even though Tadjo claims that she has "not recovered from Rwanda" and that "Rwanda cannot be exorcised," she is able to reflect on her relationship to the genocide and put its tyrannical

weight and trauma at a distance, which does not mean that she is not haunted
by it (*Ohundam*, 119). Rather than a suspicious limitation to literary accounts of
the genocide, this distance should be interpreted as a salutary difference making possible an intersubjective et collective recognition of a traumatic experience that otherwise lacks social mediations, that is to say social visibility.

To subscribe to the impossibility of speaking from a survivor's perspective is not without consequences. It requires an examination of the narrative
implications and duties this enunciative schism implies between survivors
and those who seek to disclose their words, acknowledge their wounds, and
relay their demands for justice while fulfilling a duty to remember. One of the
principal challenges for the authors of "Fest'Africa" is then to negotiate within
their works narrative strategies that make this gap imaginable without negat-
ing its "relational difference" (Derrida, *Writing and Difference*). In addition
to writing from a position that differs existentially from that of the survivor,
their literary testimonies to the genocide of the Tutsis need to make the readers reflect on the deferred and relational status of the meaning they confer to
the genocide and its aftermath. As we will see in our reading of the various
narrative strategies through which authors position themselves in relation to
other voices and mediations bearing witness to the genocide, the notion of
"positionality" is central to underscore and evaluate the ability of the literary
endeavor to fulfill a duty to remember.

Since it is impossible to comprehend what survivors have experienced or
to occupy their position of enunciation, Tadjo's, Diop's, and Lamko's narratives are careful to make readers aware that their writing both differs from
the event to which they bear witness and defers its meaning. Highlighting this
relation of non-coincidence and belatedness becomes, then, an imperative
and a challenge for these authors who must then solve the following dilemma:
how to create narrative configurations that measure the consequences of
being unable to bridge the gap from which they write—and we read—while
relaying the words and suffering of those who can no longer speak, or put
their traumatic past at a distance. Here is where the literary imagination and
its strategies can reveal themselves allies rather than sources of distrust and
testimonial distortion.

As Sarah Kofman, in *Smothered Words*, underlines in her reading of Robert
Antelme's *The Human Race* (1946), to narrate his survival in a concentration
camp, Antelme had to use literary strategies to convey the disturbing otherness
of his experience. In a post-genocide enunciative context, literary mediation
and imagination proves to be a powerful venue for memorialization. Literature
can therefore function socially as a cultural space for negotiating the gap between genocide survivors' stories and their interlocutors, since we are too often
prone to protect ourselves by declaring survivors' experiences unimaginable

and culturally ob-scene. This refusal to face what survivors have experienced tends to proclaim that their knowledge and experiences are unwelcome in our accepted imaginary because they challenge our sense of self and our imagined community. Even though we will never be able to fully comprehend and imagine, the fact is that by refusing to try to envision ourselves from a radically different perspective, we will never perform the work of "hospitality" that is required of us, since we refuse to be interrupted by the foreign experience of the survivor whose language doesn't coincide with ours. Thus, by refusing to see ourselves interrupted, we ultimately fail in our writers' and readers' duties as hosts for those who seek to reaffirm their belonging to a shared humanity. Through this unwillingness to revisit the limits of our cultural scene, we not only refuse to acknowledge the limits of our collective imaginary but also reproduce the exclusion of any experience and suffering that is a priori ob-scene to our reassuring lenses and its dead angles. Ultimately, the existential distance and narrative difference that characterize Tadjo's, Diop's, and Lamko's position of enunciation are thus both a chance and a limitation in their attempt to pass on to us the stories of those who, too often, never find the means to voice these "smothered words" that suffocate them:

> How can one speak of the "unimaginable"—that very quickly became unimaginable even for those who had lived through it—without having recourse to the imaginary? And if, as Robert Antelme says, literary artfulness alone can overcome the inevitable incredulity, is testimony not impaired by the introduction, with fiction, of attraction and seduction, where "truth" alone should speak? Robert Antelme's book *The Human Race* . . . underscores the need for fabulation, for the selection of events and therefore of writing, when trying to communicate unbearable truths. . . .
> Very quickly, in fact, those who could not stop recounting, telling one true story after another . . . realized that a gap had opened up between the detainees of the camp, who "from now on were going to be a prey to a kind of infinite, untransmissible knowledge," and the liberator, the American who came from another world, clean, strong and well nourished, and whose "ignorance was enormous" (*HR*, p. 289; translation modified). As if they belonged to different species, they could no longer understand each other; they no longer shared the same values, the same points of reference. A gap that the word "frightful" or "unimaginable" uttered by the American could not bridge, since their effect was to suggest to the detainee that he had been understood, that just with a few words, the other has been able to "grasp" everything and to form about the unknowable and the untransmissible, a definitive and reassuring opinion. . . . How then can one tell that which cannot, without delusion, be "communicated"? (Kofman 43–45)

As Kofman's reading of Antelme underlines, the challenge for Tadjo, Diop, and Lamko resides not only in their enunciative position, which puts them on the side of the "American." They also must face the reluctance of other "Americans" to listen and to expose themselves to those who have suffered "unimaginable" violence and embody a "useless knowledge" in the eyes of those who are not ready to challenge the limits and principals that define their own knowledge, as Charlotte Delbo asserts. Thus, narratives which aim to bear witness to an experience likely to be sanctioned as unimaginable, frightful, and ob-scene need to anticipate readers' resistance to imagine, and use various narrative strategies to make readers acknowledge survivors' humanity and belonging to a shared community despite the schism that leaves their experience at the threshold of the readers' grasp and understanding.

Notes

1. Pasteur Bizimungu resigned in 2000 when Kagame took control of the government. In 2004, he was sentenced to fifteen years in prison, accused of "criminal association, misappropriation of public funds and incitation to civil disobedience" after he tried to create a political party independent of the FPR who had put him in power in 1994. In 2006, he was pardoned by Kagame who had been elected president in 2000 by the Rwandan Parliament after Bizimungu's resignation and then reelected president in the first national election in 2003 with 95% of the votes.

2. For more information on human rights issues in Rwanda in 1998, see Human Rights Watch World Report of 1999 <http://www.hrw.org/worldreport99/africa/rwanda.html>.

3. Regarding this operation see Alain Tasma's film *Opération Turquoise* (2007). See also *Rapport de la Commission d'Information sur le Rwanda*, presided over by Paul Quilès to define the military operations led by France, other countries, and the UN in Rwanda between 1990 and 1994. This document can be found on the French government website: <http://www.assemblee-nationale.fr/dossiers/rwanda/r1271.asp>. Countering this official version, see the findings of La Commission d'Enquête Citoyenne <www.enquete-citoyenne-rwanda.org>, edited by Laure Coret and François-Xavier Verschave, *L'horreur qui nous prend au visage. L'État français et le génocide au Rwanda* (2005). Finally, see the report issued in 2008 by the Rwandan commission presided over by Jean de Dieu Mucyo: "Commission Nationale Indépendante chargée de rassembler les preuves montrant l'implication de l'État français dans le génocide perpétré au Rwanda en 1994."

4. For an analysis of the media coverage of the genocide of the Tutsis in France, see François-Xavier Verschave, "Dix ans de désinformation" (2005) and Jean-Paul Gouteux, *'Le Monde', Un contre-pouvoir? Désinformation et manipulation sur le génocide rwandais* (1999).

5. AFP and Reuters May 7–8, 1998.

6. This episode of the genocide inspired the film *Shooting Dogs* directed by Michael Caton-Jones (2005). For an analysis of this film, see part 3, "Screening Memory and (Un)Framing Forgetting."

7. Regarding the denial of the genocide of the Tutsis in Rwanda, see especially part 3, "Screening Memory and (Un)Framing Forgetting."

8. Mikhail Bakhtin, "The Problem of the Text in Linguistics, Philology, and Human Sciences: An Experiment of Philosophical Analysis" (103–158) in *Speech Genres and Other Late Essays* (1986). On the concept of "dialogic relation," see especially pages 125–126.

9. Ferdinand Nahimana was a preeminent ideologue of President Habyarimana's inner circle, the *akazu*. He was a co-founder of the Coalition for the Defense of the Republic (CDR), an openly pro-genocide Hutu Party. Since 1979, Nahimana's articles justified discrimination and promoted hatred against Tutsis and moderate Hutus. He was especially at the origin and in control of "Radio Télévision Libre des Milles Collines" (RTLM). The ICTR has found him guilty for his hate speech on radio, as one of the main ideologues who promoted the genocide and was fully aware of the consequences of his speeches.

10. Léon Mugesera was a member of Habyarimana's Hutu MRND party and the vice-chairman of the party for the prefecture of Gisenyi. In a speech given on November 22, 1992, Mugesera told one thousand party members that they should kill Tutsis since "we the people are obliged to take responsibility ourselves and wipe out this scum." In the same speech, Mugesera went on to say about the Tutsis: "Their home is Ethiopia. Let's find them a shortcut to get back there. That's the Nyabarongo River." This inflammatory anti-Tutsi speech played a major role in creating the conditions that made genocide possible in 1994.

11. See my reading of Laub's conception of the practice of "co-ownership" exposed at the end of part 1, "The Testimonial Encounter."

9

Between Highlights and Shadows: Tadjo's Entries

I N HER EFFORT TO PLUNGE HER READERS INTO THE HEART of post-genocide Rwanda, Tadjo opts for a hybrid and polyphonic narrative. Her writing alternates short entries that form a travel journal and a succession of short stories bearing witness to the sites and stories she gathered throughout her two trips to Rwanda. This hybrid and dialogic configuration has the merit to add to her own perspective many other voices, since she quotes numerous survivors, some perpetrators, and gives voice even to the dead. *The Shadow of Imana: Travels in the Heart of Rwanda* weaves various genres—the travel journal, the short story, the portrait—implying that none of them alone is able to render the event and its aftermath and that different reading pacts, subjective investments, and readiness to believe must be mobilized.[1] Through this narrative orchestration that favors diverse voices and perspectives, Tadjo explicitly refuses to reproduce a Eurocentric position that exoticizes the Other, since the "I" of the observer is constantly opposed to the "Them" of the observed, who are relegated to the third person and have no proper voice.[2] By immersing her voice and position of enunciation in those of her Rwandan interlocutors who also speak in the first person, Tadjo erases any hierarchy and alterity in her attempt to assert a common belonging to a shared humanity—the very commonality that the genocide has attempted to destroy. Her narrative is driven by the imperative to make us aware that it is our duty to overcome our reluctance to acknowledge the ob-scene violence humans can unleash against other humans if we so desire and to reassert our shared humanity and belonging to a common and binding *Human Race* as Antelme's testimony suggests.

The Shadow of Imana opens with numerous entries offering very objective accounts of memorial sites, encounters, discussions, and thoughts that punctuated her journey throughout Rwanda. By asserting an autobiographical relationship between the author and the object of her writing, Tadjo's travel log grounds the veracity of her narrative and her authorial legitimacy in the lived experience of the author. By adopting this genre, Tadjo positions herself as a witness to the genocide's aftermath and a witness to survivors' witnessing. Moreover, as a genre that favors a chronological account and reading, the travel log stages a progression interrupted by pauses where the author reflects on the weight of her encounters. This complementariness between description and thoughts interrupting each other throughout her journey allows the reader to follow Tadjo's deepening understanding of Rwanda's society and history as she tries to fulfill her duty to remember. This alternation between factual inventory and subjective thinking in Tadjo's narrative echoes the dual practice of witnessing and the central role of "interruption" that characterizes her position as indirect witness to the genocide—a position which resembles our own.

For Tadjo, what is at stake in her writing and our reading is a mutual duty to face our reluctance and fear of knowing and, once we decide to no longer confine the experience of the genocide to the "unimaginable," to act upon this knowledge and the malaise it generates. Our fear finds its source in the ob-scene difference it instills within our social scene, making it no longer possible to believe in the fantasy of remaining immune or disconnected to past, present, and future genocides: "Are you prepared for this incredible encounter with death distorted by cruelty? For one day we must stop in our tracks to look ourselves in the face, set off in search of our own fears buried beneath apparent serenity" (10). In her opening pages, Tadjo underlines the necessity of interrupting oneself and points toward a conception of reading that echoes Derrida's analysis of unconditional hospitality and the ethical duty it imposes on the host: "Occasionally, someone will reveal a secret to you that you have not asked to know. Then you are crushed under a burden of knowledge too heavy to bear. I could no longer keep Rwanda buried inside me. I needed to lance the abscess, lay bare the wound and bandage it" (*Shadow* 3). Furthermore, through the testimonial encounter her writing attempts to generate, Tadjo suggests that readers like herself must learn to go on haunted by a knowledge that requires us to envision ourselves as heirs of a traumatic past that continually calls for new forms of responsiveness and positionality. This might be the paradox in light of which Tadjo invites us to reconsider our relationship to the haunting knowledge to which survivors of genocide expose us, once we cease to consider their past unimaginable and their present incommensurable with our cultural scene—which is our way to silence them and declare their insight useless.

Tadjo's journal entries are regrouped in two series, "The First Journey" (1 79) and "The Second Journey" (79–118), which depict some of the defining tensions of the genocide's aftermath and expose the complexity of the divergent responses to this legacy. These purely indicative titles signal Tadjo's intent to deprive readers of any preestablished meaning that could offer some predetermined guidance as we *Travel in the Heart of Rwanda*'s struggle with the aftermath of the genocide. With no given interpretation in hand prior to our journey through Tadjo's words, we find ourselves in an hermeneutical darkness, compelled to make sense of her entries on our own. It is ultimately our role to connect the fragmented snapshots and heterogeneous voices Tadjo stages and most often passes on without any comment, leaving us at the threshold of any possible meaning. In her desire to implicate her readers, Tadjo's positioning evolves throughout the two journals as she limits herself more and more to passing on excerpts of complementary and even conflicting testimonies gathered during her travels. In a certain sense, she functions more and more like an archivist or *une passeuse de paroles* (a messenger) who limits her role within the process of writing history to the selection of what she sees as worthy of memory in her fight against the destructive hatred that menaces our humanity. It is then up to us, her readers, to define progressively the place and resonance we are willing to give to her account of the genocide's legacy. By gradually eclipsing herself in her journal entries in order to transfer the responsibility of interpretation to her readers, Tadjo's writing lays out a strategy to "overcome [our] inevitable incredulity" by forcing us to imagine the possibility of a meaning where, first, we only wanted to see the "unimaginable." This impulse to cast genocide as ob-scene experience and knowledge betrays the fantasy that we could remain outsiders, informed at a safe distance, knowing without having to act upon this knowledge. But, as Tadjo reminds us, once we have met and listened to survivors, their stories become ours, their lives can no longer be kept outside from ours. Through the testimonial encounter, we see ourselves interrupted and forced to redefine the thresholds of our cultural scene and belonging to a shared humanity.

At the same time, by electing this first-person narrative genre that implies and often stages the presence of an "I," Tadjo reminds us that we see Rwanda's past and present through her eyes. She could have opted for other genres more prone to erase or mask her signature behind the mapping and archiving work her writing performs. At the same time, Tadjo does not abuse the rhetorical power of witness position, of "having been there and having seen it with her own eyes," acutely aware of the gap separating her from the possibility to fully grasp what she tries to pass on through her writing. In her travel logs, on the contrary, she not only limits her authorial role to select and relay testimonies of Rwandans, but also goes so far as to question

"Fest'Africa"'s writers' ability to overcome the "frightening" schism between their world and a post-genocide society where common points of reference and belief about social interaction can no longer be taken for granted. Though she is aware that her views might be misleading if projected uncritically on Rwanda's society, Tadjo affirms, as does Antelme's title, *The Human Race*, the existence of a single and shared humanity despite the recurrence of ideologies capable of legitimizing genocidal ideology. The inhuman would then be defined by Tadjo as the refusal to live according to this commonality—which does not mean identity—and to embrace an ideology promoting a hateful refusal of a shared humanity. The affirmation of this commonality not only counterbalances the subjectivity of her narrative but, since survivors' experiences and words engage us all, also forces readers to imagine these traumatic experiences that exceed their own yet still remain within the realm of a shared humanity. In this sense, while *The Shadow of Imana* invites us to acknowledge unbridgeable differences, the recognition of these differences should not lead to the fear of the Other or his rejection to the realm of the "unimaginable." On the contrary, this encounter with experiences that exceed our thresholds should foster our understanding of a shared humanity and motivate us to imagine and implement the social conditions of an inclusiveness based on our human differences.

While Tadjo often reiterates the purpose of her writing—fighting any ideology based on the hatred and fear of the Other—she sometimes questions the relevance, the accuracy, and the insightfulness of her own account of Rwanda's challenges. In her first journal entitled "The Writer," Tadjo, at one point, pauses and reflects on the pertinence of writing envisioned as a social practice to bear witness to an event such as the genocide of the Tutsis: "Genocide is Evil incarnate. Its reality exceeds any fiction. How can one write without mentioning the genocide that took place? . . . Silence is the worse thing of all. We must destroy indifference. . . . The writer pushes people to listen to his voice, in an attempt to exorcise the buried memories" (*Shadow* 26–27). Tadjo indirectly exposes here her own conception and practice of writing as she attempts to bear witness to Rwanda's post-genocide era.[3] While she admits the limits of fiction and sympathetic writing, she is ready to work within them to bear witness to what happened and embrace writing's artfulness to oppose silence, indifference, and forgetting. The writer's social role in regard to the duty to remember to which she has subscribed consists in breaking the silence that surrounds what happened in Rwanda, to force people to imagine and to understand the genesis of genocidal violence, and to exorcise all the buried memories that consume survivors from within. In the specific context of enunciation from which she writes, Tadjo crafts a narrative that not only recognizes and confers social visibility to what happened, but also helps us to find ways to live within the present in the name of the past and not in a present haunted by an unspeakable legacy that contaminates all ability to project ourselves in the future as informed heirs of the past.

Despite the limits of writing to account for the genocide, it is imperative in Tadjo's view to impugn the discourses that confine genocide to the unspeakable and advocate for silence, declaring that any mediation of the genocide is doomed to fail and to trivialize the reality endured in a world beyond our grasp. Tadjo agrees with the warning that Maurice Blanchot issues in *The Writing of Disaster* (1980), namely that "the danger of words in their theoretical insignificance is perhaps that they claim to evoke the annihilation where all sinks always, without hearing the 'be silent' addressed to those who have known only partially, or from a distance the interruption of history" (84).[4] But she also advocates a duty to remember that refuses the obliteration of the past inherent in the genocidal project and denounces any present ideology that could create the conditions of possibility for another genocide. The duty of the writer is thus twofold for Tadjo. On the one hand, she must acknowledge the silence echoing the absence of those who are no longer there to tell their story and recognize that she cannot speak from their position and identify with their experience. On the other hand, she must break the social silence surrounding the silence of the dead to remember them, and to offer survivors a social scene where they can negotiate their personal and collective response to the haunting legacy that genocide inscribed within them. By seeking to instill within our cultural scene a recognition for the ob-scene experience and reality of genocide, works of authors like Tadjo, Lamko, and Diop force us to face what we would like to see remain "unimaginable" as they confer a visibility—though a belated and imperfect one—to what happened without having the arrogance to believe that we can fully comprehend the traumatic experience of genocide and its aftermath. To opt for silence then, despite its ethical intent to avoid any trivialization of genocide, or to refuse the possibility of inscribing this negation of mankind within the realm of humanity, runs the risk of feeding discourses that profit from survivors' silence and translate their social silence into denial.

In her search for the means to make us overcome our reluctance to confront what we do not want to identify with and hope to keep at a safe distance, Tadjo relies on a second genre, the short story. The insertion of a series of short stories allows Tadjo to give voice to Rwandans' inner feelings and unspoken thoughts between the two journals of her journeys that open and close *The Shadow of Imana*. By changing the locus of focalization in these short stories, Tadjo's writing explores the personal views of her interlocutors and dares to create characters who allow her to confer readability to the repressed feelings she suspects many Rwandans keep within themselves. Thanks to this shift in genre and gaze, Tadjo can voice the silenced tensions emblematic of the genocide's aftermath, with all its personal and collective challenges.[5]

What is at stake here in Tadjo's use of literature's artfulness and potentialities is the narrative ability to confer through fiction a social resonance to the unspoken memories, wounds, hopes, traumas, desire for revenge, injustice, forgiveness, discrimination, and absence of remorse, which all coexist while being silenced or smothered behind the official stories that Rwandans reproduce among themselves in public and, even more so, when talking to foreigners. Past actions and memories of the genocide are very sensitive issues in a society trying to implement national reconciliation and unity when more than one hundred thousand genocide suspects await trial in jail and at least half a million—out of a population of seven million—played a role in the killings. Thus, any public statement or disclosure regarding the past—be it a confession or an accusation—carries immediate consequences that transcend the issue of personal recovery and overstep the private sphere. Any testimony must therefore be envisioned within a context of enunciation where the witness faces official scrutiny and finds his or her words evaluated for their conformity or dissent with the current politics of reconciliation and implementation of justice.

When Tadjo and her fellow authors visit Rwanda in 1998, the reflex at that time to hide behind preestablished and commonly accepted versions of what happened was common practice. Perpetrators who refuse to confess their crimes with the hope that no one is left behind to tell the story obviously have this reflex, as do those who acknowledge minor crimes in order to reduce their sentencing and time in jail. But this reflex applies also to victims. Many survivors are still so traumatized that they find themselves unable to put their own words on their suffering and thus try to live in a state of denial in order to go on with their daily life, never knowing when they will have to face the devastating return of the repressed. Others, like Karl, whose wife was raped by militiamen in exchange for her own and their children's survival while he was abroad, are trapped in the past, crushed by the guilt of having survived, alive but somehow dead, haunting ghosts from an ever-present past that refuses to go away (75).

Other survivors choose to hide behind vague memories and seek to protect themselves by requesting that their testimony remain anonymous, afraid of being identified by perpetrators who might kill them for what they have seen and voiced. Some, in their attempt to rebuild their lives, simply do not want their social circle to know what they went through, afraid of rumors and of finding themselves ostracized—this being especially true for women who were raped and contracted HIV-AIDS. Words and memories do not circulate freely in Rwanda's public sphere because of the many consequences they might carry.

As one young survivor declares toward the end of the second journal, there is a gap between the official handling of the past and the personal needs of genocide survivors, for whom reconciliation is meaningless if the official politics of memorialization shadows the implementation of justice (*Shadow* 110–111). In an era of official memorialization that seeks to inscribe, not even a decade after the genocide, past events and suffering, once and for all, in "monuments of stone" to confine the genocide to an "ossified" and stable narrative, Tadjo's short stories underscore survivors' discomfort and give voice to their alternative views, which often obey imperatives that differ from those of the government. While it is crucial to confer a social visibility to the genocide and to refute the era of impunity, the current politics of memory are driven by the urgency to rebuild the nation and to implement economic and social reforms to prevent the recurrence of genocidal ideology and hatred killings. The major obstacle for survivors—who are a small minority in Rwanda—lies in the fact that a memory written in stone, while it assures a remembrance, also imposes a normative visibility to the past. Ultimately in this context dominated by the necessity to reconcile and to turn the page, survivors run the risk of being silenced as their voices are ventriloquized by official discourses and increasingly petrified in monuments and memorials that speak on their behalf. The narrative use of literary imagination and short stories might then prove culturally beneficial for voicing survivors' suppressed feelings and for rendering their "smothered words," too painful or dangerous to utter, audible.

In this context, the ability of literary fiction to blur the threshold between the public self and the inner self represents one narrative path for reaching people's consciousness and for staging the unspoken state of mind that remains generally hidden behind survivors' words: "The truth is revealed in people's eyes. Words have so little value. You need to get under people's skins. See what is inside" (11). Short stories, mostly written in the first-person, are then strategic narrative eye-openers for Tadjo, who, using the ability and speculative freedom of literary imagination, gets under her interlocutors' skin to confer social resonance to their unspoken trauma and perceptions of Rwanda's post-genocide challenges. Since the views of these different "I"s are shaped by what each of them has suffered and seen, Tadjo's short stories read like "biographems," to use Roland Barthes' concept of a fragmented approach to writing identity that privileges the description of a taste, a detail, or an inflexion as a more telling approach than an entire autobiography.[6] In each of her "biographems," Tadjo gives resonance to a defining traumatic experience and attempts to grasp its disruptive and long-lasting echoes within the present. This shift in genre, gaze, and positionality in Tadjo's writing confers a hybrid and polyphonic status to *The Shadow of Imana*, suggesting that no genre nor single voice can pretend to render the complexity of the genocide's genesis or to embrace the divergent responses to its aftermath. In these short first-person narratives staging other "eyes," Tadjo abandons the narrative position of exteriority that defines her relationship with Rwanda's reality in her journal writing. Thanks to the license that the literary imagination confers, she no longer limits herself to archiving a *pre-mediated* reality and to quoting from different dialogues she had with Rwandans. In these short stories, she projects herself under the skin of her interlocutors and characters to *re-mediate* out loud what their *pre-mediated* stories smother. Here, she dares to cross the positional gap separating her from those who saw their lives radically redefined by genocide. She takes the liberty to imagine how they envision themselves, view their daily negotiation of the genocide's legacy, and imagine their future.

This shift in positionality made possible by a shift in genre not only asserts the value of fiction to fulfill a duty to remember, but also indicates Tadjo's awareness that she can only bridge the distance estranging her from victims' and survivors' positions of enunciation through the use of fiction. While she imagines what her interlocutors—now characters—felt and endured, she does not claim to speak objectively in their name or to grasp fully their existential knowledge and trauma. Blanchot's warning regarding "the danger of words" and the importance of hearing "the 'be silent' addressed to those who have known only partially, or from a distance the interruption of history" remains, more than ever, relevant when Tadjo is writing from her own position as a witness (84). Using the illusion of intimacy and immediacy generated by first-person narrative or reported speech, Tadjo seeks to bring us closer to imagining various responses to the genocide's legacy, putting in parenthesis for the time the impossibility of rendering the insurmountable difference of her interlocutors.

In order to highlight this shift in genres and positionality, Tadjo begins with a short story entitled "The Wrath of the Dead," where she gives voice to those who are no longer in a position to tell their story. Like the Groupov's staging of the Choir of the dead,[7] this fictional dialogue between the living and the dead clearly indicates a shift in genre and highlights a new position of enunciation, since the possibility of engaging in a posthumous dialogue with the dead is contingent on the use of the literary imagination. Furthermore, Tadjo's willingness to go beyond the words and under the skin of her interlocutors requires a radical shift in focus, passing from an external focalization to an internal and omniscient one in order to pass on the smothered voices of those who survived or died. "The Wrath of the Dead," through its fictional face-to-face meeting initiated from beyond the grave, echoes then the inner dialogue most Rwandans have when it comes to facing their past and responding for and to its legacy. This repressed dialogue with one's own specters and past actions questions the role a duty to remember should and can play in today's Rwanda for survivors, perpetrators, bystanders, former exiles, or foreigners. To address the conflicting priorities between the dead and the living, Tadjo's first short story opts therefore for a haunting dialogue with the dead who, angry about the mounting indifference regarding their legacy and quest for justice, interpellate the living from beyond the grave, refusing to bow to the priorities of the living and the amnesia they require and instill (*Shadow* 41–42). Through these fictional encounters and haunting dialogues between the dead and the living, which craft social resonance to past wounds and promises progressively muted by the solicitations of the present, Tadjo also questions the finality and implementation of the duty to remember that her own writing seeks to fulfill. To what extent does she also betray the demands of the dead while pretending to fulfill a duty to remember? Since we do not remember the past for the sake of the past, how should we reconcile the duty to remember and its ethical weight with the duty to position ourselves within the constraints and priorities of the present?

The description in this short story of Kigali's haunted neighborhoods highlights the tension between the duty to remember and the desire, if not the necessity, for most Rwandans to immerse themselves fully in the present in order to survive. This dilemma is still a central issue today in Rwanda where the memory of the dead and survivors' testimonies are too often cast as an interference that precludes survivors and the Rwandan society as a whole from living fully in the present and rebuilding themselves.[8] But as another of Tadjo's characters asserts, it is imperative to keep the weight of memory and the volatile demands of life interwoven (57). The dead are angered to see their remembrance increasingly become a haunting nuisance and obstacle, synonymous with death, guilt, trauma, and hatred rather than a moral and ethical compass for the living and a source valorizing life's potentialities. Meanwhile, the dead in today's Rwanda, as in Tadjo's narrative, cannot be bypassed, since they are effectively present in every neighborhood, haunting every Rwandan's soul and each parcel of Rwanda's soil, considering many of them still wait to be exhumed. The dead thus continue to resurface literally, culturally, and symbolically in the memory of those who know how to read the scars that so many landscapes and urban sites attempt to conceal.[9] The broader issue that this fictional dialogue aims to highlight regarding the duty to remember is the necessity of inscribing the dead in the social rituals of mourning through which each society negotiates the cycle of life and death, pays tribute to those who preceded the living, and confers a presence to their absence by responding for and to their legacy.

This cycle of mourning and its rituals has, however, been disrupted by the genocide, as "The Wrath of the Dead" expresses through the mediation of a divine whose ability to hear the dead bridges the ontological gap between life and death. Called upon to appease the tension between the dead and the living, the divine sees a conflict between the rituals that need to be performed to mourn the dead and the political use of the corpses in official memorials such as Gisozi, Nyamata, Ntarama, and Murambi:

> We must bury the dead so that they may return to visit us in peace, and hide their decay and their blinding nakedness, so that they do not place a curse on us. . . . We must ask them to yield up to us the secrets of life, which becomes triumphant once more, since only the living can bring the dead back to life. Without us, they no longer exist. Without them, we fall into emptiness. (*Shadow* 45)

To fulfill the duty to remember implies, then, recognizing the interdependence between the living and the dead rather than attempting to petrify the dead into "monuments of stone" and rejecting them into oblivion to affirm ourselves alive. In *The Shadow of Imana*, the narrative use of imaginary dialogues with haunting voices from beyond the grave forces us, as readers, to face our refusal to imagine, to measure the belatedness of our understanding, and to assert the schism that exists between those who endured the genocide and those who were spared. To acknowledge this schism does not undermine the fact that, as heirs of the genocide, we all must respond for and to its haunting legacy and negotiate its power to erupt within our present, to disrupt our sense of belonging, and to interrupt our history.

Most of Tadjo's short stories follow a pattern that defers the contextualization of the dialogues they contain. This strategy places the readers in a situation of non-mastery since during our reading we must acknowledge that even though we understand the words, the "real" meaning of the dialogues staged by Tadjo can always escape us, since this meaning cannot be inferred outside of its context of enunciation, which is initially unknown to us. By only progressively revealing the context in which the words and thoughts of the characters make sense, Tadjo forces us to suspend our judgment and to acknowledge that we cannot project our world of reference on characters who have survived genocidal violence. This belatedness in our ability to confer meaning to what we read rhetorically functions as a journey into darkness meant to highlight the gap between our world of reference and the experience of victims, survivors, and perpetrators of genocide. Our attempt to immediately understand what is going on is systematically thwarted by Tadjo. Thus, at the very moment Tadjo claims to go under the skin of Rwandan heirs of the genocide, she reasserts the difference that separates survivors' knowledge from ours by deferring the possibility of conferring meaning. This narrative strategy not only mobilizes the imagination of the reader, but becomes another way for Tadjo to implicate us in the effort of making sense of genocide and finding a meaning in its aftermath. The short story "His Voice" (51–58) brilliantly illustrates this literary strategy of deferral and belatedness.

The story starts with a young woman, Isaro, who receives a phone call from someone who has the same voice as Romain, her deceased husband, and wants to meet her in a restaurant for what sounds like a date. Isaro, troubled by this similarity, dresses herself nicely to meet this unknown person whose voice is yet so familiar. The narrative conveys the impression that Isaro hasn't gone out on a date for a long time. At first, the encounter is pleasant and even though the man who called her does not resemble Romain, Isaro still seeks to find in her interlocutor the memory of her deceased husband. But soon, she gives up this mind-set and enjoys their conversation. At this moment, just when we think that the love story is taking shape, something unexpected happens. A bee comes buzzing around their heads and, perhaps attracted by the oil she put in her hair, harasses Isaro to the point that she can't take it any longer and leaves. She returns home disappointed, wondering if she will ever free herself from Romain's memory and rebuild her life. Her sleep is restless that night. We learn through her nightmares—which explicitly stage the return of the repressed—that Romain had hanged himself after he had been accused of having participated in the killing of the wife and children of a man named Nkuranya. Romain had always denied any involvement and Isaro had never pushed him on this subject. After his death, she was left to wonder what to believe since "he had taken the truth with him" and this doubt progressively became an obsession consuming her and keeping her from being fully in the present (55). The next day, Isaro decides to call the man who invited her to the restaurant to apologize for her hasty departure. He seems sympathetic to her and they decide to meet at the same place in the afternoon. At the restaurant, after a while, the man initiates a dialogue on the genocide and the relation to the past and the dead, as if he had guessed what had troubled Isaro the night before. He starts by telling her that he will never forget those who died, that no one will ever be able to replace them, that they should carry the memories of their dead within their hearts and not let their absence dictate their lives. Hoping to comfort her interlocutor and projecting her own impossible hopes, Isaro tells the man that the dead will return some day. The negative response of the man is unequivocal and he goes on by invalidating the premises of Isaro's attempt to be sympathetic: "They will never be with us again. . . . Those who have gone have left us the earth in which their bones lie buried. It is up to us to rebuild life. Our long vigil must come to an end." As Isaro realizes that her interlocutor's words are a subtle way to invite her to live fully within the present, she dares to ask him his name, signaling her willingness to enter in a relationship. To her dismay, the man answers: "My name is Nkuranya," he said. "Nkuranya." (57–58) At the very moment we believe that Isaro will be able to turn the page, that she will succeed to embark on a new relationship with a man, admit that Romain will never come back, that she shouldn't feel guilty for rebuilding her life, and that this renewal does not equate to a betrayal, the short story ends with a boomerang effect. The man in whom she sees her salvation and hope to free herself from Romain's memory is none other than the man whose entire family Romain allegedly killed! Tadjo's recurrent narrative use of belated contextualization and deferred meaning is powerfully destabilizing. We frequently find ourselves struck by an unexpected epilogue or twist in the plot at the very moment we believe that we are in familiar territory or have a good grasp and understanding of the situation.

This aesthetic of contextual deferral and delusion both destabilizes readers and forces them to engage in the making of a meaning, since most short stories start in the midst of the action—Tadjo denying any omniscient perspective or knowledge to her readers. Furthermore, this aesthetic functions as a constant reminder throughout our reading that we, as foreigners who seek to know and even to fulfill a duty to remember, never fully realize what we are exposing ourselves to, since the aftermath of the genocide radically challenges our frame of reference and the reproduction of our cultural scene. Nonetheless, as Tadjo's short stories and characters suggest, we need to find ways to perform our duty as hosts by opening our scene to this interruption of history that is the genocide, which in turn demands that we envision hospitality as "the interruption of the self by the self as other" (Derrida, *Adieu* 51–52).

> Where does this fear of the Other come from, bringing violence in its wake?
> . . . In the dark night of absolute blindness, what would I have done if I had been caught up in the spiraling violence of the massacres? . . . Rwanda is inside me, in you, in all of us.
> Rwanda is under our skin, in our blood, in our guts. In the very depths of our slumber, in our walking hearts. It is despair and the desire to come alive again. It is death which haunts our life. It is life which overcomes death. (*Shadow* 37–38)

To put it succinctly, Tadjo's challenge is to pass on to the reader what was passed on to her during her two stays in Rwanda and, through her narrative, to capture and extend the relevance of the genocide of the Tutsis beyond Rwanda. For Tadjo, the temptation to remain at a safe distance must be cast as a blinding fantasy. To demonstrate her point, she frames the issue of "difference" and positionality as a political question: the question of the Other. In *The Shadow of Imana*, Tadjo interrogates cultural and political practices of differentiation where social discourses about the Other legitimize hatred, discrimination, exclusion, and might ultimately lead to genocide. Despite the belatedness of her testimonial relationship to the event, as an heir she tries to decipher the lasting consequences of this fear of the Other when it becomes the dominant vector through which social identities are politically framed and manipulated. This focus on the rhetoric of the Other and the implicit premise that no country or culture is immune to its abuse, serves as another strategy to anticipate our reluctance and undo our resistance to admit any complicity with what happened in Rwanda. Thus, for Tadjo, the duty to remember that her writing implements is not only directed toward the dead, but also seeks to make us aware that no society, no human being, is immune to the social dynamics that were at play in Rwanda during the genocide. Addressing the issue of difference through the fear of the Other is, then, a narrative strategy that forces readers to acknowledge a troubling relationship of complicity rather than a self-reassuring relationship of sympathy. Furthermore, it is a way to identify within our present a social resonance for the duty to remember performed through her writing and to make us reflect, through our reading, on the ideological and social exclusions justified by the fear of the Other within our own communities.

Notes

1. I build here on Philippe Lejeune's analysis of the "autobiographical pact" in his attempt to define the implicit contractual relation of belief and truth-telling that binds the author and the reader in first-person autobiographies. Even if Serge Doubrovsky's concept of "autofiction" (see his novel *Fils* [1977]) suggests that Lejeune's theory is problematic because of its reliance on an absolute identity between author, narrator, and character, it remains true that readers' expectations do differ depending on the genre they are reading. See Lejeune, *On Autobiography* (1989).

2. For a more detailed analysis of this issue, see Pierre Halen's comparative analysis of Tadjo and Buch's travel narratives, "Rwanda et la question de l'altérité: à propos de deux récits de voyage" (2005).

3. See also here Sonia Lee, "Lire le Rwanda: Une lecture personnelle de *L'Ombre d'Imana, Voyages jusqu'au bout du Rwanda* de Véronique Tadjo" (2005), and Semujanga's essays, "Le Témoignage de l'itsembabwoko par la fiction: *L'Ombre d'Imana*" (2007) and in *Le génocide sujet de fiction?* (2008), the fifth chapter entitled "*L'Ombre d'Imana* ou l'intertexte du récit de voyage dans les méandres du génocide" (151–184).

4. See also Semujanga's analysis of this passage and the issue of the unspeakable in the first section of his article on Monénembo's oblique witnessing of the genocide, "Les méandres du récit du génocide dans *L'aîné des orphelins*" (2003).

5. In the four sections that are not part of her two journals ("The Wrath of the Dead," "His Voice," "Anastase and Anastasie," and "Those Who Were Not There"), the "real" identity of the characters remains ambivalent, some being fictional while others might have crossed the author's path, as it is the case for Seth (77).

6. See Roland Barthes, *Camera Lucida: Reflections on Photography* (1981).

7. See part 1, "The Testimonial Encounter."

8. Symptomatic of this injunction to turn the page and move on is this comment by former General Paul Kagame when he was Vice President and Minister of Defense, as reported by Alexandre Kimenyi: "When he was asked on National Radio on July 1, 1999, about IBUKA's complaints on the government's appointment of genocide suspects to important positions, he replied: 'Who do Genocide survivors and IBUKA think they are? They think they are so important . . . They should put their feelings aside. They should find a place where to put them, a cupboard, and lock them inside. They should not be sentimental'" ("Trivialization of Genocide: The Case of Rwanda" [2002], 11). Needless to say, trauma cannot be handled as such by most survivors and that for survivors the past remains often more present than the present and remains therefore the paradigm that defines present and future actions and requires everlasting accountability.

9. As a matter of fact, five, ten, fifteen years after the end of the genocide, victims' relatives and friends are still exhuming remains from sealed latrines, abandoned wells, and improvised mass graves to bury their dead with dignity. Wherever you go in Rwanda, survivors show you pits where friends and relatives where thrown and whose remains are sometimes still there because no relatives survived them or, if some did, they might not have the money to transfer their remains to a memorial's crypt. Regarding this process, see Ndahayo's admirable film *Rwanda: Beyond The Deadly Pit* (2008).

10

Writing as Haunting Pollination: Lamko's Butterfly

Lamko's novel, *A Butterfly in the Hills*[1] begins by a visit of the Church memorial of Nyamata. I will follow his lead, then, and begin with a historic and museographic detour before I analyze the role Nyamata's memorial plays within Lamko's haunting and provocative esthetic. By exposing Nyamata's specific history and the museographic narrative that made Nyamata's church such a powerful memorial in 1998, my intent is to offer some contextual elements to help us better understand why Lamko repeatedly stresses the haunting impact of this memorial and even goes so far as to confer to one of the victims exposed in this site an iconic status in his novel. For "Fest'Africa" director Djedanoum, the visits of the memorials were decisive moments for the authors of "Rwanda: Writing as a Duty to Remember" since they were about to create their own literary memorials:

> It was important for us to see. It was more impressive than only listening to testimonies. There, it was impossible to deny. Nyamata's church, and even more so, the former Technical School of Murambi, are staggering sites. When you have seen this, you are changed forever. You have the inhuman in front of your eyes. Rwanda is the only country in the world where corpses are exposed in such a way. The association "Ibuka" ("Remember" in Kinyarwanda) wants to keep the skeletons as they are to fight discourses of denial. Will it be possible to leave these dead as such in the future, this is the question. ("Le partage du deuil." Translation mine)

Djedanoum acknowledges here the visual violence he experienced when he had to face the partially preserved bodies and bones of so many victims,

---

sometimes left in the very place and position in which they were found. The eloquence of the remains and their large scale can be mind-blowing. The display of such a collection of corpses, skulls, bones, maculated clothes, unclaimed personal belongings, tarnished photos, and abandoned identification cards gives shape to the void and makes palpable the absence of life generated by the genocide. At these sites where massacres occurred, a memorializing gesture aims to capture, freeze, and release the call of thousands of silent cries. In memorials like Ntarama, near Nyamata in the Bisesero region, four years after the killings most of the bodies were still left as such, skeletons wrapped in filthy clothes, scattered along the wooden pews, surrounded by broken objects and rotten utensils that victims had taken with them when they sought refuge in the church. This physical experience of walking among the dead and close confrontation with the violence inscribed in the remnants of so many bodies—since Murambi, Ntarama, and Nyamata's memorials expose the remains of hundreds of victims—is an experience that does not leave one unscathed. Such physical encounter with death and hatred instills a powerful legacy in visitors capable of exposing themselves to this radical interruption of history. For Diop, the author of *Murambi: The Book of Bones*, his life was marked by an era before and after his journey to Rwanda.[2]

For Djedanoum, this embodied "museo-graphic" narrative and its powerful attestation of the violence as it is inscribed in the flesh functions as an *effet de réel* that immerses visitors in a haunting dialogue with the ultimate consequences of fear and hatred of the Other. The physical immersion of the visitor within the sites where people were massacred, combined with the display of fractured skulls, rows of deserted gazes, ankles severed by machete blows, blood stains, bullets holes and grenade impacts, constitute an overwhelming array of clues to the killings that generated such an abysmal void and silence. For Djedanoum and the other authors, the power of attestation of these memorials was such that it left no doubt in their mind that the genocide of the Tutsis occurred and that their works should expose their readers to what Blanchot designates, in *The Writing of Disaster,* "the interruption of history" as they witnessed it through its aftermath. At the same time, these memorials do not offer a clear explanation of the factors that lead to the genocide or how it was implemented, something that was all the more the case in 1998. Lack of funding at the time meant that each site could not offer a documented account of the genesis of the genocide and how one should read this violence in a historical perspective and respond to it. Foreign visitors in 1998 had to rely on local survivors who officiated as guides of the various memorials and keepers of memory. As Claude Lanzmann, the director of *Shoah*, reminds us, the sites where genocides

occurred are crucial for our understanding, but, ultimately, they do not
reveal their meaning by themselves:

> One must know and see, one must see and know. Indissolubly. If you visit Aus-
> chwitz without knowing anything about Auschwitz and the history of this camp,
> you don't see anything, you don't understand anything. Likewise, if you know
> without having been there, you don't understand either. One needs the conjunc-
> tion of both. This is why the issue of the sites is crucial.[3]

Nyamata, with its predominantly Tutsi population, was the theater of
extensive killings. The high number of Tutsis there was a result of forced
displacements that had occurred in the 1960s when the newly elected PAR-
MEHUTU government of Grégoire Kayibanda massively deported Tutsis to
this hostile and inhabited area.[4] Many Tutsis forced into this interior exile
died of hunger, thirst, and disease. As Scholastique Mukasonga recollects
in *Inyenzi or the Cockroaches* (2006), for those who, like her family, were
displaced to Nyamata in 1960, the name Bugesera "had a sinister resonance
for all Rwandans. It was a savanna almost inhabited, the home of large wild
animals, infested with the tsetse fly. It was said that the king sent there in
exile his chiefs fallen in disgrace" (19).[5] Despite harsh living conditions and
decades of educational and administrative discriminations, the Tutsis exiled
in the Bugesera succeeded to go on with their lives, progressively taking advantage of their demographic exception since they were not the minority in
Nyamata as was the case in the rest of the country.[6] At the eve of the genocide,
120,000 Rwandans lived in Nyamata, an equal number of Tutsis and Hutus.
But everything changed in 1994. "In 1994, between eleven in the morning on
Monday, April 11, and two in the afternoon on Saturday, May 14, about fifty
thousand Tutsis, out of a population of around fifty-nine thousand, were
massacred by machete, murdered every day of the week from nine-thirty in
the morning until four in the afternoon, by Hutu neighbors and militiamen,
on the hills and district of Nyamata, in Rwanda" (Hatzfeld, *Life Laid Bare* 3).
But acts of genocide against Tutsis in Nyamata did not begin solely after the
assassination of Juvenal Habyarimana on April 6, 1994.

Already in March 1992, more than four hundred Tutsis were murdered in
the region and many homes belonging to Tutsis were rampaged and burned.
After these killings, Antonia Locatelli, an Italian lay sister who had lived for
twenty-two years in Nyamata, was assassinated after she challenged, on Radio
France International, the official version the government gave of the events.
She repeatedly stated that the killings had mainly been perpetrated by members of the *Interahamwe*, a militia attached to the MRND party of President
Habyarimana who were not from Nyamata, a crucial detail that invalidated
the official account of a "spontaneous act of self-defense" by Hutus respond-

ing to the "discovery" of a "press release supposedly sent by a human rights group based in Nairobi warning that Hutus in Bugesera would be attacked by Tutsis" (Des Forges, "Call to Genocide" 42). Soon after these events, it was proven that this leaflet had been forged by members of the Habyarimana government and represented one of the pieces of the hateful propaganda plan against Tutsis relayed in the Bugesera by Radio-Rwanda during the weeks leading to the killings. Thus, two years before the genocide, on the smaller scale of Nyamata and its surroundings, extremist elements of the government tested the efficiency of self-defense rhetoric, the leading role of the militia and the army to start the killings, the degree of collaboration of local Hutu authorities, and the willingness of the Hutu population in rural areas to participate in the killings or watch as bystanders, not to mention the role of the official radio controlled at the time by the Hutu-extremist ideologue Ferdinand Nahimana.

As we begin to fathom, the fifty thousand dead haunting the Bugesera and its profaned churches of Nyamata and Ntarama embody a long and complex history that has been rewritten numerous times from different positions, reshaped for different purposes, at different moments before and after the genocide. Despite the multiplicity of narratives in which these dead are inscribed, one fact remains inalienable in its horrific materiality: fifty thousand people were slaughtered in Nyamata and the surrounding region in 1994 in less than three months, fifty thousand lives were cut short, fifty thousand dreams were crushed, fifty thousand gazes were stabbed, fifty thousand voices were smothered, fifty thousand smiles disfigured by fear and suffering, and then annihilated. How does one fulfill the duty to remember that such a reality calls for, a reality stained by death, suffering, political fights, racism, greed, opportunism, decades of impunity and discrimination, sadistic abuses and rape, but also a history that has witnessed periods of peaceful coexistence, acts of solidarity, laughter and marriages that disregarded the ethnicist divide and its recurrent political abuse? After the genocide, how does this palimpsest of physical and symbolic violence weigh on the competing representations of the genocide? Is it possible to envision a pedagogy against genocidal violence that would expose the perpetrators and complex factors that made it possible for so many to kill without nourishing a divisive ideology today, since half a million people participated to some degree in the genocide of the Tutsis and the assassination of Hutus who opposed the logic of hatred? The relationship between the "duty to remember" and the "politics of remembrance" cannot be ignored in Rwanda, where the representation of the past is intimately linked to the legitimacy of the new government's reforms and its politics of national reconciliation. While throughout Rwanda official memorials respond to the collective need for a space of mourning and remembrance, with its imperative of justice, we must question to which degree these sites that bear witness to the genocide of the Tutsis are also driven by various agendas and, thus, legitimate social exclusions and political gains.

After the genocide, the Rwandan government, led by the RPF, defined a clear politics of remembrance that identified one memorial for each of the twelve provinces.[7] Despite the initial resistance of Catholic authorities, who argued that only bishops could be buried in the crypts of sites like Nyamata, the Rwandan government took control of this church, which was the first to be transformed into a memorial site commemorating the genocide of the Tutsis. According to a document drafted in 1996 by the Ministry of Youth, Culture, and Sports who supervises the memory of the genocide, memorials such as Nyamata aim to "educate Rwandans in a culture of humanity and to advance the cause of ending genocide in Africa and the world."[8] Today, Nyamata's church is one of the official memorials that can be visited across the country, the most important being the Kigali Memorial Centre at Gisozi, inaugurated in 2004, which is a burial site for hundreds of thousands of victims.[9] In Nyamata, for several years the remains of the victims were left in the church as such. It was only in 1996 that they were progressively given decent burial or regrouped into different ossuaries. As we may anticipate, survivors' needs to mourn sometimes conflicted with the official institutionalization of memory. Nyamata's church too, in its transformation into a memorial, had been the scene of some tensions, since, despite the desire of some relatives of the victims, the government insisted on keeping several bodies on display.[10] After 2000, all the bodies of the few victims who could be identified were given an individual coffin. Today, the remains of more than ten thousand victims lie in the different crypts behind Nyamata's church. Within the church, all the wood benches are covered with piles of cloth that belonged to the victims while, on the altar, a cloth maculated with blood stains remains. This new "museo-graphic" display inaugurated after the renovation of the site in 2007 confers to Nyamata a haunting ability to bear witness to the magnitude of the void left behind by this "interruption of history" and obliteration signified by the piles of clothes and bones deserted by life. As the living walk amid these remains, they find themselves progressively immersed within the ob-scene aftermath of genocide, deprived from any reassuring distance and innocence.[11]

Among the identified victims is Théresa Mukandori, who plays a unique role in Lamko's *Butterfly in the Hills*, where she becomes a ghostly narrator to whom the author grants the enunciative authority to narrate the fate of her people. Through this indirect mode of literary witnessing, Lamko inaugurates a form of posthumous ventriloquism, as Patricia Yeager defines it: "The ventriloquism we lend to the dead, the tropes we clothe them in, can have the power to re-dress their bodies, to speak volumes" (28). In this sense, by delegating to a victim the narrative authority to tell the story, Lamko's re-presentation of the genocide not only operates a strategic *destitution* of his own authorial ability to speak in the name of the victims and a *restitution* of the voices of those who are no longer there to tell the story, but also the *institution* of a discursive space capable of functioning as a literary memorial to pass Théresa Mukandori's fate and demands on to us.

> I am now a butterfly, an enormous scorched-earth colored butterfly, begot by neither man nor woman, but by anger. I emerged from the void of a ghost and from the desiccated body of an anonymous woman lying among the cadavers piled inside one of the church/genocide-museums. Before the chaos came, the whole world knew me; I was the object of adulation. I inhabited the body of a real queen: "The Queen of the Middleworld." (13–14)

This haunting voice of a deceased queen, originating from beyond the grave, opens *A Butterfly in the Hills* and questions the actions and rituals of the living with sarcasm and irreverence. To keep alive the spirit of the Tutsi queen she was before being raped, mutilated, and killed in Nyamata's church, she transforms herself into a butterfly, born out of anger, to torment and haunt the living as they visit Nyamata's memorial where her mutilated cadaver is exposed as a proof of the ideology of hatred enacted five years earlier. Mortally betrayed in her former life by her trust in men's words and her belief in the sacredness of their institutions, she now denounces the hypocrisy and the opportunism that distort the memory of the genocide that engulfed her:

> All these louts, these clowns of all shapes and sizes who were making me out to be some museum piece would come in and examine me and smell my carcass and either pinch their noses or get overcome with nausea. They all pissed me off. I was determined to subject them to a wide range of tortures, to give free rein to my holy, violent anger, to use all my ghostly powers to shake them to their roots!
>
> And let no one be outraged by my brazenness. My dealings with my visitors had not always been fraught with virulent animosity. For months I had tried to be even-handed and distribute honors fairly among these dear guests who had come to visit this church/cemetery/museum officially listed now as "Genocide Site Number 12."
>
> I had paid tribute to the good people who had come and shed a tear, and felt a bit of my suffering meandering through their dazed souls. I had clearly heard the vengeful frenzy of the most agitated among them as they throbbed in spasms of indignation. I had sympathized with the discomfort of those who by some strange association felt guilty, their fingers running through their hair and scratching bewilderedly at their bodies. But I had not failed to denounce the people who shamefully turned their heads away from an unpleasant and disgusting sight. (23–24)

The desecrated, raped, and mutilated body from which the spirit of the Queen of the Middleworld frees herself in Lamko's novel, while inspired by Théresa Mukandori's displayed corpse, acquires a new dimension here. No longer silent monument, Mukandori's literary double is a ghostly figure who denounces those visitors who feign sympathy, demonstrate compassion and interest, but who, in the end, close their eyes to questions the social and historical function of the memorial in which her torn body is exhibited, but also draws the readers attention to the blind spots and dead angles within institutionalized memory. As such, the Queen of the Middleworld narratively and ideologically embodies the figure of the specter as Régine Robin describes it in her essay *The Saturated Memory* when she analyses the issue of anachronism: "The specter, the phantom, connoting the returns of the repressed, but also all the forks, paths not followed by history, the defeated, the abandoned solutions, the smothered utopias. Here the specter represents the third space that will allow transmission of a part of the heritage, the open past as it still has something to tell us and conversely. The endeavor of absence against the fullness of presence, the inscription of loss and ruin, the trace of loss against saturated memory" (56. Translation mine).

The reason for Mukandori's recurrent presence in the works of Tadjo, Diop, Lamko, and others is partly due to the fact that she had been identified by name, but even more strikingly because of the way in which she was killed. It is no coincidence that her fate is also narrated in the opening pages of Tadjo's journal, which adopts a quasi forensic mode to testify to her horrific death by multiplying short descriptive sentences—as if any images and metaphors were implicitly declared inappropriate and indecent after an oxymoronic image compares Mukandori's cadaver to "an enormous fossilized fetus":

NYAMATA CHURCH
Site of genocide.
Plus or minus 35,000 dead.
A woman bound hand and foot.
Mukandori. Aged twenty-five. Exhumed in 1997.
Home: the town of Nyamata.
Married.
Any Children?
Her wrists are bound, and tied to her ankles. Her legs are spread wide apart. Her body is lying on its side. She looks like an enormous fossilized fetus. She has been laid on a dirty blanket, in front of carefully lined up skulls and bones scattered on a mat.
She has been raped. A pickaxe has been forced into her vagina. She died from a machete blow to the nape of her neck. You can see the groove left by the impact. She still has a blanket over her shoulders but the material is now encrusted into the skin. (*Shadow* 11)

In the eyes of many authors, the violence to which her body bears witness symbolizes the radical and horrific consequences of genocidal ideology, namely that the complete extermination of a social group requires the radical destruction of that group's ability to have descendants, to have a legacy, an uninterrupted history. Reflecting on the vivid and haunting role this body had in his writing, Lamko stresses its iconic status and ability to represent the fate of millions of anonymous victims:

> One image was haunting me, the image of the corpse of a raped woman in a church with a stake in her vagina. This image remained glued to my memory. I was tormented by this image when I left Rwanda in 1998 and it constituted the point of departure in my writing. It has not been an easy endeavor because I usually write at night and this is the time of the day when ghosts suddenly surface, especially when I had to remember all these sites of the genocide with all these bodies without tombs. ("Fest'Africa au Rwanda." Translation mine)

Haunted by this image, Lamko adopts a radically different approach from Tadjo in his literary attempt to fulfill the duty to remember to which both have subscribed. While Tadjo's writing abandons the use of metaphor to adopt a clinical and objective gaze, Lamko does just the opposite. In Tadjo's text, the disturbing oxymoron comparing Mukandori's cadaver to "an enormous fossilized fetus" is both synonymous with her irrevocable death and the death of metaphor as an appropriate trope to confer social readability to the ob-scene violence of genocide. For Lamko, on the contrary, the challenge is to create metaphors that can literally bring Mukandori back to life by transcending Tadjo's oxymoronic dead end. Adopting Paul Ricoeur's view on the relationship between language and metaphor—namely that a type of narrative imagination "generates and regenerates meaning through the living power of metaphoricity"[12]—the "fossilized fetus" gives birth to a butterfly in Lamko's novel. Thanks to the regenerating power of the metaphor in the wake of death—a power equivalent to metempsychosis in this case—Lamko's writing frees Mukandori from her fossilized and silenced position of enunciation. By giving birth to a butterfly eager to tell her story on her own terms, Lamko resuscitates a petrified victim and unleashes her "monumental" suffering. His writing frees a voice from the grave to pollinate our "imaginative capability of perceiving history" so that we can respond to the haunting legacy Mukandori's narrative spectre forces on us. Lamko, therefore, implements a conception of "testimonial literature" whose social and historical function is defined by Felman and Laub as follows:

> The specific task of the literary testimony is . . . to open up in that belated witness, which the reader now historically becomes, the imaginative capability of perceiving history—what is happening to others—*in one's own body*, with the

power of sight (of insight) usually afforded only by one's own immediate physical involvement. (100)

A symbol of resurrection, the butterfly, to which Théresa Mukandori gives birth in Lamko's novel, signals the failure of the genocidal project aiming to annihilate the Tutsis of Rwanda. The rebirth of this Tutsi queen as a butterfly must indeed be read as a symbolic rebuttal to one of the most hateful metaphors used by the pro-Hutu extremist journal *Kangura*, which asserted in March 1993 that all the "cockroaches" had to be killed, since "a cockroach cannot give birth to a butterfly. It's true. A cockroach gives birth to another cockroach. . . . The history of Rwanda clearly shows that a Tutsi is always the same, that he has never changed. The malice, the wickedness are what we have known in the history of our country."[13] Finally, as her name suggests, the Queen of the Middleworld has the power to inscribe the haunting voices of the dead within the present of the living to keep the victims' memories and quest for justice alive. The authors who gave Mukandori a literary tomb did so hoping to acknowledge her abominable suffering, but more importantly, seeking to keep her disturbing past present and to refuse her social obliteration by those who silenced her. Diop recounts: "When we learned that her name was Théresa Mukandori, I saw everyone writing it down. In essence, this meant, and here we were talking a little bit to the killers: 'You wanted to kill her, but through our writing, we will make her live again.'"[14]

At stake between Tadjo and Lamko's radically different representations of the "same" reality is then the meaning each of these authors wants to assign to this monumental and embodied suffering in order to affirm within their readers' present a number of values and lessons to which they believe the cadaver of Théresa Mukandori points. As Tzvetan Todorov asserts in his critique of Claude Lanzmann's film *Shoah*, the relics of the past do not contain in themselves their meaning but require from the living a poetic work of representation and interpretation that emplots the past:

> When history serves as the point of departure for the poet's fictions, the poet can take certain liberties with the exact course of events so as to reveal their hidden essence: therein lies the superiority of poetry over history, as Aristotle pointed out long ago. . . . At the same time, a work of art is also a declaration of values and, as such, inevitably takes a moral and political stand. The choices of these values can be ascribed to no one but the artist: facts hold no lessons in themselves and their meaning is never transparent; it is the interpretation the artist gives to these facts that is responsible for the judgments embodied in a work. (*Facing the Extreme* 273)

The cadaver of Mukandori does not, then, embody its meaning nor reveal it by itself. Only its artistic, cultural, political or historical representations embody its meaning(s), since these mediations offer, through their interpretative lenses, specific values, meanings, and lessons for use by the living, as Groupov's subtitle to the play *Rwanda 94* suggests.[15] The question that arises then is this: What lessons does *A Butterfly in the Hills* call us to respond to as it provocatively emplots this obscene past and its aftermath to confer to them unprecedented visibility within our present?

As a tenacious agitator advocating for all the voiceless victims in an era of grand-sounding memorialization, the butterfly's iconoclastic stature signals the authors' refusal to let survivors' ongoing trauma be dismissed. The disturbing past they embody should not be socially or politically frozen in official monuments, silenced by guided tours, and distorted or even eclipsed by the priorities and interests of the living. As the Queen declares, the issues linked to the representation of the genocide are "monumental" in all the meanings of the term:

> Stakes here were monumental. I could not allow my story to be distorted. That is why I had quickly decided to grow a head, and a chest, and a belly and eyes and three pairs of legs and . . . butterfly wings. I chose to inhabit the body of a large scorched-earth colored butterfly, with dark stripes, to effect a simple metamorphosis that would allow me to move from invisibility to visibility, from a state of disembodiment to one of embodiment. It had been a simple matter after my rape and murder, five years ago. A *muzimu* knows neither obstacles nor limits. (28–29)[16]

In order to stage the politics of memory at play within the duty to remember and to contextualize what it means for the living to honor the dead, Lamko's narrative offers a guided tour of Nyamata's memorial leading to a direct encounter with Théresa Mukandori's fate and spirited reincarnation. Lamko's narrative is told through the interactions and reactions of four characters who symbolize different points of view, distinct experiences, and divergent interests.[17] Nonetheless, the fact that their respective trajectories lead them all to the same memorial five years after the fact signifies without ambiguity that the genocide of the Tutsis represents for all of them a common crossroad. Needless to say, most of them despise the idea that their history/History has anything to do with the trajectories of others, since they see themselves either as victims, foreign saviors, or innocent bystanders when the question of responsibility for the genocide of 1994 and its legacy is addressed.

The first protagonist present in Nyamata's memorial is Védaste, a Tutsi who escaped death in 1994 and sees himself today, as do many others, as a keeper of memory and a guide.[18] The second is an obnoxious "*muzungu*" [white man] who leads a delegation of French "penpushers" inquiring about France's role in the genocide. This delegation is an explicit reference to the commission led by Paul Quilès whose report in 1998 cleared the French army and its government of any crimes or complicity in the genocide and reaffirmed that many Rwandans were saved in the western part of Rwanda thanks to the French "Opération Turquoise" during the last weeks of the genocide. Quilès' report failed to mention that the lives saved were mainly those of perpetrators fleeing to Zaire and killers who had massacred numerous Tutsis or planned their execution. Finally, completing the quartet composed by the French delegation, the survivor Védaste, and the Queen of the Middleworld's corpse and reincarnated spirit, is Pelouse, a young Rwandan woman who has lived her entire life in Paris in exile. As we learn immediately, Pelouse is the Queen's niece, who had seen her aunt several times when she visited Paris. Five years after the genocide, Pelouse has accepted to be the photographer for the French delegation, seizing this opportunity to discover her native country and to learn the fate of her aunt from whom she has not heard since 1994.[19]

The confrontation that takes place between these characters at the memorial site offers a unique space to explore the personal uneasiness and political tensions surrounding the duty to remember a genocide and its aftermath. Reading *A Butterfly in the Hills* impels us then to reflect on what it means to become heirs to an obscene violence through memorials, be they physical sites or textual mediations. As Jackie Assayag underlines in her analysis of the social, political, and anthropological functions of memorials and museums devoted to extreme violence, the call for a "duty to remember" within a collectivity or a nation is valuable and necessary, but it is important to remember that this injunction is always subordinate to a "politics of memory" that might achieve just the opposite of what it claims when it equates "Never again" with "Never forget":

> From now on, a "politics of memory" defines to various degrees all contemporary collectivities. This is not without risk, in light of the injunction of this "duty to remember" that nourishes the cycle of eternal revenge against the enemy, the obviously irreducible Other. The members of one community run the risk of seeing themselves vampirized by the ancestors to the detriment of descendants' liberty. The "duty to remember" as it is practiced, meaning erected as an intangible dogma, can in the end contribute to the reinforcement of racism and anti-Semitism because its hyperbolic and abstract emotion depoliticizes a long and complex history. (20)[20]

Therefore, when the post-genocide government decided to transform Nyamata's Catholic Church into a memorial site, the museographic displays and narratives developed to maintain present the legacy of genocidal violence as an unforgettable crime—after decades of impunity—were not only a discourse about the past but, equally important, also a discourse about the present social and political reforms implemented in the name of the past. At play in Nyamata's memorial is not only the creation of a site allowing a collective work of mourning and a work of remembering through the recording of events, the gathering of testimonies, the identification of victims, the display of evidence, and the preservation of remains in order to assert publicly the failure of the genocidal ideology seeking the physical, social, cultural, and historical eradication of the Tutsis of Rwanda; in addition to the rituals of mourning and the archival work attesting to the perpetration of the genocide, this memorialization also seeks to acknowledge the ethical and political necessity to negotiate collectively the traumatic legacy of the genocide by reaching out to the various constituencies of Rwanda's present society—survivors, perpetrators, bystanders, exiles who came back from Uganda, Europe or Congo, various old and new diasporas, ordinary citizens, investors, officials, widows, or orphans[21]—as well as to the foreign countries whose national histories were intimately linked to Rwanda's and who, by and large, still are.

A Butterfly in the Hills stages many of these various points of views, interests and trajectories by favoring a polyvocal narrative where numerous characters appear and exit the story after they interact with the main protagonists whose paths crossed in Nyamata's memorial—Fred R., doomed to an eternal exile, being the exception. Facing so many competing perspectives and testimonies on the "same" past, Lamko's main characters must both address the violence perpetrated during the genocide and its aftermath and address each other's symbolic violence as they compete to establish their version of history as the legitimate one. The French "*muzungu* with layered jowls" must portray France's military operations in Rwanda between 1990 and 1994 in such a way as to fully exonerate the French government. Pelouse, the young Rwandan in exile, represents the perspective of the Tutsi diaspora, a character who did not directly experience the genocide and who, once back in Rwanda, feels "foreign" to the reality she finds in her homeland as it no longer corresponds to her idealized vision. Védaste, who officiates as the guide of the memorial, simultaneously embodies the view of Nyamata's survivors and the view of his employer, the government. As the keeper of an official institution of Rwanda's memory, his version must, among others, conform to the government's perspective and agenda of national reunification. Finally, the butterfly inhabited by the spirit of Pelouse's aunt, the Queen of the Middleworld, incarnates the haunting perspective of the dead and their quest for justice. Thanks to her ontological and spatial duplicity, she functions throughout the novel as a fluttering and disturbing presence among the living. As a ghost freed from any social conventions and political agendas, she dares to express her feelings and thoughts, having only to report to the dead. Refusing to be confined to the story that her violated and mutilated body is presumed to enact, her metamorphosis grants her magical powers that help her counter all those who attempt to distort her experience:

> I had decided to take back the Word and to print it directly on the consciences of these two unusual visitors in its unabridged, unexpurgated, original form. I couldn't take any more of these altered, doctored speeches, any more of these insipid solos that reeked of smuggled goods and requiems. Besides, from as far back as Lyangombe's reign, the old adage has decreed: each of us is lone witness to his life's tale, the sole true reflection of his face, for he alone has known the weariness that drew the rings beneath his eyes. The story of my life is mine and mine alone. It is the story of a queen and, above all, the story of a vagina: a vagina with a tree thrust up into it. (31)

For the Queen, leaving to others the right and ability to tell her story would be a second death, a social death. Determined to defend her right and ability to tell her story on her own terms, the Queen of the Middleworld stuns the survivor Védaste when he tries to use her story to get Pelouse's attention and forgets the *raison d'être* of his testimony. Infuriated by his misappropriation of her sufferings, she interrupts his story bearing witness to the interruption of history and leaves him speechless, declaring that she will regain possession of her story. The second chapter ends on this transgressive and surreal position of enunciation that confirms the Queen of the Middleworld in her new and self-appropriated status, as she reclaims the right to be the narrator of her own story. The following chapter demonstrates just that. It propels us back to April 1994 as the Queen recounts in the first person how she was killed. This posthumous narration represents both a testimony to her rape and gruesome murder by Father Théoneste and the performative demonstration of her new positionality regarding the mediation of her past. Unlike Tadjo, in Lamko's novel the Queen of the Middleworld narrates her rape and killing over several pages. She uses the first-person narrative, which generates a disturbing intimacy for the readers and multiplies vivid metaphors to render her suffering palpable to the readers' imagination.

The fact that Lamko's narrative confers to the Queen of the Middleworld the posthumous ability to narrate her own death must be seen here as a symbolic gesture through which his writing emancipates the Queen's memory from the horrific sexual and ideological violence to which Father Théoneste subjects her. Moreover, by allowing the Queen to narrate vividly and in great detail from her own perspective what she has endured during her long rape and agony, Lamko gives her the enunciative power to harass and respond posthumously to her killer as she counter-objectifies him at the very moment he reduces her to a sexual object. Furthermore, in the Queen's eyes and account, her killer negates his own humanity as he tries desperately to negates hers, becoming ultimately the victim of his own hatred and lust. As she has auto-proclaimed herself the sole authorized narrator of her story, the Queen enunciatively emancipates herself from the position of passive victim as she comes back to life as an uncompromising narrator who heckles her torturer and questions our will to knowledge:

> And you, Mr. Holy Man, your insatiable sexual appetite will shrivel away beneath your testicles. Go ahead, have me. Can't you see how my eyes are sparkling with tenderness; can't you see my iris aglow, the victorious moon in eclipse? Look at my lips. They are like yours, the space between their fullness like the opening of uncontrollable desire. And the dimples in my cheeks, these valleys that hold the fires of the Karisimbi volcano, do they not make of me a goddess? Time defies space, scoffs at the passing of days and moons. It is like the time of potential fecundity, only babies are not delivered by storks, although we don't tell children that. So go ahead. Run your fingers through my heather hair, Mr. Holy Man. It is rooted in the age-old turf. I no longer know if I am to scream with happiness, drop to the ground to kiss your toes, kneel to adore you, or anoint your feet and wipe them dry with my hair . . . Take my moans and make them into the new *kyrie eleisons* of your sacred, eternal, perfect youth. I shall forever hold my tongue about your libidinousness. There will be neither gorillas rumbling in the forests nor flights of wagtails in the eucalyptus trees. But hear this: your unbridled quest will know no end, for it is merely insatiety you seek, for you too are but mortal man. You know not your hour. When the moon has risen and the ululation of the owl has ripped through the clearing, the cormorants will leave the waters off Mombasa. They will come and drop down onto the plateau, with their gizzards torn asunder by the poisoned breath of the fatal wind. Rivers will run dry beneath the roots of the hills. The Earth will begin to growl. It will open explosively wide and will not subside until lumps of blood are released onto the sides of the volcano. The Earth will strangle you. Amen! (43–44)

After Védaste and Father Théoneste, the third person she persecutes is the French *muzungu* for his endless demonstration of France's innocence,[22] attitude of genocide denial, and racist ideology, until he at last acknowledges the wrongdoing of his country during Murambi's visit. The fact that he breaks his glasses as he shamefully lowers his gaze while facing the exhumed bodies of Murambi's victims that the French army helped to bury in mass graves before playing volleyball on top of them, eloquently symbolizes the interruption of his predefined gaze. This new way of seeing, of documenting, and of fulfilling his duty to remember is not without challenges for the *muzungu* who must now invent the means to perform a cultural and memorial hospitality where he envisions himself as an heir of this genocide and no longer as the foreign and neutral observer he has never, in fact, been:

> She had made up with the *muzungu* with the jowls of opulence in Murambi. Pelouse had stared long and hard at the French flag that had been flying there ever since Opération Turquoise, and repeated the guide's words: "Fifty thousand people were killed in these SOS classrooms. The soldiers who came here with Opération Turquoise had to use bulldozers to push the thousands and thousands of bodies into common graves. But several hundred of them, conserved in the clay, were unearthed and now lie in classroom / museum / cemeteries. As irrefutable proof."
> The *muzungu* with the jowls of opulence lowered his eyes. His pince-nez slipped off his nose and cracked on the red lateritical soil. He was overcome with a feeling of guilt as vast as his homeland. (140–141)

Finally, the Queen of the Middleworld harasses her niece until she abandons her preconceived perceptions and ceases to operate as the photographer of the official French commission, reproducing through her *clichés* a representation of the genocide that only reinforces a sensationalist perception and racist framing of what happened:

> What the hell was a Negro lady with a camera doing here? Come to shoot up on emotion, maybe? To get something to feed the insatiable appetites of the opulent? My anger raged anew! This century of the couch potato, irresistibly drawn to sensationalism, stuffing itself on virtual reality! A century that craves man's misery and savors it through the medium of TV screens and camera lenses. They are closet cannibals, and how much more tender and juicy it is when it's Negro fare, succulent black meat served up as steak tartare. (24–25)

In order to free Pelouse of her preconceived gaze and ideological role as photographer, which precludes her from recognizing the cadaver of her aunt because she is unable to see with her heart the object of her quest, the Queen multiplies supernatural interventions throughout the novel. Progressively, she helps her niece understand and see the reality and meaning behind the pictures she takes and undo their deceptive power of attestation, since they cannot go beyond appearances. As a ghost, the Queen speaks to her niece through her dreams and encourages her to free herself of all the normative rules and expectations that shackle her ability to be herself. She trains her to see through her own eyes instead of reproducing an inherited gaze that occults the belonging she seeks to find through her journey:

> You are faced with three ways of fulfilling yourself, and don't know which to choose. The first is called *it's necessary*; the second: *you have to*; the third, *you*

can. Nature can't stand a void . . . I am not the one who made up this way of perceiving life. I am a mere onlooker, just an onlooker. There is no possibility of not choosing, either; that's an illusion.

. . . *it's necessary* and *you have to* both tend to deny who you are rather than make you who you are. *You can,* on the other hand, . . . If you push back the limitations imposed by *it's necessary* and *you have to,* you will discover in that effort the strength you need to act. Once you have escaped from the shackle that is your body, you will find yourself in the furrow of timelessness . . . where you will sow your seed. That is where real life is lived, because you yourself will have created it and adorned it with captivating freedom. (88–90)

Ironically, Pelouse's quest, symbolized by her desire to find the tomb of her aunt in order to become a true heir (144), had been fulfilled since the beginning without her knowing it, since at the time of her visit to Nyamata she had been unable to see through her cultural and historical blindness. As the novel progresses, the Queen closes the lens of Pelouse's camera, washes away the notes she took for the commission, and provokes a state of crisis. Opening her heart and eyes thanks to her journey throughout Rwanda's post-genocidal society, Pelouse can finally see for herself and abandon the desire to find the tomb of her aunt as she discovers that the Queen had always already been in her, a haunting aunt indeed: "I am with her . . . inside her. And have been since the first day" (207). Through her numerous encounters with survivors—especially with Cracked-skull Muyango—her family ties to the Queen, and her genuine will to knowledge, Pelouse progressively emerges as the heir who truly seeks to understand the aftermath of this legacy to which the living have the duty to respond. She doesn't fear seeing herself interrupted or forced to re-envision how she sees herself and the past as she tries to respond *to* and *for* the legacy that is passed on to her by signing *in* her own name.

By staging these various voices and gazes that document the genocide and promote its remembrance in divergent ways, Lamko's narrative forces us to question the very lenses through which we can fulfill the duty to remember that we are called upon to perform. Furthermore, since she embodies the limits of photography as an "objective" medium for documenting and understanding genocide, Pelouse allows Lamko to position his writing in regard to other modes of representation. In Lamko's eyes, photography—like other "objective" mediations—cannot capture the essential reality and human suffering behind the visible scars and marks it documents, but requires a caption that Lamko's text aims to provide poetically. While acknowledging that literature does not resuscitate the past nor substitute itself for it—since the writer is always "paraphrasing history"—Lamko professes in his exordium to *A Butterfly in the Hills* that literature functions as a necessary counterpoint to confer social visibility and resonance to genocidal violence and suffering.

> Three months gives you thirty days multiplied by three. Then you have to add in two or maybe three more, depending on whether it's a leap year . . . that is, if you're including February. And if you know your math, thirty times three gives you ninety. Tack on another ten to get a round number and you come up with a hundred. Then if you multiply that by ten, and then again, and again by ten, you get a million, which, if you prefer to have a more respectable average, can be divided. . . .
>
> Adding, subtracting, multiplying, dividing, whatever the operation, there is always something that gets carried over. And of course accounting often falls victim to the need to prove something.
>
> As for units and formulae, if you are in a hurry and want to move with the speed of the times, you can use abbreviations. For example, it is accepted practice to use dm for decameter, and dl for deciliter, and $H2O$ for hydrogen dioxide.
>
> On the other hand, it is totally unacceptable to abbreviate with "the deaths of many." That's because "many" includes women, and old people, and newborns, men, life, hope, eternity and so on.
>
> Of course, if you really want to stir up the gurgling, muddy bottom of this dried out pit, if you really have the guts to arouse the horned serpent sleeping down there on its coiled tail, if you really want to risk bringing to the surface the potent, nauseating odors of that slime . . .
>
> The mathematical rendering ends down there; now is the time for poets, the time to turn a polyphonic vocation into arpeggios of cacophonic suffering.
>
> And yet, here, I have only one right: that of paraphrasing history. (11–12)

This clash between competing memories in Lamko's novel is in direct response to the fact that in 1998, while the authors of "Rwanda: Writing As a Duty of Memory" spent two months collecting the testimonies of survivors, deputies of the official French commission inquiring about France's involvement in the genocide refused to listen to survivors during their visit of Murambi's memorial. For the deputies of this commission, the duty to remember regarding France's role in the genocide of the Tutsis could only be fulfilled by the French government itself in order to maintain its sovereignty over its national memory. Thus, according to French deputy Pierre Brana, a dialogue with survivors was not needed since the bodies of the victims told "the" story: "It was not a refusal to listen to the testimony of these people. . . . after what we have seen, words would be superfluous. . . . It is true that the spectacle was so eloquent that words seemed useless."[23] In fact, what the French commission was attempting to avoid were questions as to why some perpetrators—such as Laurent Bucyibaruta, the former prefect of Gikongoro that includes Murambi—were able to find refuge in France and why the French army unthinkably built a volleyball field on top of Murambi's mass grave during "Opération Turquoise." While Bill Clinton made at least a short stop in Kigali's airport to acknowledge his mistakes and show remorse in 1998, France sought only to legitimize an official representation of the genocide to exonerate itself of any wrongdoing, despite having been the main backer of former President Habyarimana's genocidal regime. One of the lessons that Lamko's novel offers is that, in a highly polemical context of memorialization, the signs of genocidal violence exhibited by the piles of bones, the rows of skulls, and the untouched corpses do not contain the *whole* meaning of the story to which they tragically point and that they always run the risk of being "vampirized" (Assayag) or ideologically taken hostage as the survivor Muyango warns the French penpushers when they travel to Bisesero: "History loses nothing through repetition, when the recounting is accurate. What is repugnant for history is to be held hostage to the truths of the people in power, who would torture it, pluck out its wings and its feet, toss it into some sauce pan and cook it up to their tastes, that is to say, to the detriment of the victims" (116). Thus, we must imperatively listen to the survivors who are able and willing to tell their story in their own terms, which is the endeavor that the Queen is performing by pollinating the consciousness of the living, hoping that her testimony, thanks to its power of interruption, can help us to flourish socially and culturally despite its haunting weight.

Thus, Lamko's guided tour of the Nyamata church, set in 1999 in his novel, not only echoes the author's own visit of the memorial in 1998 and its haunting effect but also forces on us an awareness that the representation of the genocide of the Tutsis must be approached as a polemical arena where survivors always risk being silenced and dispossessed of their story for political reasons. In Lamko's eyes, the legacy of this genocide is then both personal and political. It is shaped as much by personal experiences and collective histories as by national memories and political interests. Hence, in its attempt to function as a cultural keeper of memory, *A Butterfly in the Hills* cannot aspire to become a literary memorial without questioning its intertextual nature and genesis. There is a need to address what is obliterated in the other versions of history with which Lamko is in dialogue as well as what his writing seeks to favor as it fulfills the duty to remember. Finally, by raising doubts about the motivation behind each character's views, *A Butterfly in the Hills* also provocatively scrutinizes the reader's own gaze, which is not immune to morbid voyeurism, denial, and forgetting. Like Pelouse, we must, in our textual encounter with the genocide, evaluate the demands of this traumatic legacy within our present and engage in a critical work of remembering to address the socio-historical conditions in which we are required to remember. As heirs, we must define ourselves through our responses for and to a past whose disturbing resonance always runs the risk of being muted or too nicely orchestrated. Thus, we must make ours the lesson of hospitality that Lamko stages through Pelouse the photographer and the heir, namely, as Sontag highlights in *Regarding the Pain of Others*, that it is up to us—the communities of listeners and readers—to craft the resonance of the interruption of history to which survivors' testimonies bear witness: "The photographer's intention do not determine the meaning of the photograph, which will have its own career, blown by the whims and loyalties of the diverse communities that have use for it" (39).

The Queen's visceral reaction against her "faithful companion in misfortune," Védaste, can be read as an implementation of this critical *work of remembering*. If the Queen goes as far as propelling Védaste into "an epileptic seizure that had him shaking convulsively," it is because he was increasingly relying on "mannered circumlocutions, politically correct and socially clean" (30). Reclaiming the right to tell her story, she does so in a far more transgressive style—a style whose poetic obscenity mirrors the culturally ob-scene violence she has endured and that her cadaver exhibits. Nonetheless, the Queen's choice for an obscene esthetic is not to be confined to the realm of mimicry. Her provocative tone and use of crude images is part of a narrative tactic that exercises a calculated violence on the reader as she foresees our strategies of denial and anticipates our abilities to euphemize the disruptive effects of the violence with which she confronts us. As Parrau's reading of Tadeusz Borowski's short stories underlines, to exercise a calculated violence on the readers when bearing witness to experiences such as the Goulag or genocide might be valuable in certain cases:

> The author deliberately exposes his reader to a calculated violence: the purpose is to forbid him to identify with the stereotypical figure of the victim, to undermine the reader's imaginary and misleading effects of reading through an imposition of truth as brutal as possible. If there is a part of provocation in *This Way for the Gas, Ladies and Gentlemen*, it must be understood in the etymological meaning of the term, the one that resides in the Latin verb *provocare*: "calling outside," the reader being effectively called to step outside of the representations that protect him from the truth of the camps. By immersing his reader in the very cruelty of the truth . . . Borowski wants to make him feel what, within this truth, radically shatters the points of reference that lie at the foundation of our experience, our world of "normal" human beings. (152–153).[24]

In this light, Lamko's provocative esthetic must be read as an invitation to see *in* and *through* the graphic images and irreverent metaphors used by the Queen of the Middleworld, a call to acknowledge the impossibility of identifying with her. Moreover, her provocative narration calls us to re-envision our ways of seeing and reevaluate what they leave culturally and ideologically in the margin, if not obliterate. The antagonisms, polemics, and sharp disagreements between Lamko's main characters over the ob-scene past that binds them form a narrative device forcing us to question any reassuring and commonly accepted mediations of the genocide, including the author's own.

One of Lamko's contributions to "Rwanda: Writing as A Duty to Remember" resides then in his ability to engage readers to reflect on the process of memorialization in which his writing and our reading participate. Since the memory of the genocide of the Tutsis in Rwanda does not enjoy the same consensual recognition as the Holocaust, it is crucial for these authors to address within their works the social and political roles their "writing" and our "reading" might play when defined as a duty to remember. Any call for a duty to remember should therefore go hand in hand with another call that values the never-ending process through which the relevance of a selective reading of the past is reasserted. Thus, while responding to the *duty to remember* that the project called for, Lamko's *Butterfly in the Hills* engages in a provocative *work of remembering*, acknowledging the contextual meaning of its mediation and the necessity to take into account former and contemporaneous representations of the genocide. Aware that any process of memorialization also risks institutionalizing forgetting, Lamko consciously reflects on this inherent tension as it pertains to memory and its limits. Furthermore, through its haunting and provocative style that gives voice to the dead, Lamko's writing of history discloses "the role of limits," as Berel Lang defines them, "the point at which the representation of limits begins to shape the limits of representation" (302–303).

If Lamko chooses to set his narrative in 1999, the same year he wrote it, rather than during the perpetration or immediate aftermath of the genocide, it is to situate his writing clearly in the present from which he attempts to re-present history or paraphrase it as a poet. Since his novel represents the past, it also represents a call to action that transcends the mere act of remembrance and favors an ongoing quest for a more nuanced and challenging sense of truth and justice. Once more, to help us in our encounter with extreme violence and genocide, authors like Lamko embrace the power and potential of literature in order to offer a symbolic and social space that not only acknowledges what happened but also aids us in reflecting on the legacy of the genocide within our present. Thanks to an esthetic that combines iconoclasm and poetry in order to inscribe the ob-scene violence of genocide within our cultural scene, *A Butterfly in the Hills* seeks to make of us informed heirs to the genocide as we define our actions and sense of belonging in the name of the past.

Ultimately, it is our duty as readers to remember that the testimonies collected by the authors of "Rwanda: Writing as a Duty to Remember," as well as the stories they crafted to relay the words and suffering passed on to them, bear witness to what can happen when the politics of hatred and the impulse to demonize the Other make human beings lose sight of their shared humanity. A famous quote from the survivor and poet Félicien Ntagengwa asserts the centrality of this issue as it welcomes visitors in numerous memorials throughout Rwanda: "If you had known me / And if you had really known yourself / Then you would not have killed me."[25]

A Butterfly in the Hills, in its unique ability to generate crisis in its readers' minds by forcing us to acknowledge what happened as not *unimaginable* but rather as *unacceptable*, represents essential reading in the study of the genocide's legacy. Lamko's iconoclastic and haunting esthetic makes it impossible to see genocide victims without being profoundly destabilized. According to Jean-Michel Chaumont, this intense and lasting discomfort is a prerequisite for inscribing within our cultural imagination the ob-scene reality and ever-present possibility of genocide as a dissolution of the fundamental bond of human cohesion and social interaction:

> Like the victims, we have received this information as unimaginable; more precisely, as *factually impossible* and *ethically unacceptable*. Later on, we had to resign ourselves to admit on an empirical level that this had been possible, since it took place, but continued to appear *intolerable* on an ethical one. Since then, we live in an irreducible *tension* between the factual recognition of what happened and the ethical protest that it should never have happened. Like any profound state of crisis, this tension provokes a global upheaval: it paralyzes critical thinking, it shatters our certainties and values, it forces us to revise the norms that guide our thoughts and actions. (299. Translation mine)

This is the crisis that Pelouse, as the genuine descendant of the Queen of the Middleworld, and we, as readers of *A Butterfly in the Hills*, must confront as we seek to restore our trust in a world where genocides have occurred and where their possibility remains ever more present. Reading, as a duty to remember, requires of the living a categorical denunciation of any ideology promoting the hatred of an Other. At stake is not only our present willingness to remember a disturbing past but, more importantly, also our willingness to take action, to engage in dialogue with genocide survivors in Rwanda, and to acknowledge the role we play in Rwanda's politics of memory and reconciliation. Only by committing to this imperative and its accompanying discomfort can we start to respond to the dead and begin to tend to the sacredness of our shared humanity.

Notes

1. All the quotes for Lamko's novel *La Phalène des collines* have been translated from the French by Arthur Greenspan under the title *A Butterfly in the Hills*. Since his translation has not yet been published, the page number refers to the French edition published by the Serpent à Plumes (2002).

2. See for instance Diop, "Le Rwanda m'a appris à appeler les monstres par leur nom" (2000).

3. Thanks to Laure Coret for having brought this interview of Lanzmann to my attention. "Le Lieu et la Parole." Translation mine.

4. PARMEHUTU is the acronym for "Parti du Mouvement et de l'Emancipation Hutu" (Party of the Hutu Movement and Emancipation) created by Kayibanda in October 1959. For a detailed political analysis of this period, see Gérard Prunier, "The Hutu Republic (1959–1990)" in *The Rwandan Crisis: History of a Genocide* (1997), 41–92.

5. Translation mine. Henceforth, all quotes from Mukasonga's works are my translations. See also her second testimony, *La femme aux pieds nus* (2008), where she describes her family's daily life in the Bugesera between 1960 and 1994 and pays homage to her mother who succeeded, thanks to her resourceful personality, to raise her family in this extremely challenging context.

6. Despite the difficulty to set exact numbers of people belonging to the three categories identified as Hutu, Tutsi, and Twa due to numerous displacements and waves of exile between 1959 and 1994, it is agreed that Hutu represented 80–85% of the population, Tutsi 15–18%, and Twa 1%. Legally, children acquired the "ethnic" identity of the father. These "ethnic" categories, which had been politicized and perverted throughout the colonial era and by the two postcolonial regimes of Kayibanda (1959–1973) and Habyarimana (1973–1994), were immediately banned on August 4, 1994, by the new RPF government. Nowadays, to use these categories in the public sphere for political purposes constitutes an act of divisionism, a crime that has been severely prosecuted in Rwanda since 2002. As Lars Waldorf underlines, "The law defines divisionism in sweeping terms as 'the use of any speech, written statement, or action that divides people, that is likely to spark conflicts among people, or that causes an uprising which might degenerate into strife among people based on discrimination' (Rwanda 2002a: Article 1)" (407).

7. The administrative division of Rwanda into twelve provinces was reformed in 2006 in favor of a system of four provinces, in addition to Kigali.

8. Quoted in Susan Cook, "The Politics of Preservation in Rwanda" (2005).

9. With the help of Aegis Trust and in collaboration with the National Museum and Kigali City Council, two international centers of reflection and learning have been created: the Kigali Memorial Centre at Gisozi (inaugurated in 2004) and the Murambi Genocide Prevention Centre (inaugurated in 2007). For additional information see <http://www.kigalimemorialcentre.org/index.php> and <http://www.aegistrust.org>.

10. Diop points toward the conflicting priorities and desires between relatives of the victims and the government's politics of remembrance in the case of Thérésa

Mukandori: "Her brother wanted her to be buried properly but the government begged him to understand the necessity to show all this" ("Entretien avec Boubacar Boris Diop" 2001). In his novel he also mentions this divergence in needs and priorities regarding mourning: "'Theresa's brother is one of the Nyamata survivors,' said the caretaker again. 'He wanted a decent grave for his sister, but the authorities pleaded with him to leave her body as it was, so that the whole world could see it'" (*Murambi* 73).

11. For a general overview of the institutionalization of the genocide's remembrance, see Célestin Kanimba Misago, "Les instruments de la mémoire. Génocide et traumatismes au Rwanda" (2007).

12. "Paul Ricoeur. Interview with Richard Kearney" (2004), 129. Regarding Ricoeur's conception of the metaphor, see his groundbreaking essay, *The Rule of Metaphor: Multi-Disciplinary Studies in the Creation of Meaning in Language* (1978).

13. Quoted in Chrétien, *The Great Lakes of Africa: Two Thousand Years of History* (2003), 324.

14. "Entretien avec Boubacar Boris Diop par Marie Bernard" (2001). Translation mine.

15. On this issue, see also Martin Jay's article, "Of Plots, Witnessing, and Judgments" (1992).

16. A *muzimu* in Kinyarwanda means a ghost, a spirit back from the dead. In traditional Rwandan culture there is a ceremony called *Guterekera* dedicated to the ghosts to assure that they do not harm the living. Thanks to Berthe Kayitesi for her insight regarding this ritual.

17. A fifth main character, Fred R., is not directly present at Nyamata's memorial, since he is exiled from Rwanda and the living. As it does with the Queen of the Middleworld, Lamko's novel also grants ghost status to Fred R., another of the genocide's dead doomed to live in perpetual exile. His fate alludes to the tragic destiny of Major General Fred Rwigema, the military commander of the Rwandan Patriotic Front, who died in combat in October 1990 after thirty years of exile.

18. On the survivors who watch over the burial sites and memorials of the victims of the genocide of the Tutsis, see Eric Kabera's remarkable documentary, *Keepers of Memory* (2005).

19. For another complementary analysis of Lamko's novel, see Semujanga's seventh chapter of *Le génocide, sujet de fiction?* (2008) entitled, "'La Phalène des Collines entre Éros et Thanatos ou l'art comme résilience du drame'" (219–257).

20. Translation mine. Henceforth, all quotes from Assayag's work are my translations.

21. Regarding this issue see Phil Clark and Zachary D. Kaufmann eds., *After Genocide: Transitional Justice, Post-Conflict Reconstruction and Reconciliation in Rwanda and Beyond* (2009); Nigel Eltringham, *Accounting for Horror. Post-Genocide Debates in Rwanda* (2004); and Johan Pottier, *Re-Imagining Rwanda: Conflict, Survival and Disinformation in the Late Twentieth Century* (2002).

22. See Lamko's caricature of this Cartesian abuse of reason to demonstrate that France is neither guilty nor responsible (95–98).

23. Quoted in Vénuste Kayimahe (2002), 11. Translation mine.

24. Philip Gourevitch's title, *We Wish to Inform You That Tomorrow We Will be Killed With Our Families: Stories from Rwanda* (1998), echoes Borowski's provocative *This Way for the Gas, Ladies and Gentlemen*, both using polite formulation conforming social etiquette to bear witness to ob-scene realities. Their readers are left speechless when they measure the discrepancy between their mannered use of language and the gruesome violence they describe.

25. "Iyo uza kwimenya / nanjye ukamenya / ntuba waranyishe." Félicien Ntagengwa was a poet, master of ceremonies, and teacher. He was deported in the Bugesera in the 1960s, survived the genocide, and died in 2007.

11

Polyvocal Dismembering:
Diop's Remembering of Murambi

In *MURAMBI, THE BOOK OF BONES*, the fate of Théresa Mukandori also surfaces within the narrative, but in a very different context. She first appears alive, in a random conversation narrated from the point of view of her friend Jessica who escorts her when she seeks shelter in Nyamata's church after having heard rumors of retaliation and killings against the Tutsis in response to the president's assassination. Their dialogue is just one among many others in Jessica's short "testimony." It joins those of Michel Serumundo and Faustin Gasana in offering the three vantage points that compose "Fear and Anger"—the opening section of Boubacar Boris Diop's book. Through these three testimonies, all focused on the first days of the genocide in April 1994, Diop juxtaposes three different "I"s who depict the "same" reality from heterogeneous perspectives. Furthermore, the trajectories of these different testimonial "eyes" do not cross even though they are all bound by the same event, the genocide of the Tutsis in Rwanda.[1]

First comes the story of Michel Serumundo, a Tutsi who, as he returns home by bus from work, learns that President Habyarimana has been killed. Once at home, he slowly realizes that this time the Hutu extremists would not "be satisfied with just a little blood," since they had the perfect excuse to kill all those that the RTLM has portrayed for months as traitors and enemies of the country (11). Trying to reassure his wife Séraphine, Michel says that she should not worry because "the whole world is watching" (9). But he knows this is wishful thinking. Just by judging his own response to the suffering he watches in the media, he can already foresee the indifference and the racist clichés that will allow the world to close its eyes or simply look the other way

(9–10). Michel Serumundo's testimony of "his" April 6, 1994, functions like an establishing shot in cinema since he bears witness to Habyarimana's death, highlights the existing tensions between his family and their Hutu neighbors who are listening to RTLM's propaganda while their son is among those setting roadblocks throughout Kigali. But Serumundo's thoughts in this opening testimony also echo a certain guilt that inhabits Diop and the other African writers of "Fest'Africa"'s project. Like Serumundo, Diop didn't hear the cries of the Tutsi victims in 1994 and only realized that a genocide was taking place when it was over. In contrast with Lamko's novel, Diop denounces not only the indifference and racist preconceptions of the West but also the attitude of many Africans who looked the other way in 1994. Embarrassed by the clichés these killings would revive in the world regarding Africa, many Africans were more concerned with the detrimental effect of this genocide on how they would be perceived than with stopping it. Finally, Serumundo stresses the fact that no country in the world is immune to the possibility of genocide. All readers are therefore not only invited to learn what happened in Rwanda but also to learn from it. This is precisely why Diop's novel testifies to this history with the hope to function, as Serumundo's name phonetically suggests in French, as a *truth serum* for the *world/monde*. Michel Serumundo's opening testimony thus operates like a foreword in disguise, since it establishes a minimal historical context, interpellates both Western and African readers, and conveys the ethical reason that drove Diop to write his novel, namely to confer retrospectively a cultural visibility to a genocide that had been off-screened in 1994 with the hope that writing as a duty to remember represents a potent serum against the recurrence of genocide.

The second testimony in "Fear and Anger" introduces the views and thoughts of an *Interahamwe*, Faustin Gasana, two days after the beginning of the genocide. As he and his militiamen are at the eve of launching systematic killings, he visits his ailing father who has always embraced the Parmehutu ideology as the portrait of Grégoire Kayibanda hanging over his bed attests.[2] While he updates his father about the ongoing events and the plans to kill all Tutsis of Rwanda, the old man tells him that this time, unlike in 1961, they must succeed and leave no one behind or they will end on the wrong side of history. As he listens to his father's warnings, Gasana can only agree with the old man with whom he shares this deep hatred for the "cockroaches." At the same time, Gasana acknowledges that it will be difficult to succeed in carrying out the genocide, since many of the young men who joined the militia are not as ideologically motivated and disciplined as he, more interested in having fun, getting drunk, and taking advantage of the power and unlawful privileges they can enjoy as *Interahamwe*. Nevertheless, despite this admission of the implicit failure of the genocidal project,

nothing deters him from "going to work." In his view, there is no other option since, according to his interpretation of history, cohabitation with the
Tutsis is impossible: "I've always known in becoming an Interahamwe that
I might well have to kill people myself or perish under their blow. That's
never been a problem for me. I've studied the history of my country and
I know that the Tutsis and us, we could never live together. Never. Lots
of shirkers claim otherwise, but I don't believe them. I'm going to do my
work properly" (18–19). The focus on the dialogue with the father positions
Gasana as the product of thirty years of anti-Tutsi propaganda. Moreover, it
allows Diop to situate the genocide in historical perspective and to educate
the reader about Rwanda's past, at least as it is perceived and understood by
Hutu extremists ready to kill without any remorse or guilt, even though they
know that they are doomed to fail. If Gasana's perspective radically opposes
Serumundo's, Diop is not impartial in their juxtaposition, since the source
of Gasana's world view is an ailing man, no longer as robust as in his youth,
lying in his bed, half blind, pus seeping from a wound. Even in the eyes of
his own son he is repulsive. Cast in this light, Diop's narrative sanctions the
values that Gasana embodies as the heir to an ailing and anachronistic ideology which will, however, still prove lethal in its desperate attempt to inflect
Rwanda's history through genocide.

    After these two antagonistic "testimonies" that convey the views and
thoughts of the victim and the perpetrator, Diop introduces a third position
in the person of Jessica who has joined the RPF and operates as a spy in the
regions controlled by the Rwandan Army Forces and the *Interahamwe*. As a
spy, Jessica provides the perspective of a Tutsi who decided to fight openly the
Habyarimana's regime. Narratively, she provides a highly knowledgeable perspective since she possesses information to which others, including Théresa
Mukandori, have no access. In this sense, Jessica allows Diop to introduce in
disguise a quasi-omniscient perspective without having to resort to an omniscient narrator who would ruin the rhetorical intimacy of the first-person
narrative and the kaleidoscopic opening of *Murambi, The Book of Bones.*
Thanks to the secret messages to which she has access, Jessica functions as an
"I" with ubiquitous "eyes" capable to communicate historical facts. While Jessica embodies an active form of resistance and an ideological position clearly
opposed to Gasana's views, she also does more. By providing a broader overview of the situation in these first days of the genocide and highlighting the
swift coordination behind the killings, she also performs a narrative resistance
that counters those who contest the planned nature of the genocide—a reading of history that often leads to the denial that a genocide against the Tutsis
occurred in Rwanda.

Once Jessica and Thérésa reach the church of Nyamata, Jessica leaves her friend there even though she knows that this is exactly what the perpetrators were hoping. But what better option was there to offer, since Jessica could not reveal her sources and real identity without putting herself and the RPF in jeopardy. Guilty and hoping for the best, Jessica returns to Kigali using her fake Hutu identity to pass the roadblocks, and narrates the events unfolding in the capital: the deserted streets, the RTLM hatred messages and hip music that inundate the streets and the minds, the systematic assassination carried out by the presidential guard against Hutu politicians who belong to the opposition, the killing of ten Belgian UN peace keepers to prompt a pullout of the UNAMIR, and the French backing of the interim government in order to stop the RPF from taking over Kigali. Jessica's testimony therefore underlines from the outset the premeditated nature of the genocide, which is everything but a spontaneous outburst of revenge sparked by Habyarimana's assassination (28–29). At the end of her history lesson, Jessica underlines the common denominator that links the three voices and trajectories opening up Diop's novel in a polyvocal mode:

> Ever since 1959, every young Rwandan, at one moment or another in his life, has to answer the same question: Should we just sit back and wait for the killers, or try something so that our country can go back to being normal? Between our futures and ourselves, unknown people had planted a sort of giant machete. Try as you might, you couldn't ignore it. The tragedy would always end up catching you. (30–31)

By opting for three voices deeply immersed in the unwinding of the genocide, Diop's narrative asserts the impossibility of remaining outside of history or of claiming the privilege of being a bystander who occupies a neutral position. Furthermore, by opting for a juxtaposition of first-person narratives, Diop performatively bans the enunciative possibility of being "above" the furor of history and able to provide an omniscient and detached perspective on this history. Thus, *Murambi* refuses the rhetorical means used by numerous historical narratives that erase the presence of the "I" in an attempt to create the illusion that the past is speaking for itself and that these narratives only echo an objective and preexisting knowledge of the past. As we will see with Cornelius, the main character of the narrative that takes place in 1998 and who represents a *mise en abîme* of Diop's attempt to fulfill his duty to remember, the impossibility to position oneself outside or above history extends to any writer who seeks to bear witness to the genocide of the Tutsis. Thus, if writing is to be seen as a duty to remember, it can only perform this duty by subscribing to the duty to position itself clearly regarding the legacy it

aims to pass on through its representation of the past. As Ann Curthoys and
John Docker stress in their introduction to *Is History Fiction?*, there is no such
thing as an unmediated representation of the past:

> The historian does not assume or claim omniscient knowledge, or suggest that
> the historical sources can be read and presented as if the past is speaking in the
> present, unassisted, unmediated in extensive and complex ways. It is possible to
> respond to the challenge of cultural theory with a desire to explore the possibili-
> ties of kinds of historical writing that seek to relate multiple narratives, and to
> self-reflexively foreground our awareness of our present relation to the past. (6)

The polyphonic construction of *Murambi* echoes without any doubt this desire to "relate multiple narratives," as Diop refuses not only to hide the "I"s
through which the past is mediated to us but also refuses the possibility of an
omniscient narrator who would hide behind the facts by giving the impression that the referent of its writing speaks for itself. On the contrary, *Murambi*'s configuration highlights and explicitly addresses within the narrative the
negotiated and polemical process that lays behind any representation of the
past. The very construction of *Murambi* represents in itself a historiographic
statement through which Diop dramatizes the conditions of possibility of his
own attempt to fulfill a duty to remember through writing.

The book is composed of four parts. The first and the third are a juxtaposition of individual testimonies written in the first person. These short
testimonies offer antagonistic and complementary vantage points regarding
the genocide and stage characters whose ideologies and interpretations of the
events radically clash. First, "Anger and Fear," as we have seen, juxtaposes the
voices of Michel Serumundo, a Tutsi victim; Faustin Gasana, a Hutu *Interahamwe*; and Jessica, a Tutsi woman who joined the RPF. The third section,
"Genocide," follows the same narrative pattern, conferring a visibility to the
killings through the following testimonies: Aloys Ndasingwa, a Hutu killer
who participated in the massacre in Nyamata; Marina Nkusi, a young woman
whose father, a Hutu, refused to kill Tutsis in the first place before he changed
his mind for fear of retaliation against his family; Rosa Karemera, an old Tutsi
woman hated by her Hutu neighbor Valérie who saw in the genocide an opportunity to mount a personal vendetta to get rid of Rosa; Joseph Karekezi,
a Hutu doctor who is Cornelius's father; Colonel Étienne Perrin, a French
officer who participated in "Opération Turquoise," which deployed soldiers
in Murambi, and who had a long discussion with Joseph Karekezi; and finally
three more testimonies by Jessica, who continues to enjoy a privileged status
thanks to her narrative status as a spy and to the testimonies she gathered.

The second and fourth part of the book, written in the third person, tells
the story of Cornelius, a Hutu expatriate who, after twenty-five years in exile,

comes back to his native country in 1998 to find out the fate of his family and plans to write a play on the genocide. Cornelius's relatives lived in Rwanda in 1994 and are presumed dead since he has not heard from them since the genocide. Jessica is the only character who appears in both time frames—1994 and 1998—as she happens to be one of Cornelius's childhood friends from the period before he left the country in 1973 because of his father. At that time, Doctor Joseph Karekezi, a Hutu who married a Tutsi, was sympathetic to the Tutsis and refused the Parmehutu ideology of discrimination as was the case for Gasana's father. This noble attitude led him to be ostracized by those in power and persecuted as a "traitor" the year Habyarimana launched a coup to take power and used, yet again, the Tutsis as scapegoats for all the ills affecting Rwanda. Cornelius's story is divided into two parts: "The Return of Cornelius" and "Murambi." The first part narrates his arrival in Kigali, his reunion with childhood friends, and the visits of several memorials. The second part narrates his encounter with his uncle Siméon Habineza, one of the rare survivors of Murambi, and his return to his native place where the fate of his family had been sealed, and indirectly his own legacy as well.

This alternation between first- and third-person narratives in addition to the multiplication of voices and perspectives allows Diop to disseminate his narrative authority, since the voice of the narrator telling Cornelius's story is only one among many others. How shall we then understand this enunciative dismembering within the remembering process that Diop's writing seeks to fulfill? First, as Cornelius stresses toward the end of his quest, conferring a readability to a genocide requires exploration of unusual modes of representation in order to stress the extra-ordinary and ob-scene nature of the event: "A genocide is not just any kind of story, with a beginning and an end between which more or less ordinary events take place" (179). By refusing a linear chronology, an omniscient narrator, and an esthetics that seeks to make the events of the past speak for themselves as if they were unmediated, Diop's novel refuses the reassurance of causality and the fantasy of mastery it provides to the readers as they face genocidal violence. In other words, Diop's esthetic offers a "cubist representation" of the genocide, since no single vantage point possesses the entire truth and meaning of the event. His novel underlines the fact that the genocide can only by approached through a polyvocal narrative combining and confronting complementary and antagonistic perspectives. Even though not all perspectives are cast as being equal and genuine, it is ultimately up to the reader to make sense of these multiple mediations by taking a position within this coexistence of heterogeneous views. Diop therein reasserts the importance of positionality both for himself and for his readers and invites us to reflect on the relationship between narrative and history as understood by Felman and Laub: "Can contemporary narrative historically bear witness, not simply to the impact of the Holocaust but to the way in which the impact of *history as holocaust* has modified, affected, shifted the very modes of the relationship between narrative and history?" (95)

The second time Théresa Mukandori appears in *Murambi, The Book of Bones*, she is dead. Jessica is again present, but the scene of their posthumous reunion happens in a radically different context. Four years have passed since Jessica escorted her friend to Nyamata's church, and now Mukandori's corpse lies before her eyes, graphically exposed in Nyamata's Memorial:

> "Her name was Théresa. Théresa Mukandori. We all knew her very well," answered the caretaker. The young woman had her hair pushed back and the scream extracted from her by the pain had been frozen on her still grimacing face. Her magnificent tresses were disheveled, and her legs wide apart. A stake— of wood or of iron, Cornelius didn't know, he was too shocked to notice—had remained lodged in her vagina. (73)

This time, Théresa's fate is told through the narrator's perspective, which follows Cornelius's trajectory. If Jessica accompanies Cornelius to Nyamata and makes him visit the memorial, it is part of a plan defined by his uncle Siméon Habineza to prepare him gradually for the revelation that he will have to face when he goes to Murambi and finds out the fate of his relatives. The face-to-face with the remains exposed in Nyamata is meant to provoke an interruption within Cornelius, to make him both question his preconceived perception of the genocide and realize the arrogance of his intent to write *their story* from a position of exteriority—not so much because he is Hutu, but rather because he is foreign to what happened in 1994 and has only an intellectual understanding of what survivors have endured and still suffer through. How dare he come back after twenty-five years and think he can "know" what the genocide has been and what the traumas of its aftermath are. Thus, by making him visit Nyamata's church, Jessica forces Cornelius to gain a better grasp of the gap separating him from the reality to which he wants to bear witness and to reevaluate the ends of such a project.

Nyamata's visit functions then as an historiographic seism that rattles the foundations of Cornelius's pretentious intention to tell the story of the dead. He is so shocked that he can no longer distinguish what he sees— wood or iron?—overwhelmed by the violence that emanates from Théresa Mukandori's cadaver. This visit makes him realize that he can no longer fulfill his duty of memory if he does not first reevaluate the position from which he bears witness and the limits of writing as a venue to fulfill a duty to remember. Cornelius clearly mirrors Diop's trajectory in 1998 and echoes his belated encounter with the genocide's aftermath. But as a character he is also animated by a sincere willingness to know. He finds himself haunted by this past that remains full of doubts as long as nobody has told him exactly what happened:

> In disparate fragments, scenes of the past and present crossed each other in his mind. He sensed how difficult it was going to be for him to put some order into his life and he didn't like the idea. To come back to one's country—to be happy there or to suffer—was a rebirth, but he didn't want to become someone without a past. He was the sum of everything he had experienced. His faults. His cowardliness. His hopes. He wanted to know, down to the very last detail, how his family had been massacred. In Murambi, Siméon Habineza would tell him everything. He had to. (43–44)

As a *mise en abîme* of the writer's challenges and duties in post-genocidal Rwanda, Cornelius's dependency on Habineza's testimony also constitutes an important statement by Diop regarding the enunciative authority of the survivors without whom the possibility of performing a duty to remember would remain a dead letter. Moreover, that Cornelius needs to visit other sites such Ntarama and Nyamata and meet other survivors before arriving in Murambi to meet his uncle underlines the fact that those who are foreign to the genocide—like Diop and the majority of his readers—cannot understand the meaning and the experience of genocide from their experience alone. As Felman and Laub underline in their analysis of Camus's *Plague*, "The event (The Plague, the Holocaust) occurs, in other words, as what is not provided for by the conceptual framework we call 'History,' and as what, in general, has no place in, and therefore cannot be assimilated by or integrated into, any existing cultural frame of reference" (103). Thus, envisioning an event such as a genocide requires re-envisioning and reworking the evidence of our personal and cultural frames of reference and engaging in an initiatory journey that will progressively prepare us to hear and to perceive an experience which is *a priori* ob-scene to our social scene and to our sense of self. Cornelius's journey then not only mirrors Diop's but also ours, as we follow this foreign character whose ignorance and willingness to know echoes our own.

Within the narration of history, Cornelius, as the writer's double, constantly revives a metanarrative inquiry on the limits of writing and the conditions of possibility that inform the process of passing this traumatic past on to the readers. In this sense, within the polyvocal remembrance that his writing performs, Diop introduces a work on remembering that reflects on the author's own position and voice. As Cornelius tells Jessica, his journey represents a return synonymous with a self-reflexive "return on himself"— *un retour synonyme de retour sur lui-même*. Like her, he is also an heir to this history that has been marked by a discourse of mutual hatred between Hutus and Tutsis. Nonetheless, even if both are defined by this past, both have the

choice—or, in fact, the duty—to transcend the inherited determination of
this past by refusing to reproduce its logic of hatred. As Cornelius underlines,
the past does not contain the meaning of their present; it is up to them to
shape it: "I went back to studying the history of Rwanda. But I didn't find any
answers there. The documents prove that the Hutus and the Twas were oppressed long ago by the Tutsis. I am Hutu but I do not want to live with that
legacy. I refuse to ask the past more meaning than it can give to the present"
(66–67).

For Cornelius, then, writing constitutes one of the social spaces where he,
as an heir to such a traumatic legacy, can explore and forge the possibility of
undoing the logic of hatred passed on to him. Haunted by this past, Cornelius
decides that he can only liberate himself from the paralyzing weight that has
been passed on to him by facing it in order to generate within the present new
social relationships and modes of coexistence. Cornelius therefore represents
a Hutu whose response to an inherited past radically differs from Gasana's as
he attempts to define his own position by refusing the social reproduction of
this heinous legacy. As one of his interlocutors tells him, "In life . . . what is
essential is for each one of us to be true to himself" (52). But in order to do so,
one must know one's past, since one can only be true to oneself through one's
response *to* and *for* the past we inherit and not by obliterating or repressing it.

After the encounter with the dead of Ntarama and Nyamata and the interruption this proximity with death and genocidal violence generates within
Cornelius, Jessica tells her friend that his uncle wanted him to confront physically and visually the horrific consequences of genocide to prepare him for the
implications of the truth she was about to reveal to him regarding what happened in Murambi and what really constitutes the legacy to which Cornelius
must respond as its heir:

> "It's about your father, Doctor Joseph Karekezi. He's not dead Cornelius. . . .
> Tomorrow you're going to Murambi, and you should know that your father
> organized the massacre of several thousand people there. The Carnage at the
> Murambi Polytechnic, that was his doing. You should also know that he had
> your mother, Nathalie Kayumba, your sister Julienne, your brother François,
> and all his in-laws killed there. . . ."
>
> Cornelius' head was on fire. He was buzzing with all kinds of feelings and
> confused ideas. He was certain only of one thing: from that day on his life would
> not be the same. He was the son of a monster.
>
> "You must have found my idea of a play out of place, Jessica."
>
> "Not really. I simply took it as a sign of the extent to which you considered
> yourself innocent."
>
> Now, his return from exile could no longer have the same meaning. From
> now on, the only story he had to tell was his own. The story of his family. He

had suddenly discovered that he had become the perfect Rwandan: both guilty and a victim. (76–78)

As a subtle allegory of Diop's self-positioning in regard to the genocide, Cornelius's trajectory serves to underscore the realization that having been abroad and silent while the genocide occurred does not guarantee a status of innocence, quite the contrary. As he learns that his father was the mastermind who planned and carried out the killing of close to fifty thousand Tutsis at the Polytechnic School of Murambi—including his spouse and children— Cornelius comes to understand that the story of the genocide of the Tutsis is *his* story and that he must, as an heir to this past, respond *for* and *to* it as he attempts to respond to this haunting legacy *in* his own name. As his uncle Habineza will tell him in the last section of the book: "You've come back and difficult moments are awaiting you. You know what has happened, and we suffer a lot, even if we don't show it. Some feel guilty for not having been killed. They wonder what fault they committed to still be alive. But you, try to think about what is yet to be born rather than what is already dead" (143).

The revelation that he is "the son of a monster" dramatically reformulates Cornelius's identity and positionality, since he can no longer believe himself to be in a position of exteriority to the ob-scene violence and aftermath of genocide and must rework his symbolic and personal scene to incorporate the legacy that his father has passed on to him. Or, to put it another way, far from confirming the scene of his identity and his preestablished sense of belonging, his return from exile reveals itself to be more the opposite: "His return was almost becoming another exile" (150). At the same time, the inscription of this ob-scene legacy within his history does not mean that Cornelius loses any agency in his ability to respond to the past he has inherited. On the contrary, instead of continuing to fantasize himself foreign to this genocide, or at least innocent if not only a victim, Cornelius addresses the state of denial in which he maintained himself and that in fact prohibited him from having an informed agency. Now that Jessica's revelation interrupted his belief that the genocide is an ob-scene reality, he finds himself in a position where he must act on *his* history and forge within *his* present the means to oppose the social and political reproduction of discourses and views that made him "the son of a monster." The interruption that has shaken Cornelius's identity and sense of belonging must therefore be extended to the duty to remember since Cornelius must envision himself as an heir for whom the past must remain "forever" within the present so that the present "never again" mirrors the past!

Furthermore, through Cornelius's quest, Diop highlights that the meaning of the past does not reside within the past nor within its relics—be they as powerful as Thérésa Mukandori's cadaver—but in the heirs' willingness to know and to position themselves within the dialectic of remembering and forgetting that is at the very heart of "Fest'Africa"'s project. In his commentary on Todorov's essay on the abuse of memory, Ricoeur identifies two major consequences linked to the inherent dialectic of remembering and forgetting within the writing of history.[3] First, he underlines that archives and historical sources, even though they are authentic, do not reveal their meaning *by* themselves since their interpretation is contingent on the historical narrative they allow and in which they find themselves inscribed. Second, he shows that archives and sources should not be envisioned *for* themselves but in the light of the responses they are able to generate regarding the legacy they pass on to question us within our present and future order of things. Todorov's essay highlights for Ricoeur both the social pertinence and potential abuse of historical discourse driven by the search for goodness and justice:

> This concern links up with the preceding discussion thanks to a most judicious piece of advice from Todorov, to extract from the traumatic memories the exemplary value that can become pertinent only when memory has been turned into a project. If the trauma refers to the past, the exemplary value is directed toward the future. What the cult of memory for the sake of memory obliterates is, along with the aim of the future, the question of the end, of the moral issue. (*Memory* 86)

Cornelius's trajectory reflects this, as he progressively discovers the impossibility of writing from an innocent position after he rightfully declares that the past does not predetermine the present and that any heir must perform his right to reformulate the value and pertinence of the past in relationship to the priorities of the present. Diop defines the end and intentionality that drives Cornelius's willingness to know and his desire to pass on the ob-scene knowledge he inherited and had to accept as an inherent part of his own history, his own scene:

> Cornelius was slightly ashamed of having entertained the idea of a play. But he wasn't giving up his enthusiasm for words, dictated by despair, helplessness before the sheer immensity of evil, and no doubt a nagging conscience. He did not intend to resign himself to the definitive victory of the murderers through silence. . . . He would tirelessly recount the horror. With machete words, club words, words studded with nails, naked words . . . because he saw in the genocide of Rwandan Tutsis a great lesson in simplicity. Every chronicler could at least learn—something essential to his art—to call a monster by its name. (*Murambi* 179)

If calling "a monster by his name" is one way to answer "the question of the end" raised by Todorov and Ricoeur in relation to the narratives bearing witness to the genocide of the Tutsis, how does this act relate to the ethical and moral imperative "never again!"? While the duty to remember constitutes a necessary injunction to ensure that "never again" such horrors will happen, it does not represent sufficient assurance that the factors and ideologies leading to future genocides will be identified, denounced, and fought in a timely manner with all the political and collective will this requires. Moreover, the injunction of the duty to remember as the path to fulfill the ethical plea that "never again" a genocide should occur runs the risk of eclipsing the other ends that narratives about extreme violence serve. Thus, our exposure, perception, and understanding of genocidal violence must also be defined by the critical dialogue that a representation of the genocide is able to provoke regarding the ends served by the duty to remember it claims to fulfill. As long as a narrative bearing witness to genocide is unable to generate such dialogue among the living about their ability to live together thanks to—and not despite—their differences, to advocate for justice and restitution for survivors, or to offer a space of mourning aimed at socially reconciling survivors with those who have not suffered their endeavor, the duty to remember will remain a rhetorical injunction that lacks social resonance because it fails to translate its ethical imperative into reality.

Toward the end of the journey that allowed him to discover that the genocide's history was an integral part of his personal story, Cornelius redefines the end of his writing as a means to confer visibility and generate social resonance for all the victims who were killed while no one heard their cries and who, today, risk falling into oblivion: "It was too soon to throw them into the darkness of the earth. Besides, every Rwandan should have the courage to look reality in the eye. The strong odor of the remains proved that the genocide had taken place only four years earlier and not in ancient times. As they were perishing under the blows, the victims had shouted out. No one had wanted to hear them. The echo of those cries should be allowed to reverberate for as long as possible" (147). Envisioned in the Francophone context of the novel's publication and "Fest'Africa"'s collective project, it is not only Rwandans who should face the remains of the genocide to address its aftermath, but also the heirs of "the Old Man"—François Mitterrand—who epitomizes the racist views that aim, ideologically and culturally, to maintain the genocide of the Tutsis ob-scene to the French historical scene and identity:

> Cornelius thought of the Old Man. "In those countries a genocide doesn't mean much." Probably not even a detail. The Old Man. A bitter heart. A cold spirit. A curt voice. Offended, they say, to discover all too late that he was, after all, mortal. . . . History would bring him down a peg or two. But in the end it didn't matter very much. Cornelius felt only the slightest bitterness. He was confident of the future, of its long memory and infinite patience. Sooner or later, in Africa

and elsewhere, people will say calmly, "Let's talk about the hundred days in Rwanda again, there is no unimportant genocide, Rwanda, *neither*, is not just a minor detail of contemporary history." (177)

In this sense, Diop's novel makes a concerted effort through characters such as the French colonel Étienne Perrin of underscoring that the genocide of the Tutsis is an integral part of French history and belongs to its present cultural scene; it thus demands that the heirs of "La Françafrique" respond to this past whose cadavers are still eloquently visible. The works of Tadjo, Lamko, and Diop represent then an attempt to generate an interruption in the denial that the genocide of the Tutsis represents an integral part of France's history, as well as of the history of our shared humanity. Through the cultural inscription of the ob-scene within the literary scene of their works, these authors invite us to respond to our own strategies of denial and exclusion as we face the mirrors they hold out in front of us so that, like Cornelius, we can re-envision our response to the past as informed heirs, no longer in denial as we shape our present responses to its legacy. As Young argues in *Writing and Rewriting the Holocaust*, "Contrary to those who see the world and its representations operating independently of one another, 'life' and 'life-in-writing'—catastrophe and our responses to it—have always interpenetrated; in this way, literature remembers past destructions even as it shapes our practical responses to current crisis" (4).

The diverse mediations of the genocide created in 1998 by the writers reunited by Djedanoum and Coulibaly are not only the result of a reflexive and critical dialogue with representations of the genocide encountered during their two-month residency in Rwanda, but also the performance of a will to confer social visibility and political resonance to a genocide committed off-camera and whose legacy faces various forms of denial. Animated by the desire to fulfill the duty to remember victims and survivors through their writing, these authors have become the heirs of survivors' memories of the genocide. As such, their collective project, "Rwanda: Writing as a Duty to Remember," must be envisioned as a social and symbolic space that functions like a scriptural museum bearing witness to the most extreme violence that can be perpetrated by humans against other humans. In her analysis of the museography of such extreme violence, Assayag identifies three necessary ends a "Seismography of Terrors" must fulfill to be pertinent in the wake of a century marked by the failure to prevent the repetition of genocide and crimes against humanity:

> To cultivate a common memory of the horrors within the museographic frame is a way to fill the "gap," to restore dignity by averting abjection thanks to a display that fulfills three functions: to offer a space of public dialogue so that the

acts of violence are voiced or shown and publicly identified with those who committed them; to provide a moral teaching through "hybrid forums" capable of making heard, freely or coercively, the meaning of past events to the generations who did not live them; finally, to give justice to victims by identifying the perpetrators on a stage that stands as a live recreation of the national disaster. . . . The finality is also ethical and prophylactic, political and social, because it delivers a message of vigilance and hope that advocates for the generalized acceptance of the inadmissible character of actions that one can neither suffer nor accept. (11)

To offer a space of public dialogue, to provide a moral teaching, and to give justice to the victims are indeed the ends that are at the foundation of the works of Tadjo, Lamko, and Diop. By bearing witness to the genocide through narratives that explore the potentialities of a polyvocal dismembering of this traumatic past, each of them seeks to interrupt us so that we face our various strategies of denial and silencing that ultimately lead to the recurrence of genocide. Reminding each society of its essential fragility, these works generate a social discussion helping us acknowledge that we can no longer claim innocence, that the genocide of the Tutsis is part of our inheritance, and that, as such, it requires of us a response. Like Cornelius, we can no longer assert that the history of the genocide of the Tutsis is not ours; we can no longer cast it as ob-scene to our historical scene.

Notes

1. For another complementary analysis of Diop's novel, see Semujanga's "*Murambi* et *Moisson de crânes* ou comment la fiction raconte un genocide" (2006).

2. Grégoire Kayibanda was the first president of Rwanda after the independence and the founder of the PARMEHUTU (Party of the Hutu Movement and Emancipation) in October 1959.

3. Todorov's original passage states: "The work of the historian like every work on the past, never consist solely in establishing the facts but also in choosing certain among them as being more salient and more significant than others, then placing them in relation to one another; now this work of selecting and combining is necessarily guided by the search, not for the truth, but for the good" (*Les Abus de la Mémoire*, 50). Quoted in Ricoeur *Memory, History, Forgetting* (2000), 86.

III

SCREENING MEMORY, (UN)FRAMING FORGETTING: FILMING GENOCIDE IN RWANDA

I can only hope. Because you know, you make a film, and the rest is what people make out of it. But I do hope that this film will help the comprehension of what did happen in 1994 in Rwanda and . . . will help people feel that what is happening on the other end of the world, it's part of them as well. It's their story, whether you live in L.A., in Timbuktu, or in Japan. . . . So I hope the film will provoke those thoughts and will help further discussions. It's not a film that you can just consume and then forget about.

Raoul Peck

12

No Neutral Shooting

N EARLY FIFTEEN YEARS AFTER THE GENOCIDE of the Tutsis in Rwanda, seven fictional films have conferred a cultural visibility to the series of events that killed nearly one million people in the span of three months: *100 Days* by Nick Hughes (2001), *Hotel Rwanda* by Terry George (2004), *Sometimes in April* by Raoul Peck (2004), *Shooting Dogs* by Michael Caton-Jones (2005), *Un Dimanche à Kigali* [*A Sunday in Kigali*] by Robert Favreau (2006), *Opération Turquoise* by Alain Tasma (2007), and *Shake Hands with the Devil* by Roger Spottiswoode (2007). None of the seven films produced so far is directed by a Rwandan, even though many of them were created with the help of Rwandan co-scriptwriters, actors, technicians, or historical consultants. The vast majority were directed by Westerners making their first films about Africa—the exception being Raoul Peck, who made two films about Patrice Lumumba in 1991 and 2000, and, to a certain extent, Nick Hughes, who worked as a cameraman in Africa for a number of years. As to the location where the films were shot, all but *Hotel Rwanda* were filmed in Rwanda and, to the extent possible, on the actual sites where the events they chronicle took place: the church in Kibuye for *100 Days*; Kigali, the Church Sainte Famille, and the Hôtel des Mille Collines for *Sometimes in April* and *A Sunday in Kigali*; the École Technique Officielle of Kicukiro (ETO) for *Shooting Dogs*; Bisesero and the Lake Kivu region for *Opération Turquoise*; the capital and the country of the thousand hills more broadly for *Shaking Hands with the Devil*, which uses multiple panoramic shots and bird's-eye views. As Raoul Peck highlights, filming in Rwanda, on the very sites where the genocide was committed, is not an insignificant decision, since the genocide of the Tutsis occurred off-camera.[1] This media and journalistic obliteration is precisely what Peck—like the other directors—attempt to remedy by "re-mediating" what occurred off-screen at the time:

> I couldn't imagine doing this film anywhere else than in Rwanda. . . . And I wanted to do it with the people of Rwanda. I wouldn't feel at ease to tell their story without telling it with them, with their acceptance, with their encourage-ment, and their participation. . . . Each location you see in this movie is real. Those scenes happened in those very locations, and of course, it gives another quality that is beyond cinema for me since . . . for a genocide there is no image, it happened behind doors. All the journalists left within the first two weeks, so there is no real image of what happened in Rwanda during these 100 days. (*Sometimes in April* "Audio Commentary")

Even if these films were shown in Rwanda through public screenings, at the Amahoro stadium in Kigali for instance since there is no movie theater in Rwanda, these cinematic representations are mainly directed at Western au-diences.[2] It is then in this context of production, distribution, and consump-tion largely determined by Western eyes, voices, references, and values, to say nothing of Western interests and capital, that we have to ask ourselves what history lessons these films actually seek to convey?

In my analysis of these cinematic representations of the genocide of the Tutsis, I work from the notion that denial is an inherent component of every genocidal project and that one of its ideological strategies is to invert the posi-tions of victims and perpetrators. In the case of Rwanda, the perpetrators of the genocide often attempt to obliterate their responsibilities and actions by casting themselves as innocent citizens caught in a civil war launched by the RPF in October 1990, as patriotic Rwandans who only acted in self-defense, as ordinary men and women who never planned the massacre of the Tutsis of Rwanda nor denied the Tutsi minority its very right to exist.[3] Thus, in the post-genocidal context of production and cultural circulation of the films witnessing the genocide of the Tutsis, it is imperative to focus on the history lessons they convey and how they shape our understanding of this past that occurred for most of us "off-screen." It is important to keep in mind that each film selects certain events that took place before and after the genocide and articulates them along with those that occurred during the one hundred days of the slaughter, which started on April 6, 1994. In each film, the personal-ized *history* through which we are invited to reflect on the genocide's *History* rests upon an arrangement of images and plot according to a particular set of themes and issues, which not only represent a memorialization of the past but also a deliberate positioning within the present. Because these movies are aimed at Western viewers who know next to nothing about Rwanda, except maybe that the country was the scene of a genocide, they put forth a version of history that both conditions what is judged to be worthy of memory and determines the lenses that give the genocide of the Tutsis the possibility of readability. Off-scene narrative voices in the opening minutes often serve as history lessons to viewers, as do "informative dialogues" functioning as encyclopedic pauses, "historical epilogues," the staging of sites of memory, the invocation of historical characters at the heart of the fiction, and the use of visual or radio archives. This multifaceted pedagogical device aims at inserting the action of the film into a specific socio-historical context and creating the illusion of reality that tends to make viewers forget they are watching a cinematic re-presentation. If these history lessons constitute one of the films' central aims, it is in part because they define the interpretive framework from which it becomes possible to make sense of characters' actions and to evaluate their decisions in an unprecedented context shaped by extreme historical events.

In conferring visibility to a disturbing past, these cinematic memorials—through their selective reading of history, their categories of perception, and their narrative logics—re-present a past for which barely any existing live footage exists, since all TV crews and all quasi journalists left Rwanda during the first week after Habyarimana's death. As it was the case for the works of "Rwanda: Writing As a Duty to Remember," the films discussed here have the merit to fill a void and raise a consciousness of what happened in Rwanda in 1994—a useful premise, which does not however guarantee a comprehensive understanding of what happened. The moment these cinematic representations offer a vision of the past, they also mask and exclude certain facets of the history to which they bear witness and therefore, often against their initial intent, institute a form of forgetting, if not illegitimate revisionism of history. As Sontag's analysis of photography in *Regarding the Pain of Others* reminds us—and this is even more true for cinematic re-presentations of a past that has barely any visual traces—"the photographic image, even to the extent that it is a trace, (not a construction made out of disparate photographic traces), cannot be simply a transparency of something that happened. It is always the image that someone chose; to photograph is to frame, and to frame is to exclude" (46). Similarly, while shooting a movie is to frame and edit in order to create traces to fill a cultural void and indifference, in the case of the genocide of the Tutsis, it is also a process that excludes some facets of this complex past and naturalizes what is worth being seen and thus remembered. Precisely because of this inherent tension between inclusion and exclusion lying at the core of all mediations of the past, these films can, despite their ethical and genuine motivations, reinforce discourses denying that a genocide occurred in Rwanda. The issue is then to evaluate to which extent cinematic

representations of the genocide of the Tutsis in Rwanda, despite their desire to confer a cultural and historical visibility to an obscene past within
a Western audience, might see themselves recuperated against their will by
deniers of this genocide? It is within this framework that I favor the analysis
of the directors' narrative choices, the dialogue between both historical and
imaginary characters, the selections of information given to viewers and their
historical veracity, the enactment of historical characters, the cast and credits,
the use of archival material or testimonies to create a "real" effect or, on the
contrary, the refusal to stick to factual reality in order to question the very act
of re-presentation.

In a post-genocidal context in which disinformation and denial are always
present as the continuation of genocide through other means, and contradictory versions attempt to make meaning out of images to impose an official
version of history, a number of these films position themselves as "historically
authentic" by advertising the fact that they are based on witnesses' stories.
Whether it be through a subtitle, as is the case in *Hotel Rwanda: A True
Story*, through a reference to autobiography, as is the case in *Shake Hands
with the Devil: Based on the Best-seller by Lieutenant General Roméo Dallaire*,
or through an opening statement, as in *Shooting Dogs*: "This film is based on
real events and was made at the locations depicted," these legitimating state-
ments aim to undermine the distinction between cinematic re-presentation
and the historical events to which they refer. Furthermore, such realist claims
seek to obliterate the *mediated* nature of reality within their representations
and make the viewers rhetorically believe of the possibility of an unmediated
immediacy and intimacy in the depiction of history. To frame a cinematic
representation of genocide by signifying at the beginning and at the end of
the movie—as it is the case for *Hotel Rwanda* and *Shooting Dogs*—that the
film is based on real lives and depicts real events, is not without consequences.
As Gary Weissman points out in his analysis of *Schindler's List*, not only does
such a focus on authenticity blur, if not collapse, the distinction between reality and re-presentation, but this "*special effect* of the real" also, paradoxically,
shifts the focus away from the event depicted to narcissistically celebrate the
ability of the film to "be" (the) real: "In representations of the Holocaust and
Nazism, a fascination with the blurring of borders between fact and fiction,
real and simulation, and the present and the past competes with an interest of
the Holocaust itself" ("Fantasy of Witnessing" 296).[4] Moreover, the recurrent
mention that a cinematic representation is based on a "true story" to lessen
its fictional perception, conceals the fact that the witness's retelling of history
is also already a mediated version of "reality." As Lang underlines in his essay
"The Representation of Limits," if the facts do not speak for themselves, nei-

ther do the authors or filmmakers who confer them a readability and visibility through their reliance on a figurative discourse and space:

> Whatever else it does, figurative discourse and the elaboration of figurative space obtrudes the author's voice and a range of imaginative turns and decisions on the literary subject, irrespective of that subject's character and irrespective of— indeed defying—the "facts" of that subject which might otherwise have spoken for themselves and which, at the very least, do not depend on the author's voice for their existence. The claim is entailed in imaginative representation that the facts *do not* speak for themselves, that figurative condensation and displacement and the authorial presence these articulate will turn or supplement the historical subject (whatever it is) in a way that represents the subject more compellingly or effectively—in the end, more truly—than would be case without them. (316)

Like the literary works published in the realm of "Rwanda: Writing as a Duty to Remember," if resorting to witnesses constitutes indeed a legitimate approach, basing a film's veracity on a single source might, however, raise a series of issues. Indeed, each individual memory is shaped by the personal relation the survivor seeks to establish between his traumatic past and his present situation. Because of his specific scars, trauma, loneliness, hopes, and desires and also because of his conscious or unconscious use of culturally connoted tropes and politically loaded metaphors, no single survivor's voice *alone* can pretend to tell the *whole* truth of the events by claiming a metonymic status.[5] As Rousso highlights, it is important to acknowledge that no single memory can comprehend and metonymically speak as the "collective" or "national" memory, which are ideological and sociological constructs: "Memory is plural, moreover, in that distinct memories are generated by different social groups, political parties, churches, communities, language groups, and so on. Thus 'collective memory' might seem to be a figment of the imagination, or at any rate little more than a misleading composite of disparate and heterogeneous memories" (*Vichy* 2). Thus, all cinematic representations of history that base their representational legitimacy on a single individual's memory too often mask that this memory is itself socially and ideologically positioned and partial. The rhetorical use of promoting one personal trajectory to embody the *whole* truth of the event and its remembrance must then be viewed as much as a structuring of remembrance than a "structuring of forgetfulness" because of its metonymical abuse within the representation of history (*Vichy* 4).

The privileging of authentic heroic or exceptional figures by some films wishing to portray the genocide of the Tutsis risks therefore institutionalizing an obliteration of the victims, since the majority of them become "a mere backdrop to melodramatic private affairs" (Kaes 208). Relegated to the background of the image and the plot, their blurred visibility is then only intermittently interrupted when a visual and narrative "deep focus" stages all the characters at very different depths of the image in focus to give them all equal importance and status. As de Baecque remarks in his analysis of films after Auschwitz, the danger of a representation that favors a heroic trajectory and the "shallow focus" it implies, lies in the *trompe l'œil* it generates. This visual and ideological obliteration of the victims is not inconsequential in its impact on our understanding of genocide:

> Cinema plays its role: it filmed the camps the day after, documenting the traces of death; it made those traces public to people in their living rooms across the country; it served as proof, conviction, testimony. But cinema also thwarted its mission of truth: it fashioned heroic behavior to hide all those—anonymous, women, children, common men, Jews and non-Jews—who never came back. It did not want to see a system of genocide, a politics of Final Solution. It tried to forget and to make us forget. (63)[6]

Unlike the films that base their authenticity on a privileged witness—whether it be Paul Rusesabagina or Roméo Dallaire—*Sometimes in April, A Sunday in Kigali,* and *100 Days* broadcast their fictional nature. Favreau's film based on Gil Courtemanche's novel *A Sunday at the Pool in Kigali* (2000) presents itself as "A fiction inspired by real events,"[7] and Hughes's film, *100 Days,* is self-defined as "A story of love and brutality set in the midst of an event the world is still trying to come to terms with—the genocide in Rwanda." In positing a relationship with history that does not try to silence its fictional premises to confer a visibility and readability on what happened, these films advocate a different pact with their viewers—one that rejects the abuse of memory that *Hotel Rwanda, Shooting Dogs,* and *Shake Hands with the Devil* uphold in valuing a realistic aesthetics that seeks to hide the crafted elements of their portrayals in order to make them "simply transparency of something that happened" . . . in short, mediations pretending to mediate an unmediated reality (Sontag 46).

Rousso's critical approach in his analysis of the conflicting Gaullist and Pétainist memories about a "same" past in *The Vichy Syndrome* will serve as a point of departure for my analysis. He defines the object of his reflection as: "The history of memory, that is, the study of the evolution of various social practices and, more specifically, of the form and content of social practices whose purpose or effect is the representation of the past and the perpetuation of its memory within a particular group or the society as a whole" (3). This critical perspective provides a pertinent analytical frame, though the films studied here constitute and institute very different "memories" that aim at maintaining the memory of a past while affirming its actuality. Nonetheless, as I have shown in the case of literary and theatrical mediations of the genocide, it is crucial not to limit oneself to an approach that celebrates the duty to remember without questioning its motive and the conditions of its possibility. To imagine that any representation is valuable by virtue of the fact that it challenges the forgetting in which the West has plunged the genocide of the Tutsis in Rwanda would be to forget that different memories of this past compete to institute the legitimate representation of this genocide—some even seeking to deny its very existence. Adopting Rousso's view, we must accept that there is no neutral or objective position from which to shoot a movie regardless of the cinematic strategies, historical research, and use of survivors' testimonies. Extending Rousso's analysis of the position of the historian to film directors bearing witness to genocide in Rwanda, we need to analyze why those who seek to document the tensions between different contemporary memories emanating from divergent social groups cannot aim for the status quo as they confer social visibility and readability to these tensions:

> Whether professional or amateur, the historian is always a product of his own time and place. He stands at a crossroads in the byways of collective memory: on the one hand he, like any other citizen, is influenced by the dominant memory, which may subconsciously suggest interpretations and eras of research; on the other hand, he himself is a "vector of memory" and a carrier of fundamental importance, in that the vision he proposes of the past may, after some delay, exert an influence on contemporary representations. (*Vichy* 4)

In the context of the genocide of the Tutsis in Rwanda, the films that have so far been produced have, like professional works of historians, professed themselves to be the privileged vectors of memory. However, in diffusing certain representations of the past and inflecting them with memory lapses, these films have managed to "ossify" within a Western audience some cultural references, categories of perception, explanations, and rationales susceptible to playing into different forms of genocide denial. In this sense, it is important to examine these films through their pretense of showing the reality of the genocide that occurred in Rwanda to determine whether or not they invite their audience to think about the bias and limitations of their cinematic mediations, the context in which they were produced, and even how they position themselves in regard to competing representations of the genocide. In other words, do these films attempt to put forth a realist esthetic to pass as neutral and objective as they fulfill a duty to remember, abusing the trope of hypotyposis,[8] or do they invite us to question their modes of representing the genocide in order to raise an awareness that any mediation of the genocide has to address the issue of denial by positioning itself?

Shooting Dogs' opening offers here an insightful example to further our understanding of this issue. To explicitly state, as does *Shooting Dogs*, that "this film is based on real events and was made at the locations depicted," posits a particular kind of referential contract with the audience, which has significant consequences. In this context, failing to mention that certain main aspects or characters are fictional becomes a silencing of the film's rewriting of history for the sake of a pseudo authenticity whose value is purely rhetorical—if not commercial—and no longer referential. According to the journalist Linda Melvern, author of *Conspiracy to Murder: The Rwanda Genocide* (2006) and *A People Betrayed: The Role of the West in Rwanda's Genocide* (2000), Michael Caton-Jones falls into this rhetorical pitfall. Melvern blames Caton-Jones and his co-director and co-producer David Belton for explicitly stating at the film's start that the events shown in the film are true when most of the main characters were invented to suit the script's needs or to answer to the BBC's expectations—the BBC having financed the movie. If most of the events on-screen are accurate, two falsifications or additions are at the heart of the polemic. First, no BBC team stayed at the École Technique Officielle (ETO) until the Belgian contingent of the MINUAR left. Second, no white priests stayed at the ETO to die with the Rwandans after the Belgian forces left. These two details are important, because they tend to relativize, if not erase, the West's resignation during the 1994 genocide. Making viewers believe that some journalists did go to the ETO and stayed, knowing that their presence might dissuade the militias from attacking, is a serious form of illegitimate rewriting of history according to Melvern, since the BBC, much like other Western media, quickly repatriated its teams, contributing to the possibility of an off-screened genocide:

> The failure of the Security Council of the UN to act responsibly is one of the great scandals of the 20th century. The failure extends to the Western media, including the BBC; inadequate reporting contributed to indifference and inaction. It was not a glorious moment for BBC news. Yet, due for release next week, is a BBC-financed film about the genocide, *Shooting Dogs*, starring John Hurt as a brave British priest. The film is billed as an "authentic recreation," shot on location with Rwandan extras playing the roles of the Interahamwe militia. The film is said to be based on the "true story" and "real events" that took place in the first days of the killing. The story centers on a massacre at a school, the École Technique Officielle (ETO), where Belgian peacekeepers abandoned thousands of people, ordered by the Belgian government to help, instead, with the frenzied evacuation of all expatriates. A BBC journalist is present at the school and challenges the peacekeepers as they leave, using the word genocide to describe what is happening. But this is fiction. There was no BBC film crew at ETO. There were no BBC film crews in Rwanda in those crucial early weeks. Nor did BBC news

broadcasts tell the world a genocide was underway. In April 1994, as the massa-cre took place, the BBC was reporting the evacuation of expats and the renewed civil war between "tribal factions." *Shooting Dogs* shows a shocking disregard for the historical record. It was not until 29 April that the word genocide was used by the BBC. ("History?" March 19, 2006)

This notorious resignation of the media is all the more serious because it made mobilizing public opinion impossible, even as nongovernmental organizations working in Rwanda were far more rapidly and accurately documenting the nature and scope of the massacres (Chaon 163 and Hilsum 167–187). As for the fictional priest who decides to die among the Rwandans he served for thirty years, he functions as a narrative and ethical counterpoint for the Church's resignation as a political institution and for the young Eng-lish teacher's fear of dying as he flees, despite his promise never to abandon his Rwandan students. As a white expiatory victim, Father Christopher thus exonerates the Church's dishonest compromises during the genocide and Westerners' cowardice in evacuating Western citizens and then ordering the UN to abandon the ETO and the thousands of Tutsis within its doors, know-ing that this retreat was a death sentence.[9]

The various audio commentaries and supplements on the DVD versions of most films also attest to their inclination for a realist esthetic when they implicitly ask witnesses to give the films their stamp of authenticity through their memories and narratives. In repeatedly orienting discussion toward representations' loyalty to the "truth," these commentaries naturalize a realist ideology that, on the one hand, seems to believe in the possibility of repro-ducing history, and, on the other hand, chooses to turn the ability to make the genocide's reality coincide with its filmic representations into what is at stake in these representations. The audio commentary in *Shake Hands with the Devil,* in which Roger Spottiswoode invites Roméo Dallaire to comment on the film, which is based on his autobiography, illustrates the DVD supple-ments' rhetorical function in making the demand for realism the determining criteria in defining the value of a film trying to depict a historical truth or a social reality. The fact that the discussion constantly returns to Spottiswoode's ability to realistically reproduce Dallaire's actions and movements or to ac-curately reconstruct the decorum of 1994 symptomatically indicates that the film's value and its capacity to communicate the "truth" of the genocide rest in its realism. The problem with this realist esthetic is the fact that it grounds its legitimacy not on an assumed and explicit interpretation of history, but, on the contrary, constructs its legitimacy in making the audience believe that its representation of history is neutral because it is supposedly mimetic. This belief in a possible mimesis tends to overshadow any reflection on the reality

of the mediation in creating the illusion that the filmed events speak for themselves. The esthetics of films like *Shake Hands with the Devil* or *Hotel Rwanda*
close then their eyes to the cinematic legacy of the Holocaust's representation
as defined by Anton Kaes in his essay "Holocaust and the End of History": "If
it is agreed that the cataclysmic mass destruction that occurred a half-century
ago defies not only historical description and quantitative determination but
also rational explanation and linguistic articulation, then a new self-reflexive
way of encoding history is called for" (208). In this sense, these discussions
that focus on the ability to authentically represent certain historical details,
dialogues, events, or discourses wind up not only masking the films' interpretive work, but also overshadowing their conditions of production. Thus, these
"making of" supplements function more as self-celebratory smokescreen than
a work on remembering—failing to question out loud the films' conditions of
production, the use of certain cinematic techniques, and the diegetic choices
made to bear witness to the genocide of the Tutsis.

Since no mediation of the past can say or show everything, it is important to discuss how each film about the genocide defines what is worthy of
memory—in other word, what is included in the film's diegetic world and
what remains off-camera, voiceless, and relegated to forgetfulness. Believing
in a mimetic representation of the past to understand it constitutes a dangerous fantasy, because this kind of realism then becomes an esthetic that forbids
us from thinking about the reality of its mediation. That is to say how what
is portrayed as reality is produced through a scripting and screening that
attempts—or not—to hide its selective positionality, historical omissions,
and ideological silencing.[10] In the conversation with Spottiswoode, if most of
the time Dallaire plays the game comparing his experience's "reality" to the
film's "image" in order to lend it authenticity, Dallaire also reminds us on
several occasions that two main dimensions of his experience of the genocide
are misrepresented or euphemized in Spottiswoode's film—a hiatus which,
precisely, tends to make the intolerable bearable despite the realistic and frequently raw scenes in *Shake Hands with the Devil*:

> This film is successful because it is not as clean and aseptic as *Hotel Rwanda*, for
> example. Here, the script is solidly anchored in reality. Nonetheless, two aspects
> make the reality of the terrain more terrible than the film's version. First, it's the
> frequency and number of massacres and the genocide's ladder. In the film, we
> see several scenes of massacre, but you have to multiply that number by ten to
> get the number of deaths there were. The church scene in which there was the
> massacre [Gikondo] is pretty close to reality. The volume was really unnerving.
> You didn't just walk next to numerous bodies, but piles of cadavers. Second, the
> smell. I don't know how you can reconstitute that in a film, the smell. (Roméo
> Dallaire in "Audio Commentary")

Dallaire's remarks here are important, because for him it is not the liberties the film's script takes with his autobiography that are disturbing. For example, he thinks the imaginary scene in which he is pictured lacerating his own thighs with a razor blade to confer a visibility upon the violent culpability that inhabited him during his mission's failure is both original and pertinent to communicate his inner feelings. For Dallaire, the incommensurability between the "reality of the terrain" and the film's "mediation" resides rather in the impossibility to reconstruct the smell and the magnitude of the genocide on-screen. In this sense, the "Audio Commentary" that grafts the real Dallaire's view on the cinematic representation of himself "offers both a surplus of reality meant to supplement and confirm the realism of the film's narrative and a syncretism of fiction and reality that destabilizes both the real and the fictional" (Rothberg, *Traumatic Realism* 239).

Through their respective choices, the cinematic representations of the genocide select the facets of this traumatic and contested history worthy of memory, but in so doing, they edit and naturalize that which passed in silence. In this sense, it is primarily through what these films leave off-screen and omit that they become prone to drifting toward genocide denial by promoting an unquestioned work of forgetting. At stake then are the narrative models and reading grids these films actualize in their filmic configurations of the genocide's memory. As Jean-Christophe Klotz suggests in his documentary *Kigali, Images against a Massacre* (2005), the challenge faced by every meditation on genocide can be summed up in this simple question: "How can you frame it? How can you make it fit within the frame—*Comment faire rentrer cela dans le cadre?*" If Klotz is reflecting simultaneously on the power of his images to inflect the course of events they document in April 1994 and their memorial power to keep the past at the heart of the present Rwandan society ten years later, Klotz's question applies both analogously and differently for fictional films. Analogously, to the extent that fictional films must also select what is worthy of memory according to what status they wish to give the past in the present, defined here by the diegesis, the plot, and the visual field. Differently, because the power of images is subordinate to plot coherence and picks up immediately on the duty to remember, since the films' relationship to the events they chronicle is always retrospective, if not posthumous. Thus, in spite of their willingness to stick to historical events, what is judged to be worthy of memory in these fictional films definitely derives more from narrative models that are socially acceptable in their depiction of state violence, from cultural expectations linked to representing extreme violence, from a refusal (or not) to fall into a voyeuristic and indecent realism, or from budgetary and technical constraints inherent to all cinematographic production. Finally, we must not forget that these films' esthetic is determined by their belonging to a very particular history of Western cinema inaugurated by Holocaust films. As de Baecque recalls, the movies filmed in the concentration and extermination camps of the Third Reich constitute a pivotal moment in cinematic history:

> Modern cinema was born from these images of the camps, which have never stopped working in it, resurging in other forms—camera-gaze, pausing on images, documentary embedded in fiction, flash-back, montage, contemplation, malaise—these specifically cinematographic figures that testify to the obsessive presence of the palimpsest of concentration camps. (66)

Despite their laudable intentions to inform and sensitize different audiences, to clearly identify the guilty, and to condemn the complicit attitudes of certain Western governments and the international community, these films can become problematic in terms of the means they use to communicate the violence of genocide and its political nature. Do the voice-over and in-dialogue history lessons, the selective use of fictional and real archives, the main character choices, the hierarchical organization of speakers or the layout of chronology with its ellipses and blanks—do all these elements allow the deniers of the genocide of the Tutsis to re-appropriate these films in order to give weight to their historical revisionism? Thus, at the very moment that these films seek to unframe forgetting by screening the specificity and historicity of this genocide, do they nonetheless manage to see themselves recuperated by those they precisely oppose?

In this sense, as Semujanga shows in his analysis of the foundational texts that made genocide thinkable in Rwanda and, so, possible, "Using the word 'genocide' is therefore a moral act: it condemns the murderer. The performative dimension of the word is so important that the speaker uttering 'genocide' says also, and necessarily, 'I condemn the murder'" (*Origins* 50). How this ethical imperative is implemented by films targeting Western viewers who know very little about the genocide of the Tutsis becomes then a major issue. It is indeed imperative for these films to initiate us to the complexities of a history both foreign to us and intimately linked to our respective national histories even though we do not want to admit this shared past and the responsibilities it entails. The danger is to limit our understanding of this genocide—and therefore the premises of our condemnation—to a simple inversion between the two antagonistic positions at the core of any genocidal ideology. We cannot advocate for a condemnation rooted in a dichotomy of hatred, which would invert and thus reproduce a stigmatization of the Other because it is precisely this conception of identity politics rooted in a mutual exclusion and hatred that lead to the killing of the Tutsis. This inability to overcome this inversion and its dualistic vision of history and antagonistic social relationship is precisely what Benjamin Sehene calls *The Ethnic Trap*. Therefore, one crucial aspect in our discussion of these films bearing witness to the genocide of the Tutsis is in the need to address how each film condemns the killers without portraying all Hutus as perpetrators and killers since such mediation would just reproduce the politics of hatred and discrimination that made—among other factors—the genocide possible.

Notes

1. As Linda Melvern underlines in "Missing the Story: The Media and the Rwanda Genocide" (2007), even when there was film and proof, no media agencies were ready to give to the killings they documented the weight and spin they deserved.

2. Of the seven films, only Nick Hughes's *100 Days* was filmed in Kinyarwanda. The 2006 DVD can be viewed in English or Kinyarwanda. None of the other movies has a Kinyarwanda version, language that is only used at times to confer an authentic flavor to the film, as is especially the case for *Shooting Dogs* and *A Sunday in Kigali* and to a lesser degree for *Sometimes in April*.

3. On the issue of denial and ideological strategies used by deniers of the genocide of the Tutsis, see Assumpta Mugiraneza, "*Négationnisme* au Rwanda post-génocide" (2009) and Hélène Dumas, "L'histoire des vaincus. Négationnisme du génocide des Tutsi au Rwanda" (2009).

4. Quoted in Michael Rothberg, *Traumatic Realism* (2000), 247.

5. This is especially true in the case of Paul Rusesabagina and his former and present political use of *Hotel Rwanda*, which is based on his testimony and led him to receive the United States Freedom Medal. For years after the premiere of *Hotel Rwanda* in 2004, Rusesabagina toured universities around the world and gained international recognition as he increasingly used his film and fame to attack Kagame's government in Kigali. Furthermore, using his status, his discourse tends to revive the Tutsis vs. Hutus divide, an attitude that can only hinder Rwandans to free themselves of the logic of racism and hatred inherited from the colonial period and used by Rwandan elites in the postcolonial era up to the genocide. See Alfred Ndahiro and Privat Rutazibwa, *Hotel Rwanda or the Tutsi Genocide as Seen by Hollywood* (2008), and the articles of William Church, director of a conservative think tank that covers the Great Lakes region, "Rusesabagina, Genocide Identity Politics" (2007) and "Rwanda: Hate Speech and Paul Rusesabagina" (2007).

6. Translation mine. Henceforth, all quotes from de Baecque's "Quel cinéma après Auschwitz?" are my translations.

7. *A Sunday at the Pool in Kigali* (2004) received in Québec an award in 2001 (Prix des Libraires). Courtemanche is a Quebecois journalist and essay writer who has been for many years a correspondent for Radio Canada in Africa and has made several documentaries on Rwanda: an award-winning documentary on AIDS in Rwanda, *L'Église du sida* [*The Gospel of AIDS*] (1993) (award for the best documentary at the

International Film Festival "Vues d'Afrique") and *Soleil dans la nuit* (1995) a series of 30 short clips featuring testimonies bearing witness to the genocide, produced for TV5 Europe-Afrique-Canada to document the first commemoration of the genocide.

8. A trope that confers a sense of immediate presence to a mediate reality.

9. For another critic of the shallow historical background and the accuracy of the facts depicted in *Shooting Dogs*, see Serge Farnel, "Sauver le chien de l'ambassade de France" (2008).

10. See my discussion of Bourdieu's concept of "symbolic violence" at the end of chapter 4, "The Hospitality of Listening as Interruption."

13

Close-up on Some
Recurrent Facts and Figures

THE HISTORY LESSONS ABOUT GENOCIDE that these films instill tend to socially institute a consensus around certain key characters, events, and
discourses that appear in most of the films and function as hinges between
the fiction and the historical reality that is its referent. Likewise, all the films
introduce, to various degrees, a number of fictional characters, despite their
purported loyalties to historical truth. These fictional characters have two
main purposes: to embody, for the sake of narrative economy and coherence
of the diegetic world, an ideological position, or, as we have already seen, to
insert a character at the heart of the film with whom a Western audience can
identify and in whom they may recognize themselves. Though it is a successful narrative process that counteracts the reflex to distance oneself in the face
of the deeply troubling and ob-scene nature of genocide, the use of imaginary
characters whose goal is to bring the audience to the heart of the genocide also
risks, in the case of Rwanda, to reproduce the heroic figure of the white man
rescuing the African.

Benefiting, in certain cases, from significant means of production and distribution, the films that chronicle the genocide of the Tutsis are privileged vectors
and carriers of memory that participate decisively in the diffusion and institutionalization of knowledge about the genocide in Rwanda. If their narratives
aim, in varying degrees, to initiate Western viewers and to give them points
of reference—dates, locations, chronology—they also privilege different moments and actors of the genocide. *Sometimes in April* covers a ten-year period
(1994–2004) by filming the main events and actors of the genocide and the significant issues of its aftermath, like justice and reconciliation, that allow viewers

to see the stakes involved. *Opération Turquoise*, on the other hand, deals only with the two last weeks of the genocide (June 19–July 4, 1994) by focusing on the divergent points of view of some of the French military and the journalist Patrick de Saint-Exupéry regarding the real goal of this highly controversial mission. Each film also invents a range of characters for the dramatic needs of the screenplay and must, in the interest of brevity and coherence, simplify the genocide's historical complexities and its political implications. Among these fictional characters, a good number of them are white—Europeans, Americans, or Canadians—so that the Western audience can identify with a self-like figure that is not the victim, the perpetrator, or a passive witness, but a witness who actively saves lives. Western viewers are called to identify with these active white characters who often embody a form of historical redemption—with various degrees of guilt—making them rhetorically more efficient to turn us into indirect witnesses of the genocide. It is worth noting that this use of various figures of the Western Self to allow viewers to envision the Other and relate to the reality of the genocide is, in itself, at the very least paradoxical. If the goal of these films is to denounce genocidal ideology, a premise of which is precisely the construction and demonization of an Other in order to legitimize this Other's obliteration in the name of the Self, we must wonder if the very privileging of Western eyes does not in itself constitute an ideological faux-pas, despite its rhetorical efficacy in captivating a targeted audience. Does this not, in effect, reproduce a subordinating relation—*une mise sous relation*—of the Other by the Self instead of seeking to forge a mutually defining relation—*une mise en relation*—between them, as Edouard Glissant conceives of in his *Poetics of Relation*?[1] Of the seven films, *100 Days*, *Hotel Rwanda*, and *Sometimes in April* are those whose main characters are Rwandans and who thus refuse to mediate a Western audience's contact and identification with the genocide of the Tutsis through the eyes of a *muzungu*. It is self-evident, however, that having Rwandan main characters is not in itself enough to evaluate the relationship created in these films as we come face-to-face with an extreme violence for which nothing has prepared us, though the potential for that extra-ordinary violence is at the heart of every society and every one of us.

In most of the films, the correlation between the character choices and the intended audience is reinforced by the historical or fictional aims and stakes favored in each of the productions—and by the director's and producer's nationality. Made with an American audience in mind, *Hotel Rwanda* presents us with Rwandan main characters, but casts American Don Cheadle as Paul Rusesabagina and replaces the too-Canadian Roméo Dallaire with Colonel Oliver, played by Nick Nolte. In addition, careful to conform to American moviegoers' expectations, the choices and script of the movie idealize the real Rusesabagina's actions and goings-on—with his mythomaniac blessing—in order to mold him into the stereotypical Hollywood hero. In portraying Rusesabagina as a hero who saved those he should have killed, because he is Hutu, *Hotel Rwanda* privileges a figure of hope in darkness and is, in that sense, a perfect African remake of Steven Spielberg's *Schindler's List* (1993).[2] These two films' success rests not so much in their ability to convey the history of genocide in a contextualized and critical fashion, but in their capacity to make the ob-scene violence of genocide bearable by telling the story through an exceptional figure. What makes these uncommon characters attractive—and thus, the danger that Schindler and Rusesabagina represent—rests in their ability to eclipse the murderous and heinous behaviors of the majority, to eclipse even to a large degree a reflection on the conditions that made the genocide possible and summoned the population's massive participation. Moreover, as Rothberg underlines in his analysis of Spielberg's film, it is the survivors who find themselves silenced and eclipsed by the election of an atypical and exceptional character: "The privileging of the exceptional survivors at the expense of the majority who had no means of escape ends by traducing the survivors themselves. The implied narrative trajectory from handsome actor to dignified survivor disallows the actual voices of the survivors—they in fact do not speak—because their stories might disrupt the seamlessness with which Spielberg has constructed his narrative of the Holocaust and its aftermath. No sense of the psychic or physical cost of survival . . ." (*Traumatic Realism* 241).

Thus, even when the idealized version of the events in *Hotel Rwanda* were questioned, Terry George continued to defend the appeal of Rusesabagina's story, remembering his exceptional status: "The Rwandan episode was a slaughter of unimaginable horror and magnitude, yet I firmly believed I had found a story that showed that even in the midst of such horror the human capacity for good can triumph" ("Smearing a Hero"). In this sense, the privileging of a heroic figure who becomes the exception makes *Hotel Rwanda* lean toward an ideological status quo—a position Rousso declared deceptive if not preposterous—even as it purports to shake up people's consciences, because at the end of the day, the humanist belief in man's goodness remains unshaken despite his unfathomable capacity to kill other men for political and ideological reasons. The success of films like *Hotel Rwanda* lies, therefore, in choosing the story of an exceptional character and a seamless script that confirm rather then disrupt an optimistic and humanistic vision of humanity—and this, at the very moment when this vision is radically questioned, if not maimed, by the reality of the narrated events.[3]

Also geared to an American audience, and produced by HBO, *Sometimes in April* highlights the significance of Washington's reluctance to recognize the massacres of the Tutsis as a genocide while also dropping a large number of American cultural and historical references to capture the audience's attention from the beginning and to impress upon viewers that this genocide does concern the United States, Peck starts off his film with a Martin Luther King, Jr. quote that implicitly poses the question of the U.S. engagement and historical responsibility, in this case, in the genocide of the Tutsis in Rwanda: "In the end, we will remember not the words of our enemies, but the silence of our friends." This suspicion of Washington's guilty silence in 1994 is then confirmed from the beginning of the film since the first character to appear on screen is none other than Bill Clinton on his trip to Kigali in 1998 when he went to Rwanda to ask forgiveness for having done nothing to prevent or stop the genocide:

> From Kibuye in the west to Kibungo in the east, people gathered, seeking refuge in churches by the thousands in hospitals and schools. And when they were found, the old and the sick, women and children alike, they were killed. Killed because their identity card said they were Tutsi. Or because they had a Tutsi parent or because someone thought they looked like a Tutsi, or slain like thousands of Hutus because they protected Tutsis or would not countenance a policy that sought to wipe out people who, just the day before and for years before, had been their friends and neighbors. It is important that the world knows that these killings were not spontaneous or accidental. It is not an African phenomenon and must never be viewed as such. We have seen it in industrialized Europe. We have seen it in Asia. We must have global vigilance and never again must we be shy in the face of the evidence. (Clinton, as cited in *Sometimes in April*)

In appealing to the symbolic and legitimating power of this archival clip, this film's opening fulfills numerous goals: first, it transposes the American viewer to Rwanda via Clinton; second, this spatial immersion is reinforced temporally by the succeeding scene when we discover, after a zoom-out, that we are not "alone" in watching the Clinton clip. Indeed, in the film's setup, Clinton's speech is viewed by a class of young Rwandan schoolchildren in April 2004; third, in signaling this spatial and temporal complicity, the film's opening inscribes the genocide of the Tutsis in American history and bars viewers from believing in their country's innocence;[4] fourth, it deconstructs the stereotype of a distant Africa, where violence is atavistic and not the result of political—and geopolitical—struggles; fifth, the discourse of the film's opening places the American—and Western—viewer not in a paternalistic role as heroic savior, but in the position of the guilty party seeking forgiveness, having recognized his/her fault and silence; finally, Peck's opening creates a bridge between American and Rwandan viewers and between the viewers' present—2004—and the genocide of the Tutsis—1994—which the film aims to make visible and intelligible by highlighting its political origins from the start.

A Sunday in Kigali and *Shaking Hands with the Devil*, on the other hand, are primarily aimed at a Canadian audience, as their critique of the Ottawa government's politics and isolation of Roméo Dallaire at the United Nations shows. Here, the spatial and temporal complicity rests on the preference for Canadian actors and characters: Luc Picard plays a young Quebecois journalist who falls in love with a Hutu woman in Robert Favreau's film, and Roy Dupuis plays Lieutenant-Colonel Roméo Dallaire in Roger Spottiswoode's film. Following the same logic, Michael Caton-Jones's *Shooting Dogs* introduces a cast of British characters and BBC journalists who, in reality, were never present at the ETO—neither before nor after the massacre that followed the Belgian contingent's departure from the school after Belgium pulled out from the MINUAR. Directed by the Haitian Raoul Peck, *Sometimes in April*—in addition to its American audience—also targets Francophone viewers through its condemnation of France's role in Africa. Repeatedly, the script points to clear evidence that the Elysée militarily supported Habyarimana's and his successors' regimes during the course of the genocide in order to maintain its influence in the Great Lakes region. Finally, co-produced by the French television stations Canal+ and France 2 and the French National Center for Cinema, Alain Tasma's *Opération Turquoise* depicts the genocide from the point of view of various French military personnel and journalists.[5] Through their different interpretations of the conflict and the priorities of their mission in Western Rwanda, Tasma interrogates the ambiguity surrounding this officially named humanitarian operation, which also happens to answer to French strategic goals in the Kivu region. If Tasma shows that the French intervention did manage to save lives, his film also unambiguously highlights that the intervention primarily benefited the Hutu perpetrators who were fleeing the Tutsi-led advance of the Rwandan Patriotic Front, and that the French army abandoned the surviving Tutsis to their fate, as was the case in Bisesero. All these films therefore share a similar premise: electing narrative strategies, plots, and casts capable to deconstruct the belief in a possible innocence or neutrality in order to implicate—emotionally and politically—their Western audiences so that they become conscious that the genocide of the Tutsis does concern them and is part of their history.

In this sense, Nick Hughes's *100 Days*, co-produced with Rwandan director Eric Kabera,[6] constitutes a significant departure from these trends. Hughes, in effect, offers a vision of the genocide that largely espouses the Rwandan government's. On the one hand, the script denounces the UN's apathy, the Catholic Church's guilt and complacency, France's complicity, and the role of extremist Hutupower militia and authorities in the implementation of this planned genocide. On the other hand, Hughes celebrates the RPF's historic role in stopping the genocide of the Tutsis and its willingness to institute a politics of national reconciliation. Filmed in Kinyarwanda and in English, this film speaks more directly to Rwandans and is also the only one that follows the tragic fate of two young Tutsis, separated and alienated by the genocide, in their struggle to survive.

In the case of the genocide of the Tutsis in Rwanda, the risk of reproducing the paternalistic and racist stereotype inherited from colonialism constitutes a serious form of historical revisionism—even denial. To the extent that the international community's apathy was one of the conditions that made the execution of the genocide possible, advocating identification with a white savior hero represents a reprehensible distortion. Allowing viewers to believe that a few exceptions like Philippe Gaillard—head of the International Red Cross delegation in Rwanda during the genocide[7]—were the norm, when in fact most Westerners were remarkable in their cowardice and resignation, constitutes a major falsification of history. If the film devoted to Roméo Dallaire sometimes tends toward hagiography highlighting his successful saving of thirty thousand people during the genocide, Spottiswoode's film also shows the extent to which Dallaire is haunted by his mission's failure and what he should have and could have done if he had refused to obey certain orders. In this regard, *Shooting Dogs* is without a doubt the film that most explicitly offers up a white heroic figure through the fictional character of Father Christopher who, after having lived thirty years in Rwanda, decides to die with the Rwandans who took refuge at the ETO when the Belgian forces of the MINUAR abandoned them to the machetes of the *Interahamwe* surrounding the school. The young British teacher who has joined Father Christopher at the eve of the genocide embodies the other choice: to flee for fear of dying. If Father Christopher is a heroic figure, he does not, however, manage to save the genocide victims, and, in this sense, his sacrificial heroism rather symbolizes a coherent ethical and moral position that contrasts greatly with and further critiques the international community's hypocrisy.

The cast of main characters in the movies aimed at Western audiences is an equally telling marker of the relationship these filmic mediations on the genocide seek to establish with their audiences. The only film whose two main characters are Tutsi is *100 Days*, which follows the story of a young couple and their family living in the Kibuye region. *Hotel Rwanda* and *Sometimes in April* both foreground a mixed couple in which the wife is Tutsi, and the Hutu husband rejects the genocidal ideology—Peck's script further complicates the story by introducing a Hutu brother who works at the pro-Hutu Radio Télévision Libre des Mille Collines (RTLM) and winds up being tried at the International Criminal Tribunal for Rwanda (ICTR) located in Arusha, Tanzania. *Shooting Dogs* and *A Sunday in Kigali* pick a different kind of mixed couple: in the first case, a young English teacher in love with a Tutsi student at the ETO; in the second case, a Canadian journalist in love with a Hutu woman who keeps being mistaken for a "dirty Tutsi" because of her relationship with a white man and her physique of stereotypically "Tutsi features." Finally, at the other extreme are *Shaking Hands with the Devil*, which is about Dallaire, and *Opération Turquoise* whose main characters are all French.

This quick close-up on the main characters aims at highlighting two points. First, it is at the very least paradoxical that the only movie screening a Tutsi couple is the least known and least distributed even though it came out in 2001, three years before *Hotel Rwanda*. That *100 Days* came out and remains almost unnoticed once again demonstrates that a film's success depends more upon its advertising and distribution and its conformity to certain cultural and ideological expectations than it does on the pertinence of the history lessons it promotes. Second, the fact that most of the movies depict mixed couples—Tutsi-Hutu, Tutsi-Muzungu or Hutu-Muzungu[8]—supports the general perception that Tutsis and Hutus who opposed the genocidal regime would have been equally victimized. The under-representation of Tutsi victims generated by the over-representation of Hutus persecuted for their political actions is a two-edged sword. On the one hand, it undermines the easy generalization that all Tutsis were victims and all Hutus perpetrators. On the other hand, it creates an inverse distortion of history in suggesting that the vast majority of Hutus tried to save the Tutsis—a type of "Hutu redemption" echoing the fantasy of "white redemption." The decision not to make most of the main characters Tutsi victims is defensible. First, it avoids the problem I rejected above of creating homogenous dichotomies where all Hutus are perpetrators and all Tutsis are victims. Second, this decision makes explicit the fact that all the Hutus in Rwanda had a choice and had to make highly consequential decisions. These stakes are at the heart of *Sometimes in April*, which screens two couples: first, Augustin, a Hutu captain in the Rwandan army and Jeanne, his Tutsi wife, and second, the symbolic couple Augustin and Honoré, and his Hutu brother who takes a radically different course during the years leading up to the genocide: Augustin refuses to play a role in the killing, despite expectations that he must participate as a Hutu officer, while Honoré becomes one of the principle voices of the RTLM.[9] Third, to the extent that most of the films condemn the UN and the West's inaction and complicity, the over-representation of fictional white characters is justifiable in that it allows for points of identification and elicits feelings of sympathy from viewers, and maybe even a sense of historical culpability.

If certain facts and actors appear to be historically and narratively inevitable, they nonetheless take on a different status, subordinate to the coherence and to the plot in which they occur. Besides the figure of the Tutsi victim with whom Western viewers would not dare identify because she is persecuted for

who she is rather than for her actions, four other emblematic figures recur
in most of the movies. Strongly connoted and morally defined in each of the
scripts, these figures allow the director to position characters relationally and
to introduce the possibility of moral judgment in a context of extreme violence and extraordinary circumstances. The first of these figures is *the figure of
evil* or *the executioner*, collectively enacted by the *Interahamwe* and individually by Colonel Théoneste Bagosora, chief of the presidential guard, primary
planner of the genocide, and influential member of the *akazu*,[10] a political
circle consisting of people close to those in power and Habyarimana's family. Second is the *figure of the liberator*, collectively enacted by the soldiers of
the Rwandan Patriotic Front (RPF) or individually by General Paul Kagame,
head of the RPF, whose members were primarily Tutsi exiles who had fled
the country since the 1960s and Hutus trying to overthrow Habyarimana's
regime. The third figure is that of *the just and the resistant*, embodied by the
Hutus who reject the ideology of Hutupower and refused to take advantage
of the opportunities of ethnic discrimination and hatred; Agathe Uwilingiyimana is an emblematic example—Hutu politician, multi-partisan and prime
minister in April 1994, she was one of the first Hutus to be assassinated for her
overt opposition to the ethnic dictatorship and her willingness to go through
the correct political channels to name a presidential successor after Habyarimana's death. Finally, there is *the muzungu figure*, the benevolent Westerner
who is frequently overwhelmed by the historical events and the complexity
of the political situation. Lieutenant Colonel Roméo Dallaire embodies this
figure as commander of the United Nations Mission to Assist Rwanda forces
(MINUAR), the symbol of the international community's political position.[11]

These four figures, which frame that of the victim, each represent distinct
existential, ethical, and political choices, which outline a range of possible positions in the plots of the films. By introducing four cardinal points embodying
explicit ideological values, these figures allow us to evaluate main characters'
decisions and to measure the consequences of their actions in a postcolonial
society racially and politically polarized. Embodied by different historical or
imaginary characters according to each script, these four cardinal figures also
suggest that understanding the genocide of the Tutsis means seeing the Tutsis
and the Hutus as non-homogeneous groups. Each film indeed significantly
deconstructs binary (di)visions (Hutus vs. Tutsis and White vs. African) and
the fundamentally racist worldview they naturalize. One of the challenges the
directors of these movies face rests then in the need to document the political abuse of this binary (di)vision without reinforcing or naturalizing it—a
(di)vision in which one group's social definition presupposes an ontological
difference from the other group against which it defines itself as its negation.
Each of these films must therefore document the political and ideological use

of this essentialist logic of differentiation without contributing to its social reproduction or reinforcement. Failing to highlight that this racist (di)vision is socially constructed and subjected to social change runs the risk of reinforcing the hatred of the Other to the point of crisis, rendering the destruction of the Other thinkable, necessary, and acceptable in the name of the Self and self-defense. By invoking, in addition to the figure of the victims, these four figures—*the executioner, the liberator, the just,* and *the muzungu*—and the positional and relational grid they embody within the diegetic world, most of the films on the genocide of the Tutsis manage to transcend a polarized and dualistic view of Rwanda's society and to demonstrate the political nature of the genocide. Privileging the idea of the political, then, demands showing the genocide to be the result of a fierce battle about the elite's monopoly over power, whose ideological genesis stems back to a particular regional and postcolonial history that cannot be reduced to an ancestral interethnic conflict.

The seven films produced between 2001 and 2007 had varying success in the box office or on the national television stations for which they were produced.[12] If George's *Hotel Rwanda*, based on Paul Rusesabagina's narrative, garnered unprecedented visibility in 2004, it was not—as one might think based on its unparalleled success—the first film to deal with the genocide of the Tutsis in 1994. Before it, came *100 Days*, written, directed, and coproduced by Nick Hughes in 2001, who wanted to create a film that would show what no cameraman, including himself as he worked for the BBC in Africa, had managed to capture in 1994 and what the world wanted to forget:

> I had the feeling that I betrayed those that I filmed. I felt that, as a witness, I had a duty to testify to what the world wanted to forget. Betrayal was everywhere, the betrayal of the international community, of the humanitarian organizations, the church's betrayal and the media's. Because after the genocide, the betrayal went on. The truth did not go away; the few survivors were becoming embarrassing.[13]

Without the benefit of *Hotel Rwanda*'s budget and distribution—the main characters in *100 Days* are played by Rwandan actors—Hughes's film went largely unnoticed when it came out in 2001. Other factors also contributed to its eclipse, despite the fact that it is far more methodical than *Hotel Rwanda* in presenting the genesis and political implementation of the genocide. First, Hughes and Kabera opted for a script that does not belittle how exceptional it was to survive, nor does it present an overblown heroism where main characters save another's life by risking one's own: the vast majority of the Tutsis introduced at the beginning of the movie are massacred in the Kibuye church, and the couple Baptiste and Josette succumb to the traumatic effects of the genocide, despite their survival. Second, all the Western characters in the film are racist, indifferent, cowardly, paternalistic, or manipulated by or in cahoots with Habyarimana—no Colonel Oliver here, no altruistic Red Cross, no benevolent BBC cameraman. Eliminating all possibilities for the audience to identify with a Western hero means that *100 Days* forbids us, as Westerners, to have pity and a clear conscience without feeling guilty: the white hero who would have acted as we wish we would have if we were in a similar situation is absent—as, indeed, was the case with few exceptions during the actual genocide. Third, the film's closing allegory does not answer Western concerns, much as it dislodges the typical Hollywood *happy ending*. At the foot of a blood-red cascade—a scene which foregrounds the victims of the genocide and places their traumatic heritage in the background—a child soldier of the RPF picks up an abandoned baby, whose Tutsi mother did not want to keep it, because it was the product of a rape committed by a Hutu priest who saved her life by making her his sex slave. In screening two of the genocide's heirs—the child soldier and the child born out of anti-Tutsi hatred and rape—the epilogue of *100 Days* explicitly confronts its viewers with the collective challenge of national reconciliation post-genocide Rwandans have to face.

As vectors of memory that reach a large audience, these films play an important role in producing and transmitting a dominant view of the genocide perpetrated in Rwanda, all of them claiming varying degrees of loyalty to history. Despite the range of scripts, it is possible to list—though perhaps not exhaustively—the recurring events that implicitly institute a consensual master narrative. While this narrative consensus helps to confer intelligibility to the genocide of the Tutsis, it also imposes a normative reading grid and historical lenses to which any mediation attempting to offer a "credible" representation of this genocide must subscribe and thus exhibit, reproduce, and reinforce. These points, facts, and historical figures, which allow the genocide's story—or one version of it—to be written, are as follows: there was a unified pre-colonial Rwandan kingdom; the Hutus, Tutsis and Twas coexisted and mingled peacefully within different clans; the Germans arrived and brought with them the beginning of the colonial era at the end of the nineteenth century; white priests played a significant role in evangelizing Rwandans; in 1931, the Belgian colonial administration instituted ethnic identity cards; in 1957, the "Bahutu Manifesto" was published with the consent and help of the Catholic Church; in 1959, the Hutu "social revolution" occurred with the blessing of the Belgian administration; Rwanda gained independence in 1962 with the first massacres taking place during that decade; in 1973, Habyarimana took power through a coup d'état, benefiting the northern Hutus; the RPF triggered war in October 1990; shortly after, the extremist newspaper *Kangura* published the "10 Muhutu Commandments"; in August 1993, the Arusha agreement was signed; January 10, 1994, a fax to the UN headquarters revealed that armed militiamen were ready to kill the Tutsis and anyone opposing the regime; April 6, 1994, President Habyarimana was assassinated; the RTLM called for the mass murder of the Tutsis; the *Interahamwe* and the presidential guard joined forces during the genocide; April 7, ten UN Belgian peacekeepers were executed; Westerners were evacuated from April 9 to 14; on April 13, the Belgian contingent of the MINUAR retreated and reduced its numbers on April 21; the power-hungry Catholic Church played an ambiguous role; massacres occurred at roadblocks, in churches, marshes, and forests throughout the hills of the whole country; the United States and the UN displayed major semantic hypocrisy, refusing to see "acts of genocide" as "genocide" for more than two months; at the end of June, with the French-led Opération Turquoise, a flow of Hutus fled to Zaire; the RPF took Kigali on July 4; at the end of the genocide in 1994, the International Criminal Tribunal for Rwanda (ICTR) was created, and the local *gacaca* tribunals were put into place in 2001 throughout Rwanda to accelerate the implementation of justice for the majority of people suspected to have participated in the genocide.

In using a narrative model based on a handful of emblematic characters, each script selects and prioritizes, then, certain of these "key" events according to its plot and length—two hours or so for most cinematic representations of the genocide of the Tutsis. In doing so, each film puts forth its own temporal depth and historical knowledge, and elects a system of socio-political causality that tries to avoid abusive generalizations by increasing the number of secondary characters in order to create nuance or introduce historical events that otherwise remain off-screen because of budgetary or time constraints. Precisely because every "re-presentation" of the past makes choices according to present concerns as it employs the past to "re-imagine" it, it is necessary to examine what these history lessons choose to make worthy of memory and what they relegate to oblivion. Likewise, it is important to ask whether these lessons allow for complex thinking about the political and historical genesis of the genocide, in addition to the complexity of its execution. Finally, we must also ask whether these lessons reproduce the categories and stereotypes that fuel genocidal ideology and its denial counterpart, by legitimizing hatred, exclusion, and destruction of the Other.

Notes

1. The imposed and subordinating relation—*mise sous relation*—characteristic of the colonial enterprise institutes unilateral objectification and subordination upon the Other. A mutually defining relation—*mise en relation*—is the antidote for this colonial practice, since no one entity has unilateral power or knowledge to completely

understand others. The Self and Other at the heart of this poetics of relation thus benefit from a right to the opacity that renders them mutually incapable of being assimilated to and by the Self or Other. Therefore, there would not be a hierarchy or a relationship of unilateral domination between the two entities; on the contrary, there would be a solidarity that demands neither identification nor annexation. See especially the chapter "For Opacity" (189–194).

2. For a discussion of the controversies sparked by Spielberg's *Schindler's List*, see Michael Rothberg's chapter, "'Touch an Event to Begin.' Americanizing the Holocaust" (especially 222–247) in *Traumatic Realism* (2000). For a general overview of cinematic representations of different genocides, see Michael Dorland, "PG—Parental Guidance of Portrayal of Genocide: The Comparative Depiction of Mass Murder in Contemporary Cinema" (2007).

3. For a detailed critique of the Hollywood myth George's film actualizes through Rusesabagina's character, see Ndahiro and Rutazibwa's chapter "A Hollywood Myth" (*Hotel Rwanda*).

4. For an analysis of the U.S. political position on Rwanda, see Power's chapter "Rwanda: 'Mostly in a Listening Mode'" in *A Problem from Hell: America and the Age of Genocide* (2003). See also Steven Livingston's essay "Limited Vision: How Both the American Media and Government Failed Rwanda" (2007).

5. With *Opération Turquoise*, Tasma continues to interrogate the taboos or memory lapses of French colonial politics, since in 2005 he produced a film about the repression of the protests organized by the FLN (Front de Libération Nationale) on October 17, 1961, in Paris during the war leading to Algeria's independence in 1962.

6. Kabera is also the producer and director of *Keepers of Memory* (2005), a documentary about survivors who became guards and guides at the various cemeteries and memorials for genocide victims and who not only testify to what they went through, but also to how they are coping with the past in the present. In 2009, he co-directed and produced Juan Reina's documentary *Iseta: Behind the Roadblock*, which focuses on the destiny and identities of the victims Hughes filmed as they were killed at a Kigali's roadblock—the only footage of killers at work. In 1994, Kabera founded the "Link Media Production," which helped produce *100 Days*. He was also a local consultant for Peck for the script and filming of *Sometimes in April*. Thanks to "Link Media Production" <http://www.linkerickabera.com>, he continues to promote documentaries and short films about the Great Lakes region. For more information, see Steve Bloomfield's article, "Welcome to Hillywood: How Rwanda's Film Industry Emerged from Genocide's Shadow" (2007).

7. Gaillard was interviewed in a number of documentaries about his work in Rwanda during the genocide and narrated his experiences in "Rwanda 1994: A Testimony: 'We Can Kill as Many People as We Like, but We Cannot Kill Their Memories'" (2004).

8. One can not help to notice that the *muzungu* is always a white man falling in love with a black woman, a pattern that results from and reproduces a colonial gaze dominated by exoticized and eroticized clichés and fantasies.

9. Here is how Peck presents the antagonistic couple formed by Augustin and Honoré: "The stories I gathered in Rwanda felt at times like real Shakespearian dra-

mas. All the typical dramatic situations you know exist happened. But, in order to have a logical construction of my story, I had to connect the dots and my characters into the same emotional world. Thus at one point in the screenplay development the idea of linking these two men as brothers. And through this, I got the symbolic arc of a Cain and Abel story of these two brothers who find themselves on two different side of the tragedy" ("Interview with Raoul Peck" on the official website of the film <http://www.hbo.com/films/sometimesinapril/interviews/>).

10. In Kinyarwanda, *akazu* means "the little house" and refers to the political, military, and economic circle that monopolized power under Habyarimana, profiting the northern Hutu elite, from whom the president hailed.

11. On the failure of the UN in Rwanda, see Michael Barnett, *Eyewitness to a Genocide: The United Nations and Rwanda* (2002).

12. All of the films are now available on DVD.

13. Nick Hughes interview with Mariett Gutherz for Club-culture.com "Vues d'Afrique" 2002. <http://club-culture.com/cinema/rwandos.htm>.

14

A Pedagogy Against Forgetting
That Sometimes Forgets Itself

THE USE OF VOICE-OVER TO SUMMARIZE HISTORICAL FACTS or their textual super-imposition on maps of Africa and bird's-eye views of the hills of Rwanda, constitute one of the privileged pedagogical moments in the transmission of knowledge about the genocide and aim at transporting viewers to the site of the action. Preceding all action in the plot, these *historical summaries* define not only the minimal knowledge required to understand the conditions that made the genocide possible but also to create a conceptual and historical framework defining the diegetic world the plot will use to render the past intelligible. It is then crucial to identify the gaps and silences in these summaries and their possible failure in screening the categories that made hatred of the Other thinkable and his elimination acceptable. The second pedagogical moments I analyze here are either the *informative dialogues*, usually initiated by an ignorant *muzungu* who asks naïve questions that the viewers are most likely also asking themselves, or the *epilogues* that often provide further historical facts, biographical information, or moral lessons.

Before discussing the two pedagogical lessons that frame the plotting and screening of the genocide—*historical summaries* and *epilogues*—let us look at how two seemingly insignificant *informative dialogues* distill more or less successfully a history lesson through the bias of speakers who are clearly identified as legitimate sources of information, not to say experts. Among the first scenes in *Shooting Dogs*, Caton-Jones stages such a dialogue between a BBC journalist and the innocent Joe who just arrived in Rwanda to teach English at the ETO—Joe, being the character with whom the Western audience is supposed to identify. This dialogue takes place several days before the start of the genocide. The BBC journalist tells him about the Hutu massacre of Tutsis marching for peace under the police's indifferent eyes. To try to help Joe understand the social tensions that rule in Rwanda, she uses the following metaphor: "Tutsis and Hutus are supposed to live together like merlot and cabernet to make a wonderful Bordeaux, but I doubt this will happen when Tutsi bashing and killing remains unpunished." If this dialogue is able to show that the genocidal violence did not spontaneously start after President Habyarimana's assassination and that its genesis is grounded in politics, the metaphor is also highly problematic. First, it decontextualizes and dehistoricizes the evolution of the categories "Hutu" and "Tutsi." Second, it naturalizes and essentializes them through an organic metaphor, though they are socially constructed and politically manipulated categories. Third, it consequently makes it impossible to think of social change and in that sense reproduces the Belgian colonial administration's logic that instituted these ethnic distinctions on the identity cards in the 1930s. Fourth, it assumes a dualistic and antithetical vision of Rwandan society, which is one of the ideological premises that allows for the construction and obliteration of the Other in the name of the Self, or majority group. Finally, this metaphor assumes that the social categories "Hutu" and "Tutsi" are homogeneous, ignoring the fact that there are political tensions, regional alliances, and ethical dissensions within each group, not to mention the fact that unions between Hutus and Tutsis have long existed.

In short, this type of knowing metaphor tends to undermine social diversity and understate the historical evolution of the formation of social identities in the Rwandan context. Because of its organic nature, the metaphor also ideologically naturalizes a reading grid that obliterates the conditions of social change, the socio-historical plurality of the references from which identity evolves and from which the relationships of power define living together, whether it be before, during, or after the genocide. These types of metaphors surface in many discourses denying the genocide of the Tutsis because of their ability to simplify the complexity of Rwanda's history and society. Furthermore, thanks to the abusive and reductive rationality they advocate, they impose a binary dynamic that allows for an inversion of the victim and executioner positions. If the metaphor of "cabernet" and "merlot" is not as perverse as those that animalize the Tutsis in making them "cockroaches" that would not know how to give birth to "butterflies," as per Parmehutu propaganda, it is no less harmful in the context of an *informative dialogue*. Far from revealing the complexity of social and power relations in Rwandan society, this metaphor obscures historical and political complexity and winds up having the opposite effect from that desired.

Another example of a such dialogues is in *Hotel Rwanda*, when the cameraman Jack Dalgish, having recently arrived in Kigali—much like the viewer, since the film is in its first ten minutes—asks Benedict, a young Rwandan journalist, what distinguishes the Hutus from the Tutsis. The journalist who is, according to Paul Rusesabagina, an expert on the subject, answers the following: "According to the Belgian colonies, the Tutsis are taller, are more elegant. It was the Belgians who created that division. They picked people, those with a thinner nose, lighter skin. They used to measure the width of people's noses. The Belgian used the Tutsis to run the country, but when they left they left the power to the Hutus, and of course, the Hutus took their revenge for years of repression. Am I telling the truth Paul?" After Paul acknowledges the accuracy of Benedict's lesson of history, Jack asks Paul whether he is Hutu or Tutsi. After pausing, Paul laconically answers that he is Hutu without elaborating or questioning this mode of social classification. He does not even mention that his wife is Tutsi. The English cameraman then turns to two Rwandan women sitting at the bar and asks them the same question. One replies that she is Hutu, the other Tutsi. Taken aback and doubtful, because these two women could be twin sisters in his eyes, Jack then turns back to the expert, Benedict. The scene stops there, neither Jack nor the audience having gotten a clear sense of what distinguishes a Tutsi from a Hutu. Paradoxically, the pedagogical value of this dialogue rests in the suspension of judgment it seeks to elicit. In effect, the dialogue questions the evidence of the inherited discourses and beliefs—since these do not allow one to clearly distinguish Hutus from Tutsis—and indicates that most of the typologies and definitions that seek to distinguish Tutsis, Hutus, and Twas are based on little more than stereotypes that come with all the social and ideological implications stereotypes carry. The history lesson this scene teaches does, therefore, give the viewer grounds to doubt the possibility of being able to distinguish Hutu and Tutsi based on physical traits alone.[1]

Through these questions, Jack not only tests the present reading grids inherited from the past; he also thwarts their legitimating and racist function in the film's present. Benedict's history lesson, which traces the origin of racial hatred in Rwanda to the Belgians and reproduces a binary (di)vision that opposes Hutu and Tutsi as homogeneous social groups, thus becomes relativized and even slashed in the present of its enunciation. The Rwandans present in the scene fail to correspond to the stereotypes advanced by this version of history and the divisions it seeks to naturalize.

Nonetheless, Benedict's one innocuous sentence—"*of course* the Hutus took their revenge"—is not explicitly questioned though it perpetuates a causal, essentialist, and vengeful vision of history, by naturalizing it *of course*. Letting this interpretation of history stand is at the very least dangerous because it reproduces, via the "expert," the version of the past upheld by Parmehutu ideology, according to which Tutsis have always been meant to enslave the Hutus, whether it be during the colonial era or now in 1994—the *Inyenzi* offensive of the RPF being the latest proof of this.[2] The Hutus always see themselves as a historically victimized group who only use violence in self-defense. This legitimization to resort to violence totally obliterates the fact that the tenants of Parmehutu had been in power for more than thirty years before the genocide perpetrated in 1994. In his analysis of the words aiming to exclude and of the narratives making the genocide thinkable and acceptable, Semujanga clearly suggests that this vision of the past feeds a rhetoric of hatred, which maintains racial divisions for political ends instead of rethinking this narrative legacy to counter its abusive effects:

> These narratives of hatred, founded on an opposition between "us/them," are also constructed on a resentment about a past that needs to be avenged, even if this past is more a construction of propaganda than a sociological fact. In this, the Parmehutu is a racism that differentiates the three social groups in Rwanda (Hutu, Tutsi and Twa) according to an essentialist categorization of individuals. In this case, being born Tutsi, Hutu, or Twa means being trapped in a social and morphological configuration petrified by assumptions and stereotypes. This racial ideology, based on negative or positive morphotypes, paved the way to genocide. ("Les mots du rejet" 28. Translation mine)

In basing its causal explanation on historical revenge, this (di)vision of history instills in the present a potentially harmful ambiguity. In effect, it makes it difficult to clearly designate the executioner and the victims, since the systematic massacre of the Tutsis during the 1994 genocide is, *of course*, only the historical response to a situation that has existed for several generations—as if nothing had changed in Rwandan power relations since the Hutu social revolution of 1959 and Rwanda's independence in 1962. In the end, giving credit to this ideology of resentment and the anachronistic causality it seeks to naturalize is virtually the same as letting those who planned and participated in the 1994 genocide off the hook. Thus, despite the fact that this informative dialogue, which sets up *Hotel Rwanda*'s plot, remains valuable to the film because it casts doubt on the relevance of inherited stereotypes, it reveals itself no less problematic for its underlying assumptions and silences that tend to legitimize the ideology of Hutu historical revenge at the hands of their former "masters." This causal understanding is all the more dangerous because it obliterates the fact that the racial distinctions between Tutsis and Hutus have always been promoted and manipulated by elites—whether these be Hutu, Tutsi, Catholic, or Belgian—to particular political ends. This scene's fault then is to speak of "revenge" without righting the causal paradigm that relativizes the genocide by inscribing it in the long term. The film would have had to pierce this scene with a vision of the past that deconstructs the discourse of "historical revenge" to put forth a less mechanical vision or to give precedence to "historical opportunism," which was used successively by various political elites to take power or justify their monopoly of it by all means.

This dialogue's other shortcoming rests in the fact that, in basing its reading grid on a long-term understanding of the victims and executioners, it reproduces and naturalizes one major pillar of genocide denial. In articulating a causality between the discourses of historical periods that were not successive—the colonial period and the four years from 1990 to 1994—the genocide of the Tutsis' deniers aim at legitimating the idea that we should not speak of genocide, since we are talking about revenge and self-defense: the oppressed Hutus attacking their former Tutsi masters, an emancipatory project which is, *of course,* socially legitimate and natural. The faulty character of this writing of history lies first in the fact that it obliterates three decades during which the Rwandan Tutsis and all those Hutus who were against the monopoly of power by various Hutu regional elites were anything but "masters." Second, this reading seeks to legitimize a causality that only exists in discourse and not in reality, knowingly obfuscating the historical specificity around the victims and genocide executors, since all Rwandans occupy both positions according to the instrument that eliminates the question of political choice and the evolution of historical possibilities. Third, since all heirs of Rwanda's history would, *of course,* be inclined to either seek vengeance or maintain their power in the name of ancestral hatred or self-defense, from which no one would know how to escape, the question of personal responsibility also gets covered up. If those who chose to participate in the genocide of the Tutsis are just "victims" of a causal logic of history defined as a succession of revenges, how can we establish a sense of individual responsibility and culpability? In the end, in making the positions of victim and murderer interchangeable, when over the course of a secular chronology Hutus and Tutsis keep killing each other, the very notion of genocide is relativized, and even denied, since we would at that point not be able to speak of genocide, or at least not of a singular genocide.

Although it is undeniable that *Hotel Rwanda* played a significant role in raising awareness in the West of the genocide of the Tutsis, the film's position remains far more complicated than this first informative dialogue would suggest, not in the least because of its representation of responsibility for the genocide and Paul Rusesabagina's relationships with a number of dignitaries and militaries who planned and were responsible for the genocide. Despite the director's desire to condemn Westerners' memory lapses, to show what happened on the margins of our national histories, and to depict the reality of the genocide so that it would haunt our conscience, in its own way, *Hotel Rwanda* offers a selective, incomplete, and even misleading version of history. Thus, it is important to examine the circumstances behind the facts that surround the making of our pedagogical dialogue with Paul Rusesabagina—the man—that Terry George screens for us in a film that tells the story of a hero—Paul the character—who is clearly, though not indisputably, identified as a reliable source of information.

Through interviewing a large number of people who took refuge at the Hôtel des Mille Collines, Alfred Ndahiro and Privat Rutazibwa's recent work *Hotel Rwanda or the Tutsi Genocide As Seen by Hollywood* systematically identifies the narcissistic and opportunistic distortions that emanate from the film's account of the genocide based on Rusesabagina's testimony. According to Ndahiro and Rutazibwa, Rusesabagina knew how to capitalize on his potential audience's guilty conscience and how to use Terry George and his producer's credulity to reinvent for himself a more glorious past, one that was compatible with Hollywood's narrative demands and values. As a case in point, I will comment briefly on one apparently minor falsification that, in fact, is a telling symptom of a major distortion in the film's representation of the genocide's genesis and execution.

The episode is that of the MINUAR convoy that failed to reach the airport to evacuate some of the people who found refuge at the Hôtel des Mille Collines. When the convoy of which Rusesabagina's family is part is stopped at a roadblock, the tone escalates rapidly between the UN soldiers escorting the convoy and the militiamen. The possibility that the refugees transported by the convoy will be massacred becomes more and more real as some are being beaten and pulled out of the vehicles. In the film, the convoy is escorted by Colonel Oliver and some white Western soldiers. The people guarding the roadblock are essentially depicted as being part of the *Interahamwe* or as ordinary citizens turned "volunteer executioners" to borrow Daniel Goldhagen's term.[3] When Rusesabagina finds out from the RTLM that his family's convoy has been stopped and is threatened, he immediately calls his friend General Bizimungu, who intervenes and saves the MINUAR convoy for a bribe. In the film, we therefore see the *Interahamwe* forces back down in the face of soldiers from the Rwandan Armed Forces, who come to support the MINUAR soldiers under the command of Colonel Oliver. In his autobiography, *An Ordinary Man*, Rusesabagina confirms this version of the story, but what really happened?

Amadou Deme, a Senegalese officer of the MINUAR who was part of the convoy's escort, offers a very different version of the events in his article "*Hotel Rwanda*: Setting the Record Straight" (2006). According to Deme, the first falsehood is related to the fact that the MINUAR contingent escorting the convoy was made up of Ghanaian and Tunisian soldiers who comported themselves very professionally. Second, the Rwandan army via General Bizimungu never played a role in this event. In fact, it was George Rutaganda, the second vice-president of the *Interahamwe* who, after a long and tense discussion with the forces holding the roadblock, managed to convince them to let the convoy through unharmed so it could return to the Hôtel des Mille Collines. Third, it was Deme himself, the MINUAR officer, who came up with the idea of going to get Rutaganda, who lived near the roadblock. Rutaganda was greeted with hostility at the barricade, because it was obvious to the murderers there that he was trying to save friends and thus preventing them from "working," that is to say killing their alleged common "enemies."

This scene is a good summary of Rusesabagina's form of opportunistic historical revisionism. He narcissistically gives himself credit for initiating the saving phone call to Bizimungu, even though this phone call never happened, and it was Deme who, at the roadblock, took the salutary initiative that saved his family. Moreover, the savior was not the "brave and corrupted" Bizimungu, but the "bloodthirsty and fanatic" Rutaganda, as the film depicts these two key figures. Finally, the soldiers who were protecting the refugees from the Mille Collines and Rusesabagina's family were Ghanaian and Tunisian—thus no white redemption in sight here. The question that arises from these inconsistencies is most glaringly: what is the motive behind this form of distorted rewriting of history? Does it go beyond the necessary simplifications of history for the needs of the script? Might it lead to some form of genocide denial?

If the first falsification—that of the initiative to contact a "savior"—is part of Rusesabagina's constant string-pulling mythomania and narcissism, the film's choice of savior in this scene is all the more disturbing. Why replace Rutaganda with Bizimungu—in the film and the autobiography? In its representation of those responsible for the genocide, *Hotel Rwanda* on several occasions creates a distinction between the role the presidential guard played, the role the Rwandan Armed Forces (RAF) played, and the role the *Interahamwe* and ordinary killers played. In *Hotel Rwanda*, the *Interahamwe* with Rutaganda at their head are depicted as primarily responsible for perpetrating the genocide. Rutaganda is depicted as an unscrupulous business man, bloodthirsty, fanatic, power-hungry, who goes so far as to suggest in the movie that Paul's "friends," Bizimungu and Bagosora, will be overthrown by the *Interahamwe*. In this sense, the militia is perceived as an uncontrollable force that commits most of the massacres while Paul's "friends" are implicated but to a far lesser degree because they are willing to save Tutsis and other potential victims. This representation of the *Interahamwe* as the principal planners and executors of the genocide is misleading to the extent that it obfuscates the political origins that tie the militia to Habyarimana's National Revolutionary Movement for Development (*Mouvement Révolutionnaire Nationale pour le Développement* MRND)—and consequently to the state's political power, whether it be under Habyarimana or his successors. Furthermore, it conceals the intimate collaboration between the army and the militia in planning the genocide—Bagosora, Bizimungu and Rutaganda, all together, having been among the primary planners.[4] This reversal of the facts tends to eclipse the roles of the army and of various other politicians in planning and executing the genocide. In this sense, this form of illegitimate historical revisionism dangerously flirts with genocide denial to the extent that the political and administrative genesis of the genocide is clouded, and its execution is falsely attributed to a minority of opportunistic and power-hungry Hutus belonging to the *Interahamwe*—a militia whose political connection with the Habyarimana's regime is silenced.[5]

Notes

1. The fact that the perpetrators of the genocide had to control the identity cards in order to verify their victims' appropriate status as Hutu-Tutsi-Twa is another proof that this racial vision and division between Hutus, Tutsis, and Twas does not follow physiological criteria. For more on this subject, see the excellent history lesson written by Jacques Delcuvellerie, director of *Rwanda 94* who plays himself the "historian" in the play.

2. The term *Inyenzi* means cockroach in Kinyarwanda. See, for example, Scholastique Mukasonga's testimony, *Inyenzi or the Cockroaches* (2006), which describes how this terminology was put in effect by the end of the 1950s and became culturally imposed to legitimize the "Hutu majority's" monopoly over power.

3. Regarding this issue of "ordinary citizens" becoming genocide perpetrators, see the second volume of Hatzfeld's trilogy, *Machete Season: The Killers in Rwanda Speak* (2005); Mukagasana dialogue with perpetrators in *Les blessures du silence. Témoignages du génocide au Rwanda* (2001); and the depositions and testimonies collected by Laure de Vulpain during the 2001 trial in Belgium of four Rwandans accused of crime of genocide, *Rwanda, un génocide oublié?* (2004). One section of her book, "Génocidaires ordinaires" (45–56), focuses on this issue of ordinary perpetrators.

4. See Des Forges, *Leave no One to Tell the Story: Genocide in Rwanda* (1999), chapters 5–7 entitled: "April 1994: 'The Month that Would not End'," "The Organization," and "Extending the Genocide." Rutaganda was sentenced to life in prison by the ITCR on May 26, 2003, and Bagosora was found guilty of genocide, crimes against humanity, and war crimes, and sentenced to life in prison by the ICTR on December 18, 2008. For additional information and current updates regarding the past and current trials of these planners of the genocide of the Tutsis consult the remarkable site of Trial Watch, <http://www.trial-ch.org/>, to follow more than 500 trials regarding human rights abuses cases, among them those of Cazimir Bizimungu, Pauline Nyiramasuhuko, Félicien Kabuga, or Wenceslas Munyeshyaka, which are still on trial or have only been indicted in 2009.

5. This reading of history also appears in another key scene, namely that in which the half-drunk and fanatic *Interahamwe* chase some Tutsis to the entrance of the Hôtel des Mille Collines, throwing a bloody helmet of a UN peacekeeper at Colonel Oliver's feet, scene suggesting that ten Belgian MINUAR soldiers have been assassinated by the *Interahamwe*. In fact, they were tortured and savagely killed by members of the presidential guard after the guard atrociously assassinated Prime Minister Agathe Uwilingiyimana in the morning on April 7. At the end of the film, the same scenario recurs when Bizimungu's soldiers directly intervene at the hotel to chase off the *Interahamwe* about to execute the Tutsis and Hutus who were on their lists. Finally, in the film's last scene, the *Interahamwe* are once again shown killing and pillaging everything in their path during their retreat, forcing an exodus of most of the Hutu population in the midst of the RPF's advance.

15

Historical and Contextual Trompe-l'œil

I F WE TURN NOW TO THE OTHER PEDAGOGICAL MOMENT that characterizes the
beginning of most of the films, what happens in *Hotel Rwanda*? The
film opens on a black screen with a voice-over of an audio extract from the
virulent RTLM, bypassing a "historical summary" in favor of reproducing an
archive that exemplifies Hutupower's extreme violence and the climate of racial hatred against the Tutsis that Hutu propaganda instilled in the Rwandan
population:

> When people ask me, good listeners, why I hate all the Tutsis, I say, read our
> history: the Tutsis were collaborators for the Belgian colonists. They stole our
> Hutu land, they wiped us. Now they have come back, these Tutsi rebels; they are
> cockroaches, they are murderers. Rwanda is our Hutu land. We are the majority.
> They are a minority of invaders and traitors. We will squash their infestation.
> We will wipe out the RPF rebels. This is RTLM, Hutu power radio. Stay alert!
> Watch your neighbors.

Because this extract is the first reading of Rwandan history the film offers—
and no other discourse is introduced to counterbalance or relativize RTLM's
genocidal ideology and its reading grid—this introduction to the subject opens
certain interpretive drifts to criticism. The opening offers a vision of Rwandan
history that revolves entirely around the ancestral (di)vision between Hutus
and Tutsis—as if no other forms of sociability had existed or were possible.
In this sense, *Hotel Rwanda* does not give itself, nor its viewers, the means to
screen the ethnicist reading grid of the past and risks of reproducing in the
end a (di)vision of history on which present discourses denying the genocide

thrive. Thus, *Hotel Rwanda*'s screening does not necessarily screen the ideology it pretends to denounce, or more bluntly: screening—*porter à l'écran*—is
not necessarily synonymous with screening out—*faire écran*. Though this introduction to the historic subject matter is shocking in its rhetorical violence
and ability to grasp the viewers' attention, it does not explicitly question a
number of the points at the heart of Parmehutu ideology: first, the fact that
Hutus were the native and original people of Rwanda; second, that Hutus
would then have the right to eliminate the invading Tutsis in the name of
self-defense; third, that Hutus are the "majority" which is a democratic decep-
tion since this "majority," is defined racially and demographically and not by
popular vote; finally, that the RPF forces are rebels, nostalgic for the colonial
era, invaders who could be eradicated the way one eradicates an invasion of
cockroaches without lending the least bit of credibility to their actions. If *Hotel
Rwanda*'s opening is problematic in more ways than one, it is because it reproduces an ideological propaganda without offering a discursive or contextual
counterpoint that would allow viewers to inhabit a critical distance and not
be limited to indignation in the face of the RTLM's violently heinous propaganda.

Once again, George's script stops short, much as is the case in the dialogue
between the BBC cameraman and Benedict, which seeks to clarify the difference between Tutsis and Hutus—this second history lesson failing to fully
deconstruct the RTLM's discursive categories and logic that open the film.
By omitting an explicit critique of these social categories that support the
existence of a Hutu nation, a majority population, historic resentment, and
the logic of revenge that these notions naturalize, *Hotel Rwanda* lends itself to
more than one recuperation by deniers, even though paradoxically it grants
the genocide of the Tutsis unprecedented visibility in the West, offers a history lesson that exposes the violence of the genocidal ideology, and questions
the political use of the racist Rwandan social classification system. As Louis
Bagilisha suggests in "Discourses of Negation, Denial and Politics," one form
of denial exemplified in *Hotel Rwanda*'s two history lessons is that, despite
recognizing that a genocide occurred, the script is unable to screen out certain
perverse categories of representation. Therefore it reproduces the discursive
logic that the tenets of different deniers' discourses depend upon in their attempt to relativize the causes of the genocide and confound the attribution
of responsibility:

> To make genocide relative by explaining it through an atavism of social violence
> and ethnic wars denies its radical singularity. A singularity which does not ap-
> pear in the "comparative approach" of deaths and suffering, but that does reside
> in its status as a political project of the State. A State project that has an ideologi-
> cal and historical genealogy and pursues the intention to exterminate a human

group fixed in an "identity" defined by the genocide's executioners. (740–741. Translation mine)

As highlighted before, the relative failure of *Hotel Rwanda* to demonstrate without any doubt that the genocide is the result of a "political project of the State" resides in the fact that the principal responsibility of the killings is attributed to the *Interahamwe* whose collusion with Habyarimana's party is silenced, leaving the door open to many innocent officials, not to mention the risk of dissolving the "radical singularity" to which Bagilisha points. In this regard, as we will see later, *100 Days* or *Sometimes in April* are salutary counter-examples.

What about the history lessons that begin most of the other films, then? Do they allow us to think of the genocide as a "political project of the State"? Do they offer up a minimal knowledge from which we cannot only interpret and evaluate characters' choices and actions, but also think about the genesis and execution of the political project at the foundation of the genocidal enterprise? To the extent that they do not interrupt the action and do not need to subscribe to the limitations of realist dialogue, do these historical introductions refuse to diminish genocide's political complexity to a series of fallacious causalities: interethnic war, atavistic racism, historical revenge of the oppressed, or even a majority's right to self-defense? In other words, do these summaries of history overturn the reductive dichotomies according to which there are only two possible positions, two irreconcilable and fixed social identities to occupy in Rwandan society?

Of the seven films, *Hotel Rwanda* is the only one that, in using the RTLM extract to introduce Rwanda's history, avoids a preliminary historical summary whose message is clearly assumed by the script and not delegated to a legitimate narrator or historical character within the diegesis. For my purposes here, I will discuss three of the six existing historical summaries. Many of them invoke the same events, appeal to similar historical lenses or rest on identical rationales in terms of their pedagogical aims and their interactions.

Favreau's film *A Sunday in Kigali* opens with a highly condensed synthesis—the description of the genocide and its origins get four lines: "On April 6, 1994, the Rwandan president Habyarimana Juvénal's plane is shot down by two missiles. The president's guard and its militias take action. This is the beginning of the genocide. Three months later, the Rwandan Patriotic Front's (RPF) victory ends the killing. Most of the 800,000 victims were ethnic Tutsis" (Translation mine). In starting with Habyarimana's assassination and making it the triggering event of the genocide, this summary espouses a communally accepted script used by many narratives, films, and documentaries about the genocide. This version of the events is attractive in part because it offers a clear course of causality that reduces the genocide's origins to a unique event. This oversimplification of the cause of the genocide functions as a rhetorical trompe l'œil that renders Rwanda's past intelligible and eliminates its complexity as well as its historical contradictions. In reducing all the factors that made the genocide possible to a single cause, the summary boasts of a narrative self-sufficiency that eclipses the form of amnesia it simultaneously propagates instead of accounting for the history that preceded the president's assassination. In actuality, the assassination cannot in and of itself explain what set off the genocide—many presidents are assassinated without genocide ensuing.

The rhetorical power of Favreau's summary also rests in the binary opposition between the "presidential guard and its militias" and "the Rwandan Patriotic Front," as if there were no other forces present in 1994. History and Rwandan society are thus read according to a binary logic of exclusion. Another gap in this summary rests in the fact that it does not clearly state that the genocide was aimed directly at the Tutsis. The summary does recognize that "most of the 800,000 victims were ethnic Tutsis," but is that a demographic coincidence? A political misfortune? Finally, since there is no mention of other social identities, what of the Hutus and the Twas? How can viewers make sense of most of the victims' ethnic identity, since the "Tutsi" identity only has a meaning in a relational context?

A Sunday in Kigali's historical summary is, in this sense, a perfect example of a narrative whose pertinence rests on its internal coherence—which provides a clear and reductive causality coupled with a dualistic view of the dehistoricized power relations—rather than on its correspondence to the social reality it purports to explain. The value of summaries like this one rests in the illusion of intelligibility they provide viewers so that they feel themselves to be in familiar territory as they venture onto the ground of a Rwanda they otherwise know nothing about. Thanks to the performative power of these summaries, there is then, at least in theory, the promise in Rwanda of a communally shared rationality and morality, which is at least encouraging to viewers as they are about to realize that by definition, genocide destabilizes the very idea of shared humanity in its negation of a part of humanity.

In *100 Days*, the historical summary is superimposed on aerial images of Rwanda, whose soundtrack is a song by Cécile Kayirebwa, one of the most famous Rwandan singers who openly supports the RPF, celebrating their sacrifices and successes in songs like "Inkindi" (the name of a strong and proud fighter) or "Instinzi" (victory).[1] This script is original, because the historical summary does not come at the start of the film. Three abruptly juxtaposed dialogues precede it—dialogues the mayor of Kibuye has with a representative of the government, a Catholic priest, and the Hutu population in his community. Despite the absence of a description of a specific context for these dialogues—beyond the fact that they take place in Kibuye—this prelude unambiguously signals that the genocide is being planned with the Church's blessing. The police chief's words to the mayor leave no doubt about what is expected of the Hutus in Kibuye:

> Let me tell you the facts: All over Rwanda people are organized. Even here in your town [Kibuye], people are rising to this challenge. You must understand that the decision of this new government has made. You have been told, ordered, that the first enemy, before the rebels, is the Tutsi population. Do not wish some of them dead. We are going to kill them all. That is the most important. All. (*100 Days*)

The dialogue between the mayor and the priest underscores then, after the State's planning, the Church's complicity in supporting Parmehutu ideology and power, closing its eyes to the rest, taking refuge in a hypocritical neutrality rather than opposing the genocide. Taking up the question of war crimes, the priest offers the following assurance, that in cases of genocide, the Catholic Church remains "neutral," as it was—supposedly—during the Holocaust: "In the last war, the Germans committed many terrible crimes. Now, the Americans also committed terrible crimes. But we don't remember them because the Americans won." The priest's conclusion follows: "God does not take sides, does not pick a camp." The film's script continually denounces this hypocrisy. In the Rwandan context, claiming neutrality by remaining passive when the institution one represents is perceived as a source of authority and redemption is a form of active complicity in a country in which 90 percent of the population was practicing Christians in 1994—the highest percentage in all Africa.

100 Days denounces this active implication of the Catholic Church on two occasions. The first instance in which the church is implicated is in its resignation—not to say collusion—when, before the massacres start, the white priest leaves Kibuye with the representative of the genocidal government after the latter had informed the mayor of Kibuye of his "duties" and had finished planning the genocide in the region. These two figures of authority are symbolically reunited side by side in the French military convoy sent to evacuate Westerners and the Rwandan friends of the French government such as Habyarimana's wife and members of her family (Opération Amaryllis). Next, the church's implication in the genocide is shown through the episode where Father Kennedy, a young Hutu priest, suddenly becomes head of his parish after his white superior flees the country and abuses his new power. The young and opportunistic ecclesiastic then works in collaboration with the authorities to lure the Tutsis in his parish into the arms of the *Interahamwe*. He then abuses his newfound power to force a number of Tutsi women to

become his sexual slaves in exchange for his protection.[2] Through the historical parallel of the Catholic priest and his theory of repentance, Hughes's script
does not merely denounce the Church's hypocrisy; it suggests an ideological
complicity between the Church's discourses and genocide of the Tutsis deniers
who advocate the notions of double genocide and self-defense. In declaring
that historical truth is always written by the winners, who erase all traces of
their crimes, the priest relativizes—not to say, he completely denies—the
Holocaust's specificity since it is shown as one war crime among others.
The priest thus implicitly invites the mayor to see the planned genocide of
the Tutsis as a war crime—and not a crime of the State—which is to say as
a legitimate, equal counterpoint to the Hutu deaths at the hands of the RPF
during wartime between 1990 and 1994.

The second dialogue between the mayor and the priest introduces the second major rhetoric of denial after the theory of double genocide or mirrored
killings, namely the notion of self-defense. In this context, the systematic
massacre of the Tutsis is indeed a sin, but because it is also an act of collective
self-defense, it is a sin that can be tolerated so long as the sinner is prepared
to confess and ask forgiveness for his crimes: "Killing is wrong. But you are
entitled to defend yourself. The teaching of the Catholic Church is quite clear
on this point. God forgives us our sins provided we confess, we repent, and
we seek forgiveness." The Catholic priest's words thus wipe away the mayor's
final scruples that were keeping him from following the government's orders.

This opening of *100 Days* unambiguously shows that the Church failed in
its mission, not only through its collusion with the Parmehutu ideology of
genocide, but also in encouraging and preferring the impunity that benefited
anti-Tutsi propaganda from the 1950s onward.[3] The priest, thus, unabashedly
gives the mayor the ethical green light in assuring him that the extermination
of Tutsis in the context of the war against the RPF amounts to self-defense,
and thus is a forgivable sin. What follows is the scene in which the mayor delivers his speech exhorting the Hutu population to "get to work," eloquently
concluding the film's preamble, which underscores the fact that a genocide
is, before all else, a State affair whose execution requires the backing and participation of a society's principal institutions. In addressing the Hutus of his
town to encourage them to wipe the country "clean" of the Tutsis, the mayor
of Kibuye is depicted on-screen, framed symbolically and symptomatically,
on his left by the army, and on his right by Father Kennedy, the young Catholic priest who embodies the vilest opportunism. As one of the key sentences
of his speech suggests, the population has nothing to worry about because the
decision to exterminate the Tutsis was made for them, as testifies the legitimating presence of the representatives of all forms of institutionalized power:

The rebels are destroying our country, but we know who supports them. Their supporters are among us. Waiting. Waiting to be your masters again. The Tutsis came here. They refused to live with us, to marry us or to share power with us. There is only one solution. They must go! So that they can never come back. You are going to clean the land for your children. You must not be frightened, the decision has been made for you. You only have to do it once. But it has to be done once and for all and it will be forgotten. Get rid of the women and their baby rats. Don't leave any rats for the future. The time for work is now. What we have been waiting for is happening. Hutu Power! Hutu Power! (*100 Days*)

Thus, before even offering a historical summary, *100 Days* starts by affirming that the genocide is primarily a State project and not a byproduct of an ethnic war. This state project is made possible not only by racist ideology, the elite's desire to maintain its monopoly over power, a social imaginary dominated by a radical logic of mutual exclusion, but also by the participation of these three pillars of institutionalized power: the State, the Army, and the Church— without whom, the majority of the population would neither consider legitimate the decision to exterminate a specific part of the population, nor would find it possible to perpetrate mass murder in the utmost impunity at the heart of a society. The preamble of *100 Days* thus has two major pedagogical benefits. First, it calls the audience's attention to the behind-the-scenes institutional work that went into planning the genocide of the Tutsis and to the fact that its planning required a coordinated indoctrination and supervision of the population. Second, it also deconstructs the causal perception that summaries like the one in *A Sunday in Kigali* reproduce—summaries that depict the genocide of the Tutsis as a spontaneous or nationalist killing spree after President Habyarimana's assassination on April 6, 1994.

The historical summary that then follows, superimposed upon the aerial views that celebrate the beauty of the country of the thousand hills with Cécile Kayirebwa's voice singing "Indamukanyo," a melody that welcomes young and old,[4] is, however, highly problematic. Its abusive generalizations undermines the pedagogical accuracy of the film's beginning, which eloquently underscores the political and institutional genesis of the genocide.

Bound by volcanoes and lakes, Rwanda is so small, it is lost between the plains of East Africa and the Congo jungle. The land keeps two tribes, the Hutus and the Tutsis. Years ago, the Tutsis ruled Rwanda, but the Hutus overthrew their master. For thirty years, the Hutu elite disguised their wealth and the people's poverty by teaching that the Tutsis were the cause of all Rwanda's troubles. Then Tutsi rebels invaded and waged war: the Hutu rulers plotted genocide. (*100 Days*)

This caricaturesque history lesson undermines the reading grid offered up by the three dialogues that precede this reading of the past and its vision of Rwandan society. First, talking of a "lost country" reproduces an exotic vision of Africa and all its ensuing stereotypes inherited from the colonial-era explorers adventuring themselves into the "Heart of Darkness"—Joseph Conrad's legacy still vividly impregnating our imaginary. If Rwanda really is such a "small" and "lost" country, why would France have bothered militarily supporting its regime? Second, to talk of "tribes" in defining the Hutus and the Tutsis is ethnological nonsense, because the Hutus, Tutsis, and Twas—the third so-called "tribe" that the summary leaves out—lived together sharing the same language, religion, and culture in the pre-colonial era amid different clans that were all part of the same kingdom.[5] In the case of Rwanda, we therefore cannot speak of separate tribes defined by different genealogies or royal filiations as is the case in bordering countries like the Democratic Republic of the Congo.

Third, this summary, like many others, draws no distinctions between these two "tribes," as if all Tutsis had been masters and all Hutus, slaves or serfs during the colonial era, before this relationship of domination was reversed in the 1960s. Hughes' summary also strangely does not even mention the Belgian colonial era, which profoundly altered the Rwandan social imaginary, its political climate, and its administration of power—not to mention the essentialization of ethnicist modes of positioning. Finally, in presenting the 1990 RPF attack as the event that triggered the genocide of the Tutsis, this summary dangerously slips toward relativizing the genocide by making it a military "response" to the RPF attack. Following this causal logic, certain deniers would not fail, perversely, to suggest that the RPF bears primary responsibility for the genocide in advancing the following argument: "if the RPF had not attacked Habyarimana's government in 1990, there would not have been a genocide in 1994." In his conclusions of the investigation of the attack on Habyarimana's plane on April 6, 1994, the French judge Jean-Louis Bruguière defended and promoted this same reasoning, accusing Paul Kagame of being responsible for Habyarimana's death and, consequently, for the genocide of the Tutsis. This inversion of the victims and executioners is inherent to genocidal ideology and its denial leanings based on the notion of self-defense. For genocide deniers, one of the foundational twists of their rhetoric consists in always depicting the real target of genocide—here the Tutsis—as the perpetrators, the masters, the aggressors, or the invaders. Because it does not critically deconstruct the categories and logic that undergird its interpretation of the past, Hughes's historical summary is, in fact, an emblematic example of a discourse offering up a history lesson that slants its goals and lends power to interpretations that play with different forms of denial actually opposed by the film.

Among the historical summaries of the films produced so far, the one that begins *Sometimes in April* is unquestionably the most detailed and thought-out—keeping in mind that these summaries obey various constraints of genre, length, production, reception, need to capture attention, and so on. Through its nuanced historical lenses, its precise information, and visual screening, this summary not only depicts the political nature of the genocide, but also locates it in a complex historical and political context, refusing to reduce the genocide's genesis to a causality of revenge, a triggering event, or secular interethnic hatred. In *Sometimes in April*, the historical summary proceeds from the bottom to the top of the screen in short paragraphs, whose background is a chronological succession of maps of Africa—the first map dating from the beginning of the colonial era, subtly replaced by maps of the next centuries. The spatial readability introduced by the use of cartography is, therefore, not fixed in time, and highlights the fact that Africa's very readability evolves over centuries, and that Rwanda's actual borders were not always what they are today and are the result of a long history. The zoom-in that progressively narrows viewers' field of vision not only turns the map of the African continent into a map of Rwanda in order to situate the country; it also indicates the transformation and cutting up of pre-colonial kingdoms into countries defined by borders fixed at the 1884–1885 Berlin Conference. Through this montage that enlivens and historicizes the evolution of kingdoms and borders, Peck creates a spatial and temporal frame that allows viewers to imagine the genesis of the genocide of the Tutsis in light of the region's colonial heritage and the evolution of power relations in Rwandan society—the planning and execution of the genocide representing from then on the most extreme and pathological actualization of Rwandan power relations. The opening summary goes as follows:

> For centuries, the Hutus, Tutsis, and Twas of Rwanda shared the same culture, language and religion. In 1916, Belgium took control of Rwanda from Germany and installed a rigid colonial system of racial classification and exploitation. By elevating the Tutsis over the Hutus, they created deep resentment among the Hutu majority. In 1959, the Belgians handed control of Rwanda to the Hutu majority. With independence came decades of institutionalized anti-Tutsi segregation and massacre. Hundreds of thousands of Tutsis and moderate Hutus were forced into exile.
>
> In 1988, some of these refugees formed a rebel movement called the Rwandan Patriotic Front (RPF) to reclaim their homeland. In 1990, from their base in Uganda, the RPF launched an offensive against the Hutu regime that was stopped with French and Belgian military support. A deadly cycle of war and massacre continued until 1993, when the United Nations negotiated a power-sharing agreement between the two sides. To protect their power, hard-line

Hutu extremists resisted the implementation of the agreements and planned one
of the most terrifying genocides in history. (*Sometimes in April*)

Because it is always possible to criticize a summary for its brevity and its
choices, since summaries must by definition hyper-selectively order facts and
events, it is most important to examine the historical lenses the summary uses
in selecting what is worthy of memory. These lenses simultaneously create
depth in terms of temporality, social categories, and the discursive logic that
supports the past's readability and its uses in the present. In this capacity,
Peck's summary is exemplary. First, it is the only one that mentions the existence of three social groups—Hutu, Tutsi, and Twa—during the pre-colonial
period, and does it by intoning that they did not constitute distinct ethnicities
or tribes since they belonged to the same culture, shared the same language,
and believed in the same god *Imana*. Second, it highlights the Belgian colonial era's defining role in transforming Rwanda's social categories into ethnic
categories. This rupture of the legitimate markers through which Rwandan
society thinks about the political sphere and defines the distribution of power
is radical in the sense that it created a shift from a socio-economic and clan-
based (di)vision of society to an essentialist and racial (di)vision of society.
Extolling the "racial superiority" of the Tutsis through the 1950s, the Belgian
administration instituted an irrevocable logic of discrimination in Rwandan
society, since the possibility of social recognition and political legitimacy will
forever now depend upon "race." Third, the fact that this summary mentions
the Belgians' paradigm shift and the reversal of their allegiance during the
independence era calls viewers' attention to the opportunist nature and the
ideological uses of these "racial" categories. In the face of Tutsi aspirations for
independence, the Belgians suddenly decided to democratically support the
"Hutu majority" leaving their previously favored Tutsi elite empty-handed:
the discrimination against the Hutus up until then legitimized in the name of
a supposed *ontological superiority* of the Tutsi gives way to this other form of
institutionalized racism, namely that of the Hutu *demographic majority*.

At this point in his summary, Peck should have more explicitly denounced
the concept of a "majority" to the extent that it rests on an essentialist and
racist view of Rwandan society and is in no way the result of a democratic
process—much in keeping with the reasoning behind the supposed innate
Tutsi superiority. Fourth, the history lesson we are offered is the only one,
along with Tasma's summary in *Opération Turquoise*, that provides some
insight on the formation of the RPF in establishing a relationship with the
exiles of the 1960s—an army that, in the other summaries, seems to emerge
out of nowhere. Peck and Tasma are also among the very few who do not immediately qualify the RPF as "rebels"—a de-legitimizing epithet that assumes

Habyarimana's government's point of view—and who mention the French military role during the RPF's advance in 1990.

Finally, *Sometimes in April*'s summary avoids the trap of gross generalizations by refusing the logic of a dualistic opposition between two homogeneous and unified groups, the Tutsis and the Hutus. Peck's summary clearly indicates that, if the genocide's genesis is inscribed in a history that reaches back to the colonial era and an international geopolitical context, it is above all because of a political elite consisting of extremist Hutus doggedly opposed to sharing power, as stipulated by the Arusha accords signed in 1993. This point is key, because it tells the viewers outright that the genocide's origins hearken back to political and State affairs, and not to a racial or ethnic conflict, or even a historical causality grounded in the revenge paradigm. In making politics and power hunger the paradigm for thinking about the genocide's inception, Peck's summary subordinates its reading of the past to the succession of struggles and events in which the control of power was at stake—struggles that, over the course of different regimes, fashioned the legitimate categories of authority and politics in the Rwandan imaginary. In this sense, the summary effectively communicates the idea that the genocide was not spontaneous, nor was it triggered by Habyarimana's assassination, or a historical revenge or action of self-defense, but it is a State project motivated by a thirst for power that requires premeditated and minutely planned courses of action. In the "Making of" comments, Peck is quick to underline that "genocide doesn't happen like the first day of the first atrocities. There is a sort of mechanism which is put in place years before." This vision leads Peck's script to follow the historical summary with a montage of excerpts on the colonial era starting with the 1959 film *Imana's Sons* and archival images steeped in the Belgian colonial newsreels. The excerpt from *Imana's Sons* primarily highlights the misunderstanding at the heart of the first encounter between the colonizers and Rwandans: the official archival segments display the pitfalls of the *mission civilisatrice* by showing images of anthropologists measuring the Rwandans in order to classify them according to their morphological (di)visions, or the Belgian king Beaudouin visiting Rwanda to make sure that his colonies were being well handled. These images render any form of nostalgia for the colonial enterprise impossible, showing them not as a civilizing mission, but as an enterprise motivated by "arrogance, avidity, and power." Thus, far from having created civility between Rwandans or having brought them civilization—as if Rwandans were deprived of it before the colonial period—the Belgian administration's heritage was a racial and essentialist (di)vision that made different Rwandan elites into pawns and later played a key role in the possibility of thinking about, legitimizing, planning, and, finally, executing the genocide of the Tutsis in 1994.

After pedagogical moments identified as *informative dialogues* and *historical summaries*, what about the *epilogues*? What fantasy of closure do they betray? Is their function to repeat the story screened by History with a capital "H"? Is it to offer a follow-up on the main or historical characters beyond the temporal frame covered by the script? To maintain this traumatic past's actuality by inscribing it in the audience's present? To communicate legal information since genocidal crimes are imprescriptible? Or is it to promote reflections on morality or an injunction that equates a duty to remember with a duty to denounce?

Let us begin this time with *Sometimes in April*'s epilogue: "By day 100 of the genocide, close to one million people had been killed. 82 people have been charged by the International Tribunal for Rwanda. To date, 20 have been convicted and sentenced to prison terms. Of those who watched the genocide unfold, and did nothing to stop it, no one has been charged. . . . Never Forget." This historical assessment concludes the succession of death estimates that pop up throughout the film to highlight the extent and speed of the massacres—"Day 1: 8,000 people killed," "Day 65: 620,000," and "Day 77: 716,000 people killed." Peck's epilogue estimates the final number of lives claimed by the genocide. If he does not mention at this point in the film that most of the victims were Tutsis, it is because there is not much room for doubt about the identity of the vast majority of the victims. The second part of the epilogue echoes the theme of demand for justice, one of the major points throughout the film, because on a number of occasions, Peck's script positions the audience as members of the jury judging one of the film's main characters, Honoré, a Hutu intellectual tried by the ICTR in Arusha for his anti-Tutsi speeches and calls to murder on the RTLM radio waves. In returning to this quest for justice and its meager balance sheet in 2004, Peck suggests that the question of responsibility for the genocide remains wide open, since only a small fraction of the genocide's planners and participants were arrested, tried, and sentenced. The end of the epilogue reengages the theme introduced in the Martin Luther King quote at the film's start, namely, what happens to those who remained silent during the genocide's course. If some, like Bill Clinton, came to apologize, no one was accused of crimes against humanity for his/her passivity, cowardice, or egoism, which makes all of those who remained silent guilty to the extent that their resignation was an inherent part of what made the genocide possible. The concluding sentence of Peck's epilogue—"Never Forget"—comes at the end of the film credits and represents both a duty to remember and an ethic injunction by resounding in the audience's minds "never forget" as the necessary premises of "never again." *Sometimes in April*'s final lesson thus is not limited to a retrospective evaluation that is only about the past; rather it also seeks to call the audience's conscience—and even their culpability—to task so that these million deaths do not become a lesson lost on the living.

Shooting Dogs' epilogue does also offer an explicit moral lesson during the final scene when Marie, one of the rare ETO survivors, reunites with Joe in England five years after the genocide. After Joe admits to his cowardice—because he left Marie when the Belgian soldiers left the ETO on April 11, too afraid to die despite his promise to stick with her—Marie reminds him of their responsibility as survivors and witnesses: "We are fortunate. All this time we have been given. We must use it well." This injunction is also directed at the audience, since Joe's rhetorical function is to be a Western mirror so that we can grasp our own resignation. Caton-Jones's short epilogue mentions the genocide's death toll, but it also gives the death toll of the ETO massacre that occurred right after the Belgian forces left the school that had become a refuge for those chased by the *Interahamwe* surrounding the compound. In this way, the assessment returns to information mentioned in the film but that the script does not explicitly show: "On April 11, 1994, over 2500 Rwandans abandoned by the UN at the ETO were murdered by extremist militias. Between April and July of that year, over 800,000 Rwandans were killed in the genocide." The categories used here to designate the executioners and the victims do highlight the political dimensions of the genocide in making the extremist militias responsible for the massacre, but the assessment neither makes explicit the militias' affiliation with Hutu extremist political parties like the MRND and the CDR, nor does it account for the army's role in the ETO massacre. As the lengthy title Linda Melvern uses in one of her articles where she criticizes Caton-Jones's film makes clear, *Shooting Dogs* is far from explicitly stating what happened: "History? This film is fiction. A new BBC film telling the 'truth' of events in Rwanda only compounds the original sins of the West's media" (2006). Here is the central argument used by Melvern in her critique that started a second main controversy around Caton-Jones's film in the British press:

> The depiction of the massacre at ETO upon which *Shooting Dogs* is based is misleading. It was not a screaming and rampaging mob of machete-wielding youths who killed those sheltering at the school. It was far more chilling. After the Belgians withdrew, the 2,000 people were herded on a death march, an operation coordinated by senior officers of the Rwandan military, soldiers trained at European military academies. Among them were the conspirators of the genocide, officers who, for three years, had been plotting the slaughter. . . . The victims of the ETO massacre were killed in a gravel pit by the Presidential Guard, who sealed the exits, allowing the militia to use their machetes in order to save on ammunition. ("History? This film is fiction")

In addition to this inaccuracy, the historical lenses of *Shooting Dogs'* epilogue fail to accurately represent the (di)vision that radically polarizes the Tutsis and the Hutus, since the executioners are extremists and the victims Rwandans. This representation introduces another misconception, since we could then rightfully simply talk—as it is too often the case—about a genocide of Rwandans or a Rwandan genocide. In this way, the epilogue here obliterates the genocide's specificity, since the Tutsis alone were systematically killed for who they were and not for their actions or their political opposition to Habyarimana's regime and Hutu power ideology. Once again, brevity is not the best recipe for screening interpretive drifts and unwanted re-appropriations.

Right after the final assessment in *Shooting Dogs*, a dedication honors the victims and survivors of the ETO, a way in which Caton-Jones can show that his film is participating in the duty to remember by conferring to certain episodes of the genocide, for which there is barely any filmic documentation, a cinematic and cultural visibility: "This film could not have been made without the participation and generosity of the survivors of the massacre at the ETO. The film is dedicated to them and to all who lost their lives in the genocide." In bringing image and text together, *Shooting Dogs* concludes on a series of portraits paying tribute to the survivors of the ETO who participated in the making of the film and consented to "reliving" this traumatic past, despite the suffering that comes with reliving their role in the events. It is, perhaps, at this moment that Caton-Jones's film most effectively and loyally actualizes his desire to depict a story based on real facts and events filmed on the very location in which they took place. At the same time, as Rothberg has shown in his critique of the sequences showing those who were saved by Oskar Schindler at the end of Spielberg's film—sequence filmed in color and identified as "The Schindler Jews today"—the very fact that these survivors are shown without being given the ability to tell their story is highly problematic and seems more justified by a rhetorical impulse to assert the film's fidelity to the depicted reality: "The porousness of the boundaries between narrative and history within the film may be intended to enhance the confusion between the film as a whole and the history that is its referent, but instead it reduces the survivors to nonspeaking extras in their own lives" (*Traumatic Realism* 241).

The longest epilogue is in the only film that does not give a historical summary in the beginning, namely *Hotel Rwanda*. Here, the epilogue's length is due to that fact that it contains biographical, legal, and historical information:

Paul Rusesabagina sheltered 1268 Tutsis and Hutus refugees at the Mille Collines Hotel in Kigali. Paul and Tatiana now live in Belgium with their children Roger, Diane, Lys, Tresor and their adopted nieces Anaïs and Carine. Tatiana's brother, Thomas and his wife Fedens were never found.

In 2002, General Augustin Bizimungu was captured in Angola and transported to the UN War Crime Tribunal in Tanzania. At the same tribunal, the *Interahamwe* leader Georges Rutaganda was sentenced to life in prison.

The genocide ended in July 1994, when the Tutsi rebels drove the Hutu army and the *Interahamwe* militia across the border into the Congo. They left behind almost a million corpses. (*Hotel Rwanda*)

Terry George's epilogue has three distinct parts. The first is a sort of biographical recap that tells viewers what happened to a number of the characters in the film. This section stems from the fact that the film focuses on one specific episode in Paul Rusesabagina's life—from the eve of the genocide to the moment when he and his family are evacuated to the zone controlled by the RPF during a prisoner trade-off organized by Colonel Oliver (alias Roméo Dallaire). This biographical recap also feeds the "reality" effect, which gives the film legitimacy and emotional power, since the simple mention that a character's life continues beyond the movie's context asserts in the audience's mind that there is no difference between the character in the film and the real Paul Rusesabagina. Here again, the epilogue reaffirms "the porousness of the boundaries between narrative and history" with all the rhetorical power gained by a film when "based on a true story"—autobiographical grounding that many posters of *Hotel Rwanda* or DVD covers do not fail to mention explicitly.

The epilogue's second part conveys the fate of the two figures who were portrayed in the film as having been the genocide's primary planners, namely General Bizimungu and the head of the *Interahamwe*, Rutaganda. If we rely solely on the information given in *Hotel Rwanda*—here and elsewhere—which does not include, as is the case with *Sometimes in April*, any information on the judicial gaps of the ICTR's achievements in 2004, we might imagine that all guilty parties were apprehended and the worst of them sentenced. In this sense, *Hotel Rwanda* closes off judicial record in terms of the prosecution of those responsible for the genocide, failing to account that the fight for justice is far from over and that we—Western viewers—might have a role to play, as Peck's epilogue suggested. The third part of the epilogue looks back to the end of the genocide, since the film ends with Rusesabagina and his family's evacuation and not the end of the genocide. Following *Shooting Dogs*'s example in stating the number of deaths, here there is no specific mention of the fact that Tutsis accounted for the vast majority of the "million cadavers."

To conclude this section about the history lessons in the different films about the genocide of the Tutsis in Rwanda, I would like to return to Swedish writer Sven Lindqvist's quote that ends Tasma's film *Opération Turquoise* and serves in his film as epilogue. This quote comes right after the young French soldier has the ethical realization that "neutrality is disgusting. It is the

worst of lies"—a conclusion which the audience should also have reached by
that point, especially because we are meant to identify with this young man,
who, like us, is dropped in Rwanda and slowly realizes the deeply ambiguous
nature of the humanitarian mission in which he is participating. Thus, the
history lesson we are given is a moral lesson as well, because once again, it is
worth remembering that in the context of genocide, neutrality can only be a
fallacious option: "It is not the lack of information, which misleads us. What
we are lacking is the courage to understand what we know and to draw the
consequences thereof" (Sven Lindqvist. Translation mine). Consequently, the
different epilogues these films offer, with various degree of success, do not
invite us to *turn the page* away from this chapter of history. Instead, they dramatize the human consequences that ensue when we prefer to *turn our heads,*
hoping that it will all be over soon. . . . Unfortunately, this does not happen,
and we must, then, *in return*, look at the political and ethical consequences
that this genocide, as an "interruption of history," imposes on our present
actions and beliefs.

Notes

1. The three Cécile Kayirebwa songs used in *100 Days* are called "Indamukanyo"
(Greetings), "Urubamby'ingwe" (Melody on Pastoral Life), and "Iribagiza" (Striking
Beauty). All are from her album *Amahoro*, which means "peace" in Kinyarwanda.
Opting for a symbolic approach that provokes empathy rather than a realist aesthetic,
Hughes also uses these songs as soundtracks for massacre scenes. Kayirebwa's voice
and music give the victims of those killings a melodious and nostalgic voice rather
than reducing them to cries of suffering and agony.
2. Father Kennedy's character is largely inspired by Father Wenceslas Munyeshyaka's criminal actions during the genocide when he was at the Sainte Famille Church
in Kigali. Despite the fact that he was accused of genocidal crimes by the ITCR, he
found refuge in France in November 1994, and has lived there since, continuing his
church duties with the blessing of the French government and the Catholic Church.
This character also appears in Peck's *Sometimes in April* and is at the heart of Sehene's
novel, *Le feu sous la soutane: Un prêtre au cœur du génocide rwandais* (2005). For more
on this, also see African Rights' report 9, "Father Wenceslas Munyeshyaka: In the Eyes
of the Survivors of Sainte Famille" (1999).
3. For more information on the Catholic Church's role in the genocide and its
relationship with genocide denial, see Jean Damascène Bizimana's work, especially,
L'Église et le génocide au Rwanda: Les Pères Blancs et le négationnisme (2007), and "The
Catholic Church and the Tutsi Genocide: From Ideology to Negation" (2008). See
also Carol Rittner, John K. Roth and Wendy Whitworth eds., *Genocide in Rwanda:
Complicity of the Churches?* (2004)

4. Thanks to Gilbert Ndahayo for having taken the time to translate this song's lyrics for me. The melody is full of nostalgia, as the section Hughes uses shows: "I came to say hello/ Because I miss you/ I came to greet you, the youth/ I came to greet you, the elder/ My voice sounding high/ Up to the garden sky of Rwanda/ I came to greet you/ With the chorus of this song . . .".

5. See Servilien Sebasoni, *Les origines du Rwanda* (2000) and in Catharine Newbury, *The Cohesion of Oppression* (1988), her chapter, "Statebuilding in Precolonial and Colonial Rwanda" (21–70).

16

Ob-Scene Off-Screened:
A Genocide Off-Camera

THE POTENTIAL OF FICTIONAL FILMS to create an unprecedented visibility and memorial conscience for a genocide that long remained off-screen culturally and in the Western media is all the more important because very few images were filmed during the main phases of the genocide. Nearly all the Western journalists left Rwanda very quickly, evacuated by French forces in Operation "Amaryllis" from April 9 through the 14 or during the retreat of most of the UN Belgian troupes.[1] The quasi absence of media coverage this retreat caused allowed the genocidal regime to operate in broad daylight, without worrying about being caught on camera. It also contributed to a growing sentiment of total impunity in the Hutu population, which was encouraged to participate broadly in the killing. A look at the most significant documentaries on the genocide turns up ten or so filmed sequences that recur showing piles of bodies along the side of the road or by roadblocks—images taken at the beginning of the genocide—or hundreds of cadavers piled up and decomposing in churches, stadiums, or hospitals, if not floating in rivers—images taking toward the end of the genocide or in the areas captured by the RPF.[2]

According to *100 Days* director Nick Hughes, the filmed sequences that show direct killing number no more than three. In Rwanda as a BBC cameraman in April 1994, he filmed one of them. Filmed from the roof of the French School in Kigali, this sequence shows two Tutsi women being killed with machetes and displays the murderers' nonchalance and comfort with their actions. This clip is unique and documents a violence unheard of despite the distance between the camera and the events, and it was used in the opening of the documentary *"Kill them All!" Rwanda: the Story of an "Unimport-ant" Genocide* as well as in Groupov's play *Rwanda 94* in which a journalist interrogates—through the screening of these rare images—the symbolic representation of the genocide and its reception.[3] Hughes's sequence is also referenced in *Hotel Rwanda* when cameraman Jack Dalgish decides to leave the hotel to film the killings in Kigali and he comes back with similar footage to Hughes's. The quasi absence of images documenting the massacres during the first weeks of the genocide—and the impossibility of really investigating the people caught in that rushed footage—means that the victims remain anonymous, grim representatives of a history their bodies are not necessarily able to tell.[4] It is only in 2007 that Hughes went back to Rwanda to enquire about the identity of the victims whose death he captured on film, the fate of their relatives, and about the identity of the perpetrators. Juan Reina and Eric Kabera filmed this powerful journey through which Hughes aims to personalize the anonymous victims he filmed from a distance by immerging himself in the intimacy of their stories and families in order to conjure these ghostly presences who have haunted him since 1994. Hughes co-produced their documentary entitled *Iseta: Behind the Roadblock* (2008), a remarkable film advertised as "A documentary on the only Tutsi genocide footage" that portrays the core tensions and silences defining the Rwandan society fifteen years after the genocide and the challenges remaining in order to achieve re-unification and reconciliation among all Rwandans.

The fact that there are no images of the perpetration of the killings, if we except Hughes's footage, is paradoxically seen by some survivors as a chance. As Innocent Rwililiza underlines in Hatzfeld's account of the reconciliation process in Nyamata after 2003, the existence of such images would be a re-current source of shame tarnishing the memory of the dead and humiliating those who survived:

One almost never see pictures taken during the killings . . . This is most for-tunate, because images of the killings under way—I could not bear that. . . . It would be degrading. And a photo of little gatherings of supplicants beneath the papyrus, of hacked-up people crawling to moisten their lips in marsh water, or even famished old folks clawing the dirt for scraps of manioc? Pictures of our monkey life in Kayumba or their reptile life in the marshes would be inhuman. It would pile pain on the sufferings of the survivors suffering and be useless be-sides. Because those pictures would make nothing more explicit to people who did not experience the genocide, and would simply illustrate a dance of death. (Rwililiza quoted in Hatzfeld, *The Antelope's Strategy* 98–99)

Despite their power to shock public opinion, are then the few images depict-ing bodies along the roadside able to be more than just an illustration of the deadly trace left by a macabre "dance of death"? Are they able to indicate that the genocide of the Tutsis' final phase has begun? To foreign eyes, there is no visible distinction between the Tutsi bodies and those of the Hutus who opposed Habyarimana's regime and were also systematically executed during the early days so that no Hutu voices would speak against the killing of the Tutsis and prevent the massive participation of the general population. As the only BBC correspondent who stayed in Rwanda during the whole genocide and was, at times, the only foreign journalist in Kigali, Mark Doyle admits that the cadavers, in themselves, did not offer up the scope and political rationale behind the executions that were taking place:

> I have to admit that during the first few days, I, like others, got the story terribly wrong. Down to the ground, up-close—if you could get close enough, safely enough—it did look at first like chaos. I said so. I used the word chaos. What I could see clearly in the first few days was the shooting war between the Rwandan Patriotic Front (RPF) and the government, and the dead bodies. It was not clear who had killed whom, not at first. . . . In a way, the shooting war was easy to describe. The genocide war took a little longer to confirm. But I got there in the end . . . within little more than a week of the beginning of the killing on 6–7 April, there were clear references to government-backed massacres of ethnic Tutsis and Hutu opponents of the regime. In other words, within the first few weeks of the killing, there was reportage from the field sketching out the true nature of the massacres. (145)[5]

Moreover, as Tom Giles suggests in his article on the media's failure in Rwanda, the vast majority of Western correspondents in Africa were in South Africa in 1994 to cover the election of the first black president—an event far more attractive and less chaotic than the Arusha accords and the massacres that preceded and followed Habyarimana's assassination in Rwanda ("Media Failure" 236).

In *Hotel Rwanda*, the disillusioned Jack Dalgish and Paul Rusesabagina have a conversation about the power of images and media to alter the course of events they are covering—and the media and political invisibility to which the genocide of the Tutsis is confined:

> Paul: I am glad that you have shot this footage and that the world will see it. It is the only way we have a chance that people might intervene.
>
> Jack: If nobody intervenes, is it still OK to show?
>
> Paul: How can they not intervene when they witness such atrocities?
>
> Jack: If people see this footage, they'll say "Oh my God! This is horrible!" And then they go on eating their diners. (*Hotel Rwanda*)

Beyond their metonymic power, the urgency these images should communicate—since more often then not it was not hundreds, but thousands of people who were killed daily throughout the country—is likely to remain a dead letter in the absence of any explanation regarding the genesis of the filmed events. Even more troubling is that when a commentary or an investigation provides a precise context giving meaning to an image by restoring the off-screen view that made it possible, the same unreceptive end seems to prevail. As Edgar Roskis highlights in "A Genocide Without Images: Whites Film Blacks," even the rare journalists and photographers who stayed in Rwanda were only rarely able to convince editors to publish their reports and photos: "The photographers' brute and unembellished images and the simple testimonies left editors indifferent. Patrick Robert returned to Paris at the beginning of May, having sold barely a single photo. . . . It was only on May 18 that a photograph of the Rwandan atrocities made the first page of a French newspaper, *Le Quotidien de Paris.*"

Showing the "Rwandan atrocities" does not guarantee a readability and intelligibility of the political project to exterminate the Tutsis, since one can prevent people from seeing the social reality by depicting it through clichés that dress up the genocide's political project as a tribal, interethnic conflict. In this sense, although inscribing the massacres into the visual field is only one necessary condition to unframed forgetting, it is not enough to pull the genocide of the Tutsis out of its off-screened cultural and media status. Indeed, the power relations defining the context that made the genocidal violence thinkable and possible can, themselves, remain off-screened, as Jean-Paul Gouteux suggests in his critique of the French press:

> In regards to Africa, there is a journalistic tradition that limits information to ethnic clichés, without any analysis worthy of that name and, certainly to echo France's African politics, without criticism. The French media is never interested in the deep questions about Africa. The cultivated image is that of ethnicity and tribalism, which is to say that they speak only of the form and means of these political manipulations, never of the political manipulations themselves. In France, the media remain obedient, and opinion is always under control. ("Génocide rwandais: La presse française." Translation mine)[6]

In this context of media and politics, where the imposition of a dominant and legitimate view of the genocide is at stake, the question of the extent to which the genocide of the Tutsis was kept off-camera or off-screened is not limited to a media cover-up. As Bee Bee Bee reveals in *Rwanda 94* over the course of her discussion with the survivor of the Holocaust Jacob, the question of invisibility above all returns to a willingness to know. If there is no desire to know,

there is no individual or political will to confront the consequences that follow from acquiring this knowledge, and no recognition of the expectations
and actions this knowledge demands.[7] In the face of the moral obligation to
intervene—since information is not lacking—any attempt to claim innocence
through ignorance is an act of guilty hypocrisy, because this ignorance and reproduction of the ob-scene is individually or politically maintained: "There is
no truth possible where nobody listens with the most intimate parcel of one's
skin. . . . The person who doesn't want to know will never know" (*Rwanda
94* 80).

A *Sunday in Kigali* stages numerous occasions to reflect on the power of
images and the off-screening of the ob-scene reality and aftermath of the
genocide. The main character Bernard Valcourt is a Quebecois journalist
who comes to Rwanda to make a documentary about AIDS in the months
immediately preceding the genocide. Staying at the Hôtel des Mille Collines,
he falls in love with the young Rwandan waitress Gentille, a Hutu who is incessantly accused of being a "dirty Tutsi" by the *Interahamwe* because of her
relationship with the *muzungu* with the fancy camera and her stereotypically
"Tutsi-looking" physique, according to the RTLM's heinous radio propaganda. When the genocide starts, Valcourt marries Gentille, symbolically
abandoning his position as an observer and sealing his destiny with those he
has come to film. Throughout the film, the numerous scenes in which Valcourt meditates on his camera's value and potential constitute a *mise en abîme*
of images' power to mediate, which self-reflexively also apply to the images
the film's audience is seeing on-screen.

After the historical summary that narratively and visually relates Habyarimana's plane assassination and the beginning of the genocide, the film opens
with a scene, which is, as such, emblematic. It highlights the problematic
nature of the very image we are seeing while dramatizing its anachronistic
relationship with the genocide's reality, which it purports to seize and communicate. This retrospective account of the event and the media belatedness
is depicted chronologically first in the script, because the film begins on July
15, the very day that the RPF declares victory and the genocide nears its end.
This is also the day Valcourt finally manages to return to Kigali to find out
what happened to Gentille, after being stuck at the Rwandan border for three
months following his evacuation in the beginning of April. Immediately after
he has been dropped off by a truck at the Mille Collines, he runs into a man
who is holding one of the genocide's victim's skull. Neither man speaks or
looks at the other. The man who is carrying the skull, completely ignores
Valcourt's presence as Valcourt watches him, petrified and incredulous before
this ghostly apparition.

As his shock dissipates, the journalist comes back into his own body and to his documentary gaze and reflexes. He quickly takes his portable camera out of his bag and films the man from behind for a few seconds before interrupting his archival gesture, as if suddenly realizing its vanity. This scene shows that Valcourt—and the audience—arrives too late, after the events are over: the violence embodied in that skull cannot be captured from Valcourt's vantage point, from behind, in the wake of the genocide. It is also not insignificant that Valcourt sees a survivor is holding a skull without being able to capture this encounter into his camera's visual field. To the extent that Valcourt only films the survivor from behind, the survivor's body functions as a screen that hides the skull he is holding in his hands and therefore symptomatically maintains the ob-scene violence of genocide off-screen. Occupying this mediating position between the skull and Valcourt, the survivor stands not only as that keeper of a traumatic memory, but also as the mediator without whom Valcourt cannot gain access to the ob-scene history that just ended, which the skull symbolizes. Thus, at the very beginning of Valcourt's long quest through the ruins of Rwanda to find out what happened to Gentille, he finds himself in a relationship of dependence on the survivor and witness, and not in a position of mastery or objectification. In passing by Valcourt without even looking at this *muzungu* who has returned once the genocide is over, and in turning his back to the camera when the white man wants to film him, the man holding the skull lets Western viewers know that the genocide survivors are not expecting a thing from those who turned their backs on Rwanda during the massacres. By not glancing at Valcourt—and so by extension, at the film's audience—this survivor tells us that we do not deserve the courtesy of being recognized, greeted, or welcomed, especially not after having looked away—our humanity having failed in our absence in Rwanda.

Finally, this scene is also a way for Favreau to position himself as a cinematographer in contrast to the media in terms of their visual representation (or lack thereof) of the genocide in Rwanda. Indeed, the fields of vision of Favreau and Valcourt's cameras diverge here, where at other points in the film they coincide, since we are invited to look through Valcourt's camera, whose images take up the whole screen forcing us to adopt his vantage point. This reflexive screening, which puts two cameras and two gazes into play, can highlight the image's double relationship to the genocide and its image and can definitely suggest a complementary—rather than antagonistic—relationship between Valcourt's journalistic approaches and Favreau's cinematic screening of memory and unframing of forgetting. For Valcourt, who was evacuated at the very beginning of the genocide and did not come back until it was all over, the history this skull embodies is that of guilt; a guilt fed by the fact that the genocidal violence and the trauma the skull suggests are confined to an off-camera memorial space, since there are virtually no visual images of the genocidal events. For Favreau, heir to the genocide's visual obliteration, the cinematic approach represents one of the means that can symbolically remediate this absence of media images in conferring—through the bias of the artistic freedom of all creative work—a cinematic visibility to what was initially culturally obscured and politically off-screened. In offering up a visibility to what remains elusive and off-screen to Valcourt's camera's vantage point, Favreau essentially positions his camera as one of the avenues through which it is possible to retrospectively inscribe that which remained until then off-screen and ob-scene—for political or cultural reasons—into a society's imagination and memory.

Nonetheless, this complimentary relationship does not suggest an immediate recovery of the genocide's witnesses' and victims'—dead and alive—experiences. Valcourt and Favreau's images in effect uphold two anachronistic and mediated relationships with the reality they seek to capture. Thus, the impossibility to identify with the victim's experience that retains its opacity or, as Chambers would put it, symbolizes the "haunting power of the residual" (*Untimely* 223).[8] The genocidal violence is only accessible to us through its traces, such as the skull and the testimony of the survivor who carries the traumatic heritage the skull embodies. Thus, if Favreau's and Valcourt's mediations come together in their anachronistic relationship to this opening event in *A Sunday in Kigali*, their abilities to depict the past are not interchangeable. Before the black—or rather white—screen that Valcourt symbolizes, fictional films have a memorial and ideological role to play in the sense that they can undo the forgetting surrounding the genocide—a media invisibility, which effectively supports many genocide deniers' discourses for which a traceless past allows to question any statement about the existence of a genocide of the Tutsis, even going so far as to say that it never occurred. Furthermore, like the authors of "Rwanda: Writing as a Duty to Remember" who introduce a self-reflexive "work of remembering" within their attempt to confer a resonance to the genocide,[9] Favreau's screening of the genocide through Valcourt's quest stages a similar self-reflexive screening regarding the film's own ability to frame genocide.

Since Favreau was not only present after the genocide but also before the killings were systematically carried out after April 6, what about the power of images and the camera before the event? How does the film stage the role of Valcourt's camera during this period when he was directly filming the mounting violence and tension, after having finished his AIDS documentary? At one point, as political tensions escalate and massacres begin to be executed long before Habyarimana's assassination, Gentille asks Valcourt why he insists on filming what threatens their lives when he knows that doing so risks his own life:

Gentille: Why do you stay?

Valcourt: Because words are not enough. We have to create images to end this folly.

Gentille: You think you can do it?

Valcourt: In all honesty, no, but I don't have the right not to try.

Valcourt's skepticism here prevails over his capacity to influence the course of events in accomplishing his duty as a journalist snatched up by the unfolding genocide—a testimonial posture which does not at this moment emerge out of a duty to remember since its aim is contemporary to the event and not retrospective. As the French filmmaker Klotz—who was present in Rwanda at the beginning of the genocide before being shot and evacuated—articulates in defining the stakes of *Kigali: Images Against a Massacre* (2005), the question all journalists must answer in the context of genocide is: "What can images do against the deliberate will to eliminate a whole segment of the population and against popular cowardice. . . . We have to realize that in the face of events that are beyond the imaginable, journalistic objective discourse and neutrality can no longer stand" ("Le Papillon face à la flamme").[10] Along these lines, not only does *A Sunday in Kigali* chronicle a planned genocide, it also chronicles a planned media failure and images' inability to change the course of the history they are documenting.

This failure is underlined at numerous occasions throughout the film. First, when Valcourt comes to Rwanda in early 1994, he symptomatically seeks to document the wrong epidemic, as remarks one Tutsi living with AIDS for whom the real sickness is not viral, but the politically propagated epidemic of hatred between Hutus and Tutsis that has festered in Rwanda for more than a half-century. The cause of the image's failure here comes back to the fact that images tend to reproduce a reading grid corresponding to the existing social and cultural gaze and its pre-determined framing. Second, several days before Habyarimana's assassination, a Rwandan friend advises Valcourt to not only leave the country but also to give up his belief in the power of journalistic images and resign himself to the fact that "a camera is no match for machetes"! Third, when he is trying to leave Kigali with Gentille several days after the genocide has started by getting on one of the planes sent to evacuate Westerners, before they get to the airport their convoy is stopped at a roadblock. Valcourt then comes face-to-face with the Hutu cameraman he had hired to film his AIDS documentary during the months leading to the genocide, unaware that he is a Hutu extremist. The cameraman, now the head of a group of *Interahamwe* that controls the roadblock, picks out Gentille and forcefully removes her from the group as Valcourt begs him to spare her until another militiaman strikes him unconscious. Still unconscious, Valcourt is—without his consent and against his will—evacuated from Rwanda without knowing what happened to Gentille whose fate is then pushed off-screen. This scene and Valcourt being knocked unconscious symbolically capture the literal and figurative journalistic blackout of the West during the genocide. The scene also implements a radical inversion of power relations since the Hutu cameraman essentially communicates to Valcourt that "he is no longer boss of anything" and the *Interahamwe* now have an exclusive oversight regarding who dies and lives. Symbolically blocked at the border for three months like the international media, Valcourt then cannot return to Kigali—or to himself and his role as an archiving witness—until July 15, the end date of the genocide marked by the RPF's victory.

If *A Sunday in Kigali*'s script tends to confirm Valcourt's lack of photographic power in the face of the machete's power, what does this tell us about Favreau's film, which grounds its rhetorical, didactic, and affective force on its identification with Valcourt's failed desire to intervene and change the course of history, or at least the trajectory of some Rwandans? Is every retrospective and fictional imaging equally destined to dwell in failure? In the first place, *A Sunday in Kigali*'s script forces its Western audience to recognize its own guilt and historical indifference through Valcourt's successive failures. Moreover, upon returning to Kigali after the genocide's end, he can only conclude that the irreparable was committed, and a new era is opening before him—that of the duty to remember. He must pursue this according to the genocide's remaining traces and witnesses, which he forces himself to identify and confront. Favreau's film thus performatively screens what the media left off-camera during the 1994 genocide, since the script, which adopts Valcourt's vantage point, does not depict what happened during the three months where he was not in Rwanda. In this sense, the script clearly shows that the genocide's off-screening or media-induced invisibility can only be partially re-mediated through testimonies from survivors, who guard the memories Valcourt incessantly seeks, haunted as he is by a desire and fear to know what happened to Gentille. Nonetheless, conferring a previously non-existent visibility to the genocide through the bias of testimonies is not a form of redemption or reversal regarding what happened. When Valcourt finally finds Gentille, she is a living dead who asks him to help her commit suicide because her life is agonizing after what she went through. The image's power, therefore, does not rest in its capacity to alter the course of events it documents, nor does it rest in its ability to retrospectively reconstruct what was obliterated or destroyed. No redemption here. The power of filmic images is rather linked to actualizing the cultural and cinematic means to prevent those who died from dying a second time—that is to say socially, by remaining off-screened from the collective memory that frames not only what is worthy of memory but also the heritage in the name of which the living position themselves.

Valcourt's position as an anachronistic witness in regard to the genocide's actuality and its victims' memories is brilliantly imprinted in two dramatic scenes at the end of the film: Gentille's rape and her burial. In the first of these scenes, Valcourt imaginatively and empathically "relives" Gentille's rape through the traces left behind in the room where she was sequestered and tortured, putting his hands on the bloody imprints hers left behind. The montage's coming and going between the present and the past, however, only partially makes up for the genocide's blackout, because Gentille's martyrdom is only shown through the spectral and mediated artfulness of shadow puppetry. In this sense, Valcourt—and the audience—is positioned as the heir of a traumatic past that will always haunt him, because its initial invisibility can never completely be overturned, and he will never be able to come to terms with Gentille's experience—the victim's suffering only coming out through a play of shadows.[11]

In regard to the question of realism, *A Sunday in Kigali* can be viewed as a screening of the failure of the realist illusion, since Valcourt cannot relive the reality of Gentille's ordeal but only her suffering through his imagination. In this sense, Favreau distances himself from the realist esthetic by clearly suggesting through Valcourt's quest that it is impossible to create a relationship of immediacy with the genocidal experience, since it only comes through the mediated and belated mode of shadow puppetry or testimony. In addition, as Valcourt's trajectory suggests, it is important to unravel the realist tyranny, because it reproduces people's belief that any work on remembering constitutes an interference in the representation of reality, and even a betrayal. By leaving Gentille's killing—a metonymy for the genocide's perpetration—first off-camera to signify its blackout and, then, only visible retrospectively through its shadows—a lesser degree of obliteration than a blackout—Favreau's esthetic opposes realism and its ideological trompe l'œil where reality and its filmic mediation are one and the same. Thus, within his own cinematic mediation of the genocide, Favreau exhibits the inadequacy of his belated account of genocidal trauma. For Chambers, the very gesture of acknowledging this cultural and representational "im-pertinence" of our cultural mediations to confine past historical trauma instills a ghostly dynamic within the duty to remember, which makes the past even more a haunting presence: "The legacy of historical trauma, then, ... is not just shame, ... but also the figure or symbol, the relay through which language's hauntedness, its inability adequately to represent, becomes haunting language, whose testimonial power ... is difficult to ignore because it is a shameless enactment of anomaly, of im-pertinence" (*Untimely* 231),

As Jacques Rivette remarks in his critique of Gillo Pontecorvo's film on the Nazi extermination camps, *Kapo*'s (1960) major flaw—as with any film that claims at being loyal to the reality of the genocide because it is based on testimony—is to appeal to a realist esthetic and a heroic dramatization—a figure prevalent in films like *Hotel Rwanda* and *Shake Hands with the Devil*:

> . . . for many understandable reasons, absolute realism or what can stand instead of cinema is impossible here; all attempts in this direction are necessarily unsuccessful ("thus immoral"), every effort at reconstitution or at derisively making up is grotesque, every traditional approach of the "spectacle" emerges out of voyeurism and pornography. The director must temper reality, so that what he dares present as "reality" can be physically bearable for the audience who can then only conclude, maybe unconsciously, that, of course, it was hard, these Germans, what savages, but the whole is not intolerable, and by being good, with a little shrewdness and patience, you could deal with it. At the same time, we slowly get used to the horror, it trickles into the customs, and will soon be part of modern man's mental landscape; next time, who will be able to be surprised or indignant at what will have in effect ceased to be shocking? (Rivette 67. Translation mine)

The will to erase the film's materiality as a medium, like resorting to fiction to create an effect of reality, constitutes not only an "immoral" rhetorical gesture, but also perpetrates a "symbolic violence" against the audience. As Bourdieu shows, this violence is characterized by a discourse that seeks to naturalize and legitimize a memory—whether it be a witness's or one constructed in the movie—by hiding the fact that memory, far from being a mimetic or transparent representation of the past, is above all the product of and response to a social struggle in which the legitimate representation of the genocide of the Tutsis is at stake. It is necessary to denounce mimetic realism, because that esthetic attempts to short-circuit all reflections on the image's positioning and the limits of its power in mediating reality. As Bourdieu remarks, a text's or film's degree of reflexivity about its own mediation of reality attracts our attention to its conditions of possibility and thus invites us to reflect on how our perception of the real is grounded to the reality and materiality of our perception. Thus, a film or a discourse "that takes itself as an object draws attention less to the referent . . . than on the operation that consists of referring to what we are doing. . . . This reflexive return, when it is accomplished . . . is somewhat unusual or insolent. It breaks the charm, it disenchants. It attracts our attention to what the process of representation forgets and makes us forget. . . . This reflexive return thus creates a distance that threatens to annihilate the belief, as much for the speaker as for his audience . . . . (*Leçon* 54-55. Translation mine)

If *A Sunday in Kigali* draws our attention to the task of filming the genocide, it is by giving us a cameraman who is forced to rethink the power of images and the impertinent relationship to reality he fosters through his camera's bias, and by adopting a non-linear chronology through which the script creates a critical distance between itself and its belated representation of the genocide. Moving away from a chronological narration of the genocide, in effect, is a refusal of one of the most powerful rhetorical mechanisms that gives coherence to the unfolding of historical events, namely the principle of causality. Favreau and Peck are the two directors who refuse to depict the genocide chronologically and thus try to make their mediations relevant without appealing to tactics that tend to naturalize the representation of reality by appearing to follow the course of events when, in fact, the script chooses those events and determines their course and order.

The power of images is thus redefined or rather its question reframed in *A Sunday in Kigali*, since it has to be rethought through the mediating and retrospective relationship we wish to establish with the reality of genocide—a reality which our own cannot fully comprehend or frame, though that does not mean that we must not seek to know it and grant it social recognition. Whether we are trying to make this past visible or whether we are seeking the different positions that representing this past allows for the living, screening the genocide means providing space for the dead and responding to and for their legacy as we seek to respond in our own name. The dialogue with the past is thus always primarily a dialogue among the living who inherit this past and to which and for which we must respond. As the French historian Arlette Farge asserts in *The Taste of the Archive* (*Le Goût de l'Archive* 1989), the mediations of the past that we collect, archive, and produce are not primarily intended to keep the past alive but are, rather, contested and contesting sites through which we dialogue in the present and project ourselves in the future in the name of the past, and the way we frame its memory.

> One does not resuscitate lives that are lying in the archives. But this is not a reason to make them die a second time. The room for maneuver is narrow to elaborate a narrative that neither erases nor dissolves them, but keeps them available. . . . The taste of the archive is visibly an errant journey through the words of others, the quest of a language able to save their relevance, maybe it is even an wandering through today's words . . . in order to articulate a dead past through a language and produce an "exchange among the living" (De Certeau). (145–147. Translation mine)

This imagistic burial rite that generates dialogue among the living is screened in the film's final scene. Valcourt is on Gentille's tomb, showing the now orphaned Désirée, the clips he filmed of her and Gentille before the genocide. That he is showing these archived images to Désirée is additionally significant, because she is the daughter of his Rwandan friend who told him on the eve of his death at the hands of the militia that "the camera is no match for machetes." If Valcourt's camera could not save his friend or his wife or prevent his friend's daughter from becoming one of the genocide's orphans, it is nonetheless a powerful force against obliterating and forgetting what the genocidal ideology sought to bring about with its machetes. As they became archives, Valcourt's pre-genocide images, as sepulchers testaments, serve to fight genocidal denial because they culturally and ideologically represent—in both senses of the term—a presence, even if it is in the devastating mode of recollection. To use Roland Barthes' distinction between the "punctum" and the "studium" of a photograph, the images that Valcourt shows Désirée on Gentille's tomb keep the genocide's victims from being denied that they had existed, not only by their "studium" but also in maintaining their presence among the living in the "punctum" as defined by Barthes in his analysis on photography: "The Photograph does not necessarily say *what is no longer*, but only and for certain *what has been*. This distinction is decisive" (Barthes 85).

The camera's power thus rests in its ability to resist the cultural and historical obliteration the machetes create. In this sense, Valcourt's images, though they do not manage to change the course of events, do acquire testimonial and archival value in preventing Gentille's physical death from amounting to her social death as well. The power of images, as defined in a film like *A Sunday in Kigali*, lies in their capacity to function as archives against the genocidal project's goal of obliteration and its ideology of denial. Thus, in showing the images of Gentille on the camera screen at her burial—which at that moment is not filming anything but reproducing the archived trace of the one who is no longer there, yet whose memory is still present in the "punctum" mode—*A Sunday in Kigali* affirms the need to confer visibility upon the suffering and the victims who were kept off-screen so that this invisibility does not translate in the genocide's erasure from memory. If Valcourt's camera failed against machetes in 1994, Favreau's hope is that his camera will not fail against this other weapon that works hand in hand with the genocide's perpetrators, namely the deniers' machete that seeks to shortcut any voices and images bearing witness to the genocide of the Tutsis in Rwanda either by doubting their accuracy and authenticity or maintaining them culturally ob-scene.

During the years that lead to the genocide and during its perpetration, another media outlet played a crucial role: the Radio Télévision Libre des Mille

Collines (RTLM),[12] also referred to as "radio-machete." In the films about the genocide, the extensive broadcasting by RTLM contrasts radically with the Western media's blackout. In all the films, RTLM functions as a recurrent source of sonic contamination within the Rwandan visual field. If in the midst of the genocide, "the camera is no match for machetes," how does the camera fare against the "radio-machete"? Broadcasting in Kinyarwanda, RTLM made itself, from July 1993 onward, the Parmehutu ideology's soapbox in increasingly virulent ways. The station perpetuated a visceral hatred of *Inyenzi* by constructing history lessons where the Hutus are the only true Rwandans, while depicting the Tutsis as historical invaders and casting the RPF's 1990 attack as the latest proof of this reading of Rwanda's history. During the genocide, RTLM played an even more active role not only in calling the Hutu population to armed defense and to go to "work," but also in spreading regular "updates" that documented the dead and indicated the killers the location of the remaining "cockroaches," so they could be killed. The Western media's misperception of what was unfolding and their rapid off-screening of the killings contrast sharply with RTLM's saturation of the Rwandan radio waves and is a recurring theme in the cinematic representations of the genocide, as *Hotel Rwanda*'s opening frame attests. With few exceptions, the films all use extracts from RTLM broadcasts—in Kinyarwanda or in translation—to show that the State propaganda's impact on the population was one of the conditions that made the genocide possible. Be it through scenes showing groups of Rwandans gathered around radios or through panoramic and bird's-eye view shots of Kigali with RTLM's heinous messages voiced-over, each of the films depicts the climate of ideological saturation that pervaded during the period leading up to the genocide on April 6, 1994. The diegetic and non-diegetic use of RTLM becomes, then, for filmmakers a way of showing that nothing about this genocide was spontaneous, since it required so much propaganda to condition the population and not only make the genocide possible, but worse, also acceptable in the majority's eyes. In *Shooting Dogs*, for example, an RTLM extract is used to establish a correlation between images of Kigali's deserted streets and RTLM's role as a privileged medium for the genocidal ideology that made people believe all Tutsis were RPF rebels, which legitimized their extermination: "The time has come to do our duty! The army cannot do their job alone, it is up to you the people! Go to the roads. Work at the roadblocks!" (*Shooting Dogs*).

In *Sometimes in April*, Peck gives RTLM an even more central role, since one of the main characters, Honoré—a Hutu whose brother Augustin married a Tutsi—is one of the radio hosts for RTLM, diffuses the genocidal discourse, and, ten years after the genocide's end, is prosecuted by the ICTR in Arusha. In one of the first scenes of the film, the camera follows Honoré in

the RTLM studios as he prepares to give his "history lesson" just days before
the genocide started:

> DJ Max: Remember, a cockroach cannot give birth to a butterfly. Cockroaches
> will always give birth to cockroaches. Be vigilant. They are among us. Those
> *Inyenzi*, they are devils.
>
> Honoré: You just listened to the famous DJ Max, as always speaking the truth.
> Now, dear listeners. . . . Yesterday we spoke about how the *Muzungu*, the Ger-
> man and Belgian colonists chose the Tutsi invaders as proxies for their dirty jobs.
> Forced labor, raising of heavy taxes on those poor peasants, and the whipping.
> We Hutus, will we ever forget the whipping? Will we, my dear listeners? I beg
> not. For these scars will never heal. But the days when a Tutsi king or *Mwami*
> is imposed upon the Hutus is passed. For we have sworn never to let them rule
> over us again. Never. . . . Those cockroaches can't hurt us! We'll hunt them
> down, wherever they are. (*Sometimes in April*)

If at the beginning of this history lesson the filming is initially a close-up on
Honoré to clearly identify him as a spokesperson for the genocidal ideology,
by the middle of his speech, Peck's camera leaves the studios and gives the
audience a traveling aerial view of Rwanda's fields and hills to illustrate the
propagating power of RTLM's indoctrination. This long traveling shot, during which we continue to hear Honoré's "history lesson," ends at an arms
warehouse, where uniformed soldiers distribute guns and machetes to Rwandans listening to Honoré on their portable radios. In this scene, Peck not only
visually links Honoré's speech with its consequences by juxtaposing the two
within the same visual field; he also refutes the free speech argument and the
unawareness of the effects of one's words, that they were only expressing their
personal opinions without ever having killed anyone with their own hands—a
defense strategy that Honoré and many others intellectuals used during their
trials in Arusha to claim their innocence.

If the international media's resignation during the genocide's first week
was undeniably the impetus for the genocide of the Tutsis longer term's
media invisibility, journalists' return to Rwanda around the end of June in
the realm of the French *Opération Turquoise* or in mid-July after the RPF's
victory paradoxically contributed to reaffirming this initial obliteration rather
than correcting it. Indeed, when the Western media really became interested
in the genocide, nearly two million Rwandan Hutus were fleeing toward Zaire
(which is today the Democratic Republic of the Congo) to escape the RPF's
advance. In the eyes of the French media, this massive exodus created an
"unprecedented humanitarian crisis" caused by the RPF's "black Khmers" in
the Goma region. Thus, yesterday's executioners became today's victims and
vice-versa!

In *Kigali: Images against a Massacre*, Klotz brilliantly depicts this inversion by first showing an excerpt of the French news about the Hutu exodus toward Goma in the Turquoise zone: the report presents this exodus as a desperate attempt by Hutu civilians to escape the RPF rebels' reprisals. The French news' commentary thus not only makes all Hutus into victims and Tutsis into murderers, but it legitimizes France's politics in Rwanda and the strictly humanitarian nature of *Opération Turquoise*. Klotz then repeats the same images with his commentary to restore the information obliterated in 1994— that many of the genocidal murderers who killed nearly a million people were hiding among the runaways: the *Interahamwe*, soldiers from the Rwandan Armed Forces, representatives of the civilian authorities, and ordinary killers who acted out of opportunism. Moreover, to affirm that this exodus created an "unprecedented humanitarian crisis" testifies to the degree to which the genocide, which had only just ended, had been off-screened: as if a genocide that killed nearly 70 percent of all the Tutsis living in Rwanda was not a "precedent" of great enough proportions, compared to the hyper-mediated crisis developing in Goma. When Patrick de Saint-Exupéry, a French *Figaro* journalist,[13] was interviewed in the documentary *"Kill them All!" Rwanda: The Story of an "Unimportant" Genocide*, he denounced "this fascinating memory lapse" in the international community and the manipulation of information at play in the French media:

> During *Opération Turquoise*, there was a complete focus on the refugees' drama, on the cholera in Zaire. . . . The world's gaze was fixed on the cholera, Goma, and three kilometers from that you have a country whose hills were plastered with cadavers. They were everywhere. Only Goma existed, next door, nothing had happened, it didn't exist. . . . The cholera was springing up, that was the most important thing, as if everything could be reduced to that and the rest could be erased. (Translation mine)

Sometimes in April's script also exposes this media sleight of hand at the genocide's end when, under the UN's oversight, in the West's public opinion the "sudden" humanitarian effort in the Hutu refugee camps in Zaire eclipsed the very same international forces' resignation during the genocide of the Tutsis. Thus, in intervening under the guise of a humanitarian mission to support the Hutus in the refugee camps in Zaire after refusing to intervene to help the Tutsis end the genocide, the West and its media confounded victims and executioners. Numerous media portrayed the "RPF rebels" as murderers and not as the armed forces that ended the genocide, while the Hutu refugees in camps were shown as "victims" of an "unprecedented humanitarian crisis"! In Peck's film, we find the same American political advisors, among them people like Prudence Bushnell, who tried in vain to convince the political elite to intervene during the genocide, now easily convincing the U.S. government to finance a humanitarian operation, indecently called "Operation Hope"! At the end of the official meeting, piqued by the politicians' opportunistic turnaround, an intelligence officer tells Bushnell off-record: "It is too bad the CNN factor didn't kick in a little bit sooner." This late arrival on the scene through history's false door generated long-standing misunderstandings on the identity of victims and executioners. It contributed a great deal to what Chaumont calls "the competition of the victims" in the Great Lakes region and favored historical lenses prone to legitimize the notion of double geno-cide and that of tribal, interethnic, or civil war. Thus the off-screening affect-ing the genocide of the Tutsis was only reinforced—and not remediated—by the hyper-mediatization of the humanitarian crisis in the Hutu refugee camps in Zaire. This double standard helped legitimize a reading of history in which the genocide's executioners and victims are indistinguishable from each other, because all Rwandans took turns being both.

One young American accompanying a humanitarian convoy in Kibuye in *100 Days* makes a comment that is emblematic of this media and semantic confusion. The scene takes place toward the end of the genocide. Hutu civil-ians, *Interahamwe* militiamen, and the authorities who participated in the massacre of the Tutsis have taken refuge in the very church where, months be-fore, after the Belgian forces left the country, they massacred every last Tutsis in Kibuye and buried them in a mass grave next to the church. In this allegori-cal version of *Opération Turquoise* and the UN's aid to the Hutu refugees— the Kibuye church standing in for the Goma camp—Hughes dramatizes the grim role reversal, the executioners now seeking refuge to benefit from UN protection in the very place they massacred Tutsis in hiding. An American, who is aiding in the humanitarian effort and who controls the arrival of sup-plies, remarks to one of the genocidal killers: "People are so nice here. It's re-ally a marvelous place!" This obliteration of the massacre that occurred in the very same place just weeks earlier, indeed, testifies to the invisibility in which the genocide of the Tutsis was draped and how the over-mediatized humani-tarian effort to help Hutu refugees only reinforced this truncated version of history where yesterday's executioners are today's victims and vice-versa. This confusion does little more than fuel deniers' desires to uphold the notions of double genocide and self-defense.

Notes

1. On April 8, France authorized operation "Amaryllis" to evacuate nearly 1,500 threatened people, but not all were Westerners, as the first plane to leave Kigali seated

43 French citizens and 12 Habyarimana family members. This seriously calls into question the French official account of the facts according to which the French military had orders to evacuate only Western citizens. Furthermore, it displays the privileged ties between the Elysée and Habyarimana's regime. For more on the French military's abandonment of threatened Rwandans, be they Tutsis or non-cooperating Hutus, see Vénuste Kayimahe's testimony (2002). Kayimahe is a Tutsi who was hired by the French government at the French Cultural Center in Kigali and was abandoned by his employers who were obviously conscious of what awaited him after their departure. See also the documentary of Raphaël Glucksmann, David Hazan, and Pierre Mezerette, *"Tuez-les tous!" Rwanda: Histoire d'un génocide "sans importance"* (2004), and Robert Genoud's films *La France au Rwanda* (1999) and *Rwanda—Récit d'un Survivant* (2001), which chronicles Kayimahe's survival.

2. Greg Barker, *Ghosts of Rwanda* (2004); Robert Genoud, *Rwanda: How History Can Lead to Genocide* (1995); Raphaël Glucksmann, David Hazan, and Pierre Mezerette, *"Tuez-les tous!" Rwanda: Histoire d'un génocide "sans importance."* (2004); Fergal Keane, *Valentina's Nightmare: A Journey into the Rwandan Genocide* (1997); and Danièle Lacourse and Yvan Patry, *Chronicle of a Genocide Foretold* (1996).

3. As I have discussed in part 1, in Groupov's play, the European journalist Bee Bee Bee is supposed to produce a TV show on the genocide. After much research, she decides that she must start the show with an 8-minute montage of sequences filmed during the genocide or shortly after it. She believes that she must show the facts and events without commenting on them so as to show what a genocide is—a systematic massacre of a segment of the population. She refuses to use any speeches, ambient sounds, or music to restore the images' brute materiality, but her montage does opt for one sonic moment in which an increasingly heavy silence is interrupted several times by an RTLM excerpt singing the Hutu's joy at massacring the *Inyenzi* and asking God to help them eliminate the Tutsis from Rwanda. In addition to the text published in 2002, a film version of *Rwanda 94: An Attempt at Symbolic Reparation for the Dead through the Living*, directed by Marie-France Collard and Patrick Czaplinski, is now available on DVD (2007). For a more detailed analysis, see part 1, "The Testimonial Encounter."

4. In "Exhibit 467: Genocide Through a Camera Lens" (2007), Nick Hughes talks about the circumstances around filming this sequence, what it represents to him, and the investigation he carried on after the genocide to find out the identity of the victims he caught on tape.

5. For more on this topic, see also Melvern's article, "Missing the Story: The Media and the Rwandan Genocide," which examines how the April 9 massacre in the Gikondo parish church in Kigali—the first large-scale massacre of Tutsis discovered by the MINUAR—was covered in the press after one of the MINUAR soldiers took photos to document the massacre of several hundred Tutsis by the *Interahamwe*, the Rwandan army, and civilian members of the parish. Jean-Philippe Ceppi's article, printed on April 11 in *Libération*, which at least had the explicit title "Kigali Open to the Fury of Hutu killers," appeals to the term "genocide" to qualify the Gikondo massacre that was aimed against the civilian Tutsi population. Unfortunately, this article is an exception, because the term "genocide" subsequently disappeared from the media for several weeks during coverage of the events to which Rwanda fell prey.

240 Chapter 16

6. For more on the French press and media, see Gouteux, *'Le Monde', un contre-pouvoir? Désinformation et manipulation sur le génocide rwandais* (1999). For information on the American press, see Steven Livingston, "Limited Vision: How Both the American Media and Government Failed Rwanda" (2007). For information on the African press, see Emmanuela Alozie, "What Did They Say? African Media Coverage of the First 100 Days of the Rwandan Crisis" (2007).

7. For a more detailed analysis of Bee Bee Bee's discussion of the willingness to know and the role audience, witness interlocutors, and readers play in the cultural and political off-screening of genocide, see in part 1, chapter 6, "Becoming Heirs and Going on Haunted."

8. On Chambers' concept of the "residual" see, in part 1, the end of chapter 5, "Staging the Ob-Scene."

9. See part 2, "Dismembering Remembering: 'Rwanda: Writing as a Duty to Remember'."

10. Klotz's documentary autobiography, *Kigali: Images against a Massacre* (2005), is to this day the best reflection on the power of images to change the course of events they document. His script is similar to Favreau's in *A Sunday in Kigali.* Klotz was in Rwanda before the start of the genocide to make a documentary, and when the genocide started, he decided to stay in the convent where he was working and where many Tutsis took refuge. He was, therefore, able to film the negotiations between the priests and military as well as the militiamen. During one of the operations to intimidate the priests so that they would stop protecting the Tutsis, Klotz was shot in the leg and was then evacuated. Two days after he left, the militia broke into the convent and massacred all the Tutsis there. Unlike Valcourt, Klotz only returned to Kigali ten years later to find out the fate of those he archived in 1994, hoping that some survived. Using a portable video-player, Klotz shows the images he shot before he was evacuated and asks people living near the convent or relatives of those who died there if they recognize any of the people he filmed and if any of them survived.

11. This blackout of the actual killings echoes the analysis of Innocent Rwililiza, one of the genocide survivors interviewed by Hatzfeld: "A genocide must be photographed before the killings—to show clearly the preparation. . . . And the genocide can be photographed afterward . . . to convince disbelieving minds and thwart negationists. But the intimate truth of the genocide belongs to those who lived it, and so does the right to withhold this truth, for it is not something to be shared with just anyone" (*The Antelope's Strategy* 100).

12. For more on RTLM, see Jean-Pierre Chrétien, Jean-François Dupaquier, Marcel Kabanda and Joseph Ngarambe eds., *Rwanda: The Media of the Genocide* (2002) (especially 56–82 about the birth of extremist media), and also Allan Thompson, ed., *The Media and the Rwanda Genocide* (2007).

13. Patrick de Saint-Exupéry published *The Inadmissible: France in Rwanda* (2004), a book written to denounce the fact that in September 2003, the French Minister of Foreign Affairs, Dominique de Villepin, spoke of "the genocides" committed in Rwanda, thus legitimizing the thesis of the double genocide and a reading of history that ultimately denies the genocide of the Tutsis in Rwanda.

17

The Heir or the Return
of the Off-Screened

SOMETIMES IN APRIL IS CHARACTERIZED by a constant back-and-forth between
the three months of the genocide and its ten-year anniversary, which is
both the script's present and the audience's since the film came out in 2004.
This montage, oscillating numerous time between the present in which the
past is commemorated and the traumatic experience of the genocide, creates
a distancing effect that ironically engages the audience. *Sometimes in April*
does not seek to submerge its audience in the genocide by eliminating a critical analysis on the temporal, spatial, and affective distance that both separates
us from and relates us to 1994. The choice of main characters also attests to
this pact, since there is no *muzungu* figure with whom the Western audience
would be called to identify—thus feeling the genocide's relevance through
them. If the genocide affects us, then, it is according to a different logic than
those of identification and belief that define a realist esthetic. As Peck confides
in his interview, the act of fracturing the narrative with temporal jumps between past and present, much like presenting multiple characters' trajectories
like fragments of a mosaic, aims at ruffling the Hollywood esthetic that values
identification with a heroic figure and a smooth, linear, and uninterrupted
representation of the real: "Hollywood knows how to get you so emotionally
involved that you have no space for your own thinking. I could have had you
crying the whole time, but I wanted to make a movie that didn't shut my
brain out" (Interview with Joy Press, 2005). In this sense, Peck's polyvocal
and polytemporal script is opposed to any mediation parading as a historical
discourse by virtue of giving a singular and privileged memory metonymic
value. In other words, Peck's reliance on multiple trajectories and historical

locations, combined with his use of a dialogue between present and past, refute the rhetorical power of simplification, generalization, and symbolic imposition that metonymy employs in explaining relationships of power and a given society's history.

How, then, should we understand scripts that opt for a diegetic world characterized by the *huis clos* and, in that sense, offer a spatial metonymic representation of the genocide? Three films fit in this category: *100 Days* takes place in Kibuye and its church, *Hotel Rwanda* unfolds at the Hôtel des Mille Collines, and *Shooting Dogs* is situated at the École Technique Officielle (ETO) in Kicukiro. If the question of production costs is not a negligible explanation, other motives also play into the decision to only use one location. In locking characters and audience into a closed location from which they cannot escape, these films impose a mimetic relation that dramatizes the fact that most of the genocide's victims quickly found themselves trapped in locations previously considered to be safe havens. If the Hôtel des Mille Collines held up its promise to the extent that it benefited from an uninterrupted UN presence and the indirect protection of the Belgian and French governments, the other schools and establishments protected by the UN at the beginning of the genocide became death traps for those who found refuge in them after the massive cutback in UN forces present in Rwanda. The churches also did not play their historical role as sanctuaries, as they had since the 1960s during times of *Muyaga*, or "bad winds."[1] Nonetheless, one of the inherent dangers in using a closed-off location for the site of a representation of history is that most of the historical events related to the plot happen off-screen, and, thus, the representation risks silencing the genocide's complexity, simplifying it to the extreme, or obliterating it entirely since it primarily resided outside the bounds of the film's frame, imageless, even denied.

Obviously *Hotel Rwanda* resorts to the spatial metonymy of the *huis clos* for budgetary reasons and to maintain its realism, since it was not shot in Rwanda. But more fundamentally, it does so because this esthetic of enclosure and entrapment in a single location helps dramatize the script devoted to Paul Rusesabagina's trajectory as he took control of the hotel and tried to find ways to get out of the "hell" surrounding him and save his family and other people who were hiding at the hotel. In this movie, the closed staging affirms the film's focus on Rusesabagina and his attempt to not let himself be caught in the torments of History unfolding outside the hotel compound. During the whole film, he tries to inflect history by finding means to escape with his family his foretold fate. Depicted as a character who saved those to whom he gave hospitality—even though this version of his autobiography has been highly contested by many survivors who were at the Mille Collines during the genocide[2]—can his cinematic and iconic trajectory function as a pertinent metonymy of the genocide of the Tutsis? In other words, can *Hotel Rwanda*'s Paul Rusesabagina metonymically function as a "narrative host" to the victims? The answer is clearly no. Not because he is a Hutu married to a Tutsi, but because his trajectory, social status, and personal connections make him everything but *An Ordinary Man* who could represent the norm. In this sense, he is "exceptional" indeed, not only for the reasons highlighted in the cinematic rewriting of his actions as manager of the Hôtel des Mille Collines but also to appease the audience. Needless to say that the genocide of the Tutsis becomes far more bearable when mediated through an exception—a Hutu survivor who was able to call Belgian high-ranked politicians, who was able to dialogue with top officers involved in the genocide, who could call them and bribe some of them—rather than the norm. The norm were the ordinary Tutsis who were powerless, persecuted for who they are, trapped in churches, hiding in marshes, running through woods, killed point blank or by machete at roadblocks without any leverage to entertain the possibility of a dialogue.

Peck's script, which follows the trajectory of a fictional family that is not so different from Rusesabagina's—a Hutu husband, Tutsi wife, and the threat of death—avoids this metonymic trap in various ways. First, the script is built around the radical opposition between two Hutu brothers—Augustin and Honoré—which adds complexity to the family's narrative. Second, Peck interweaves the fate of Augustin, whose wife and children were killed during the genocide, with two survivors he meets after the genocide and whose testimonies add different perspectives to our understanding of what happened and raise the issue of justice, since one testifies at the ICTR in Arusha and the other at a *gacaca*. Third, he stages the main characters' trajectory in different locations to account for the different ways in which the genocide was perpetrated in the capital compared to the rural areas or the marshes. Finally, Peck's script is based on a dual temporality—1994 vs. 2004—that tears the imaging and screening of history from the strings of the linear realist esthetic and poses them as a struggle over their legitimate representation of the genocide. *Sometimes in April*'s diegetic world, thus, exposes the viewers to a spatial multiplicity, a temporal heterogeneity, and a polyvocal witnessing that frees Peck's cinematic representation from the metonymical trompe-l'œil characterizing many other films.

After the opening history lesson, the film's action begins in April 2004 and thus makes the audience's present coincide with the main characters'. The genocide's tenth anniversary serves here as a symbolic and memorial bridge between survivors and the film's audience—a relationship that a banderole filmed during this sequence explicitly suggests: "April 7, 2004. National Day of Remembrance." Even more specifically, in starting the film with Bill Clinton's 1998 repentance speech, Peck orchestrates a face-to-face encounter between his Western viewers and the genocide of the Tutsis' heirs. As analyzed earlier, the zoom-out following the beginning of Bill Clinton's speech uncovers the fact that we are not the only ones watching the speech that had occupied the full screen at the scene's start, but Rwandan students are also watching in a class devoted to commemorating the genocide and reflecting on its legacy. At the end of the speech, the teacher, Augustin, encourages his students to ask questions. The camera's slow pan across the room, showing us the students' immobile faces looking straight into the camera, signals a shift in our positioning and viewing. We turn away from the initial positioning of the camera suggesting a "seeing with" while Clinton's speech was played to a more confrontational "face-to-face" once the speech is over. During this panned shot, the students' heavy and immobile gazes probe the audience members' conscience, which, following Clinton's speech, can no longer deny the possibility of an analogous historical connectedness, not to say guilt. Thus, if the genocide of the Tutsis is a history that concerns us, it is above all because we are also its heirs, since these young Rwandans' traumatic history is also ours.

The two main characters in *Sometimes in April*, Augustin and Honoré, two Hutu brothers on opposing trajectories during the genocide, not only embody the figures of the just and the perpetrator but also the figure of the *heir*. During the genocide, Augustin is an officer in the Rwandan Armed Forces, husband to a Tutsi, father of three, and who refuses to espouse the Parmehutu ideology of hatred despite the risks this entails. Opposing this *figure of the just* is his brother Honoré, an intellectual who works for RTLM and who represents the *figure of the perpetrator* because of his speeches that celebrate the Hutu majority, the ideology of self-defense or Tutsi hatred, and because of his calls to the true Rwandans to go to "work" for their country. If the characters are designed to explicitly show that the genocide is a political and ideological enterprise—since being Hutu does not explain or justify anything—these two Hutu brothers' trajectories invite not only to go beyond an ethnic or racial reading grid of the genocide, but also to address the aftermath of the genocide. The brothers' survival makes them heirs who must, according to Derrida, negotiate the genocide's traumatic consequences and legacy by answering both *to* their past and *for* their past actions in order to answer in their name.[3] In order to dramatize these two heirs' face-to-face encounter ten years after the genocide, the script severs their trajectories in 1994 through the death of Augustin's wife and three children. Trapped in their house in Kigali because of the roadblocks that prevent Tutsis and Hutu "traitors" like Augustin from escaping, Augustin asks his brother Honoré to take Jeanne and his two sons—his daughter being in a religious school outside of Kigali—to the Hôtel des Mille Collines, since Honoré can move freely owing to his notoriety on RTLM radio waves. Honoré reluctantly agrees to do this for his brother. Unfortunately, on the way he encounters a roadblock where the soldiers do not know him, and they execute Jeanne and the two boys in front of his powerless eyes. If Jeanne survives this massacre to die later on in the genocide, Honoré realizes at that moment the effect of his words and runs away. The brothers do not see each other again after that day. Although Augustin knows that Jeanne and his two sons are dead, he does not know the circumstances around their deaths—his brother Honoré being the sole keeper of that knowledge.

In 2004, Augustin is teaching while Honoré is being held at Arusha where he is tried by the ICTR for having promoted and diffused the genocidal ideology during his shows at RTLM. If they are bound together by the trauma of Jeanne and the children's deaths, though for different reasons, the brothers embody the difficult dialogue of national reconciliation that the Rwandan heirs of the genocide must engage, since they have no choice but to live together. When the film starts, these two heirs have not seen or spoken to each other in ten years. One of the film's central storylines, then, is, on the one hand, for Honoré to recognize his responsibility in the genocide and on the other for Augustin to agree to see his brother again, to reestablish a dialogue with him, and decide to confront his brother's knowledge about the circumstances surrounding his family's fate. As Augustin's internal monologue at the beginning of the movie suggests, April is the month to remember and face the absence that haunts survivors' hearts: "Yes it is April again. Every year in April the rain season starts, and every year, every day in April a haunting emptiness descends over our hearts. Every year in April, I remember how quickly life ends. Every year I remember how lucky I should feel to be alive. Every year in April I remember." The use of the conditional here is symptomatic of the fact that Augustin is not able to be fully alive among the living. Despite his survival, a part of him stays in the land of memory, among the dead—a hiatus the film underscores through Augustin's resistance to marry his new partner, Martine Kamanzi, who tried unsuccessfully to save the life of his daughter Anne-Marie.

The script's originality rests here in the fact that the brothers' relationship is not limited to the opposition between the just and the perpetrator. This duality emerges out of mutual dependence when these polarized figures realize that they are not only united by the same past, but also that they need each other to negotiate their response to this traumatic past and the different positioning it requires from them. In fact, if Augustin wants to live in the present, he must confront his brother who holds the key to his past—and also to a certain degree out of it—because knowing what happened to Jeanne and his two sons is the only way for Augustin to rebuild himself and be fully within the present. Taking refuge in ignorance and hiding behind the fear of knowing provokes in Augustin a feeling of paralysis and might ultimately lead to self destruction from within. Honoré, on the other hand, while he must recognize his responsibility for the role he played in the genocide, needs his brother's recognition to move on. It is imperative for him Augustin knows that he did everything he could to save Jeanne and the kids, but that the genocidal monster borne out of his own words slipped out of his control and turned against those he wanted to protect. In this sense, the two brothers are heirs of the same haunted and haunting past, though for different reasons, which excludes them from the world of the living. This relationship of interdependence is embodied by the letter Augustin receives from his brother toward the end of the first scene in the film, when he returns home after his teaching. Thus, the day he uses Clinton's speech to generate a discussion with his students about the genocide, he receives a letter from his brother demanding him to come to Arusha in Tanzania where Honoré is jailed and put on trial so that he can tell Augustin what happened to his wife and children. Furthermore, to give more weight to the sincerity of his invitation to reopen a long overdue dialogue—since both brothers haven't talked to each other for many years—Honoré acknowledges his role in the genocide and states that now only truth can somewhat ease his guilt. If the film's first sequence introduces us to Augustin in the classroom where the video of Clinton's speech is playing and ends with Augustin reading this letter—a juxtaposition that underlines the impossibility to draw a line between public and private discussions when facing the aftermath of the genocide—the second sequence depicts Honoré during his trial in Arusha in 2004. Following much hesitation after Honoré's letter, Augustin finally decides to go to Tanzania, ten years after the genocide, to meet his brother and confront his knowledge of the past. When Augustin gets to the tribunal to hear Honoré's confessions, he takes a seat in the section reserved for the public, behind tinted glass that allows him to see Honoré without being seen. Even through the classic montage that alternates between the two brothers' point of view, Peck dramatizes their painful reconnection. They are in the same place, the tribunal, but they are still separated by the tinted glass that symbolizes a double ignorance: Honoré ignores whether his brother is present as he admits his role in the genocide; Augustin ignores that, his brother's knowledge about the past events led to the death of his loved ones. The opaque glass separating them thus comes to embody the fact that at this point in the film, the two heirs have not yet found the resources and means to extract themselves (or each other) from the double interior monologue that respectively imprisons them and prevents them from engaging on the path of dialogue and, maybe, reconciliation. One of the challenges for these two heirs united by the same traumatic past will rest in their mutual willingness to destroy this tinted glass that cuts Honoré off from society and protects Augustin from the past's wreckage while preventing him from living fully in the present.

Only after this second sequence depicting Honoré's confessions at Arusha in 2004 without the knowledge of his brother's presence does the film flash back to 1994, landing us in the RTLM studios a few days before the start of the genocide. The script then narrates the course of events in a linear fashion, occasionally flashing forward to the present in Arusha to show us how Augustin eventually manages to overcome his fear of knowing what happened to his family. Not until the very end of the movie does Augustin find the strength to meet up with his brother and hear the exact circumstances under which Jeanne and his two sons were killed, despite Honoré's efforts to save them. If Peck's script from the beginning does not leave any doubts about Jeanne and the children's fate, it is not until Honoré's confessions and his brother's willingness to know and confront his brother's testimony that their initial off-screen status ends for Augustin and the audience.

The originality of *Sometimes in April* compared to most of the other films about the genocide of the Tutsis—*A Sunday in Kigali* being here another exception—rests in the fact that Peck screens the return of what was off-screened by refusing the temptations of realism that seek to erase the distance between the cinematic mediation and the actual events. In highlighting different figures of the heir, Peck, on the contrary, integrates the temporal distance between the genocide of the Tutsis and his audience (and himself) as the critical distancing the genocide's heirs need to come to terms with the past. In this sense, in starting the film in 2004, Peck's anachronistic script makes the tenth anniversary of the genocide the present from which it is possible to remediate the cultural obliteration surrounding the genocide of the Tutsis and representations that continue to mask its political and ideological nature. In the "Making of *Sometimes in April*," Peck explains that he was not interested in one single story, but trying to convey the whole political background of the genocide. In one word, he was not interested to make a film that would be seen as a sort of *Black Schindler's List*. In inscribing the genocide of the Tutsis retroactively in the audience's present and in making the Western audience responsible, via Clinton's preliminary speech, Peck's script forbids us from circumscribing the genocide's heritage to the figures of Augustin and Honoré. Moreover, because there is no heroic figure along the lines of Rusesabagina or Dallaire who comes to save the victims from their impending death, the audience cannot feel relieved of its responsibility and guilt. In this sense, *Sometimes in April* positions its audience at the heart of a dual relationship. On the one hand, it is a relationship of sympathy toward the different heirs of genocide with whom we cannot identify, because they are survivors whose experience is incommensurable to ours, and on the other hand, it is a relationship of identification with this other heir, Bill Clinton—the mirror for our own historical resignation, as various sequences in the film remind us.

Refusing a realism that would submerge us in the past and would allow us to believe in this comfortable illusion that we are just looking at an ob-scene reality that concerns us only from a distance, Peck's script makes the effort to inscribe the genocide of the Tutsis in American history, French history, and in the international community's history via UN decisions. From there, the scenes that depict Clinton's confessions, the retreat of the UN troops, the American government's hypocritical explanations in deferring for as long as possible the use of the word "genocide" to avoid an intervention, the military collaboration between France and Rwanda, the Mitterrand portrait on the back of the extremist newspaper *Kangura,* or even the evacuation of the genocidal murders by French troops during Opération Turquoise constitute the main exhibits that Peck's script uses to forbid us from believing in the possibility of our innocence.

Once we embrace the perspective of the heir, there is no more neutral position possible for us as spectators, since the very fact of having been spectators in 1994—instead of intervening—is precisely what defines our historical culpability. The return of the off-screened in *Sometimes in April* thus operates in a dual process of critical recognition—a process in which the relationship between different heirs of the genocide is at stake as they negotiate their relationship with the past and the resonance they wish to give it in the present through their positioning among the living. On one side are the survivors who must try to distance themselves from the past that haunts them while recognizing the facts and acting accordingly. On the other side are the audience members who must recognize that they, too, are "historical" heirs of the genocide of the Tutsis and that this genocide is an integral part of their history, whether they want it to be or not. In both cases, any claim to innocence is a form of denial. Thus, ICTR's judicial proceedings against Honoré, accused of being one of the channels for the genocidal ideology through his RTLM radio shows, are not limited to this one character, according to Peck's script. The return of the off-screened that unfolds during these proceedings cannot, in fact, be separated from the process Peck's script stages to denounce our good conscience and to break down our reassuring strategies of amnesia to avoid a face-to-face with the ob-scene, its ghosts and the haunting power of the residual they instill within our present. Fundamentally, by freeing the viewers from the realist fantasy of representing what history *is,* the ideological value of Peck's esthetic is that his polyvocal and anachronistic mediation dismembers the question of remembering from any essentialist claims and reframes it by focusing on the production of history, "how history *works*"

(Trouillot 25). From this process, two fundamental injunctions arise. First, like Augustin, we must begin by rejecting the false comfort of ignorance and innocence—which recreates in various forms the genocide's obliteration from our cultural scene—by confronting this past that concerns us and by re-envisioning its aftermath as being part of our history. Second, as the film's epilogue suggests—a scene where Augustin's new partner, Martine, a survivor, overcomes her fear and decides to testify publicly in a *gacaca* to identify some of the genocide's perpetrators—the return of what was suppressed into invisibility demands that we fully assume our roles as heirs by rejecting silence and neutrality within our respective communities. From there, when the *gacaca* judges ask those who are present if anyone recognizes these men accused of having killed more than 120 young girls in a Catholic school, they are also addressing us, the audience, since we have at this point of the film also "seen" what happened. Thus, when the survivor abandons her silence to testify and bear witness to the genocide, Peck's script enjoins us to do the same in the name of the responsibility that comes with our position as historical heirs: "Who recognizes them?" "I do. My name is Martine Kamanzi. I was there. I am a survivor."

Notes

1. *Muyaga*, meaning "bad winds," was the term used to refer to the massacre of Tutsis (Mujawayo, *La Fleur de Stéphanie* 22).

2. See Ndahiro and Rutazibwa, *Hotel Rwanda or the Tutsi Genocide as Seen by Hollywood* (2002).

3. Regarding the concept of the "heir," see part 1, chapter 6, "Becoming Heirs and Going on Haunted," where I discuss Derrida's interview with Roudinesco, "Choosing One's Heritage" (2004).

Epilogue

ON TURNING THE PAGE

Beware of those who were hoping to make a clean sweep of the past thanks to the reconciliation process . . . For some time now, some politicians and anonymous citizens are suggesting, by an annoyed smacking of their lips, that "we must all move on now. Yes, 'it' happened, and we understand that this is terrible for you, but we have to move on now . . ." These people think that, today in our country, twelve years later, the question of our survival occupies too much space, because it is no longer the country's priority. However, if the survivors are fiercely attached to the memory of the genocide, it is not for ideological reasons, but "simply" because they cannot, as survivors, move on to something else. Thus, obviously, they are an encumbrance. You have a country that needs to move on and you, the survivor, you are a little bit like the tumor that prevents it from claiming it is healthy.

Esther Mujawayo (*SurVivantes* 217)

18

Testimony, Memory, and Reconciliation in the Era of *Gacaca*

FOR THE SURVIVORS OF THE GENOCIDE OF THE TUTSIS, the social conditions of bearing witness to their past are a constant source of potential conflicts and social disruptions, since the mediation of their suffering is intimately linked to political and ideological visions and divisions that are still vivid in contemporary Rwanda. Thus the tensions surrounding the possibility of enunciating such a traumatic past cannot be confined to the private sphere or limited to the survivors' psychological resilience and narrative ability to foster social recognition for their loss and suffering. As Weine emphasizes in his analysis of testimonies bearing witness to traumas of political violence, it is "essential that this elaboration [does] not stop at some boundary just out-side of the self, and fail to consider broader social, cultural, political, spiritual, developmental, and ethical concerns and struggles" (104). Testimony repre-sents, then, one possible avenue through which victims who find themselves too often politically muted, or who have not yet found the means to inscribe their experience within the public sphere, attempt to voice the story of their suffering for themselves as individuals and for their community. By refus-ing to remain silent or silenced, survivors aim not only to keep the memory of those who died alive, but also to gain social recognition and legitimacy within the ongoing dialogues through which social memory and belonging are shaped. What might be perceived or is cast as a private and personal enunciation must on the contrary be heard and envisioned as a form of social engagement. Survivors' testimony, then, aims not only to represent the past as it has been witnessed, but at the same time symbolizes a social performance of the survivors' agency within their respective community. To bear witness to one's survival is therefore by no means a practice that can be confined to one's personal ability to remember a painful past. The attempt to voice the trau-matic legacy of the genocide and confer to its haunting imprint a readability fulfills numerous hopes: refusing the obliteration of those who died, docu-menting how the genocide was planned and carried out in 1994, asserting the end of a culture of impunity that prevailed during decades, seeking justice and social recognition, sharing a traumatic weight to alleviate its haunting grip, and overcoming a disjointed relationship with one's contemporaries. As such, testimony requires from survivors to engage in a polemical dialogue with competing discourses that institute the dominant representations of the genocide and shape the responses to its aftermath.

In Rwanda, one of the major challenges for survivors resides in the fact that the memory of the genocide is intimately linked with the current policy of national reconciliation and reunification of the country. If this politic is in-evitable and beneficial in the long term, its implementation generates among many survivors a feeling of betrayal, since the judicial process on which the possibility of achieving reconciliation relies is seen as a politicized form of justice favoring the perpetrators in the interest of the nation's future. Here is how Innocent Rwililiza, a survivor who lives in Nyamata, assesses the current implementation of justice:

> Justice comes through the application of law, and the law would bring the country to its knees. . . . We can't demolish a Hutu society of more than six million people who work hard, behaving humbly and obediently, in order to satisfy a few hundred thousand weak and unstable survivors who grumble and will disappear, as survivors, with the next generation. And then there is a truth that has been somewhat disguised: if we, the survivors, obtain neither justice nor reparations, while the prisoners are released after being so copiously fed by the international organizations, it's because we are turning a slightly deaf ear to any words of reconciliation. (quoted in Hatzfeld, *The Antelope's Strategy* 131)

Furthermore, the social dialogue through which the memory of the past is collectively negotiated happens to take place within the realm of the *gacaca*, a judicial system where perpetrators are given an unprecedented voice and see themselves rewarded if they confess their crimes. This willingness to confess is not merely driven by feelings of guilt or remorse, but rather by the fact that the *gacaca* laws offer perpetrators the possibility to see their sentence reduced if they confess their crimes in public and engage in the government's politic of reconciliation. Furthermore, the *gacaca* jurisdictions are part of a decentralized judicial system where survivors, presumed killers, and other witnesses belonging to the same neighborhood or community are required to testify about what they saw and did during the genocide. As Mujawayo highlights, the "new *gacaca* law has drastically changed the situation: it forces you to speak. If you are hiding some information ends up being revealed by others—and sometimes by your own accomplices—one concludes that you didn't want to testify and you can be persecuted for this omission" (*Stéphanie* 70). Because of their local and participatory nature—each Rwandan being mandated to participate, to tell what they know, what they did and witnessed—the *gacaca* play a key role in the reconciliation process. They assert within the social body the end of impunity, promote a collective discussion regarding a past victims and perpetrators would never publicly address face to face, and are a preeminent vehicle to implement the restorative justice at all levels within Rwanda's society.[1]

One major consequence of the *gacaca* for survivors, as Mujawayo underlines, resides then in the fact that the narration of "what happened is no longer confined to the survivor as was the case before" (*Stéphanie* 70). Thus, in Rwanda today, those who bear witness to the genocide of the Tutsis are either survivors or the very perpetrators who transgress the implicit law of silence *ceceka*—remain silent—that prevails among suspected or convicted perpetrators. This situation represents a radical and sometimes cruel inversion of fate for many survivors who find themselves forced to ask politely, if not beg, the killers to tell them how they murdered their relatives and where their remains are. As if hearing what happened to their loved ones was not already painful enough, survivors must often endure the public humiliation to admit that, to some extent, their ability to mourn their relatives depends on the killers' knowledge, desire, and interest to speak. This dependency on the perpetrators' willingness to bear witness to what happened is an additional source of pain for survivors who, more then a decade after the genocide, seek to find the remains of their relatives to bury them with dignity. As Mujawayo highlights, to be able to put an end to the unbearable uncertainty that surrounds the death of so many loved ones is a crucial step for many in their effort to rebuild themselves: "I already told you how essential it is to be able to visualize the ultimate moments of your loved ones. It is essential and unbearable at the same time. One wants to know, and one does not" (*Stéphanie* 14).

In this restorative judicial context, the distinction that Georgio Agamben makes between the two words in Latin for "witness" finds itself challenged, if not perverted. In the *gacaca* the concept of witness is indeed extended to the perpetrators, often the only ones who know what happened. If both survivors and perpetrators are required to bear witness as "third parties"—*terstis*—it is only survivors who are asked to forgive the killers of their relatives. This demand forced upon survivors is highly problematic: first, survivors' testimonies should not be reduced to the judicial as they represent a social performance of survival; second, survivors are deprived of any authority to grant pardon when asked by repenting—and sometime opportunistic—perpetrators to forgive them, placing an additional burden on the survivors' shoulders to alleviate the weight of their own responsibility and guilt. In his analysis of Primo Levi,[2] Agamben articulates the distinction between *testis* and *superstes* as follows:

> In Latin there are two words for "witness." The first word, *testis*, from which our word "testimony" derives, etymologically signifies the person who, in a trial or lawsuit between two rival parties, is in the position of a third party (*terstis*). The second word, *superstes*, designates a person who has lived through something, who has experienced an event from beginning to end and can therefore bear witness to it. It is obvious that Levi is not a third party; he is a survivor (*superstite*) in every sense. But this also means that his testimony has nothing to do with the acquisition of facts for a trial (he is not neutral enough for this, he is not a *testis*). In the final analysis, it is not judgment that matters to him, let alone pardon. "I never appear as judge"; "I do not have the authority to grant pardon. . . . I am without authority" (77, 236). (17)

Moreover, building on Levi's assertion that survivors can only speak "by proxy" for the dead, that "the survivors are not the true witness,"[3] Agamben highlights the atypical status of genocide survivors' ability to bear witness, since here "the value of testimony lies essentially in what it lacks: at its center it contains something that cannot be borne witness to and that discharges the survivors of authority. The 'true' witnesses, the 'complete witnesses,' are those who did not bear witness and could not bear witness. . . . The survivors speak in their stead, by proxy, as pseudo-witness: they bear witness to a pseudo-testimony" (Agamben 34). Thus, to grant perpetrators the ability and authority to tell what happened only further dispossesses survivors of their story and their ability to be the legitimate tellers of what happened to them, their relatives, and their community. This explains why many survivors, if they do not publicly oppose the current politics of restorative justice, do not embrace all the constraining facets of the *gacaca* and approach with reluctance the demand for forgiveness emanating from perpetrators—a request that forces upon them a daunting dilemma requiring painful compromises between personal views and collective imperatives. Here is how Mujawayo discusses this issue with Belhaddad:

> Fundamentally, for the survivor and for the perpetrator, it is not the same forgiveness that is at play. For the perpetrator, it is a kind of salvation because it equates a certain reduction in his or her sentence: for the victim, it amounts to impossibility or sacrifice. . . . We, the survivors, often sense that the killer has the feeling he or she has to lower himself or herself when asking forgiveness. Therefore to declare that he or she regrets is less a commitment for the perpetrator.

But we have to be clear that the role cannot be inversed: the killer does make me a favor by declaring he or she is sorry, he or she does not grant me anything. . . . And ultimately forgiveness, you know, this is not the survivor's obsession. To forgive in regard to 274 lives who have been taken away. Just this sentence makes you realize the absurdity of the equation. (*Stéphanie* 126–127)

Furthermore, Mujawayo criticizes the hundreds of impersonal letters that Rwandans have received and have to accept as the confession of the killer and his demand for forgiveness: "The text never changes. Same demand for forgiveness, same goal intended, same dissociation. So far, I still haven't heard about a letter where its author accuses himself. The use of the pronoun "I," when it is used, seeks only to minimize the responsibility of the author who was acting among a group. . . . Another striking aspect in these letters is that they never mention the least regret, nor the slightest repentance for the committed crimes. Thus, ultimately, I should forgive someone who does not regret what he or she did? Therefore, in the end, here is my conclusion: Let's eventually talk about reconciliation, but let's drop the issue of forgiveness. . . . To reconcile is not to forgive" (129–130).

Furthermore, under the current climate of mandatory reconciliation, while the perpetrators are encouraged and rewarded to testify and admit their crimes, survivors are encouraged to listen and endure the revelations made by perpetrators, and, foremost, to keep the stories of their ongoing struggle with the genocide's aftermath for themselves—except during commemoration events which fulfill another political goal and social function. The other major point of contention is the limited scope of the *gacaca*'s jurisdiction, since it does not have the political authority to address survivors' needs, to enquire what they face, to discuss the issue of material reparation and compensation, or to enquire how survivors succeed or not in the daily negotiation of their trauma.

In the constraining context of enunciation that survivors face in the aftermath of the genocide, what I would like then to explore is how a series of testimonies focusing on life after the genocide assess the feasibility of the injunction "to turn the page," "to go on with one's life," and "to contribute positively to Rwanda's reconciliation and renewal." I will primarily ground my analysis in Mujawayo's testimony *Stéphanie's Flower: Rwanda Between Reconciliation and Denial* (2006), but also refer to Yolande Mukagasana's *The Wounds of Silence* (2001), and Jean Hatzfeld's *The Antelope's Strategy* (2007)—his most recent account of the life of survivors and perpetrators in Nyamata after many of those implicated in the genocide were released from Rilima's prison in 2003 and returned home.[4] The common denominator of these narratives resides in their polyvocal approach since all three combine to various degrees the author's voice and experience with numerous antagonistic perspectives—from Mukagasana who tends to remain throughout her book the voice of authority to Hatzfeld who tries to erase his presence as much as possible, limiting his intervention to the selection and collage of the testimonies he gathered in Nyamata. For these authors, the decentering of their own voice and views allows them to present a dialogic approach more prone to capture and render the complexity of the challenges generated by the coexistence of conflicting priorities, unequal material conditions, divergent expectation regarding justice, and, equally important, shared hopes, common desires for economic growth, prosperity, and peace. In order to offer such a representative spectrum of social and personal trajectories coexisting in today's Rwanda, each author talked with many, from survivors who are traumatized to the point that they see themselves as living dead, to survivors who are fully engaged in the implementation of the reconciliation process. But all three did not limit themselves to survivors' views and words, they also interviewed perpetrators and, sometimes, even the killers of their own relatives. Mukagasana confronts her children and husband's killer who denies any participation in their death and claims his innocence. Mujawayo talks with her sister and children's killers—some admitting their crimes, others not. Not a survivor himself, Hatzfeld exposes his inquiry within Nyamata's community by juxtaposing survivors' thoughts with those who murdered their relatives and were released from jail in 2003. Among the authors' interlocutors, attitudes vary greatly, going from those who deny any involvement in the genocide to this man who walks around with the skull of the only person he killed, haunted by his action. When Mukagasana asks Enos N.—who admitted the killing of one Tutsi—what these pieces of bones in his hands are, she got this response:

> Wherever I go I am holding the remains of the skull of the man I killed because, a long time after the genocide, as I was passing in front of the house of my victim, this skull spoke to me and asked me to take him along. I want to keep this skull until everything is clear in me. I need to expiate. Alas, the skull no longer talks to me. Besides, the perpetrators who shared my cell in prison broke it. They didn't want me to walk around with this skull; they were saying that it was an avowal and that I should never admit. They told me that I brought shame to them. (quoted in Mukagasana, *Les Blessures* 117)

Between these two extremes defined by denial and a haunting need to expiate, one can find some who ask forgiveness, others who confess some of their killings, some who help and even marry survivors, while others continue to harass them and mock their pain, distress, and loneliness. In their attempt to describe and evaluate the cohabitation between survivors, perpetrators, those who helped the persecuted, those who refused to embrace the Hutu-power ideology, as well as those who came back from exile after 1994—none of these groups being themselves homogeneous in their attitudes and actions—a central issue resides then in the authority each author confers to some voices while disfranchising others, less representative of his or her view on the reconciliation process. Often sharply conflicting, the meaning of the various collected testimonies is intimately subordinated to the selection and ordering process each author follows as well as the framing comments that position the authors' interlocutors, their views about their past actions, and the present reconciliation process. At the same time, as Hatzfeld underlines, there is a striking divide in the relationship survivors and perpetrators have toward the past and its remembering. This difference echoes, even more then a decade after the genocide, a radical difference born from the difficulty for survivors to see themselves again as human beings fully alive as they were before the genocide, while many perpetrators never questioned their humanity and right to live—not to mention for some their right to kill:

> Paradoxically, for the killers, their memory is intact. They are not traumatized and rarely keep the signs of what they did. Nevertheless, while they can trust their memory, they have also a suspicious relation to their memory since it can be a source of trouble. To remember is to speak. They remember, but speak only about the genocide among themselves. The complexity lies on the side of the survivors: they cannot bear lies nor stand the killers' silence, but at the same time they can not bear the truth either since it reminds them that they were weakened and animalized. Ultimately, the real problem is the one of humiliation and not the ability to remember, even though this is also a real concern. ("L'Impasse: interview de Jean Hatzfeld." Translation mine)

In 2001, after two personal testimonies focusing on the events of the genocide and narrating the killing of her husband and her children, Yolande Mukagasana published the *Wounds of Silence*, her personal attempt to undo the social silence and humiliation surrounding survivors' need to speak and to be listened with dignity. The genesis of this book is radically innovative since she spent several months interviewing both victims of the genocide and perpetrators who were waiting their trial in prison. The intent of this pioneering work was to evaluate the process of reconciliation advocated by the government's politics of national unity. Furthermore, her intent was to demonstrate that in Rwanda there are not only two homogeneous groups facing each other—the survivors and the perpetrators. A far more complex nexus of positions regarding the participation and resistance to the genocide, and its traumatic legacy needs to be mapped out and acknowledged. For Mukagasana, it is imperative to overcome any rhetoric based in the fear and the cult of the Other, since such a divisive and dichotomist perception of Rwandans can only lead to further mistrust, political manipulation, hate, and ultimately massacres. Thus, throughout her interviews, she tries to explore venues that could help Rwandans seek collectively the truth, agree how justice should be implemented, and define together the future of their society. In this regard, Mukagasana adopts a groundbreaking approach by the dialogues she has been willing to solicit between perpetrators and survivors like her. By forging and staging a discussion between Rwandans who do not necessarily speak to each other and by inscribing their voices within the same symbolic and social space of her book, *Wounds of Silence* performatively calls for a necessary dialogue among all Rwandans despite the challenges of such an endeavor. That said, the call for such a dialogue does not amount to forgetting, amnesia, and forgiveness without justice:

> The survivors of the genocide need justice to be done, in order to reclaim their dignity of human being. The killers too need justice to be done, first to be able to reconstruct themselves, and furthermore to be able to participate to the rebuilding of Rwanda's society. . . . Rebuilding. Seeking justice. Reviving trust between Rwandans. Thinking together not only in the aftermath of genocides but also at their source. There will be no humanity without forgiveness, there will be no forgiveness without justice, but there will be no justice without humanity. (*Les Blessures* 10)

More than forty large black-and-white photographic portraits depicting Mukagasana's interlocutors constitute the first section of *Wounds of Silence*. This series of portraits places the reader in a troubling face-to-face. For each photograph taken by Alain Kazinierakis, a neutral caption indicates the person's name, age, if he or she is a survivor or someone accused of having participated in the genocide currently awaiting trial in prison. A short quote offers some insight of the person's thoughts, feelings, and beliefs. Rhetorically, these short and decontextualized quotes and portraits introduce, in an impressionistic style, both the complexity of the issues that will be addressed in the second section of the book and the challenge of establishing a dialogue among all Rwandans. Finally, this gallery of intense close-ups and disturbing face to face can be seen as an invitation to reflect on the difficulty to capture visually the suffering inflicted during the genocide and, in its aftermath, the impossibility to identify who did what on the sole basis of one's appearance—a subtle way to advocate for the necessity of engaging in a collective dialogue and moving beyond the "hateful stereotypes" that were one of the preconditions of the genocide.

In the second part of her book, Mukagasana weaves together short edited excerpts of her dialogues with survivors and perpetrators. Each interview ends with a comment where Mukagasana assesses what has been said, showing either sympathy, admiration, or anger, depending on how her interlocutors

relate to their past and, in the case of presumed killers, claim or deny responsibility for their acts. Despite all the smothered words that *Wounds of Silence*
voices, Mukagasana does not allow her interlocutors to develop their position, cutting short numerous dialogues with perpetrators asserting their innocence despite the evidence against them. At the same time, Mukagasana goes
so far as to interview her former neighbor, Gaspard B., who took her children
out of their house to kill them in a nearby mass grave. During this encounter,
Gaspard claims that he did not kill anyone and just happened to be there
while others were doing the killings and that he is innocent.[5] Of course we
are not given the full interview, only excerpts followed by a comment where
Mukagasana clearly conveys her position and interpretation. One could argue
that in this very particular context of enunciation, a truthful transcription
without annotation and comment might run the risk of giving some perpetrators the chance to take advantage of the ignorance and incredulity of some
readers. In this regard, Mukagasana's constant authorial intervention can be
justified since not everyone knows how to read between the lines or decipher
the codes and references used by some prisoners in their attempt to cast their
actions as acts of self-defense in a time of war or, more perversely, denying
any involvement hoping that no survivors were left behind to tell the truth.

   Despite this limitation to the dialogic dimension of *Wounds of Silence*, the
diversity of the juxtaposed testimonies highlights in a dramatic way the difficulty of establishing a dialogue between survivors and perpetrators as well
as between survivors overall when asked to convey a representative view of
the challenges Rwandans face on the path toward national reconciliation.
Mukagasana's collage of antagonistic voices provocatively underlines how
difficult it is to unveil the truth of what happened, since each testimony is
motivated by very different, not to say conflicting, feelings and hopes, ranging
from guilt, remorse, pain, and mourning to opportunism, hatred, and hypocrisy. Her attempt to inscribe within the same symbolic space the voices of
survivors and perpetrators in order to weigh out the possibility of a dialogue
toward a restored sense of belonging and humanity ultimately highlights the
resistance and denial survivors face in their quest for the social, political, and
human recognition of their suffering. Furthermore, Mukagasana knows that
even if her project falls short in its attempt to reconcile Rwandans through the
dialogues she initiated, her book, by inscribing these marginalized voices in
the public sphere, might generate unprecedented dialogues within the Rwandan society—dialogues born from the necessity to respond to the survivors'
disturbing voices and haunting experiences: "Because they feel guilty of having not been able to save their loved ones, survivors need to know the truth.
As long as the truth of what happened is not unveiled, the victims will doubly
see themselves as victims: victims of having been the target of the genocide,

they are today victims of having been victims when the main authorities and
powers would like to satisfy themselves with an amnesic reconciliation" (*Les
Blessures* 9–10).

The social recognition of survivors' rights and needs in contemporary
Rwanda is one recurrent issue that Mukagasana highlights, aware that many
survivors silently share the feeling of being a problem, a disturbing presence,
like this orphan of the genocide who was nine years old in 1994 and who believes that paradoxically survivors "have become a problem for the Rwandan
society" (110). Echoing this view, Emmanuel M., survivor and keeper of a
memorial, goes further by linking the possibility of a national reconciliation
to the role justice and material compensation need to play within this crucial
process: "I live in misery and sorrow. We, the survivors, we are being sacrificed to the politics of national reconciliation. Our killers are the winners here.
When they come back, we need to give them their houses back, whereas they
destroyed ours and assassinated us. As for us, who will restitute our belonging? And when we testify against them, we are dead, because we live among
them. I am appalled, but I feel totally powerless. I do not believe in a reconciliation without justice" (131). Even though these views and claims date back
to 2001, they are still relevant today in the eyes of many survivors who saw
all their loved ones killed, their houses and belongings destroyed. With their
social network dismantled to the point that they do not have adequate struc-
tures of support and solidarity, many survivors have little chance to rebuild
themselves in a post-genocide Rwanda characterized by rapid economical and
urban growth and a pragmatic government oriented toward the future. For
authors like Mukagasana and Mujawayo, one of the main factors that calls for
book like *Wounds of Silence* is the fact that many survivors are facing a society
that is quick to compromise when it comes to recognize the needs generated
by the wounds of the past and prefers them to remain off-stage if voiced outside of the commemoration period. As numerous survivors interviewed by
Hatzfeld attest, the words through which survivors bear witness to the genocide and its aftermath do not circulate freely and spontaneously:

> Marie-Louise Kagoyire: "Whenever I speak to a Hutu, I try to camouflage what
> I feel. . . . Conversation with a Hutu is a delicate thing. If I say something big,
> if I speak wounding words, he will feel offended, turn his back on me, and I'll
> find myself the loser. Frankly, one feels uneasy listening to a killer's words if he
> is lying, and one feels just as uneasy if he is telling the truth. As for him, he will
> feel ashamed of what he is saying if it's the truth, yet will be equally ashamed of
> his lies. . . ."
>
> Cassius Niyonsaba: "The harsh politics of reconciliation forbid survivors to
> speak in any fashion about the killings, except when invited to give evidence,
> during ceremonies, mourning periods, or the *gacaca* trials. . . . Among us survi-

vors, we do talk about it, but with others it's impossible. Even with a foreigner, nothing is certain: there are some who might understand, but others can be mocking or aggressive. Instead of risking such defeats, it's better to close up our hearts." (*The Antelope's Strategy* 82–83)

While Esther Mujawayo and Jean Hatzfeld both give voice to men and women—be they survivors or perpetrators—whose views and actions they do not share, their narrative and rhetorical use of antagonistic voices differs from Mukagasana's by their genuine effort to expose at length their interlocutors' position and views about reconciliation and justice. At the same time, while they confer a social visibility to opinions that are not their own, their willingness to expose and understand them does not constitute an acceptance nor an endorsement of their interlocutors' agenda. The dialogic configuration of their works must be read as an acknowledgement of the social and intersubjective negotiation surrounding the legacy of a divisive past and the recognition that no one owns the truth alone, since it needs to be collectively articulated and acknowledged.

Stéphanie's Flower: Rwanda between Reconciliation and Denial opens with Esther Mujawayo's return to Rwanda and her quest to locate the bodies of her sister and her three children. Like many survivors, Mujawayo feels indebted to those who died and equates her survival to the obligation to bury them with dignity and preserve their memory. The main obstacle and source of frustration for Mujawayo resides in the fact that the possibility of honoring her dead relatives relies on the confessions of those who participated in the genocide and are now admitting some of their crimes. In the chapters relating her encounters with the three presumed killers of her sister and her family, Mujawayo narrates the difficulty to interpret their discourse and the discomfort generated by the impossibility to ever truly knowing what motivates their willingness to speak. During her participation to various *gacaca* sessions, Mujawayo evaluates the potentialities and limitation of this judicial system based on the willingness and ability of the local communities to face what happened and confront, more than ten years after the events, a traumatic past that continues to haunt their present and weighs insidiously on so many social interactions among Rwandans. What is particularly difficult for Mujawayo is that the survivors are not given the possibility to define and negotiate the rules and the conditions under which they face the perpetrators; it is the government that imposes through the *gacaca* and the policy of national unity and reconciliation a constraining context of dialogue that weighs in on what can be said, by whom, and when.

In the end, despite the confession of one man who participated in the killing of her sister and her children, Mujawayo finds herself unable to locate the bodies of relatives. In order to overcome the failure of her quest an pay tribute to the memory of the dead, Mujawayo writes her book as a memorial to Stéphanie and her children. This symbolic and performative gesture allows her to free herself from the humiliating relation of dependence in which the perpetrators' silence maintains her. Moreover, by inviting us to read her book as her sister's memorial, Mujawayo neutralizes the perpetrators' ability to prevent her to pay tribute to her dead with the hope that she will continue to suffer and live in guilt. In addition to the book's dedication as a memorial for her sister, Mujawayo identifies one other sign that maintains the memory of her sister alive: a flower that Stéphanie planted near her now destroyed house before the genocide, a flower that blooms each year and symbolizes, more than a decade after the genocide of the Tutsis, the failure to obliterate what happened and erase the memory of those who were killed for the sole reason they were Tutsis.

The second part of her book is devoted to stories and words of survivors who are fully implicated in the reconciliation process. As Mujawayo exposes their words and actions, she tries to understand the motivation behind their engagement that brings them in a daily interaction with perpetrators—a proximity that the author who lives in exile sees beyond her strength, not to mention emotionally dangerous. For Mujawayo, to engage in the reconciliation process as a survivor and to work with perpetrators represents a potentially suffocating journey for survivors who, one more time, are asked to make the impossible happen politically, socially, and psychologically: "Here is my major concern: . . . do survivors have to go through this new challenge that this constraining confrontation with their killers represent? . . . You are going to tell me, and you will be right, that some truth also exists in this challenge and that this truth is crucial for survivors. Indeed, it is crucial for us to know how our relatives have died, and especially where their bodies are, where, where, where . . . But the codified context of the *gacaca* within which this truth is revealed does it not request from us the impossible?" (*Stéphanie* 59) To illustrate this point, various chapters convey the stories of the women Mujawayo met. Each of them pays tribute to their involvement and attempts to negotiate the aftermath of the genocide: Théophilia oversees perpetrators working in the context of the Travaux d'Intérêt Général (TIG or Works of General Interest); Joséphine goes into prisons to encourage accused perpetrators to participate in the reconciliation effort by admitting their crimes; Odette works as a "judge" in a *gacaca* court; Stéphanie manages reconciliation and conflict resolution camps with the British NGO Oxfam; and so on.

Mujawayo's testimony is therefore not only dialogic thanks to her conversation with Belhaddad and her use of the second-person narrative that rhetorically positions us within the dialogic space of sharing and trust of her ttion, it is also polyphonic.[6] In *Stéphanie's Flower*, Mujawayo orchestrates a multiplicity of voices that do not necessarily coincide with her personal trajectory and views. In Weine's analysis of testimonies bearing witness to political violence and suffering, the use of a polyphonic approach is key as it highlights the dialogic foundation of testimony as a cultural practice aiming to foster a decentered space where mutual recognition and understanding can occur through the negotiation of differences: "Within one point of historical experience, even within one person's narration of surviving political violence, there are many different ways of seeing many different things, and each connects interpersonally, culturally, historically, and spiritually with many other views. . . . Thus the survivor's storytelling contains words that carry points of view that belong to a larger distributed network of experiences and meanings" (103). Furthermore, as Bourdieu reminds us in "The Space of Points of View" (1999), anyone who attempts to grasp "difficult" experiences and realities should never loose sight that they are "difficult" because they challenge our normative frameworks and the common representations that naturalize them. Thus, it "should become clear that . . . simplistic and one-sided images (notably those found in the press) must be replaced by a complex and multilayered representation capable of articulating the same realities but in terms that are different and, sometimes, irreconcilable. Secondly, . . . we must relinquish the single, central, dominant, in a word, quasi-divine, point of view that is too easily adopted by observers—and by readers too, at least to the extent they do not feel personally involved. We must work instead with the multiple perspectives that correspond to the multiplicity of coexisting, and sometimes directly competing, points of view" (3).

After having conveyed all these stories that can only raise admiration for the strength and altruism these survivors demonstrate, Mujawayo exposes her fears regarding the faith of these women and friends who all are trying to find ways to cope with the aftermath of the genocide and who do not have Esther's privileged position—as she admits herself—to live outside of Rwanda to rebuild themselves:

> During each of these encounters, I suffered, I suffered. . . . Despair: they wanted to exterminate you, you survived, but the non-sense of this reality can lead you to commit suicide. You are not dead, but you cannot believe again in your right to live as you did before. You are broken. . . . So, how do they do it Théophilia, Joséphine, Odette, Stéphanie . . . ?
>
> I came to the conclusion that to choose to implicate oneself in the reconciliation was a way for them to fight against these feelings. When you sense that your society wants to close the heavy chapter of the genocide, sometimes by rushing the process, you understand that survivors will remain in the margins. You then ask yourself the question: and in all of this ongoing process, how will I position myself? Do you want to put yourself on the side and contemplate what is done

and what is at play, like a spectator? Anyhow, as a survivor, you have nothing
more to loose. . . . Thus, instead of being excluded, you decide to be an acting
and involved victim. (*Stephanie* 205–207)

Mujawayo is concerned with the price these survivors will ultimately pay
psychologically when opting to live in this daily proximity with perpetrators.
Moreover, the fact that Mujawayo's interlocutors have neither her privileged
position of exteriority to rebuild themselves, nor a social space where they can
unload all the sufferings and atrocities to which they are heirs, only deepens
her concerns. In her comments preceding or following her discussion with
these women, Mujawayo underlines that her friends do not have—like the
perpetrators through the *gacaca*—a social space where they too could unload
all the sufferings and atrocities of which they are and become the heirs as
they are working with survivors and perpetrators: "They took the crazy bet of
wanting to get closer to these others who wanted our end. But who is getting
closer to them?" (211)

What is at stake here, ultimately, is the relationship that survivors of the
genocide are able to forge between their personal history and the official
understanding of Rwanda's past, which is currently debated and negotiated.
The risk for survivors is to find themselves dispossessed of the right and the
ability to tell their story according to their understanding and, therefore, to
be silenced and alienated a second time if unable to recognize themselves in
the new framework through which they will be asked to address their trauma
and their survival. In *Unclaimed Experience: Trauma, Narrative, and History*,
Cathy Caruth underlines this crucial negotiation between the personal
and the collective relationship to a traumatic past as follows: "The belated
experience of trauma . . . suggests that history is not only the passing on of a
crisis but also the passing on of a survival that can only be possessed within
a history larger than any single individual . . ." (71). In today's Rwanda, the
call for national reconciliation, the participation to the *gacaca* system, and a
rewriting of Rwanda's past in order to produce new textbooks constitute the
paradigmatic lenses through which the genocide's legacy is publicly addressed
and instituted. These codified contexts of enunciation define a new era in the
history of witnessing the genocide that Mujawayo summarizes as follows:

After 1994, a deafening silence petrified the entire population. The survivors
were no exception. You don't speak if you are convinced that you will not be
listened to, and moreover, when you might risk your life. But, very quickly after
the genocide, the assassination of survivors started. You see, some are forced
to speak while others are obliged to remain silent. This reality, the pressure to
remain silent for survivors or risking their lives is rarely addressed. . . . Because
of clan affiliation or of ideological certainty, the perpetrators bet a lot on the

muteness prevailing in the hills. Nobody, absolutely nobody in Rwanda could
have imagined that the killers would speak about their acts one day. . . . With the
gacaca, the testimonies are circulating. (*Stéphanie* 74)

This new era of witnessing has restrictive consequences for survivors' ability
to tell their story, to be heard socially, and to make various political demands.
The social evolution of the injunction to bear witness and the highly codified
gathering and circulation of survivors' testimony must be read in context.
Many perpetrators and survivors find themselves placed in a surrealistic
cohabitation one decade after the genocide and must invent new forms of
sociability in order to overcome the past antagonism that Sehene identifies as
"the ethnic trap." The implementation of these new forms of sociability can
only be a fragile process, as Rwandans need to negotiate complex tensions
and find means to rebuild the social nexus of their respective communities by
re-imagining their identities, their relation to history, and what is at the heart
of their common belonging. It is in this perspective that I would like to conclude in an open-ended mode by conveying some recurrent themes voiced by
many of the survivors interviewed by Mukagasana, Mujawayo, and Hatzfeld.
My intent? To highlight that the ability to turn the page is not equally shared,
nor seen as equally desirable and that the haunting legacy of the genocide,
therefore, will not go away by imposing a unique path forward or by favoring
various forms of social amnesia.

First, the major achievements of the *gacaca* cannot be disputed despite its
imperfections and recent tendency to expedite procedures and sentencing: for
the government, a clear political statement that the era of impunity is over
and a pragmatic way to convert a costly inmate population into a cheap labor
force for the common good through the TIG; for the prisoners who do not
belong to the first category of perpetrators of the genocide, the assurance that
they are also Rwandan citizens who have the right to be judged in a decent
timeframe and that they are given a chance to contribute to Rwanda's renewal
by confessing their crimes and offenses; finally, for the survivors, the certainty
that everything they say will be recorded, a chance to see some perpetrators
sentenced, but even more important, an opportunity to learn how family
members and neighbors died, where their remains lay and, thus, the hope to
find some sense of closure by burying their dead with dignity.

Second, the *gacaca* have also generated new challenges for survivors: they
must listen in public to the crimes and atrocities committed against their relatives with all the social voyeurism and humiliation it may imply; they must
remain silent and respectful when facing those confessing the murder of their
loved ones; they must accept to see their testimony challenged by the alleged
perpetrators; they must live among the perpetrators released from prison and

accept their return; and, ultimately, some survivors must live in the fear of being killed for what they have witnessed if they choose to step forward as mandated by the law. The spectrum of *gacaca*'s achievements and challenges is, therefore, complex and broad, and it is difficult to generalize, since every case is specific, depends on the location, the number of survivors, the networks of support or hostility, the material and mental status of survivors not to mention the true intentions of those who confessed or claimed their innocence.

Nevertheless, the reluctance of the government to create a compensation and reparation fund for survivors by fear of being perceived as favoring the Tutsis survivors offers a sharp contrast with the generous benefits perpetrators of the genocide receive if admitting their crimes within the new *gacaca* jurisdictions. In both cases, the same economic rational prevails, but with very different consequences and sacrifices for both groups. In the end, it is survivors who once more are asked, in the name of national reconciliation, to make the biggest sacrifice by accepting too often expedited verdicts, by facing demands of forgiveness that killers impose on them, by having to overcome the emotional stress and trauma generated by the return of so many perpetrators within their neighborhood, and by silencing their desire of a judicial system that would fully address the issue of material compensation for those who were left without a family or have suffered traumatic violence and sexual abuse that exclude them from most social networks.[7]

What is at stake here for many survivors is the refusal to die a second time by being socially smothered and seeing that behind the official claim that the era of impunity is over, the new era is not immune to selective forms of amnesia and deafness when it comes to survivors' needs and claims. Equally crucial for survivors is the social and political response to their desire to be heard when bearing witness. The progressive ability to overcome the memory of having been forced to behave in a shameful and inhuman manner in order to survive can only be achieved if there is a non-alienating dynamic between their personal memories and the official memory that is currently shaped in Rwanda and the diaspora. As Annick Kayitesi underlines in her testimony *We Are Still Alive* when she reflects on her desire to bear witness, it was crucial for her to speak "in order to gain the interior certainty that she had the right to exist for who she was. This need to bear witness is even more urgent because numerous survivors, raped girls, misunderstood adolescents are condemned to remain silent" (245. Translation mine). A survivor has to be seen and become more than a survivor to be fully alive, but it is not by turning a deaf ear on their compensations' claims and permanent need to negotiate the disruption of a traumatic past within their present that this goal can be achieved.

Even if one can understand the economic and political pragmatism motivating this approach focused on long-term policy, it is important to notice that the current political injunction to turn the page and mute any claim for a special status for survivors will ultimately disfranchise many of them. Especially affected by this exhortation to look forward are the survivors who found themselves orphaned from their former social network and unable to reintegrate another one to rebuild a sense of belonging and empowerment. This social estrangement has not only its source in the fact that many survivors found themselves orphaned but is also intimately linked to the profound demographic shifts that have reshaped the former social landscape as well as a rampant urban economy that requires an education and skills most survivors do not have in order to be part of it. Therefore, in this rapid and changing context, many survivors will not be able to contribute to national reconciliation if justice is not administrated properly and if survivors are not given adequate financial support, counseling, social help, and recognition. But equally crucial for survivors' future is the social and political assurance to find safe spaces where they can speak without fear for their lives in order to find means to negotiate their trauma.

A society that denies the needs generated by a traumatic past and refuses a specific status for survivors' needs can only produce a ticking bomb that might be dangerous in the long term. But dangerous for whom? For the survivors without any doubt. For the current government and the majority of Rwandans it may be a risk worth taking since the number of survivors unwilling or unable to embrace the politics of reconciliation represents a very small minority within the new demographic landscape of Rwanda. But is this a sufficient reason to leave so many who have seen and lived too much in the margins of tomorrow's Rwanda? This is the challenging question that Mukagasana, Mujawayo, and Hatzfeld's polyphonic testimonies raise as they expose the diversity of views in post-genocide Rwanda and the multiple ways survivors seek to be "acting victims" as they negotiate the social resonance of their traumatic past. Thus, through her dialogic and polyphonic art of witnessing, Mujawayo not only offers a memorial to Stéphanie and a voice to many survivors, but she also reminds us that to bury the dead is to honor them through the dialogues they generate among the living. What will our answer then be? Are we willing to become "acting readers and interlocutors" and face not only the experiences to which these survivors bear witness but also our own responsibilities within our respective communities and societies, so that their words and ongoing suffering will no longer remain smothered and muted?

Notes

1. Without going into the details of the *gacaca*'s laws, like the different categories of criminals, the various phases of implementation, and the modifications of the *gacaca*

law, let me just mention that those who planed the genocide, used their positions of authority and power to implement the genocide, and forced others to engage in the killings, as well as those who committed rapes, are not judged by the *gacaca* but by the ordinary judicial system. For more technical information, see the official site of the National Service of Gacaca Jurisdictions, <http://www.inkiko-gacaca.gov.rw/En/ EnIntroduction.htm>. See also Digneffe and Jacques Fierens eds., *Justice et gacaca. L'expérience rwandaise et le génocide* (2003). In *Stéphanie's Flower*, Mujawayo also devotes an entire chapter to explain how the traditional *gacaca* were redefined in the context of the aftermath of genocide in order to implement justice in a timely fashion, since more than one hundred thousand genocide suspects were awaiting their trial in jail ("Les gacaca" 47–60).

2. Primo Levi is a survivor of Auschwitz and the author of one of the most famous Holocaust testimonies, *Se questo è un uomo*, published in the United States under the title *Survival in Auschwitz* (1947), and essays such as *The Drowned and the Saved* (1986). He committed suicide in 1987.

3. Levi's famous quote that Agamben comments is also used by Mujawayo in her self-reflexive chapter devoted to testimony in *SurVivantes* (263) when she acknowledges her very privileged and atypical status in regard to those who were killed. This quote goes as follows: "We, the survivors, are not the true witness. . . . We survivors are not only an exiguous but also an anomalous minority: we are those who by their prevarications or abilities or good luck did not touch the bottom. Those who did so, those who saw the Gorgon, have not returned to tell about it or have returned mute. . . . We who were favored by fate tried, with more or less wisdom, to recount not only our fate but also that of the others, indeed of the drowned; but this was a discourse 'on behalf of third parties,' the story of things seen at close hand, not experienced personally. . . . We speak in their stead, by proxy" (*The Drowned and the Saved* 83–84).

4. For a cinematic approach of the issues raised by these works, see the remarkable film of Gilbert Ndahayo entitled *Rwanda: Beyond The Deadly Pit* (2008), the four documentaries of Anne Aghion, *Gacaca, Living Together Again In Rwanda?* (2002), *In Rwanda We Say . . . The Family That Does Not Speak Dies* (2004), *The Notebooks of Memory* (2009), and *My Neighbor My Killer* (2009), and Laura Waters Hinson's recent documentary *As We Forgive* (2008).

5. At one point the reader learns that his wife is accused of having thrown grenades in the mass graves to finish off the agonizing victims—a revelation that only reinforces the reader to question Gaspard's claim of innocence (*Les Blessures* 135).

6. For a more detailed analysis of the dialogic dynamic at play in Mujawayo's testimonies, see the end of part 1 "The Testimonial Encounter."

7. As Annick Kayitesi provocatively summarizes in her testimony, a "lot of people, lead by President Kagame, talk about reconciliation and forgiveness. The perpetrators are coming out of jail, reclaim their houses, their land. They are supposed to perform collective work to pay their debt to society. But meanwhile, the survivors to whom nobody has ever given back a single of their possessions remain those who are eternally sacrificed" (*Nous existons* 229. Translation mine).

Bibliography

African Rights and REDRESS. *Survivors and Post-Genocide Justice in Rwanda: Their Experiences, Perspectives and Hopes.* Kigali: African Rights, 2008.

Africa Rights Watch. "Father Wenceslas Munyeshyaka: In the Eyes of the Survivors of Sainte Famille." *African Rights* 9 (April 1999).

———. "Bisesero: Résistance au Génocide. Avril-juin 1994." *African Rights* 8 (April 1998).

Agamben, Giorgio. *Remnants of Auschwitz: The Witness and the Archive.* Translated from the Italian by Daniel Heller-Roazen. New York: Zone Books, 1999 [1998].

Alozie, Emmanuel. "What Did They Say? African Media Coverage of the First 100 Days of the Rwandan Crisis." *The Media and the Rwanda Genocide.* Ed. Allan Thompson. London-New York: Pluto Press/Fountain Publishers/IDRC, 2007. 211–230.

Antelme, Robert. *The Human Race.* Translated from the French by Jeffrey Haight and Annie Mahler. Marlboro, VT: Marlboro Press, 1992 [1946].

Apter, David. "Political Violence in Analytical Perspective." *The Legitimization of Violence.* Ed. David Apter. London: Macmillian, 1997. 1–32.

Assayag, Jackie. "Le spectre des génocides. Traumatisme, muséographie et violences extrêmes." *Gradhiva* 5 (2007): 7–25.

Bâ, Medhi. *Rwanda, un génocide français.* Paris: L'Esprit frappeur, 1997.

Bagilisha, Louis. "Discours de la négation, dénis et politiques." *L'Histoire trouée. Négation et témoignage.* Ed. Catherine Coquio. Nantes: L'Atalante, 2003. 731–752.

Bakhtin, Mikhail. *Speech Genres and Other Late Essays.* Translated from the Russian by Vern W. McGee. Austin: University of Texas Press, 1986.

Barnett, Michael. *Eyewitness to a Genocide: The United Nations and Rwanda.* Ithaca: Cornell University Press, 2002.

Barthes, Roland. *Camera Lucida: Reflections on Photography.* Translated from the French by Richard Howard. New York: Hill and Wang, 1981 [1980].

Bartov, Omer. "Defining Enemies, Making Victims: German, Jews, and the Holocaust." *American Historical Review* 103.3 (1998): 771–816.

Bazambanza, Rupert. *Smile Through The Tears: The Story of the Rwandan Genocide.* Montreal: Éditions Images, 2005 [2004].

Bazié, Isaac. "Au seuil du chaos: Devoir de mémoire, indicible et piège du devoir dire." *Présence Francophone: Revue Internationale de Langue et de Littérature* 63 (2004): 29–45.

Belhaddad, Souâd. "L'infinie solitude du rescapé." *Revue d'Histoire de la Shoah* 190 (2009): 397–406.

———. "Dire est impossible." *Rwanda. Pour un dialogue des mémoires.* Ed. Jean Mouttapa. Paris: Albin Michel, 2007. 165–179.

Bizimana, Jean Damascène. "L'Église catholique et le génocide des Tutsi: de l'idéologie à la négation." *La Nuit Rwandaise* 2 (2008): 249–264.

———. *L'Église et le génocide au Rwanda: Les Pères Blancs et le négationnisme.* Paris: L'Harmattan, 2001.

Blanchot, Maurice. *The Writing of Disaster.* Translated from the French by Ann Smock. Lincoln: University of Nebraska Press, 1995 [1980].

Bloomfield, Steve. "Welcome to Hillywood: How Rwanda's Film Industry Emerged from Genocide's Shadow." *The Independent* August 30, 2007.

Borowski, Tadeusz. *This Way for the Gas, Ladies and Gentlemen.* Selected and translated from the Polish by Barbara Vedder. New York: Penguin Books, 1976 [1959].

Bourdieu, Pierre. "The Space of Points of View." *The Weight of the World: Social Suffering in Contemporary Society.* Ed. Pierre Bourdieu. Translated from the French by Priscilla Parkhurst Ferguson. Cambridge: Polity Press, 1999 [1993]. 3–5.

———. *Practical Reason: On the Theory of Action.* Translated from the French by Randal Johnson. Stanford: Stanford University Press, 1998 [1994].

———. *Leçon sur la leçon.* Paris: Minuit, 1982.

Braeckman, Colette. *Rwanda. Histoire d'un génocide.* Paris: Fayard, 1994.

Brauman, Rony. *Devant le mal. Rwanda: Un génocide en direct.* Paris: Arléa, 1994.

Buber, Martin. *I and Thou.* Translated from the German by Walter Kaufmann. New York: Scribner, 1970 [1923].

Caruth, Cathy. *Unclaimed Experience. Trauma, Narrative, and History.* Baltimore, MD: The Johns Hopkins University Press, 1996.

Cazenave, Odile. "Writing the Rwandan Genocide: African Literature and the Duty of Memory." *Reconstructing Societies in the Aftermath of War: Memory, Identity, and Reconciliation.* Ed. Flavia Skov-Brizio. Boca Raton, FL: Bordighera, 2004. 70–84.

Certeau, Michel de. *The Writing of History.* Translated from the French by Tom Conley. New York: Columbia University Press, 1988 [1975].

———. *Heterologies: Discourse on the Other.* Translated from the French by Brian Massumi. Minneapolis: University of Minnesota Press, 1986 [1981].

Chalaye, Sylvie. "*Rwanda 94*, du Groupov (Belgique) et *Méfiez-vous de la pierre à barbe* de la Madani Compagnie. Que peut le théâtre face à l'horreur génocidaire?" *Africultures* 32 (2000).

———. "Entretien avec Jacques Delcuvellerie." *Africultures* 20 (1999).

Chambers, Ross. *Untimely Interventions: AIDS Writing, Testimonial, & the Rhetoric of Haunting*. Ann Arbor: The University of Michigan Press, 2004.

———. "Orphaned Memories, Foster-Writing, Phantom Pain: The *Fragments* Affair." *Extremities: Trauma Testimony, and Community*. Eds. Nancy K. Miller and Jason Tougaw. Urbana: University of Illinois Press, 2002. 92–111.

———. *Facing It: AIDS Diaries and the Death of the Author*. Ann Arbor: University of Michigan Press, 1998.

Chaon, Anne. "Who Failed in Rwanda, Journalists or the Media." *The Media and the Rwanda Genocide*. Ed. Allan Thompson. London-New York: Pluto Press/Fountain Publishers/IDRC, 2007. 160–66.

Chaumont, Jean-Michel. *La concurrence des victimes. Génocide, identié, reconnaissance*. Paris: Editions la Découverte, 1997.

Chrétien, Jean-Pierre. *The Great Lakes of Africa: Two Thousand Years of History*. Translated from the French by Scott Straus. New York: Zone Books, 2003 [2000].

———., Jean-François Dupaquier, Marcel Kabanda and Joseph Ngarambe eds., *Rwanda, les médias du génocide*. Paris: Karthala, 2002.

———. *L'Afrique des grands lacs. Deux mille ans d'histoire*. Paris: Flammarion, 2001 [2000].

Chun, Wendy Hui Kyong. "Unberable Witness: Toward a Politics of Listening." *Extremities, Trauma Testimony, and Community*. Eds. Nancy K. Miller and Jason Tougaw. Urbana: University of Illinois Press, 2002. 143–165.

Church, William. "Rwanda: Hate Speech and Paul Rusesabagina." *The Conservative Voice* January 31, 2007.

———. "Rusesabagina, Genocide Identity Politics." *The Conservative Voice* January 16, 2007.

Clark, Phil and Zachary D. Kaufmann eds., *After Genocide: Transitional Justice, Post-Conflict Reconstruction and Reconciliation in Rwanda and Beyond*. London: Hurst & Compagny, 2009.

Clarke, Bruce. "Un million de pierres au pays des mille collines." *Africultures* 30 (2000): 18–20.

Cohen, Jared. *One-hundred Days of Silence: America and the Rwanda Genocide*. Lanham, MD: Rowman & Littlefield Publishers, 2007.

Cojean, Annick. "Les voix de l'indicible." *Le Monde* April 25, 1995.

Cole, Tim. *Selling the Holocaust: From Auschwitz to Schindler: How History is Bought, Packaged, and Sold*. New York: Routledge, 1999.

Collard, Marie-France. "Le génocide continue." *Rwanda 1994–2004: des faits, des mots, des œuvres*. Ed. Laure Coret. Paris: L'Harmattan, 2005. 145–148.

Cook, Susan. "The Politics of Preservation in Rwanda." *Genocide in Cambodia and Rwanda: New Perspectives*. Ed. Susan Cook. Piscataway, NJ: Transaction Publishers, 2005. 293–311.

Coquio, Catherine. "Envoyer les fantômes au musée?" *Gradhiva* 5 (2007): 39–52.

———. *Rwanda. Le réel et les récits*. Paris: Belin, 2004.

———. "À propos d'un nihilisme contemporain. Négation, déni, témoignage." *L'Histoire trouée. Négation et témoignage.* Ed. Catherine Coquio. Nantes: L'Atalante, 2003. 23–89.

———. "Aux lendemains, là-bas et ici: l'écriture, la mémoire et le deuil." *Lendemains* 112 (2003): 6–38.

Coret, Laure ed., *Rwanda 1994–2004: des faits, des mots, des œuvres.* Paris: L'Harmattan, 2005.

———. "*Rwanda 94*, au Rwanda, dix ans après." *Rwanda 1994–2004: des faits, des mots, des œuvres.* Ed. Laure Coret. Paris: L'Harmattan, 2005. 149–158.

———. and François-Xavier Verschave eds. *L'horreur qui nous prend au visage. L'État français et le génocide au Rwanda.* Paris: Karthala, 2005.

———. and Ye Young Chung. "'Dire l'invisible.' Étude comparatiste de *Shoah* de Claude Lanzmann et *Rwanda 94, une tentative de réparation symbolique envers les morts à l'usage des vivants* du Groupov." *Drôle d'époque* 14 (2004): 179–195.

Courtemanche, Gil. *A Sunday at the Pool in Kigali.* Translated from the French by Patricia Claxton. Montreal: Vintage Canada, 2004 [2000].

Curthoys, Ann and John Docker. *Is History Fiction?* Ann Arbor: The University of Michigan Press, 2005.

Dallaire, Roméo. *Shake Hands with The Devil: The Failure of Humanity In Rwanda.* Toronto: Random House Canada, 2003.

Dauge-Roth, Alexandre. "Testimonial Encounter: Esther Mujawayo's Dialogic Art of Witnessing." *French Cultural Studies* 20.2 (May 2009): 165–180.

De Baecque, Antoine. "Quel cinéma après Auschwitz?" *Cahiers du cinéma* Hors-série (2000): 62–66.

Delbo, Charlotte. *Auschwitz and After.* Translated from the French by Rosette Lamont. New Haven: Yale University Press, 1995 [1970].

Delcuvellerie, Jacques. "La représentation en question." *Rwanda 1994–2004: des faits, des mots, des œuvres.* Ed. Laure Coret. Paris: L'Harmattan, 2005. 127–140.

———. "Une réparation symbolique: Entretien avec Jean-Christophe Planche." *Périphéries* (May 2000). http://www.peripheries.net/article245.html.

Deme, Amadou. "*Hotel Rwanda*: Setting the Record Straight." *Counterpunch* April 24, 2006.

Derrida, Jacques and Élisabeth Roudinesco. "Choosing One's Heritage." In *For What Tomorrow . . . A Dialogue.* Translated from the French by Jeff Fort. Stanford: Stanford University Press, 2004 [2001]. 1–19.

Derrida, Jacques. "Responsabilité et hospitalité." *Autour de Jacques Derrida. De l'Hospitalité.* Ed. Mahammed Seffahi. Genouilleux: Éditions la passe du vent, 2001. 131–149.

———. *Writing and Difference.* Translated from the French by Alan Bass. London and New York: Routledge Classics, 2001 [1967].

———. *Of Hospitality: Anne Dufourmantelle Invites Jacques Derrida to Respond.* Translated from the French by Rachel Bowlby. Stanford: Stanford University Press, 2000 [1997].

———. *The Instant of my Death Maurice Blanchot: Demeure: Fiction and Testimony.* Translated from the French by Elizabeth Rottenberg. Stanford: Stanford University Press, 2000 [1998].

———. *Adieu to Emmanuel Lévinas.* Translated from the French by Pascale-Anne Brault and Michael Naas. Stanford: Stanford University Press, 1999 [1997].

———. "Marx & Sons." *Ghostly Demarcations: A Symposium on Jacques Derrida's Specters of Marx.* Ed. Michael Sprinker. London and New York: Verso, 1999. 213–269.

———. *Specters of Marx.* Translated from the French by Peggy Kamuf. New York: Routledge, 1994 [1993].

Des Forges, Alison. "Call to Genocide: Radio in Rwanda, 1994." *The Media and the Rwanda Genocide.* Ed. Allan Thompson. London-New York: Pluto Press/Fountain Publishers/IDRC, 2007. 41–54.

———. ed., *Leave no One to Tell the Story. Genocide in Rwanda.* New York: Human Rights Watch, 1999.

Didi-Huberman, Georges. *Images in Spite of All: Four Photographs from Auschwitz.* Translated from the French by Shane B. Lillis. Chicago: University of Chicago Press, 2008 [2003].

Digneffe, Françoise and Jacques Fierens eds., *Justice et gacaca. L'expérience rwandaise et le génocide.* Namur: Presses Universitaires de Namur, 2003.

Diop, Boubacar Boris. "Génocide et devoir d'imaginaire." *Revue d'Histoire de la Shoah* 190 (2009): 365–381.

———. *Murambi, The Book of Bones.* Translated from the French by Fiona Mc Laughlin. Bloomington and Indianapolis: Indiana University Press, 2006 [2000].

———. "Stephen Smith, passeur du racisme ordinaire." *Négrophobie.* Eds. Boubacar Boris Diop, Odile Tobner and François-Xavier Verschave. Paris: Les Arènes, 2005. 61–101.

———. "A la découverte de notre innocence. Entretien de Taina Tervonen avec Boubacar Boris Diop." *Africultures* 59 (2004): 30–38.

———. "Entretien avec Boubacar Boris Diop par Marie Bernard." *Aircrige* (March 2001). http://aircrigeweb.free.fr/ressources/rwanda/RwandaDiop1.html.

———. "Le Rwanda m'a appris à appeler les monstres pas leur nom. Entretien." *Africultures* 30 (2000): 15–17.

———. *Le cavalier et son ombre.* Paris: Stock, 1998.

———. *Les Traces de la meute.* Paris: L'Harmattan, 1993.

———. *Les Tambours de la mémoire.* Paris: L'Harmattan, 1990.

———. *Le Temps de Tamango.* Paris: L'Harmattan, 1981.

———. *Thiaroye terre rouge* (theater). Paris: L'Harmattan, 1981.

Djedanoum, Nocky. *Nyamirambo!* Bamako and Lille: Editions Le Figuier/Fest'Africa, 2000.

———. and Maïmouna Coulibaly. "'Nous avions l'obligation morale d'aller jusqu'au bout' Entretien." *Africultures* 30 (2000): 12–14.

———. "Le partage du deuil: entretien avec Sylvain Marcelli." *L'Interdit* (November 2000). www.interdits.net/2000nov/rwanda2.htm.

──────. "Interview of Nocky Djedanoum by Chaacha Mwita." *Daily Nation* June 25, 2000. http://www.nationaudio.com/News/DailyNation/25062000/Features/I S1 htm

Dorland, Michael. "PG—Parental Guidance of Portrayal of Genocide: The Comparative Depiction of Mass Murder in Contemporary Cinema." *The Media and the Rwanda Genocide*. Ed. Allan Thompson. London-New York: Pluto Press/Fountain Publishers/IDRC, 2007. 417–432.

Doubrovsky, Serge. *Fils*. Paris: Éditions Galilée, 1977.

Doyle, Mark. "Reporting the Genocide." *The Media and the Rwanda Genocide*. Ed. Allan Thompson. London-New York: Pluto Press/Fountain Publishers/IDRC, 2007. 145–159.

Dumas, Hélène. "L'histoire des vaincus. Négationnisme du génocide des Tutsi au Rwanda." *Revue d'Histoire de la Shoah* 190 (2009): 299–347.

Eltringham, Nigel. *Accounting for Horror. Post-Genocide Debates in Rwanda*. London: Pluto Press, 2004.

Farge, Arlette. *Le Goût de l'archive*. Paris: Seuil, 1989.

Farnel, Serge. "Sauver le chien de l'ambassade de France." *La Nuit Rwandaise* 2 (2008): 185–193.

Felman, Shoshana and Dori Laub, M.D. *Testimony: Crises of Witnessing in Literature, Psychoanalysis, and History*. New York and London: Routledge, 1992.

Franche, Dominique. *Généalogie du génocide rwandais*. Bruxelles: Tribord, 2004.

Gaillard, Philippe. "Rwanda 1994: un témoignage: 'On peut tuer autant de gens qu'on veut, on ne peut pas tuer leur mémoire.'" *IRRC* 855 (2004): 611–627.

Gallimore, Rangira Béatrice and Chantal Kalisa eds., *Dix and après: réflexions sur le génocide rwandais*. Paris: L'Harmattan, 2005.

Gasengayire, Monique. "*Murekatete*, un témoignage (im)possible." *Dix ans après: réflexions sur le génocide rwandais*. Eds. Rangira Béatrice Gallimore and Chantal Kalisa. Paris: L'Harmattan, 2005. 143–160.

George, Terry. "Smearing a Hero, Sad Revisionism over *Hotel Rwanda*." *Washington Post* May 10, 2006.

Giles, Tom. "Media Failure Over the Rwanda's Genocide." *The Media and the Rwanda Genocide*. Ed. Allan Thompson. London-New York: Pluto Press/Fountain Publishers/IDRC, 2007. 235–241.

Glissant, Edouard. *The Poetics of Relation*. Translated from the French by Betsy Wing. Ann Arbor: University of Michigan Press, 1997 [1990].

Godard, Marie-Odile. *Rêves et traumatismes ou la longue nuit des rescapés*. Romonville Saint-Agen: Editions érès, 2003.

Goldhagen, Daniel. *Hitler's Willing Executioners: Ordinary Germans and the Holocaust*. London: Little, Brown and Co., 1996.

Gourevitch, Philip. *We Wish to Inform You That Tomorrow We Will be Killed With Our Families: Stories from Rwanda*. New York: Farrar, Straus & Giroux Inc., 1998.

Gouteux, Jean-Paul. "Génocide rwandais: La presse française au ban des accusés." *The Dominion* August 17, 2005. www.dominionpaper.ca/francais/2005/08/17/genocide_r.html.

———. *Un génocide sans importance. La Françafrique au Rwanda.* Lyon: Editions Tahin Party, 2001.

———. *'Le Monde', un contre-pouvoir? Désinformation et manipulation sur le génocide rwandais.* Paris: L'Esprit frappeur, 1999

Groupov (Collectif théâtral. Jacques Delcuvellerie dir.). *Rwanda 94. Une tentative de réparation symbolique envers les morts, à l'usage des vivants.* Paris: Editions théâtrales, 2002.

———. *Rwanda 94. Une tentative de réparation symbolique envers les morts, à l'usage des vivants—Rwanda 94: An Attempt at Symbolic Reparation to the Dead, For Use by the Living.* Translated from the French and from Kinyarwanda by Prajna Paramita. The book includes a double CD of the music directed by Garrett List with additional compositions by Jean-Marie Muyango. Brussels: Carbon 7 Records/Liège: Groupov, 2000.

Halen, Pierre. "Le Rwanda et la question de l'altérité: à propos de deux récits de voyage (V. Tadjo, H. C. Buch)." *Dix ans après: réflexions sur le génocide rwandais.* Eds. Rangira Béatrice Gallimore and Chantal Kalisa. Paris: L'Harmattan, 2005. 189–208.

Hatzfeld, Jean. *The Antelope's Strategy.* Translated from the French by Linda Coverdale. New York: Farrar, Straus & Giroux Inc., 2009 [2007].

———. "L'Impasse: interview de Jean Hatzfeld by Pierre Michel." *Actualité Livres—Evene.fr* October 2007. http://www.evene.fr/livres/actualite/interview-jean-hatzfeld-strategie-antilopes-977.php.

———. *Machete Season: The Killers in Rwanda Speak.* Preface by Susan Sontag. Translated from the French by Linda Coverdale. New York: Farrar, Straus & Giroux Inc., 2005 [2003].

———. *Life Laid Bare: The Survivors in Rwanda Speak.* Translated from the French by Linda Coverdale. Photographs by Raymond Depardon. New York: Other Press, 2007 [2000].

Hilsum, Lindsey. "Reporting Rwanda: The Media and the Aid Agencies." *The Media and the Rwanda Genocide.* Ed. Allan Thompson. London-New York: Pluto Press/Fountain Publishers/IDRC, 2007. 167–187.

Hughes, Nick. "Exhibit 467: Genocide Through a Camera Lens." *The Media and the Rwanda Genocide.* Ed. Allan Thompson. London-New York: Pluto Press/Fountain Publishers/IDRC, 2007. 231–34.

Huyssen, Andreas. "Monument and Memory in a Postmodern Age." *The Art of Memory. Holocaust Memorials in History.* Ed. James E. Young. New York and Munich: Prestel Verlag, 1994. 9–17.

Ilboudo, Monique. *Murekatete!* Bamako: Editions Le Figuier/Lille: Fest'Africa, 2000.

Inongo, Willy and Senga Kibwanga. *Couple modèle—couple maudit.* Durbuy: Coccinelle BD, 2001.

Jay, Martin. "Of Plots, Witnessing, and Judgments." *Probing the Limits of Representation: Nazism and the "Final Solution."* Ed. Saul Friedlander. Cambridge: Harvard University Press, 1992. 97–107.

Kabanda, Marcel. "*Kangura*: The Triumph of Propaganda Refined." *The Media and the Rwanda Genocide.* Ed. Allan Thompson. London-New York: Pluto Press/Fountain Publishers/IDRC, 2007. 62–72.

Kaes, Anton. "Holocaust and the End of History: Postmodern Historiography in Cinema." *Probing the Limits of Representation: Nazism and the "Final Solution."* Ed. Saul Friedlander. Cambridge: Harvard University Press, 1992. 206–222.

Kagame, Paul. "Preface." *After Genocide. Transitional Justice, Post-Conflict Reconstruction and Reconciliation in Rwanda and Beyond.* Eds. Phil Clark and Zachary D. Kaufman. London: Hurst Publishers, 2009. xxi–xxvi.

Kalisa, Chantal. "Theater and the Rwandan Genocide." *Peace Review* 18.4 (2006): 515–521.

———. "Le Gos au Rwanda. Entretien avec Koulsy Lamko." *Dix ans après: réflexions sur le génocide rwandais.* Eds. Rangira Béatrice Gallimore and Chantal Kalisa. Paris: L'Harmattan, 2005. 259–280.

———. and Rangira Béatrice Gallimore eds., *Dix ans après: réflexions sur le génocide rwandais.* Paris: L'Harmattan, 2005.

Kayimahe, Vénuste. "La peur des fantômes." *La Nuit Rwandaise* 3 (2009): 67–89.

———. *France-Rwanda, les coulisses du génocide. Témoignage d'un rescapé.* Paris: Dagorno/L'Esprit frappeur, 2002.

Kayitesi, Annick. *Nous existons encore.* Paris: Michel Lafon, 2004.

Kayitesi, Berthe. *Demain ma vie. Enfants chefs de famille dans le Rwanda d'après.* Paris: Editions Teper, 2009.

———, Rollande Deslandes and Christine Lebel. "Facteurs de résilience chez des orphelins rescapés du génocide qui vivent seuls dans les ménages au Rwanda (Association Tubeho)." *Revue canadienne de santé mentale comunautaire* 28.1 (2009): 67–81.

Kimenyi, Alexandre. "Trivialization of Genocide: The Case of Rwanda." *Anatomy of Genocide: State-Sponsored Mass-Killings in the 20th Century.* Eds. Alexandre Kimenyi and Otis L. Scott. Lewiston, NY: The Edwin Mellen Press, 2002. 429–444.

Klotz, Jean-Christophe. "Le papillon face à la flamme: interview de Jean-Christophe Klotz." *Evene.fr* (November 2006). http://www.evene.fr/cinema/actualite/interview-klotz-rwanda-kigali-images-massacre-kouchner-559.php.

Kofman, Sarah. *Smothered Words.* Translated from the French by Madeleine Dobie. Evanston, IL: Northwestern University Press, 1998 [1987].

Kritzman, Lawrence. "In Remembrance of Things French." *Realms of Memory: Rethinking the French Past.* Ed. Pierre Nora. vol.1. New York: Columbia University Press, 1996 [1984]. ix–xiv.

Krog, Antjie. *Country of My Skull: Guilt, Sorrow, and the Limits of Forgiveness in the New South Africa.* New York: Three Rivers Press, 2000.

Kyomuhendo, Goretti. *Secrets No More.* Lansing: Michigan State University Press, 1999.

LaCapra, Dominick. *Writing History, Writing Trauma.* Baltimore, MD: The John Hopkins University Press, 2001.

Lamko, Koulsy. "Fest'Africa au Rwanda: Un projet artistique qui a fait école. Entretien avec Koulsy Lamko. Propos recueillis par Sylvie Chalaye." *Africultures* 43 (2001).

———. *La Phalène des collines.* Paris: Le Serpent à plumes, 2002 [Butare: Éditions Kuljaama, 2000].

———. *Le Mot dans la rosée.* Arles: Actes Sud Papiers, 1997.

Lang, Berel. "The Representations of Limits." *Probing the Limits of Representation: Nazism and the "Final Solution."* Ed. Saul Friedlander. Cambridge: Harvard University Press, 1992. 300–317.

Langer, Lawrence. *The Holocaust and the Literary Imagination.* New Haven, CT: Yale University Press, 1975.

Lanzmann, Claude. "Le Lieu et la Parole. Interview par Marc Chevrie et Hervé Le Roux." *Au sujet de* Shoah, *le film de Claude Lanzmann.* Ed. Michel Deguy. Paris: Belin, 1990.

La Pradelle, Géraud de. *Imprescriptible. L'implication française dans le génocide tutsi portée devant les tribunaux.* Paris: Les Arènes, 2005.

Lee, Sonia. "Lire le Rwanda: Une lecture personnelle de *L'Ombre d'Imana, Voyages jusqu'au bout du Rwanda* de Véronique Tadjo." *Dix ans après: réflexions sur le génocide rwandais.* Eds. Rangira Béatrice Gallimore and Chantal Kalisa. Paris: L'Harmattan, 2005. 93–102.

Lejeune, Philippe. *On Autobiography.* Translated from the French by Katherine Leary. Minneapolis: University of Minnesota Press, 1989 [1975].

Levi, Primo. *The Drowned and the Saved.* Translated from the Italian by Raymond Rosenthal. New York: Random House, 1989 [1986].

———. *Survival in Auschwitz and The Reawakening: Two Memoirs.* Translated from the Italian by Stuart Woolf. New York: Summit Books, 1986 [1947].

Livingston, Steven. "Limited Vision: How Both the American Media and Government Failed Rwanda." *The Media and the Rwanda Genocide.* Ed. Allan Thompson. London-New York: Pluto Press/Fountain Publishers/IDRC, 2007. 188–197.

Mamdani, Mahmood. *When Victims Become Killers: Colonialism, Nativism, and the Genocide in Rwanda.* Princeton, NJ: Princeton University Press, 2001.

Masioni, Pat, Cécile Grenier and Alain Austini. *Rwanda 1994. Tome 2: Le camp de la vie.* Paris: Vent des Savanes, 2008.

———, Cécile Grenier and Ralph. *Rwanda 1994. Tome 1: Descente en enfer.* Paris: Albin Michel, 2005.

M'Bokolo, Elikia. *Au cœur de l'ethnie.* Paris: La Découverte, 1985.

Melvern, Linda. "Missing the Story: The Media and the Rwandan Genocide." *The Media and the Rwanda Genocide.* Ed. Allan Thompson. London-New York: Pluto Press/Fountain Publishers/IDRC, 2007. 198–210.

———. "History? This film is fiction. A new BBC film telling the 'truth' of events in Rwanda only compounds the original sins of the West's media." *The Observer,* March 19, 2006.

———. *Conspiracy to Murder: The Rwanda Genocide.* London: Verso, 2004.

———. *A People Betrayed: The Role of the West in Rwanda's Genocide.* London: Zed Books, 2000.

Miller, Nancy K. "Memory Stains: Annie Ernaux's *Shame.*" *Extremities: Trauma Testimony and Community.* Eds. Nancy K. Miller and Jason Tougaw. Urbana: University of Illinois Press, 2002. 197–212.

Misago, Célestin Kanimba. "Les instruments de la mémoire. Génocide et traumatismes au Rwanda." *Gradhiva* 5 (2007): 63–75.

Monénembo, Tierno. *The Oldest Orphan*. Translated from the French by Monique Fleury Nagem. Linçoln: University of Nebraska Press, 2001 [2000].

———. *Cinéma*. Paris: Seuil, 1997.

———. *Pelourinho*. Paris: Seuil, 1995.

———. *Un attiéké pour Elgass*. Paris: Seuil, 1993.

———. *Un rêve utile*. Paris: Seuil, 1991.

———. *Les Écailles du ciel*. Paris: Seuil, 1986.

———. *Les Crapauds-brousse*. Paris: Seuil, 1979.

Mugiraneza, Assumpta. "La dynamique discursive dans l'idéologie génocidaire." *Humanitaire* 10 (2004): 107–115.

———. "Les écueils dans l'appréhension de l'histoire du génocide des Tutsi." *Revue d'Histoire de la Shoah* 190 (2009): 153–172.

———. "*Négationnisme* au Rwanda post-génocide." *Revue d'Histoire de la Shoah* 190 (2009): 285–298.

Mujawayo, Esther. "Postface to Alexandre Dauge-Roth's 'Testimonial Encounter: Esther Mujawayo's Dialogic Art of Witnessing'." *French Cultural Studies* 20.2 (2009): 177–179.

Mujawayo, Esther and Souâd Belhaddad. *La Fleur de Stéphanie. Rwanda entre réconciliation et déni*. Paris: Flammarion, 2006.

———. *SurVivantes: Rwanda, dix ans après le génocide*. Paris: Editions de l'Aube, 2004.

Mukagasana, Yolande. *Les blessures du silence. Témoignages du génocide au Rwanda*. Photographies d'Alain Kazinierakis. Arles: Actes Sud and Médecins sans frontières, 2001.

———. *N'aie pas peur de savoir*. Paris: Robert Laffont, 1999.

———. *La mort ne veut pas de moi*. Paris: Fixot, 1997.

Mukasonga, Scholastique. *La femme aux pieds nus*. Paris: Gallimard, 2008.

———. *Inyenzi ou les Cafards*. Paris: Gallimard, 2006.

Munyandamutsa, Naasson. "Blessure invisible, une expérience déroutante." *Humanitaire* 10 (2004): 160–167.

Ndahiro, Alfred and Privat Rutazibwa. *Hotel Rwanda or the Tutsi Genocide as Seen by Hollywood*. Paris: L'Harmattan, 2008.

Newbury, Catharine. *The Cohesion of Oppression: Clientship and Ethnicity in Rwanda, 1860–1960*. New York: Columbia University Press, 1988.

Novick, Peter. *The Holocaust in American Life*. Boston: Houghton Mifflin, 1999.

Parrau, Alain. *Écrire les camps*. Paris: Belin, 1995.

Planche, Jean-Christophe. "Une réparation symbolique: Entretien avec Jean-Christophe Planche." *Périphéries* (May 2000). http://www.peripheries.net/article245.html.

Pottier, Johan. *Re-Imagining Rwanda: Conflict, Survival, and Disinformation in the Late Twentieth Century*. Cambridge: Cambridge University Press, 2002.

Power, Samantha. *A Problem from Hell: America and the Age of Genocide*. New York: Perennial, 2003.

Press, Joy. "Shadow of Guilt: Director Raoul Peck reflects on making a drama about Rwanda without cheap tears." *The Village Voice* March 8, 2005.

Prunier, Gérard. *The Rwandan Crisis: History of a Genocide*. New York: Columbia University Press, 1995.

Raharimanana, Jean-Luc. *Rêves sous le linceul*. Paris: Le Serpent à plumes, 1998.

Ricoeur, Paul. *Memory, History, Forgetting*. Translated from the French by Kathleen Blamey and David Pellauer. Chicago: The University of Chicago Press, 2004 [2000].

———. "Paul Ricoeur: Interview with Richard Kearney," *On Paul Ricoeur: The Owl of Minerva*. Ed. Richard Kearney. Aldershot: Ashgate Publishing, 2004.

———. *The Rule of Metaphor: Multi-Disciplinary Studies in the Creation of Meaning in Language*. Translated from the French by Robert Czerny with Kathleen McLaughlin and John Costello. London: Routledge and Kegan Paul, 1978 [1975].

Rittner, Carol, John K. Roth and Wendy Whitworth eds., *Genocide in Rwanda: Complicity of the Churches?* St. Paul, MN: Paragon House Publishers, 2004.

Rivette, Jacques. "De l'Abjection: Sur *Kapo* de Gillo Pontecorvo (1960)." *Cahiers du cinéma* Hors-série (November 2000): 67.

Robin, Régine. *La Mémoire Saturée*. Paris: Stock, 2003.

Rosello, Mireille. *Postcolonial Hospitality: The Immigrant as Guest*. Stanford: Stanford University Press, 2001.

Roskis, Edgar. "Une génocide sans images. Blancs filment Noirs." *Le Monde diplomatique* November 1994.

Rothberg, Michael. "Between the Extreme and the Everyday: Ruth Klüger's Traumatic Realism." *Extremities: Trauma Testimony and Community*. Eds. Nancy K. Miller and Jason Tougaw. Urbana: University of Illinois Press, 2002. 55–70.

———. *Traumatic Realism: The Demands of Holocaust Representation*. Minneapolis: University of Minnesota Press, 2000.

Rousso, Henry. *La hantise du passé. Entretien avec Philippe Petit*. Paris: Les éditions Textuel, 1998.

———. *The Vichy Syndrome: History and Memory in France since 1944*. Translated from the French by Arthur Goldhammer. Cambridge: Harvard University Press, 1991 [1987].

Rugamba, Dorcy. "Nécessité de dire." *Rwanda 1994–2004: des faits, des mots, des œuvres*. Ed. Laure Coret. Paris: L'Harmattan, 2005. 141–143.

Rurangwa, Jean-Marie Vianney. *Le Génocide des Tutsi expliqué à un étranger*. Bamako: Editions Le Figuier/Lille: Fest'Africa, 2000.

Rurangwa, Révérien. *Genocide*. Translated from the French by Anna Brown. London: Reportage Press, 2009 [2006].

Rusesabagina, Paul and Tom Zoellner. *An Ordinary Man: An Autobiography*. New York: Viking Adult, 2006.

Rusimbi, John Garuka. *By the Time She Returned*. London: Janus Publishing Company, 1999.

Rutayisere, Paul. "Le remodelage de l'espace culturel rwandais par l'église et la colonisation." *Revue d'Histoire de la Shoah* 190 (2009): 83–103.

Saint-Exupéry, Patrick de. *Complices de l'Inavouable: La France au Rwanda*. Paris: Les Arènes, 2009.

———. *L'inavouable: La France au Rwanda*. Paris: Les Arènes, 2004.

Sebasoni, Servilien. *Les Origines du Rwanda*. Paris: L'Harmattan, 2000.

Sehene, Benjamin. *Le feu sous la soutane. Un prêtre au cœur du génocide rwandais*. Paris: L'Esprit Frappeur, 2005.

———. "Dead Girl Walking." Translated from the French by Toni Wulff. *From Africa: New Francophone Stories.* Ed. Adele King. Lincoln: University of Nebraska Press, 2004. 110–121.

———. *Le Piège ethnique.* Paris: Dagorno, 1999.

Semujanga, Josias. *Le génocide, sujet de fiction? Analyse des récits du massacre des Tutsi dans la littérature africaine.* Québec: Éditions Nota Bene, 2008.

———. "Le Témoignage de l'itsembabwoko par la fiction: *L'Ombre d'Imana.*" *Présence Francophone: Revue Internationale de Langue et de Littérature* 69 (2007): 106–34.

———. "*Murambi* et *Moisson de crânes* ou comment la fiction raconte un génocide." *Présence Francophone: Revue Internationale de Langue et de Littérature* 67 (2006): 93–114.

———. *Origins of Rwandan Genocide.* Foreword by Tom Rockmore. Amherst, MA: Humanity Book, 2003 [1998].

———. "Les mots du rejets et les récits du génocide." *Les Langages de la mémoire. Littérature, médias et génocide au Rwanda.* Eds. Pierre Halen and Jacques Walter. Metz: Université Paul Verlaine, 2003. 17–35.

———. "Les méandres du récit du génocide dans *L'aîné des orphelins.*" *Études littéraires* 35.1 (2003): 101–115.

Small, Audrey. "The Duty of Memory: A Solidarity of Voices after the Rwandan Genocide." *Paragraph: A Journal of Modern Critical Theory* 30.1 (2007): 85–100.

Sontag, Susan. *Regarding the Pain of Others.* New York: Farrar, Straus & Giroux Inc., 2003.

Stallybrass, Peter and Allon White. *The Politics And Poetics of Transgression.* Ithaca: Cornell University Press, 1986.

Stassen, Jean-Philippe. *PAWA Chroniques des monts de la lune.* Paris: Delcourt, 2002.

———. *Déogratias: A Tale of Rwanda.* Translated from the French by Alexis Siegel. New York: First Second, 2006 [2000].

Straus, Scott. *The Order of Genocide: Race, Power, and War in Rwanda.* Ithaca: Cornell University Press, 2006.

Tadjo, Véronique. *The Shadow of Imana: Travels in the Heart of Rwanda.* Translated from the French by Véronique Wakerley. Oxford: Heinemann, 2002 [2000].

———. *Champs de bataille et d'amour.* Paris: Présence Africaine, 1999.

———. *A vol d'oiseau.* Paris: L'Harmattan, 1992.

———. *Le Royaume aveugle.* Paris: L'Harmattan, 1991.

———. *Latérite* (poems). Paris: Hatier, 1984.

Tal, Kalí. *Worlds of Hurt: Reading the Literature of Trauma.* New York: Cambridge University Press, 1996.

Ternon, Yves. "Rwanda 1994. Analyse d'un processus génocidaire." *Revue d'Histoire de la Shoah* 190 (2009): 15–57.

Thompson, Allan ed. *The Media and the Rwanda Genocide.* London-New York: Pluto Press/Fountain Publishers/IDRC, 2007.

Todorov, Tzvetan. *Les abus de la mémoire.* Paris: Arléa, 1998.

———. *Facing the Exreme.* Translated from the French by Arthur Denner and Abigail Pollak. New York: Metropolitan Books, 1996 [1991].

Trouillot, Michel-Rolph. *Silencing the Past: Power and the Production of History.* Boston: Beacon Press, 1995.

Umutesi, Chantal. *La paix dans l'âme.* Paris: Klanba éditions, 2004.

Uvin, Peter. *Aiding Violence: The Development Enterprise in Rwanda.* West Hartford, CT: Kumarian Press, 1998.

Verschave, François-Xavier. "Dix ans de désinformation." *Négrophobie.* Eds. Boubacar Boris Diop, Odile Tobner and François-Xavier Verschave. Paris: Les Arènes, 2005. 103–196.

———. and Laure Coret eds. *L'horreur qui nous prend au visage. L'État français et le génocide au Rwanda.* Paris: Karthala, 2005.

———. *Françafrique: Le plus long scandale de la République.* Paris: Stock, 2003.

Vidal, Claudine. "Les commémorations du génocide au Rwanda." *Les Temps modernes* 613 (2001): 1–46.

———. "Le génocide des Rwandais tutsi et l'usage public de l'histoire." *Cahiers d'études africaines* 150/152 (1998): 653–663.

Vulpain, Laure de. *Rwanda, Un génocide oublié? Un procès pour mémoire.* Paris: Editions Complexe, Arte Editions and France Culture, 2004.

Waberi, Abdourahman A. *Moisson de crânes. Textes pour le Rwanda.* Paris: Le Serpent à Plumes, 2000.

———. *Balbala.* Paris: Le Serpent à Plumes, 1996.

Waintrater, Régine. "Le temps de l'extrême: génocide et temporalité." *Revue d'Histoire de la Shoah* 190 (2009): 407–426.

———. *Sortir du génocide. Témoigner pour réapprendre à vivre.* Paris: Payot, 2003.

———, Jean Damascène Bizimana, Annick Kayitesi, Yves Ternon and Jean-Pierre Getti. "Table ronde. Dix ans après: le génocide des Tutsis du Rwanda." *Humanitaire* 10 (2004): 52–68.

Waldorf, Lars. "Censorship and Propaganda in Post-Genocide Rwanda." *The Media and the Rwanda Genocide.* Ed. Allan Thompson. London-New York: Pluto Press/ Fountain Publishers/IDRC, 2007. 404–416.

Weine, Stevan. *Testimony After Catastrophe: Narrating the Traumas of Political Violence.* Evanston, IL: Northwestern University Press, 2006.

Weissman, Gary. "A Fantasy of Witnessing." *Media, Culture & Society* 17 (April 1995): 293–307.

Wieviorka, Annette. *Auschwitz expliqué à ma fille.* Paris: Seuil, 1999.

———. *L'Ère du témoin.* Paris: Plon, 1998.

———. *Déportation et génocide. Entre la mémoire et l'oubli.* Paris: Hachette/Pluriel, 1995.

Yaeger, Patricia. "Consuming Trauma: or, The Pleasures of Merely Circulating." *Extremities: Trauma Testimony and Community.* Eds. Nancy K. Miller and Jason Tougaw. Urbana: University of Illinois Press, 2002. 25–51.

Young, James E. *Writing and Rewriting the Holocaust: Narrative and the Consequences of Interpretation.* Bloomington and Indianapolis: Indiana University Press, 1990.

Filmography

Aghion, Anne. *My Neighbor My Killer.* France, 2009. 80 mn.
——. *The Notebooks of Memory.* France, 2009. 53 mn.
——. *In Rwanda We Say . . . The Family That Does Not Speak Dies.* France, 2004. 55 mn.
——. *Gacaca, Living Together Again In Rwanda?* France, 2002. 55 mn.
Anker, Daniel. *Imaginary Witness: Hollywood and the Holocaust.* USA, 2004. 92 mn.
Barker, Greg. *Ghosts of Rwanda.* USA-Great Britain, 2004. 120 mn.
Caton-Jones, Michael. *Shooting Dogs.* Great Britain-Germany, 2005. 115 mn.
Collard, Marie-France and Patrick Czaplinski. *Rwanda 94: An Attempt at Symbolic Reparation to the Dead, for Use by the Living. Based on the Show "Rwanda 94," directed by Jacques Delcuvellerie.* Belgium, 2007. 340 mn.
——. *Rwanda: Through us, humanity . . .* Belgium, 2006. 155 mn.
——. *Ouvrières du Monde.* Belgium, 2000. 57 mn.
Courtemanche, Gil. *L'Église du SIDA. Les ravages du SIDA au Rwanda.* Canada, 1993. 57 mn.
Favreau, Robert. *Un dimanche à Kigali.* Canada, 2006. 118 mn.
George, Terry. *Hôtel Rwanda.* Great Britain-South Africa-Italy, 2004. 121 mn.
Genoud, Robert. *Rwanda—Récit d'un Survivant.* France, 2001. 52 mn.
——. *La France au Rwanda.* France, 1999. 52 mn.
——. *Rwanda: How History Can Lead to Genocide.* France, 1995. 52 mn.
Glucksmann Raphaël, David Hazan and Pierre Mezerette. *"Tuez-les tous!" Rwanda: Histoire d'un génocide "sans importance."* France, 2004. 97 mn.
Hinson, Laura Waters. *As We Forgive.* USA, 2008. 53 mn.
Hughes, Nick. *100 Days.* Great Britain-Rwanda, 2001. 115 mn.
Kabera, Eric and Juan Reina. *Iseta: Behind the Roadblock.* Great Britain-Rwanda. 2009. 57 mn.

Kabera, Eric. *Keepers of Memory*. Rwanda, 2005. 52 mn.

Keane, Fergal, *Valentina's Nightmare A Journey into the Rwandan Genocide*. Great Britain-USA, 1997. 60 mn.

Klotz, Jean-Christophe. *Kigali. Des images contre un massacre*. France, 2005. 94 mn.

Lacourse, Danièle and Yvan Patry. *Chronicle of a Genocide Foretold*. Canada, 1996. 164 mn.

Lainé, Anne. *Rwanda, un cri d'un silence inouï. Témoignages de rescapés du génocide*. France, 2003. 52 mn.

Mwicira Mitali, Daddy De Maximo. *By The Shortcut*. Rwanda, 2009. 105 mn.

Ndahayo, Gilbert. *Rwanda: Beyond The Deadly Pit*. Rwanda, 2008. 97 mn.

N'Diaye, Samba Félix. *Rwanda, pour mémoire*. Senegal-France, 2003. 68 mn.

Peck, Raoul. *Sometimes in April*. USA, 2004. 135 mn.

———. "Making 'Sometimes in April'." *Sometimes in April*. DVD, 2005.

———. "Audio Commentary with Writer and Director Raoul Peck conducted by Elvis Michell." *Sometimes in April*. DVD, 2005.

———. *Lumumba*. France-Belgium-Haïti, 2000. 116 mn.

———. *Lumumba. La mort du prophète*. Germany-Switzerland-Haïti, 1991. 68 mn.

Raymont, Peter. *Shake Hands with the Devil: The Journey of Roméo Dallaire*. Canada, 2004. 91 mn.

Reina, Juan and Eric Kabera. *Iseta: Behind the Roadblock*. Great Britain-Rwanda, 2009. 57 mn.

Spielberg, Steven. *Schindler's List*. USA, 1993. 188 mn.

Spottiswoode, Roger. *Shake Hands with the Devil—J'ai serré la main du diable*. Canada, 2007. 113 mn.

———. "Audio Commentary by the Director and General Roméo Dallaire." *Shake Hands with the Devil—J'ai serré la main du diable*. DVD, 2007.

Tasma, Alain. *Opération Turquoise*. France, 2007. 90 mn.

———. *Nuit noire 17 octobre 1961*. France, 2005. 108 mn.

Weymeersch, Eric. *Le Fils D'Imana* (scenario by Alexis Kagame). Belgium, 1959. 90 mn.

Woukoache, François. *Nous ne sommes plus morts*. Cameroun-Belgium, 2000. 126 mn.

Index

mémoire), 27, 29, 89–95, 98n3, 104–6, 153, 164

Rwanda 94. *See* Groupov

Rwililiza, Innocent, 8–9, 10, 78, 223, 240n11, 254

Saint-Exupéry, Patrick de, 184, 237, 240n13

Schindler's List, 4, 172, 185, 218, 247

Sebasoni, Servilien, 23n5

secondary witness, 9–10, 22, 28, 29–30, 36–37, 43, 45–46, 62, 67, 77–78, 83, 96, 106–10, 115–16, 158, 248–49, 263

Sehene, Benjamin, 94, 181, 220n2

Semujanga, Josias, 99nn15–16, 126nn3–4, 180, 199

Shake Hands with the Devil. See Spottiswoode

Shooting Dogs. See Caton-Jones

Shoshana, Felman, 28–29, 57–58, 63, 79, 82–83, 135–36, 157–58, 159

social dialogue. *See* testimony

Sometimes in April. See Peck

Sontag, Susan, 5, 28, 73, 146, 171, 174

Spottiswoode, Roger, 172, 174, 177–78, 187–89, 232

Stallybrass, Peter, 67

Sunday in Kigali. See Favreau

survivor, 110, 261–62; enunciative authority, 159, 255–56, 259, 266–67; guilt, 40–41, 119, 261–62, 264; loneliness, 58, 75, 79–81, 106–8, 111; shame, 41, 119, 223, 255, 259, 268

symbolic violence, 6, 20, 44, 45, 57, 73, 232

Tadjo, Véronique, 91, 106–8, 109; *The Shadow of Imana* 97, 108, 114–26, 126nn2–3, 134–35

Tal, Kalí, 26, 44, 57

Tasma, Alain, 184, 187, 189, 214, 219–20

testimony, 26–28, 37–39, 42, 81, 119–20, 253–56, 267; attestation & recreation, 44, 82–83, 159, 254, 264; belatedness, 107–8, 110, 123–25, 158, 226–27, 231, 266; dialogic space, 42, 48, 81–82; listening, 43–49, 51, 70, 77–78, 80, 83, 109, 116, 145, 269; performance of survival, 39–40, 42–43, 47–48, 58, 82, 91–92, 253–54, 265–66, 268–69; social dialogue, 47–48, 50, 58, 64, 77, 79, 107–8, 253–54, 261, 265

Todorov, Tzvetan, 136, 162, 165n3

trauma, 8, 19, 26, 28, 37–40, 42, 119, 228, 254, 259, 268–69; cultural trauma, 54, 64, 80, 231–32; enunciative trauma, 44–46, 69, 253, 266, 269

United Nations, 5, 102–3, 155, 177, 187, 192–93, 201–2, 217, 237–38, 242, 248

United States, 4–5, 11n3, 102, 185–86, 193, 237–38, 248

Uvin, Peter, 13–14

Verschave, François-Xavier, 102, 112n4

Vianney Rurangwa, Jean-Marie, 91–92

Waberi, Abdourahman Ali, 91, 93, 99n15, 105

Waintrater, Régine, 38, 42, 49

Weine, Stevan, 50, 54, 77, 81, 83, 253, 265

Weisman, Gary, 172

Woukoache, François, 95

Yeager, Patricia, 37, 132

Young, James, 90, 164

About the Author

Alexandre Dauge-Roth is associate professor of French at Bates College. He has published numerous articles on the representation of the genocide of the Tutsis in literature, testimony, and film. His work in French and Francophone studies examines testimonial literature as a genre and analyzes social belonging through historical, political, and medical readings of the body. He has explored representations of AIDS in Sub-Saharan Africa through the works of Koulsy Lamko and Fanta Regina Nacro and graft and transplant as prominent metaphors for the migrant and the host in the works of Malika Mokeddem and Jean-Luc Nancy. He has published essays on Hervé Guibert, François Bon, Georges Perec, and Claude Simon. In 2007, Dauge-Roth hosted an international conference, "Rwanda: From National Disintegration to National Reunification," at Bates College and created "Friends of Tubeho," a non-profit organization that funds educational scholarships for orphans of the genocide in Rwanda.

CPSIA information can be obtained at www.ICGtesting.com
Printed in the USA
BVOW040907210512

290596BV00002B/7/P